In Search of Inclusive Policy

In Search of Inclusive Policy

Addressing Graded Inequality

Editors

Sukhadeo Thorat

Narender Kumar

INDIAN INSTITUTE OF DALIT STUDIES, NEW DELHI

RAWAT PUBLICATIONS

Jaipur • New Delhi • Bangalore • Guwahati • Kolkata

ISBN 978-81-316-0162-4

Reprinted, 2016

Published in association with
Indian Institute of Dalit Studies
Q 3, Green Park Extension, New Delhi 110 016
Phone: 011-41643981/82 Fax: 011-41643982
E-mail: iids@dalitstudies.org
Website: www.dalitstudies.org

Published by
Prem Rawat for **Rawat Publications**
Satyam Apts, Sector 3, Jawahar Nagar, Jaipur 302 004 (India)
Phone: 0141 265 1748/7006 Fax: 0141 265 1748
E-mail: info@rawatbooks.com
Website: www.rawatbooks.com

New Delhi Office
4858/24, Ansari Road, Daryaganj, New Delhi 110 002
Phone: 011 2326 3290

Also at *Bangalore, Guwahati* and *Kolkata*

Typeset by Rawat Computers, Jaipur
Printed at Chaman Enterprises, New Delhi

Dedicated
to
Shri Arjun Singh

Contents

VII
Better-off, Worse-off and Creamy Layer

Foreword

Much earlier we have recognised that the caste-based iniquitous Indian society, particularly the Hindu society, has been a constant source of discrimination, deprivation and poverty among a large section of our population. The multiple socio-economic groups that suffer in this process include ex-untouchables, Other Backward Castes, adivasis, semi-nomadic and de-notified tribes, women, and also some religious minorities, particularly Muslims. These groups are socially and economically situated in such a way that they lack access to income-earning assets such as land and capital, gainful employment, adequate access to social needs like civic amenities, education, health, and housing; and, as result, many of their economic, civil and cultural rights remain only notional in character. The deprivation and discrimination thus get institutionalised through caste, class, gender, religious and ethnic status.

The struggle against such iniquitous social order goes back to the period of Buddha, who tried to reform the Indian society on the principles of liberty, equality, fraternity and compassion. It was followed by several social and religious reform movements, particularly the Bhakti movement, spanning from the 8th century in the south to the 11th to 16th century in the north. More recently, in the

19th and 20th centuries, several attempts were made to address the agonies of women, low-backward caste people and the untouchables. The backward castes movement by Ramaswami Periyar in the south, particularly Tamilnadu, and by Narayan Guru in Kerala, Mahatma Jotirao Phule and others in Maharashtra, and historic movement of the untouchables led by Dr. Babasaheb Ambedkar were all directed towards securing the basic human rights to them, and also attacking the caste and gender-based discrimination and deprivation. Gandhiji brought the issue of untouchability to the national level, through his own idioms and political discourse. Even adivasis were not behind in waging struggle for their legitimate rights in different parts of the country.

Independent India's Constitution could not overlook these struggles and movements that embodied the legitimate aspirations of the depressed sections of the Indian society. Knowing fully well that the general socio-economic development process might not enable the marginalised sections to equitably share the benefits of economic growth, the Constitution enjoined the State to evolve and adopt the various affirmative action programmes specifically for the excluded and disadvantaged groups of the Scheduled Castes (SCs), Scheduled Tribes (STs), socially and educationally backward classes (OBCs), and religious minorities.

The affirmative action programmes in India in the form of reserving fixed quota for the SCs, STs, and the OBCs in the public educational institutions and employment has been a perennial source of debate among the academic community in India. Those who oppose quota-based affirmative action programmes preeminently argue that along with the principle of equality, merit and efficiency are the first casualty of the reservation policy. Other arguments include that the caste is disappearing; that caste is not class; that rather than caste, economic status of the group/individual should be taken into account; that, in the case of the OBCs, creamy layer should be excluded from the benefits of the policy; and so on. They tend to support all other welfare programmes and policies for the betterment of these sections, except reserving fixed quota for them. The protagonists of the quota-based affirmative action policy attempt to counter each argument of the opponents mentioned above. Their main contention is that, since the Indian society is exclusionary in character, the reservation policy in India, in its present form, should not be viewed merely as a welfare programme, rather it essentially needs to be looked, among other things, as an *anti-discriminatory* policy.

Of late, efforts are being made to move towards social and economic development with *inclusive* policies to enable the disadvantaged and marginalised sections of the society, such as the SCs, the STs, the OBCs, women, religious minorities like Muslims, and other disabled groups, to enable them to equitably share the benefits of economic growth. There is a considerable discussion in the government and among the civil society organisations about the alternative policies and strategies for inclusive development. It is indeed gratifying to note that the 11th Five-Year Plan is committed to securing *faster and more inclusive growth.*

It is in this context that the present volume *In Search of Inclusive Policy: Addressing Graded Inequality* by Sukhadeo Thorat and Narender Kumar is the most welcome contribution. It puts together important articles written by well-known academicians and researchers which have been published in the reputed academic journals and dailies in the wake of the Union Government's decision to reserve 27 per cent seats for the OBCs in the public education institutions for higher learning. But, more importantly, it does not confine its endeavour to that issue alone. It takes into consideration and rightly so, all inclusive policies for the OBCs and other groups such as the SCs, STs, and religious minorities such as Muslims, as also Dalit Christians. What is further noteworthy, the volume contains not only different, but totally conflicting views and perspectives on the various affirmative action policies and their implications.

In somewhat lengthy introduction, the editors address and discuss the relevant issues not only with academic and intellectual clarity, but also more dispassionately. They rightly argue that the *exclusion* is the most distinguishing and defining character of the Indian society that it has acquired through the institution of caste. The caste system has not created only inequality, but as Dr Ambedkar, probably for the first time argued, it has created *graded* inequality. They scrutinise the existing theoretical and empirical literature for developing appropriate inclusive policies so as to make the Indian economy more egalitarian, polity more participatory, and overall society more humane.

The book thus comprehensively contributes to the discussion on issue under consideration, which is, by any means, both complex and controversial. I appreciate the attempt of the authors in dealing with the issue in a forthright manner.

I am confident, this work would serve as a compulsory reading to the academicians and policy makers, as also to the public at large, inasmuch as the articles included in this put forth varied perspectives, which together help understand the issue of graded inequality and inclusive policy in their totality.

Bhalchandra Mungekar
Member, Planning Commission of India

Preface

The Indian Institute of Dalit Studies, Delhi published a book *Reservation and Private Sector: Quest for Growth and Equal Opportunity* in 2005. This book came in the wake up of discussion and debate on the issue of extension of public sector reservation to private sector for the Scheduled Castes (SCs) and Scheduled Tribes (STs). This volume includes papers published in newspapers and journals. Another wave of writing on reservation came in the wake of the announcement by the government to extend the reservation which other backward castes (OBCs) enjoy in government services to central educational institutions. This announcement by the government again led to an intense discussion and debate and generated large amount of literature. This book includes 31 selected papers which were earlier appeared in various journals and newspapers. The contents of these papers vary from definition of other backward caste, to their size, their problems and alternative policies to overcome those problems. Some of the papers also discuss the issues in general terms covering the groups such as SCs, STs and religious minorities.

In the 'Introduction' to the books, the editors capture the central arguments of these papers. While there is a common thread that runs through these papers, there are also differences in terms of number of issues related to OBCs and others including the solution.

In the context of current discussion and government's efforts to develop solution to the problem of SCs, STs and particularly the OBCs and other groups like religious minorities such as Muslims and Dalit Christian, the book discuses the framework for the policy and the relevant issues. The issues that the introduction addresses are: What is the nature of Indian society in terms of its exclusionary character? Why we need to address and be concerned about the issue of social exclusion and discrimination in general and the one connected with the institution of caste in particular? What are the lessons from the existing theoretical and empirical literature for developing inclusive policies? How can we make our society, polity and economy more inclusive and participatory?

We are grateful to the editors of *Economic and Political Weekly* for the articles by Sukhadeo Thorat, Ashwini Deshpande, Yogendra Yadav and Satish Deshpande, K. Sundaram, A.R. Vasavi, Rana Hasan and Aashish Mehta, Bhagwan Das, A. Ramaiah, Satish Deshpande, S. Subramanian, K. Ravi Srinivas, Neera Chandhoke, Rohini Somanathan, Jayati Ghosh, C.P. Bhambhri, Pratap Bhanu Mehta and Kancha Ilaiah. Besides, the editor(s)/publisher(s) of the following journals/ newspapers/websites also deserve our thanks for the following articles published therein:

- Integral Liberation Bangalore for the article by Ambrose Pinto.
- Countercurrents.org for the article by V.B. Rawat.
- Rediff.com for the article by T. Pradeep.
- *The Statesman* for the article by Dipak Basu.
- The Tehelka.com for the article by Kancha Ilaiah.
- *People's Democracy* for the article by R. Arun Kumar.
- International Centre for Ethnic Studies (ICES), Kandy for the article by Partha S. Ghosh.
- CHET, Africa for the article of S. Srinivas Rao.
- Institute of Labour Studies, ILO, Geneva, for the article by André Béteille.
- www.cse.iitb.ac.in for the article by Sandeep Pandey.
- home.iitk.ac.in for the article by Amman Madan.
- World Socialist Website for the article by Kranti Kumara and Keith Jones.

Given the importance of the issue and efforts to develop inclusive policy for discriminated groups, we believe that the book will be an useful reading for researchers, policy makers and students interested in this theme. The initial tedious work of collection of papers from various sources and seeking the permission of publishers and individual authors was done by Sarbeswar Sahu and Aparimita Pramanik during their initial stay at the Institute. We recognise their contribution. Dr. Pramod Kumar from IGNOU, Sanil, Poonam and Amrita of IIDS helped in proof-reading, thanks to all of them. We also thank Narendra Kumar who compiled all the papers in a publishable form.

Our special thanks to Prof. Bhalchandra Mungekar, Member, Planning Commission of India for readily writing foreword to the volume.

Finally, we are thankful to Rawat Publications for publishing this volume in the shortest possible time.

Sukhadeo Thorat
Narender Kumar

Given the importance of the issue and attempts [illegible] inclusive policy for discriminated groups, we believe that [illegible] will be of use to [illegible] policy makers and students. [illegible] sources and seeking the permission [illegible] authors was done by [illegible] Aparajita Chakraborty during their internship at the Institute. We [illegible]

Introduction

Graded Inequality and Inclusive Policy: An Overview

SUKHADEO THORAT AND NARENDER KUMAR

The recent announcement of the government to extend the reservation for Other Backward Castes (OBCs) to centrally managed educational institutions has led to an intense discussion on the desirability of such a step. From the date of announcement in April 2006 to its final acceptance in December 2006 by parliament, the nine months period produced voluminous literature, which indeed speaks for the vibrant democratic character of our civil society. It also provides the mirror image of the thinking of the civil society on the problems of Indian society. The papers – small and large – run into hundreds. This volume puts together only selected papers on the theme of reservation for OBCs in particular and other groups in general. The subjects of these papers vary from definition of OBCs, to their size, their problems and alternative policies to overcome the problems. Some of the papers also discuss the issues in its general terms.

In this introduction, we will first deal with the central arguments of the papers included in the volume. Then, discussion will centre around the problem of social exclusion associated with multiple identities and the policy implication for building the inclusive and participatory society. In the backdrop of these papers and in the context of current discussion and efforts to develop a solution to the problem of SCs, STs and particularly the OBCs and other groups like religious minorities such as Muslims and Dalit Christians, the introduction discusses the issues of social exclusion and inclusive policy in its wider context.

Review of Papers in the Volume

The identification and definition of the OBCs goes back to First Backward Class Commission, popularly known as Kaka Kalelkar Commission, which tried to identify them on the basis of their low social position in the traditional caste hierarchy of Hindu social order, lack of general educational advancement, inadequate representation in government services, and also in the field of trade, commerce and industry.

As the recommendations of the Kalelkar Commission were not accepted, so another commission, i.e., Mandal Commission was entrusted with this task. The Mandal Commission adopted a comprehensive criteria on social, educational and economic basis. It used *eleven* indicators for identification of OBCs based on social backwardness, extent of manual labour for their livelihood, age at marriage, female participation rate, school attendance and dropout rate, proportion of matriculates, family assets, kuccha houses and source of drinking water and the extent of consumption loan. Based on these indicators, the socially and educationally excluded communities from amongst the Hindu Shudras and some of the communities of the Muslims were included in the broader category of OBCs.

Attempts were made to estimate the population of OBCs. The 1931 population census estimated the population around 52 per cent, whereas, the Kalelkar Commission (1955) did not estimate the size of this group. However, forty-seven years after 1931 census, the Mandal Commission stated that the population of OBCs, which includes both Hindus and non-Hindus, is around 52 per cent (Agrawal and Aggarwal 1991: 44). For the more recent years, i.e., 2000, the National Sample Survey puts their population figure at 36 per cent although using the restricted definition. Nevertheless, the estimate by all these sources is more than 27 per cent, which is taken for reservation for OBCs.

Attempts were also made to characterise their problem. Some papers in this volume discuss their problem and refer to the historicity of discrimination and deprivation due to caste system (e.g., Sukhadeo Thorat, Arun Kumar, Ambrose Pinto, Jayati Ghosh), backwardness in terms of poverty, education, etc. (by K. Sundaram, Ashwini Deshpande, Satish Deshpande), and heterogeneity within (e.g., by A. Ramaiah, Rohini Somanathan). Some argued that OBCs were neither stigmatised nor suffered from economic hierarchy (Partha S Ghosh) or that the present caste system lacks legitimacy in the same sense of order of hierarchy as was existent in Varna system (André Béteille).

Notwithstanding the difference, most agreed that as compared with higher castes, the OBCs suffered from relative deprivation and therefore suggested solution to their problem. Kaka Kalelkar Commission, which submitted its report in March 1955, had prepared a list of 2,399 backward castes or communities for the entire country, of which 837 had been classified as the 'most backward' and also made a number of recommendations to address their problem. This include reservation for OBCs to the extent of 70 per cent seats in all technical and professional institutions, and in all government services (proportion in service varying from 25 per cent for class I to 40 per cent for class IV) as well as in local bodies.

The Mandal Commission Report followed the Kaka Kalelkar Commission. Given the 50 per cent limit, the Commission recommended a reservation of 27 per cent for OBCs. It recommended a change in the private ownership of the means of production both in industry and agriculture, reservation including promotion in public sector undertakings both under the central and state governments and private sector undertakings receiving financial assistance from the government, and reservation in all universities and affiliated colleges (for detail see Agarwal and Aggarwal 1991).

Most of the authors of papers in this volume also suggest measures for the empowerment of OBCs, though they differ in solution. Some argue for general solution in terms of policies for the development of all the sections without reservation to OBCs. These measures mainly include free and compulsory education and other policies of economic empowerment. Some others agree for the use of general solution but also favour simultaneous use of reservation due to experiences of discrimination faced by OBCs. Others prefer reservation but with exclusion of the "creamy layer". They argue that the OBCs are not a homogeneous group, but is marked with internal differentiation and therefore the relatively better-off should be excluded from the reservation by using social and economic standing of individual within the OBCs.

Graded Inequality and Inclusive Policy

Thus, this review of the central arguments of the papers in this volume unfolds differences in the perspectives on problem of groups suffering from the social exclusion associated with caste, particularly the OBCs, and solution to their problem. There is, however, a common thread that runs through most of the papers. Most of them recognise the problem of exclusion-linked deprivation of excluded groups like SC, ST and OBC, and argue for a need to address their problem in one way or the other, although they differ in terms of solution.

In the context of current discussion and efforts to develop solution to the problem of OBCs and other groups like religious minorities such as Muslims and Dalit Christians, it is necessary that the issue be discussed in a more realistic manner. This could possibly be done only with reference to the present theoretical and empirical literature on the issue of exclusion-linked deprivation of excluded groups in India and insights from this literature. The relevant issues that need to be addressed are: What is the nature of Indian society in terms of its exclusionary character? Why we need to address and be concerned about the issue of social exclusion and discrimination in general, and one connected with institution of caste in particular? What are the lessons from the existing theoretical and empirical literature for developing remedies against discrimination? How can we make our society, polity and economy more inclusive and participatory?

In this section, we deal with some of these questions. In Indian context, we have to fall back upon Ambedkar's writings and post-Ambedkar developments in literature on the issue of social exclusion. Ambedkar had developed arguments for equal opportunity policy, in terms of reservation, in the early 1920s through 1950s drawing mainly from the theoretical developments in Political Science relating to concept of justice, and equal right during the period. A good amount of new writings have now appeared since Ambedkar developed his thoughts on the subject. These writings have further expanded the concept of social exclusion, its consequences and possible remedies. While the social science literature conceptualised general notion of social exclusion, the economists extended it to the spheres of economic and market discrimination.

Meaning of Social Exclusion and Discrimination

Before we discuss the issue related to exclusion in Indian society, it is useful to get insights on the concept of social exclusion in its general term. In social sciences literature, there is general agreement on the core features of social exclusion, its principle indicators and the way it relates to poverty and inequality (Buvinic 2005). Buvinic summarises the meaning of social exclusion as "the inability of an individual to participate in the basic political, economic and social functioning of the society", and goes on to add that social exclusion is "the denial of equal access to opportunities imposed by certain groups of society upon others" (ibid.). The definition captured the three most distinguished features of social exclusion, namely, that it affects culturally defined "groups", that it is embedded in social interrelation (the process through which individuals or groups are wholly or partially excluded from full participation in the society in which they live), and that its outcome is deprivation, low income and high degree of poverty of the excluded groups (Hann 1997; Sen 2000).

Consequences of exclusion thus depend crucially on the functioning of social institutions through network of social relations, and the degree to which they are exclusionary and discriminatory in their outcome. Social exclusion has sizeable impact on an individual's access to equal opportunity, if social interaction occurs between groups on superior-subordinate relationship. The groups focus approach recognise that people are excluded because of ascribed rather than achieved features, beyond individual agency or responsibility (Buvinic 2005) Amartya Sen draws attention to various meanings and dimensions of the concept of social exclusion (Sen 2000). Distinction is drawn between the situation, where some people are being kept out (at least left out), and where some people are being included (may even be forced to be inclûded) in deeply unfavourable terms, and described the two situations as "unfavourable exclusion" and "unfavourable inclusion". However, the "unfavourable inclusion", with unequal treatment may carry the same adverse effects as "unfavourable exclusion".

Sen also differentiated between active and passive exclusion. For the casual analysis, and policy response, Sen argued, "it is important to distinguish between "active exclusion", i.e., fostering of exclusion through the deliberate policy interventions by the government, or by any other wilful agents (to exclude some people from some opportunity) and "passive exclusion", which works through the social process in which there are no deliberate attempts to exclude, nevertheless, that may result in exclusion from a set of circumstances".

Sen further distinguishes the "constitutive relevance" of exclusion from that of "instrumental importance". In the former, exclusion or deprivation has an intrinsic importance of its own. For instance, not being able to relate to others and to take part in the life of the community can directly impoverish a person's life, in addition to the further deprivation it may generate. This is different from social exclusion of "instrumental importance", in which the exclusion in itself is not impoverishing, but can lead to impoverishment of human life.

Within the social science literature more precise elaboration of the concept of discrimination has come from the economics in the context of race and gender (Darity 1995). The mainstream economic literature throws more light on discrimination that works through market and non-market transactions and develops the concept of market discrimination with some analytical clarity. In the market discrimination framework, discrimination of a group may operate through restrictions on the entry in market, and/or through "selective inclusion", with an unequal treatment in market and non-market transactions, which is similar to Sen's concept of unfavourable inclusion.

The labour market discrimination can occur in hiring when two persons with the same employment experience, education and training but differing in some non-economic characteristic face denial in hiring. The differences are generally correlated with certain non-economic (racial, ethnic or religious) characteristics of the individual. The occupation discrimination occurs when business persons from a group are faced with quantitative restrictions to enter into the occupation of majority group, or face differential treatment in acquiring access to factors and services necessary for production and business activity.

To summarise the development in social science literature, the concept of social exclusion, thus, essentially refers to the processes through which groups are wholly, or partially, excluded on the basis of group identity from full participation in economy and society in which they live. It involves two crucial dimensions, namely, the "societal interrelations" (causing exclusion) and their "outcome" (causing deprivation). For understanding the nature of exclusion, therefore, the insight into the societal interrelations and institutions of exclusions is as important as the outcome in terms of deprivation for excluded groups. It is also necessary to recognise that in "group exclusion", people are excluded because of their group identity and not because of individual attribute. Therefore, we need to recognise distinction between exclusion of an individual and exclusion of a group. Exclusion of an 'individual' is different from "exclusion of a group". Individuals often get excluded from access to economic and social opportunities for various reasons specific to them. Likewise, individual often gets excluded from employment due to lack of required education and skill. Individuals also get excluded from having access to higher education due to lack of minimum qualifications required for the job. Similarly, people get excluded from access to input and consumer market due to lack of purchasing power. Thus, exclusion of an individual has no connection with his or her social and cultural identity. In case of exclusion of group, however, individuals with certain social and cultural identity such as social origin like caste, ethnicity, religion, gender or colour, are excluded from having access to sources of income, employment, education, civil rights and other social needs. Thus, "group exclusion" is based on social and cultural identity of persons, irrespective of the attributes of individuals within the social/cultural group.

This has important policy implications. While in case of "individual exclusion" the focus will have to be on enhancing the individual capabilities in the form of pro-poor policy, while in case of "group exclusion" the focus of the policy will be targeted on the group as a whole covering all individuals in the social/cultural group.

Caste and Social Exclusion

This theoretical literature and the insights from it are quite relevant in understanding the exclusion in Indian situation. In India, exclusion revolves around the societal institutions that exclude, discriminate, isolate and deprive some groups on the basis of group's identity like caste, ethnicity, religion, gender and others.

The nature of exclusion associated with the caste system particularly needs to be understood and conceptualised as it has been the basis of reservation policy for SCs, STs and OBCs and there is growing demand to extend it to similar groups like religious minorities such as Muslims and low castes converted to Islam and Christianity.

Theoretical attempts in social and economic interpretation of caste system recognise that caste as a system of social and economic governance is determined by certain customary rules and norms, which are unique and distinct (Akerlof 1976; Scoville 1991; Lal 1988; Ambedkar 1936 and 1987). The economic organisation of caste system is based on the division of people in social groups (or castes) in which the economic rights of each individual caste are pre-determined or ascribed by birth and made hereditary. Entitlement of economic rights is, however, unequal and hierarchical. The economic rights are unequally assigned and therefore entitlement of rights get narrower and narrower as one moves down in caste hierarchy from high to low caste. The system also provides for a community-based regulatory mechanism to enforce the system through the instruments of social ostracism (or social and economic penalties), and reinforces it further with the justification from some philosophical elements in Hindu religion such as theory of karma and rebirth based on the notion of eternity of soul (Lal 1988; Ambedkar 1936 and 1987).

The caste system's fundamental characteristic of fixed social and economic rights for each caste, with restrictions for change, implies "forced exclusion" of one caste from the civil, economic and educational rights of other caste. Exclusion in civil and economic spheres thus is internal to the system, and is a necessary outcome of its governing principles. In the market economy framework, the occupational immobility would operate through restrictions in various markets such as land, labour, capital, credit, other inputs, and services necessary for any business and education.

This interpretation of caste system implies that in its original form, unlike many other human societies, the caste system does not recognise the individual and his/her distinctiveness as the centre of the social purpose. In fact, for the purpose of rights and duties, the unit of the Hindu society is not an individual (even the family is not regarded as a unit in the Hindu society, except for the purposes of marriages and inheritance). The primary unit in the Hindu society is caste, and hence, the rights and privileges (or the lack of them) of an individual are on account of his/her being a member of a particular caste (Ambedkar 1987). Also, due to the hierarchical or graded nature of the caste system, the entitlements to civil, economic and educational rights for different castes become narrower and narrower as one goes down in hierarchical ladder in the caste system. Various castes in their rights and duties get artfully interlined and coupled with each other in a manner such that the rights and privileges of the higher castes become the causative reasons for the disadvantage and disability of the lower castes, particularly the untouchables and other backward castes located at the bottom of caste hierarchy. In this sense, a caste does not exist in a single number, but only in plural (ibid.). Castes exist as a system of endogenous groups, which are interlinked with each other in unequal measure of rights and relations in all walks of life. Castes at the top of the order enjoy more rights, at the expense of those located at the bottom. Therefore, the lower castes, such as former untouchables and located at the bottom of the caste hierarchy, have much less economic, educational and social rights.

The caste/untouchability and ethnicity-based exclusion thus reflects inability of individuals and groups like former untouchables and OBCs and other similar groups to interact freely and productively with others and to take part in the full economic, social, and political life of a community (Bhalla and Lapeyre 1997). Incomplete citizenship or denial of civil rights (freedom of expression, rule of law, right to justice), political rights (right and means to participate in the exercise of political power), and socio-economic rights (right to property, employment and education) are key dimensions of impoverished lives.

Consequences of Social Exclusion and Discrimination

The concern about discrimination is precisely because of its linkages with underdevelopment, inequality, poverty and the potential inter-group conflict that it can lead to between the dominant and discriminated subordinated groups.

On Economic Growth

The standard economic theory of discrimination indicates that economic discrimination generally generates consequences, which adversely affect overall economic efficiency and thereby economic growth. The market discrimination leads to failure of market mechanism, which in turn induces inefficiency due to misallocation of labour and other factors among firms and economy.

Factor immobility also brings segmentation of the markets. In case of caste system, for instance, fixed occupations by not permitting mobility of human labour, land, capital and entrepreneurship across castes, the system creates segmented markets and brings imperfections in each of these markets. Thus, far from promoting competitive market situation, it creates segmented and monopolistic markets. Labour and capital fails to shift from one occupation to another even if the wage rate and rate of return (on investment) are higher in the alternative occupations. Factor immobility brings gross inefficiency in resource allocation and in economic outcome (Ambedkar 1936 and 1987).

Economic efficiency is also affected by reducing job commitment and efforts of workers who perceive themselves to be victims of discrimination and by reducing the magnitude of investment in human capital by discriminated groups. In caste-based segmented markets, the economic efficiency is thus lower than in the model of perfectly competitive market economy (Birdstall and Sabot 1991).

Factor immobility also leads to unemployment, which is typically associated with the customary rules governing employment in various occupations (Ambedkar 1936 and 1987). By not permitting the movement of labour between occupations, caste becomes a direct cause of much of voluntary unemployment for higher caste and involuntary unemployment for low caste persons. The higher caste Hindus would generally prefer to be voluntarily unemployed for sometime than to take up an occupation which is considered to be polluting. For the lower castes, on the other hand, the restriction to take other caste occupation will compel them to remain involuntarily unemployed. Thus involuntary unemployment in the case of lower castes and voluntary unemployment in the case of higher castes is one of the negative outcomes of the caste system.

The economic efficiency of labour suffers severely in another manner also. Insofar as the division of occupations is not based on individual choice, the individual sentiment, preference and the natural aptitudes have no place in it. The social and individual efficiency requires us to develop the capacity of an individual to the point of competency to choose and make once own career. The principle of individual choice is violated in the caste system insofar as it involves an attempt to appoint a task to an individual in advance, selected not on the basis of training or capacities but on the caste status of the parents.

Further, some of the occupations are considered socially degrading which reduce the social status of persons engaged in them. Forced into these occupations on account of their caste origin, people do not derive job satisfaction. In fact, such occupations constantly provoke them to aversion, ill-will and desire to evade (Ambedkar 1936). The caste system also disassociates intelligence from work and creates contempt for physical labour. The dignity of physical labour is nearly absent in the work ethics of the caste system. The lack of dignity of labour thus affects the incentive to work adversely. This implies that the caste system (as an economic organisation) lacks several elements, which are required to satisfy the conditions for optimum use of resources and optimum economic outcome.

On Inequality, Poverty and Inter-Group Conflict

This brings us to the consequences of discrimination and exclusion on income distribution and poverty. The consequences of the caste system in terms of inequality and poverty are more serious than that for economic growth. Since the access to sources of income and economic reward under the caste system is determined by unequal job assignment of rights, the result is an income distribution generally skewed along caste lines (Lal 1989). Ambedkar argued that whatever may have been the original purpose behind the origin of the caste system, but later as it evolved in its classical form it certainly involved an economic motive, the purpose of which is income maximisation through coercion rather than economic efficiency of any sort (Ambedkar 1936 and 1987). The manner in which the customary rules and norms regarding rights to property, occupation, employment, wages, education, social status occupation and dignity of labour are framed and defined, they involve denial of educational, social and economic rights, and resultant deprivation and the poverty of the lower castes. Economic and educational disparities in general and poverty of lower castes like former untouchables and OBCs in particular, is a direct outcome of the unequal assignment of rights under the caste system.

There is an additional social and political cost of caste-based social exclusion. By exacerbating current inequality between groups, and by contributing to its perpetuation from one generation to the next, it also fosters inter-group conflict (Birdsall and Sabot 1991).

Caste-based discrimination in access to sources of income and human development of subordinate groups thus has potential for inducing inter-group conflict.

Dynamics of Exclusion and Discrimination

The caste system as an institution has also undergone a significant change from its original form, which has been discussed in the preceding section. Only a few have ventured to explain the dynamics of the caste system. Akerlof's economic model of the caste system emphasised that the provision of social ostracism (with penalties involving social and economic boycott and isolation) against the violation of customary rules of caste system acts as the main deterrent for any change. The fear of being socially and economically boycotted and isolated acts as an imminent force for the survival of the system. This implied that there are social costs associated with change, which discourage the caste system from being dynamic in nature (Akerlof 1976). Scoville emphasised the role of the economic cost involved in the enforcement of the caste system. Enforcement of the system involves economic cost – transaction and enforcement – and these costs are too high for the individual members to break the rules of the system (Scoville 1991). Scoville thus locates the reasons for rigidity of the caste system into enormous economic costs, which inhibit the change in the customary rules governing the caste system. This implies that in situation of low economic costs, the inefficient rules governing the caste system would change and make the system dynamic.

The "cost and efficiency" explanation however remained silent about the other motive behind the discrimination. Marxist and Ambedkar explanations go beyond the costs and efficiency and emphasize the role of social, educational and economic gains of monopolisation accruing to the higher caste persons as reason for continuation of the caste system. The higher caste people will continue to support the caste system as long as it brings gains for them in social, economic and educational spheres. The customary rules governing the social and economic relations and those relating to education under the caste system would change, if the alternative (or new) rules yield higher economic and social gains to the higher castes. Conversely, traditional rules would continue if the alternative or new rules yield lesser gains to the higher caste persons.

Ambedkar further added that the change in the ideas about human rights and equality also induces the change in the social relations, in so far as the concept of human rights and justice involved under caste system is contrary to the modern tenets of human rights and justice.

Thus, the prevailing theoretical literature indicates that the changes in caste system will depend on the relative magnitude of social costs (in terms of social isolation/standing), economic costs (that is, transaction and enforcement costs), and the social and economic gains associated with change. It will also depend on the extent of acceptability of the modern ideas about human rights, justice and equality. The lesser gains to the higher castes in the exiting system (compared with gains in system governed by new rules) and the low social and economic costs of such change will induce change in the traditional social and economic relations of the caste system. Similarly, the recognition and pursuit of human rights and justice will also induce the change in the system. Conversely, if the gains to higher castes in social, education and economic spheres in the traditional system are higher and the cost of change is high and also the notion of human right and justice as prevalent among the masses is against the progressive norms of human rights, there will be less incentive for higher castes to go for change.

Remedies Against Social Exclusion: Free Market versus Interventionist Policy

Given the adverse consequences of economic and social discrimination, reducing discrimination is thus a worthwhile strategy because it is likely to increase economic efficiency and growth, and reduce poverty and inequality and also minimize the potential for conflict between the groups. How to overcome the discrimination has been the central concern of social and economic theories. Two alternative solutions have emerged in the economic literature. One theoretical strand predicts that, in highly competitive markets, discrimination will prove to be a transitory phenomenon as there are costs associated with discrimination to the firm/employer, which result in lowering the profits. Firms/employers, who indulge in discrimination, face the ultimate sanction imposed by the markets. The theory sees the resulting erosion of profits as a self-correcting solution to eliminate discrimination. Thus, this view would suggest promotion of competitive markets to reduce economic and social discrimination.

However, others argued for different policy to overcome economic and social discrimination. The proponents of this view argue that there are several reasons why economic discrimination might persist over long periods. Firstly, even if the markets are sufficiently competitive, the exclusion and discrimination will still persist. The existence of decades of labour market discrimination in high-income countries attests to that. Secondly, in reality, not all markets are competitive. Indeed, in most of the economies, the market is highly imperfect and is governed by oligopoly and monopolistic situation, which gives power to the firms to discriminate at will.

The limitation of the competitive market as solution is summarised by Darity and Shulman (1989) as under:

> *"The analytical stance of the mainstream neo-classical economists is characterized as methodological individualism and it presumes that economic institutions are structured such that society-wide outcomes result from an aggregation of individual behaviours. It presumed that if individuals act on the basis of pecuniary self-interest then market dynamics dictate equal treatment for equal individuals regardless of inscriptive characteristics such as race. Consequently, observed group inequality is attributed to familial, educational, or other background differences among individuals who are unevenly distributed between social groups. The causes of a dissimilar distribution of individuals between social groups may be genetic, cultural, historical, or some combination thereof. The differences in cultural attributes include the value families and neighbourhoods place on education, attitudes, and work habits. The historical refers primarily to the impact of past discrimination on current inequality. In contrast, economists who may be classified as methodological structuralists do not accept this interpretation. Structuralism as an analytical method holds that aggregate outcomes are not the result of a simple summation of individual behaviours, but rather arise from the constraints and incentives imposed by organizational and social hierarchies. In this view, individual behaviour achieves its importance within the context of group formation, cooperation, and conflict. Economic and political outcomes are thus a function of the hegemony exercised by dominant groups, the resistance offered by subordinate groups, and the institutions that mediate their relationship. Discrimination, in this view, is an inherent feature of*

economic system. Competition is either not powerful enough to offset the group dynamics of identity and interest, or it actually operates so as to sustain discriminatory behaviours. Discrimination is due to the dynamics of group identification, competition, and conflict rather than irrational, individual attitudes. Market mechanisms, far from being relied upon to eliminate discrimination of their own accord, must be scrutinized and pressured to further the goal of equality of opportunity".

These two views have different policy implications to overcome discrimination. A view which predicts discrimination to be self-correcting argues for strengthening competitive market mechanism. The alternative view asserts that market discrimination will persist, despite the presence of competitive market forces or for other reasons, therefore, the interventionist policies will be necessary. In their view, correcting discrimination would require legal safeguards against discrimination and policies for equal share in various spheres. It calls for state interventions, not only in land, labour, and capital market but also in product and consumer market and social needs such as education, housing and health, as the discriminated groups face discrimination in multiple spheres in transactions canalised through market and non-market channels.

Empowerment versus Equal Opportunity Policy

We are caught in discussion over developing reservation policies for groups and communities suffering from social, educational and economic exclusion associated with caste, ethnicity, gender and religious identity. Experience of half a century of economic development has brought to surface the exclusionary character of Indian society and its consequences for excluded groups. The alternative ways of overcoming the deprivation are suggested by the social scientists engaged in the discussion, particularly in the context of issue of reservation in private sector and extension of reservation for OBCs in educational institutions and similar demand by lower castes converted to Islam and Christianity and certain religious minority groups like Muslims. Two alternative sets of remedies, which can be grouped into the strategies of "social and economic empowerment" and of "equal opportunity" emerged from the discussion.

The policy of social and economic empowerment is essentially directed towards improving the ownership of capital assets like agricultural land, capital for business, entrepreneurial skills, and educational level and skills of discriminated groups. These measures are supposed to enhance the capacity of discriminated groups to undertake business and their employability through education and skill development to seek good quality employment. It appears that there is also a general recognition of need to empower the discriminated groups such as lower castes, particularly the former untouchables, women and some religious minority groups, for denial of equal economic rights to them in the past. However, when it comes to giving equal opportunity through instrument of reservation and similar methods, it does not find similar favour. It is argued that the labour and other markets and educational institutions generally work in neutral manner and access to markets are therefore determined by merit and efficiency alone. As such, there is no need of safeguards against possible market and non-market discrimination. Thus, while the policies for general social, educational and economic empowerment of discriminated groups are favoured, those ensuring equal share and participation in terms of reservation are marked with differences.

What are the insights from the theoretical and empirical literature on this policy issue. It is necessary to recognise that the problem of discriminated groups like SCs, STs, women and religious minorities is dual in nature. First is the lack of access to income earning capital assets like agricultural land and capital for business, quality employment and education and skills due to denial of the same in the past for long periods of time, the consequences of which are visible today in the form of inter-group inequality in several indicators of human development. Second is the continuation of the discrimination in the various markets and non-market transactions in the present, in some forms, if not in its full original forms. This is particularly the case of lower castes in Hindu society. Therefore, the discriminated groups require dual solution – a set of remedies for improving the ownership of land and capital assets, quality employment and education as compensation for that denial in the past, and another set of remedies to provide safeguards against discrimination in the present. While the first remedy is based on the justification of the principle of compensation for denial of rights in the past (the consequences of which are visible in the present), the second set of remedies is based on the assumption of providing safeguards against the discrimination in the present, in various market and non-market transactions and ensuring the due share and participation in employment, education, business, legislature and other supportive services.

It is expected that the policy of social, educational and economic empowerment will help to enhance the capacity of discriminated groups to take advantage of ongoing social and economic progress. Improved access to income-earning assets will improve the capacity and enable to undertake business activity. Education and skill development is expected to increase employability and help them to get jobs in private and public sectors.

However, it is necessary to recognise that economic and educational empowerment alone will not suffice; it will only empower the discriminated groups to enable them to make use of the ongoing economic and social progress, but will not ensure the ultimate use due to continuing discrimination in market and non-market transactions including the supply of social needs such as education and health. In the absence of equal opportunity policy in the form of reservation, the discriminated groups may continue to face discrimination in the form of denial of access in private employment, education, business and civil amenities, like housing and water and other spheres. It is precisely for this reason the complementary equal opportunity policy (complementary to the policy of general economic empowerment) is developed, in the form of reservation to ensure them the due share in employment, education, selectively in capital for business and, housing and water and other amenities, in addition to the policy of social and economic empowerment. The complementary nature of these two policies will ultimately help the historically discriminated groups to receive due share in economic and social progress.

Graded Inequality and Nature of Inclusive Policy

The development of "inclusive policy" thus requires use of both policies, namely policy of social and economic empowerment and policy of equal opportunity (in the form of reservation policy). However, formulating the reservation policy for various caste groups of Hindu and non-Hindu societies needs to take into account features of the caste system in terms of its exclusionary character with wider social and economic consequences on different castes within the Hindu fold.

Let us first discuss the features of the caste system in the context of inclusive policy. The core governing principle of the caste system is not the inequality alone but the "graded inequality", which implied hierarchical unequal entitlement of rights to various castes. Entitlement of rights being hierarchically unequal, every caste (except for the higher caste group) suffered from a degree of denial and exclusion. No rights could be universal. However, in the given framework of social relations, the loss of rights was not uniform across caste groups. As one moved down in the caste hierarchy, the rights and privileges also got reduced. By implication the caste located at the bottom of caste hierarchy suffered the most. The hierarchical structure determined privileges and obligations of different caste groups in a given network of social relations making disadvantage of lower castes became advantage for higher castes.

The system of graded entitlement to rights results in disparities in social, economic and educational conditions of different caste groups. The lesson we ought to learn from this is that given the differential impact on each caste, the policy against discrimination and deprivation needs to be caste-specific and governed by specific social, economic and education conditions of each caste. Thus, while the general exclusionary character of Hindu society, in which every caste suffers (except the higher caste) from denial of rights in differentiated manner, will require a common policy of social inclusion, to ensure equal participation for all castes in various spheres of society, however, additionally, it will also have to be combined with group specific policies of inclusiveness. By implication equal opportunity policy will necessarily be different for different caste groups depending on the nature of discrimination faced by them and their social, economic and educational conditions.

It has to be recognised that Indian society is characterised by multiple forms of exclusion associated with group identity like caste, ethnicity and gender, religion in various spheres of our society, polity and economy. Therefore, it requires an inclusive policy to overcome deprivation associated with caste, ethnicity, gender, religion and other forms of exclusions. It appears that the development experience of the last fifty years or so indicates that social and economic development has benefited the various groups in differentiated manner and therefore those who experienced exclusion or derived limited benefits from social and economic development are now seeking solution to their group-specific problem.

How to develop inclusive policy for different groups suffering from exclusion associated with caste, ethnicity, religion and gender is an issue, which is being currently discussed by the policy makers in India. The lesson from the literature is that the nature of inclusive policies for India will have to be necessarily guided by the nature of an exclusionary character of Hindu and non-Hindu communities of the Indian society. The policy framework will have to be governed by the forms and spheres of discrimination and their consequences on the discriminated groups.

As regards the Hindu society, as mentioned above, the principle of "graded inequality" implies that not all castes suffer equally from hierarchical entitlement of rights. While the castes located at the bottom of caste hierarchy, namely, the former untouchables suffer the most, the OBCs follow closely. The OBCs probably did not suffer from untouchability and residential and social isolation as much as the former untouchables did, but historically they too faced exclusion in education, employment, and certain other spheres. In case of non-Hindu communities, some elements of Hindu caste system seem to have been carried forward and spillover into the converted religions, and therefore the lower castes converted to Christianity and Islam (like the lower castes converted to Buddhism and Sikhism) also faced discrimination, although not in a similar fashion as the Hindu low castes did.

Certain religious minorities, particularly the Muslims, also probably face discrimination as a religious group in a number of spheres, as reflected in their lower performance with respect to relevant human development indicators. Similarly, the women face exclusion as a category of population but it varies depending on their caste, class and religious background. Some groups such as tribal and semi-nomadic tribal communities also suffer from isolation and exclusion due to their ethnic background.

Due to variations in the forms and spheres of discrimination, the consequences on the deprivation and poverty across various discriminated groups also vary. Although unlike SCs/STs, there are limited studies on discrimination of other discriminated groups, however, the visible presence of inter-group inequality in various indicators of human development points towards the consequences of historical discrimination, reflected in differential access to income-earning assets, property, business, employment, education, and civil rights in varying degree to various castes. Therefore, although all of them require measures to compensate for denial of equal rights in the past and also necessary safeguards against discrimination (in some forms if not in all of its original forms) in the present, however, the equal opportunity policy in the form of reservation, in its essential elements, may vary depending on the nature of discrimination faced by each of these excluded groups and their present social, educational, economic and political standing.

The inclusive policy for the discriminated groups essentially will have two aspects. First, insofar as the bulk of discriminated persons also happen to be the poor, it will require pro-poor policies of general nature. Among the general policies, the special programmes to improve the skill and education level to enhance the employability of these sections are most important. Since these sections particularly the SCs, the STs, the OBCs and women, were denied rights to education in the past, it is necessary to use measures to compensate for denial of equal rights in the past. The other groups like religious minorities, especially Muslims, also suffer from lower education, hence similar measures are necessary for them as well. Besides, education, the general policy will also involve measures to improve the ownership of income-earning capital assets as some groups as a whole or some sections within the groups lack access to assets, again, due to denial of ownership of such assets in the past. Also, it will require measures to provide social needs like housing, health and the like.

Secondly, in addition to the general pro-poor policy, it will have to be supplemented by the equal opportunity policy. The general policy will be necessary to compensate the discriminated groups for denial of equal rights in the past. However, given the fact that they continue to suffer from exclusion and discrimination in society, polity and economy in some form, if not in their original traditional form, in the past, it is necessary to provide legal safeguards against present discrimination as well as pro-active measures to give them the fair share in various spheres of society, polity and economy. The equal opportunity policy will have to be necessarily in the form of reservation to ensure fair access to employment, capital assets, and social needs like education and housing, civil and cultural rights and other spheres.

The experiences of various countries, including our own, indicate that governments have used few measures separately or in combination as part of equal opportunity policy. It generally constitutes few components. Legal safeguards against discrimination in multiple spheres of society, polity and economy is the first necessary step. This generally takes the form of law against discrimination such as Civil Rights Act in USA or Civil Rights Act in India (formerly known as Anti-Untouchability Act, 1955 and Prevention of Atrocities Act, 1989). Such Acts are necessary to provide legal safeguards so that in the event of discrimination, an individual could take recourse to these legal provisions. However, it has also been recognised that although the legal provisions are necessary pre-conditions to overcome the discrimination, legal safeguards are not adequate enough. It is recognised that laws cannot overcome the consequences of historical exclusion in the past, in terms of denial of basic rights in education, in access to income earning assets, employment, civil right and other spheres. Thus laws have their limitation in overcoming the consequences of exclusion and discrimination suffered by the discriminated groups in the past which also continue in the present. In fact, the consequences of discrimination in the past and present are reflected in poor performance of the discriminated groups with respect to necessary indicators of human development such as educational level, ownership of income earning assets, employment both in private and public sectors, as well as their participation in executive, governance and legislature in the centre and the states.

Therefore, the equal opportunity policy will require specific policy measures to ensure equal share and participation of discriminated groups in various spheres of society, polity and economy such as legislature, executive, employment in private and public sectors, education and other public spheres in the form of reservation. The reservation policy will ensure their due share in income earning assets, employment in private and public sectors, education, civil amenities like housing and other services and also executive (including decision-making and monitoring). This compensatory policy is necessary to break the inter-generational cumulative transmission of the disadvantaged.

Besides the policy of equal access in employment, education and legislature, equally important is their participation in executive and administration in decision-making and monitoring. The representation of discriminated groups becomes meaningful through their own representation and participation in administration and decision-making process at all levels, as it brings their experiences as well as sensitivity in the whole process. Therefore, participation of the discriminated groups in the governance at all levels, from legislature to making of policies, and their execution and monitoring, is necessary. Representation and participation in governance of discriminated groups is thus central to both inclusive policy and inclusive society.

There are constitutional, legal and other mechanisms which have been used internationally and nationally to operationalise the two dimensions of equal opportunity policy, namely, reservation in employment, education, legislature, public housing and other spheres and equal share and space in executive, administration for decision-making and monitoring. It is imperative that the provisions with respect to equal rights and protection against violation of rights need to be embodied in the Constitution. If a society practices discrimination, then, the impetus for change should come both from the state and the civil society. The private initiative by civil society in the form of reforms of society and other initiative for equal human rights are necessary. However, it is obligatory on the state to take steps by making provisions in the Constitution, with clear statement of responsibility on the state to develop policies against exclusion and discrimination and undertake measures to compensate the discriminated groups.

To put in brief the inclusive policy will involve three necessary components. Firstly, it should include general pro-poor policy for the welfare of poor as a whole, including the discriminated groups. Secondly, the equal opportunity policy for discriminated groups with two measures, namely, law against discrimination and pro-active measures in the form of reservation to give equal share in income earning capital assets; in public and private sector employment; in education and housing; and, participation in governance through fair share in legislature, executive and administration with necessary provisions in Constitution and the laws. It is necessary to recognise that while there shall be some common features of inclusive policy cutting across all discriminated groups, however, the equal opportunity policy will have to be of different nature for different discriminated groups such as SCs, STs, OBCs, semi-nomadic and de-notified tribes, a specific discriminated religious minority, women, physically challenged and other categories depending on the form and nature of discrimination suffered by each one of them and their social, education and economic situations. Since our society, economy and polity are characterised by exclusions and isolation of various types and magnitudes, it is imperative that a comprehensive inclusive policy to ensure the representation and participation of hitherto excluded sections to receive the gains of social and economic development is necessary. The polity, society and economy will have to be more inclusive and participatory, only then can democracy as a means of governance would become meaningful for one and all.

Making the Excluded Groups Visible in Statistics

Improving the ability to gather data disaggregated by caste, gender, ethnic background, religion, disability and other features associated with exclusion is a basic step for governments in promoting inclusion. Such information is necessary for better programme design and for more effective targeting and programme evaluation (Buvinic 2005). Several countries in Latin America and elsewhere include questions on the ethnicity and race in their population censuses. In addition, specialised household surveys are conducted, which include questions about the changing situation of excluded groups. In India, it is necessary that National Statistical Data System which includes population census and specialised household surveys such as National Sample Survey, National Family Planning and Health Survey and others should include specific questions related to excluded groups covering their situation and also the nature and forms of discrimination in multiple spheres.

References

Agrawal, S.P. and Aggarwal, J.C. (1991): *Educational and Social Uplift of Backward Classes*, Concept Publications, Delhi.

Akerlof, George (1976): "The Economics of Caste and of Rat Race and Other Woeful Tales". *Quarterly Journal of Economics*, XC.4. November 1976.

Akerlof, George (1980): "The Theory of Social Customs, of which Unemployment may be one consequence", *Quarterly Journal of Economics*, XCIV-4, June 1980.

Ambedkar, B.R. (1987): "The Hindu Social Order - Its Essential Features" in Vasant Moon (Ed.), *Dr. Babasaheb Ambedkar: Writing and Speeches*, Department of Education, Government. of Maharashtra, Vol.3, pp. 95-115.

Ambedkar, B.R. (first Published 1987): "Philosophy of Hinduism", Vasant Moon (Ed.) *Dr. Babasaheb Ambedkar: Writings and Speeches*, Department of Education, Government of Maharashtra, Vol.3, pp. 1-94.

Banerjee, Biswjit and Knight J.B. (1985): "Caste Discrimination in Indian Urban Labour Market", *Journal of Developing Economics.*

Bhalla, A. Lapeyre, F. (1997): Social exclusion: towards an analytical and operational framework. *Development and Change*, 28: pp. 413-433.

Birdsall, Nancy and Sabot Richard (1991): "Unfair Advantage: Labour Market Discrimination in Developing Countries". World Bank Studies.

Breman, Jan (2002): "Upheaval as Resurgence of Social Darwinism", *Economic and Political Weekly*, Vol 37 (16).

Buvinic, Mayra (2005): "Social Exclusion in Latin America", in *Social Exclusion and Economic Development*, Johns Hopkins University Press.

Chakravarti, Uma (1998): *Rewriting History: The Life and Times of Pandita Ramabai*, Kali for Women, New Delhi.

Clarke, Sathianathan (1998): *Dalits and Christianity: Subaltern Religion and Liberation Theology in India*, Oxford University Press, New Delhi.

Darity, William, Jr. (Ed.) (1995): *Economics and Discrimination*, Vol. I, An Elgar Reference Collection (U.S.)

Darity, William, Jr. and Shulman, Steven (1989): "Question of Discrimination: Racial inequality in the U.S. Labour Market," Wesleyan University Press, Middletown, Connecticut

Deshi, A.K. and Singh H. (1995): "Education, Labour Market Distortions and Relative Earning of Different Religious: Caste Categories in India", *Canadian Journal of Development of Studies*, December 21

Dr. Babasaheb Ambedkar Writings and Speeches, Vol. 14, Education Department, Government of Maharashtra.

Dube, Saurabh (1998): *Untouchable Pasts: Religion, Identity and Power among a Central Indian Community, 1780-1950*, Vistaar Publications, New Delhi.

Dworkin, Ronald (2002): "Affirmative Action: Does it Work?", "Affirmative Action: Is it Fair?" in *Sovereign Virtue: The Theory and Practice of Equality*. Cambridge, Mass: Harvard University Press.

Galanter, Marc (1984): *Competing Equalities: Law and Backward Classes in India*. Oxford, New Delhi.

Haan, De. Arjan (1997): Poverty and Social Exclusion: A Comparison of Debates on Deprivation. Working Paper No. 2, Poverty Research Unit at Sussex. Brighton: University of Sussex.

Haan, De. Arjan (2003): Extreme Deprivation in Remote Areas in India: Social Exclusion as Explanatory concept, Manchester conference on Chronic Poverty, April, session "Social Exclusion, Rights and Chronic Poverty".

Harwood, Sterling (1990): "Affirmative Action Is Justified: A Reply to Newton", *Contemporary Philosophy*, pp. 14-17.

Human Rights Watch (1999): *Broken People: Caste Violence against India's Untouchables,* Books for Change, Bangalore.

Ilaiah, Kancha (1996): "Why I Am Not a Hindu: A Sudra Critique of Hindutva Philosophy", *Culture and Political Economy,* Samya, Calcutta.

Jaffrelot, Christophe (2003): *India's Silent Revolution: The Rise of Low Castes in North Indian Politics,* Permanent Black, New Delhi.

Jeffrey, Craig, Roger Jeffery and Patricia Jeffery (2004): "Broken Trajectories: Dalit Young Men and Formal Education" in *Educational Regimes in Contemporary India* (eds) Radhika Chopra and Patricia Jeffery in collaboration with Helmut Reifeld, Sage, New Delhi.

Kaur, Ravinder (2004): *The State and Social Equality: Deconstructing Reservations in Institutes of Technology,* MS, New Delhi.

Kirpal, V. and Meenakshi Gupta (1999): *Equality through Reservations,* Rawat Publications, Jaipur.

Lal Deepak (1984): "Hindu Equilibrium", *Cultural Stability and Economic Stagnation,* Vol. I Carendor, 1988 Oxford.

Moffat, Michael (1979): *An Untouchable Community in South India,* Princeton University Press, Princeton.

Nambissan, G. and M. Sedwal (2002): "Education for All: The Situation of Dalit Children in India" in R. Govinda (Ed.), *India Education Report,* Oxford University Press, New Delhi.

NCERT (2005): "National Focus Group on Scheduled Caste and Scheduled Tribe Children", MS.

Purdy, Laura. (1984) "In Defense of Hiring Apparently Less Qualified Women", *Journal of Social Philosophy* 15: 26-33.

Racine, Josiane and Racine, Jean-Luc (1997): *Viramma: Life of an Untouchable,* (translated by Will Hobson), Verso, London.

Rodrigues, Valerian (2003): *The Essential Writings of Dr. B.R. Ambedkar,* Oxford University Press, New Delhi.

Scoville, James G.L. (1991): "Towards a Model of Caste Economy" in James G. Scoville, (Ed.) *Status Influences in Third World Labour Markets, Caste, Gender and Custom,* Walter de Gruyter, Berlin and New York.

Sen, Amartya (2000): "Social Exclusion: Concept, Application and Scrutiny", Social Development Papers No. 1, Office of Environment and Social Development , Asian Development Bank.

Shah, Ghanshyam (2004): "Underprivileged and Communal Carnage: A Case of Gujarat", Manuscript.

Subrahmanian, Ramya (2003): "Exploring Processes of Marginalisation and Inclusion in Education, in Education Inclusion and Exclusion: India and South Africa Perspectives", *IDS Bulletin,* Vol. 34 (1), January.

Thorat, Sukhadeo (1996): "Ambedkar on Economics of Hindu Social Order: Understanding Its Orthodoxy and Legacy" in Walter Fernandes "*The Emerging Dalit Identity: The Assertion of the Subalterns*" Indian Social Institute, Delhi.

Thorat, Sukhadeo and Narender Kumar (forthcoming): *Ambedkar on Social Exclusion and Inclusive Policies,* Oxford University Press, New Delhi.

Thorat, Sukhadeo (with Aryma and Prashant Negi) (2005): *Reservation and Private Sector: Quest for Equal Opportunity and Growth,* Rawat Publications, Jaipur.

Thorat, Sukhadeo (With R.S. Deshpande) (1999): "Caste and Labour Market Discrimination" *Indian Journal of Labour Economic,* Conference Issue, November.

Thurow, Lester C. (1969): *Poverty and Discrimination,* The Brookings Institution, Washington, D.C.

Vasavi, A R (2003): "Schooling for a New Society? The Social and Political Bases of Education Deprivation in India", *IDS Bulletin,* Vol. 34, No1.

Weisskopf, Thomas (2004): *Affirmative Action in the United States and India: A Comparative Perspective,* Routledge.

I

Discrimination, Deprivation and Inclusive Policy

1

Paying the Social Debt

SUKHADEO THORAT

The government's initiative to bring the private sector under the ambit of reservation policy and to extend reservations to the other backward classes (OBCs) in public educational institutions has led to a renewed discussion on familiar themes, which include: Are separate policies necessary for the lower castes? If yes, what should be the nature of such policies? Why not use alternative policies, as reservations involve costs in terms of efficiency, merit and reverse discrimination. Drawing insights from theoretical and empirical literature, particularly from economics, I seek to address some of these issues in this article.

The problems of the lower castes (the scheduled castes – SCs – and the OBCs) are unique and distinct and as such have to be understood in terms of their being excluded from having equal rights in the "past". Also, such forms of exclusion, even if not in all their original forms, continue to perpetuate themselves in the "present". In social sciences literature, there is reasonable agreement on the definitive features of social exclusion and the means by which it perpetuates poverty and inequality. Social exclusion is conceived as a process, which unfavourably denies opportunities to certain groups. It is embedded in societal relations and manifests itself by "wholly" or "partially" excluding certain groups from full participation in the activities of a society. It is necessary to recognise that social exclusion based on identities is a process independent of income status, productivity or the merit of individuals. Identity-based exclusion pivots around the ethnic background of an individual and not on his economic characteristics. It is an altogether different matter that identity-based exclusion eventually leads to the economic and social deprivation.

In contextualising social exclusion in the Indian perspective, what comes to the fore is that the process revolves around certain social relations that discriminate, isolate, and deprive some groups on the basis of their identities such as caste and ethnicity. Among other things, exclusion in the Indian context is closely linked with the institution of caste. Caste, as a customary form of governance with its fundamental characteristics of fixed, unequal and hierarchal arrangement of rights, leads to the "exclusion" of one caste from the rights that the other castes enjoy.

Past and Present Exclusion

The consequences of the historical denial of rights to the lower castes still remain as residual effects and are visible in the poorer representation of the lower castes with regard to ownership of land, business, and in education. The continuation of caste discrimination in modified forms, if not in its traditional forms, also persists.

This article attempts to capture the consequences of historical denial substantiating this with statistical inferences with respect to ownership of assets and education. In 2000, the National Sample Survey (NSS) data on livelihoods indicated that only 16 per cent of the total SC rural households pursued cultivation, while the similar figures for the STs and OBCs stood at 35 per cent. Correspondingly, the households pursuing cultivation for the "others" category stood at 41 per cent (Table 1).

Similar disparities persist in cases of ownership of businesses. The proportion of households involved in business was 12 per cent for SCs, 5 per cent for the STs, and 15 per cent each for the OBCs and others. In the urban areas, this proportion stood at 27, 22, 38 and 36 per cent for the SCs, the STs, the OBCs and the others respectively. In the urban areas, the proportion of regular/salaried workers was 36-38 per cent for the SCs the STs, and the OBCs in comparison to 46.5 per cent for the others. Also, the percentage of casual labours was the highest for the SCs/STs (25%), followed by the OBCs (17%) and the others (7.4%).

Table 1

Ownership of Agricultural Land and Business – 2000

	SC	*ST*	*OBC*	*Others*
Rural				
1.Self-employed cultivator	16.4	36.2	34.7	41.1
2. Self-employed business	12	5.2	15.5	14.8
3. Wage labours	61.4	48.5	37.1	25.3
Urban				
1. Self-employed business	27.3	21.6	37.6	35.6
2. Regular/salaried	37.1	38	36.3	46.5
3. Casual labours	26.5	25.6	17.4	7.4

Source: NSS Employment/Unemployment Survey, 1999-2000.

In 2000, with regard to education too, large-scale inter-group disparities were evident from the NSS figures. In 2000, for the rural areas, the percentage of literate adults stood at 52, 56.7, 68, and 80 per cent for the STs, the SCs, the OBCs, and the others in that order. Correspondingly, the figures for the urban areas stood at 77 per cent for the SCs/STs, 86 per cent for the OBCs and a huge 93 per cent for the others.

Table 2

Current Attendance Rates (19-25 Age Groups)

(in per cent)

	SC	*ST*	*OBC*	*Others*
1. Currently not attending	93.17	92.6	91.73	50.66
2. Graduate/Diploma	4.19	3.81	4.55	13.37
Share in Total Graduate by Faculty				
1. Intermediate and below	4.8	15.09	25.08	38.19
2. Agriculture	2.61	7.01	18.18	53
3. Engineering/technology	2.06	8.74	17.18	51.1
4. Medicine	0.91	0.06	27.09	34.05

Source: NSS Employment/Unemployment Survey, 2000.

Further, in 2000, the attainment rate at the graduate/diploma level was 4.19 per cent for the SCs, 3.81 per cent for the STs, 4.55 per cent for the OBCs, and 13.37 per cent for the others. Equally stark was the share of the others in various levels of attainment: about 38.19 per cent (intermediate and below), 53 per cent (agriculture), 51.1 per cent (engineering/technology) and 34.05 per cent (medicine) respectively – which was much higher than the proportion of the others in the total population, which stood at 35.9 percentage points for the rural areas.

Conversely, the share of the SCs, the STs and the OBCs was lower than their respective proportions in the total population. The share of the SCs in various levels of attainment was about 4.8 per cent (intermediate and below), 2.61 per cent (agriculture), 2.06 per cent (engineering/technology) and 0.91 per cent (medicine) respectively, which is much lower than their percentage share in the total population. Similarly, the share of the STs in similar levels of attainment worked out to be 15.09, 7.01, 8.74 and 0.06 per cent respectively. The attainment levels were low in agriculture, engineering and technology, and medicine when compared to their respective share in the total population, which stood at 10.6 per cent for the rural population.

Likewise, the share of the OBCs in similar levels of attainment stood at 25.08, 18.18, 17.18 and 27.89 per cent. Again, the attainment rates at various levels were lower than their share in the rural population, which stood at 37 per cent. Persisting disparities in access to capital assets and education between the lower castes and the others provide an indirect evidence of the impact of past discrimination. Although systematic empirical research on the extent of economic discrimination in the "present" is meagre, studies do provide some evidence of economic discrimination in hiring and wage payment for SCs. Studies also suggest that SCs faced discrimination in various markets in rural areas. Similarly, limited evidence also suggests that the industrial employment system has been exclusionary throughout the period of modern industrial development and even today the proportion of those securing jobs through informal and personalised channels is as high as 60-70 per cent. The social composition of those securing jobs through informal channels is generally tilted favourably towards the socially better-endowed sections of the society.

Thus, the cumulative impact of the exclusion of lower castes is clearly visible in their lack of ownership of assets and low education. If the lower castes possess few land and business assets and education, it is because they do not have access to property rights and education. And, if the higher castes are seen to have more of both, it is because access to assets and education was artificially "reserved" for them at the cost of the lower castes.

International Experience

Given the evidence on inter-social group inequality and discrimination, a policy for overcoming the consequences of past discrimination and providing legal safeguards against present discrimination is inevitable. There are lessons to be drawn from international experiences, which have often been quoted for the issue of private sector reservation in India, particularly with respect to two aspects: (a) type of the economic sectors, and (b) the methods used.

First, with regard to the economic sphere, most countries have developed legal and equal access policies through affirmative action/reservation for the discriminated groups in multiple economic and social spheres.

Second, with regard to the method, at least three kinds of "procedures" are used. The first method incorporates legal protection against discrimination in the form of "anti-discrimination laws". The second method utilises equal access measures of various types known by different names such as affirmative action/reservation/fair access policies and involves proactive measures to ensure fair access to the discriminated groups. In some countries, formal and informal quota systems are incorporated to achieve equity in access to resources. However, in both aspects, the population or labour force is used as an indicator to measure and ensure the fair share of representation.

The third method is known as "reparation or compensation". It is important to understand that affirmative action/reservation policy programmes are largely designed to address the problems of present discrimination and also address the issue of cumulative impact of historical discrimination in the past. The instruments of "compensation", on the other hand, are specifically designed to compensate for the denial of property rights and education to the discriminated groups as a one-time settlement and through continuous efforts in compensatory modes.

Lessons

Adoption of these three-tier measures for the lower castes in the public and private spheres in India will largely depend on the nature of discrimination and the degree of deprivation faced by them. The residual impact of the caste system and continuing forms of discrimination in the present are not in question; there is sufficient evidence on the ill-effects of the caste system, but the question centres around the nature of interventions for securing equal rights to lower castes.

The strategy of "compensation" is possibly necessary to repay for the denial of property rights in agricultural land, business and education. Essentially, the "compensation" principle is justified on the basis of the need to repay the lower castes for the historical material losses suffered by them.

Policies for increasing the ownership of agricultural land for lower castes should be incorporated within the framework of "compensation" principles. Among other countries, the Malaysian programme to improve the ownership of agriculture land of the indigenous Malay community is an example under which large tracts of agricultural lands were acquired and distributed to the Malays as a one-time settlement. Similarly, the government in India, too, should group together government land and land acquired under ceiling laws, as well as land free from legal problems and classify them together as a "pool of common land" and redistribute it to the low castes to compensate for the historical denial of land rights as a one-time settlement.

Like in agriculture land, the lower castes, particularly the SCs, were also debarred from undertaking any business activity on account of the notions of purity and pollution. It is important, therefore, that the policies for improving business ownership by the lower castes be treated mainly in a compensatory mode – developing programmes to improve the ownership of businesses and their share in private capital.

The measures for the promotion of low caste businesses may include reservations in government and private contracts of various types and reservations in the purchases of agricultural and other products by the government and private sector. This is necessary to provide safeguards against the exclusion faced by the low caste businesses in sale of goods and services.

There is also a need to increase the ownership of corporate capital among the lower castes. In this respect, again, there is a lot to be learnt from the Malaysian and the South African experiences. The systematic redistribution of private capital ownership to a minority community was undertaken in Malaysia, whereby, the share of the Malay community rose from 2 per cent to 30 per cent over three decades. For this purpose, the Malaysian government fixed the quotas in the share capital of private companies and set up special institutions to finance the equity participation of the Malaya minority. The Malaysian experience, therefore, could guide the efforts of the Indian government to ensure that the share in the private capital of the lower castes increases.

Coming to employment policy, the pattern of employment among lower castes is such that a majority of them are primarily casual wage labourers. As a vast majority of these casual labourers are adequately represented, there seems to be no need of developing a reservation policy, but legal safeguards against selective discrimination in hiring and wage payments in the form of anti-discrimination law is necessary. In the non-farm sector (industrial and service sectors), the discrimination in employment is possibly of a high order in certain categories of jobs, if not all. Therefore, it is imperative that a strategy of legal safeguards along with reservations be developed for the non-farm sector.

Lastly, educational policies for lower castes should also be considered in the twin framework of compensation for the past denial of right to education and provision of equal opportunity against present discrimination. The lower castes need to be compensated by implementation of a comprehensive programme of education designed specifically for their empowerment. This needs to be supplemented by reservations in educational institutions of various types.

It is necessary to recognise that the exceptionally high proportion of the higher caste students in educational institutions, much above their share in the total population, has been because education was artificially reserved for them by putting entry barriers to the vast section of lower castes almost till the beginning of 20th century. Perceptibly, the present higher share of higher castes in education is the result of continuous privileges enjoyed by earlier generations, which continues on to the present generation with the denial of the same to the lower castes. It is this social debt, which higher castes owe to the lower castes that needs to be repaid by compensatory policies.

How to develop inclusive policies so that both the higher and the lower caste youth have an equal share in accessing education, is an issue. In my view, an inclusive policy which benefits both can be developed.

On Alternatives, Merit and Creamy Layer

A number of other issues related to alternative policies, merits and creamy layer have figured in the current discussion.

The first issue relates to the suggestion of using general policies to improve employability and human resource capability of lower castes instead of reservation. It needs to be recognised that lower castes need both because their problem is two-fold – namely, lack of access to fixed capital assets, employment and education due to denial in the "past", but also continuing discrimination in the "present". Therefore, it requires a dual solution. Improving education and employability alone will not help the lower castes unless it is supplemented by strategies of equal access in the form of reservations to overcome discrimination. It is not coincidental that in several countries the policies of economic and educational empowerment for discriminated groups are supplemented by equal opportunity policies of affirmative action and reservation.

The second issue relates to suggestions that reservation should be based on economic criterion rather than caste or ethnicity. Insights from theory indicate that the basis of discrimination is group identity and not economic powerlessness; in fact, identity-based exclusion from economic and social rights is the source of powerlessness. Such forms of exclusion are suffered by both relatively better-off and worse-off persons belonging to the discriminated groups. Therefore, the basis of preferential policy in favour of the lower castes needs to be based on caste.

Also, this aspect is closely intertwined with the other suggestion that preferential policies should be utilised only for the relatively worse-off sections within the discriminated groups and that the relatively better-off sections should be excluded from the purview of reservations. This view assumes that the relatively better-off sections within the discriminated groups possess enough economic strength to overcome the effects of discrimination faced by them. In my view, this is an issue, which needs careful consideration and study.

Since caste discrimination is the basis of reservation, the use of the same for relatively better-off sections from the low castes would depend largely on whether they are able to overcome the cumulative impact of discrimination due to their economic strength. Indeed, if that is the case, then, the relatively better-off sections may not need protection against discrimination in the form of reservation. But, if they continue to experience caste-based discrimination, then measures against such discrimination are necessary. As such, there is little research on this issue and in the absence of any evidence, it is too early to say whether the relatively better-off sections should be excluded from the purview of the reservation policy. This will require us to identify that critical minimum "economic level", which would enable the lower castes to overcome the discrimination on the basis of economic strength, so that safeguards in the form of reservation against discrimination are not necessary. This will vary from caste to caste depending on the intensity of discrimination.

In the case of the SCs, however, one can say with a degree of certainty that both the relatively better-off and worse-off sections suffer from discrimination, although in differing degrees and, therefore, they require protection against discrimination in the form of both anti-discriminatory laws and equal opportunity policies such as reservations. However, the better-off sections could be excluded from concessionary economic benefit, which is already being practised.

Another issue raised pertains to the supposed beliefs regarding the adverse consequences of relaxation in qualifications on issues such as productivity and educational quality. As regards employment, this has much less support in economic theory and the empirical literature. Theoretical insights, in fact, argue for interventions in the form of affirmative action to overcome market failures caused by market discrimination and to make them more competitive. At a practical level, the recruitments in the public sector under reservations in India and elsewhere are based on fulfilling some prerequisite qualifications. Studies from the US indicate that the potential effects of affirmative actions on performance, at least in the labour markets, appear to depend heavily on how they are implemented. Employers that practise affirmative action have tried to mitigate its potentially negative effects on performance by pre-screening the recruitment and hiring criterion, as well as, by special training and evaluatory efforts afterwards.

In case of education, providing admissions to persons with lesser grades does not carry the potential of affecting educational standards. It only provides low caste groups the prospect of accessing education without any significant relaxations in passing grades or marks. But despite this, other writings on these themes have overplayed the issue of merit. Much of it has come without adequate empirical evidence.

Some Suggestions

By way of conclusion I would make a few suggestions. Firstly, it is necessary to recognise the exclusionary and discriminatory character of our society and economy associated with caste, ethnicity, religion and other group identities and the need to develop remedies. However, to design appropriate policies, an understanding of contemporary forms of discrimination in multiple spheres, and their consequences is quite necessary. It becomes imperative, therefore, to undertake empirical studies on the exclusionary character of our economy, society and polity – an area which has been neglected in the mainstream social science research so far.

In fact, with respect to the theoretical and empirical literatures on exclusion, we are in a situation, which may be described as an "academic crisis", resulting in the woeful ignorance regarding the exclusionary character of our society and our inability to discuss the issue in an enlightened manner. The state in recognition of the critical issues plaguing our society has to respond with policy initiatives and, rightly so, because it cannot wait till academics come up first with the best solution. Therefore, state responses often precede both theory and empirical research, because academics have failed to come up with a research-based enlightened solution.

Further, I would also like to suggest that there is a need to set up an "Equal Opportunity Commission/Office" and bring under its purview all reservation policies related to women, the SCs, the STs, the OBCs, religious minorities, and the physically challenged under one umbrella organisation. The main objectives of this Commission should be to (a) build up a database on socio-economic profile of these groups; (b) develop policies for each of the groups and sub-groups; (c) monitor the implementation of the reservation policy and other policies; and (d) advise the government on a regular basis.

2

Caste, Inequality and Affirmative Action

ANDRÉ BÉTEILLE

I am really very happy to be here with you this afternoon but I also feel a bit daunted by the magnitude of the task that is assigned to me. I am going to talk about caste, inequality and affirmative action, all in the course of 45 minutes. These are really three separate topics, although they are related to each other. I take it that your main interest is in affirmative action and I will pay special attention to that subject. Some of you may be familiar with the programme of affirmative action in the United States and in other countries. There are many distinctive features of the programme in India, and in order to appreciate these features and understand how the programme has been faring in the last several decades, it is necessary to know something about the structure of society and the problems which the programme seeks to address.

Each one of these topics – caste, inequality and affirmative action – is large and complex. I will begin with caste, and I will try to indicate the basic features of the system. It is true that caste has given rise to a massive programme of affirmative action in India, but there are also programmes of affirmative action which have been devised in other contexts where caste does not exist. So caste has to be understood to some extent on its own terms.

Certainly, the caste system is changing. I think that is about the only point on which the specialists are agreed. What is the direction in which it is changing? There are sharp disagreements on that. Some would say, and this is my opinion, that if you take a long-term view of caste, the indication is that it is becoming weaker and not stronger, taking the system as a whole. But, there are others who would argue that state action has in fact increased the strength of caste. So, even on that point, there are disagreements among the authorities and I do not want to discuss these disagreements today – whether caste is becoming stronger or weaker, whether affirmative action is making caste stronger or making it weaker. This is an argument which is debated over and over again in India. Some say that affirmative action is essential, it is necessary in order to eliminate, or at least to reduce, the inequalities that have been inherited from the past. Others say that affirmative action in fact reinforces the sense of separate identity between members of different castes.

Now, caste, of course, is closely related to inequality but inequality is not all there is to caste. There are many other aspects of caste which need to be considered at least briefly. And inequality is not simply a matter of caste. There are other aspects of inequality in Indian society which are extremely important. In the 1950's and 1960's, after the country became independent, there were sharp disagreements between Marxists and liberal theorists as to whether, in fact, caste was the real basis of inequality in Indian society. Some would say that it was, while others would say that the real basis of inequality was the ownership, control and use of land. For the latter, it was the agrarian social structure which provided the real basis of inequality in Indian society. In other words, there are aspects of caste which can be discussed independently of the issue of inequality, and there are aspects of inequality which can be discussed independently of caste.

I will try to bring together caste and inequality and to present the programme of affirmative action in the context of our understanding of the inequalities of caste that continue to exist. Many students of Indian society have argued that caste was the country's fundamental social institution. If there was anything which gave Indian society its distinctive features, it was the caste system and caste was the basis of Hindu society over a very long period. It was very much tied up with Hindu attitudes towards ritual purity and pollution, to Hindu conceptions of hierarchy as the basic order of society, and in that sense they would say that caste is the fundamental institution of Hinduism, that it represents the social morphology, so to say, of Hindu society. Hinduism is a religion whose social aspect is expressed in the division of the population into castes and sub-castes of many different kinds.

Caste has existed in India, particularly among the Hindus, over a very long period of time. It has long been a subject of discussion, and not simply among contemporary or modern social theorists. Caste was extensively discussed in the classical literature of Hinduism which tried to explain and even to justify the system. So, there has been an elaborate discussion over a long period of time of the logic of caste, so to say. If you look at medieval European history, you will find elaborate discussions of the logic of the feudal system and the "estates". But India has a much greater continuity over time in the discussion of caste. So it was in that sense the definitive institution of Hindu society.

Caste was not confined to the Hindus and this is something which must be kept in mind. Divisions of a kind which are very similar to the divisions of caste among the Hindus have existed also among the Muslims in India and on the sub-continent over a very long period of time. When the British administrators began to construct a social map of India, they used their 10-year censuses as occasions for writing about the division of the population into its basic groups and communities. These census reports, which start from the end of the nineteenth century, provide very interesting information on the divisions and sub-divisions of Indian society. The census of 1921, which, of course, was of undivided India, had a special report on caste among the Muslim population. The detailed discussion of what the census commissioner described as caste among the Muslims generated a strong reaction from the Muslim intelligentsia who argued that caste was antithetical to the principle of Islam. How could one talk about caste among Muslims in India? But, in the course of time, most students of Indian society and of the sub-continent have come to accept that caste-like divisions exist not only among the Muslims but also among Christians and other religious communities. They also exist in incipient form among the tribal communities in India.

The division of the population into a large number of groups which were ranked in some kind of a hierarchy was found throughout India and it was not confined to the Hindus only. But, of course, it was only among the Hindus that you found not simply the practice but also the theory of caste. Over a period of 2,000 years, the Hindus had developed a model of society in which the hierarchical division of the population was regarded as constitutive of their society and indeed of human society as such. It is distinctive of caste among the Hindus that you have not only the practice of caste, not only the division of society into innumerable groups, but you also have a theory which seeks to describe, explain and justify these divisions.

When one uses the term "caste" in English, s/he is actually translating two distinct terms in the classical as well as the modern languages of India. The first term is 'varna' and the second is 'jati'. Both these have been described as caste. They are not unrelated to each other but they are not the same, and it is very important to understand the distinction between the two in order to understand the social logic of caste. The scheme of varnas has been elaborated in India among the Hindus for at least 2,000 years. It has no counterpart among the other religious communities, and that is extremely important. The theory of varna lays down the logic of the system just as many medieval texts laid down the logic of the system of estates in medieval Europe. According to these classical texts and also according to later accounts, there were four and only four varnas – Brahman, Kshatriya, Vaisya, and Sudra. These four varnas are ranked in the order shown. The distinctive feature of the system of varnas is that it was believed to be invariant, to be present throughout the country, throughout the length of the sub-continent. It was the same order, Brahman, Kshatriya, Vaisya, and Sudra which was believed to prevail throughout the country. Further, it was not only invariant; it was also believed to be permanent. The same order of the social world divided into Brahman, Kshatriya, Vaisya, and Sudra remained unchanged over the centuries.

When we look at the history of modern India, we realise that the traditional order of varnas may not change, but it becomes obsolete. Fewer areas of life tend to be governed by varna than was the case in the past. And one can see this obsolescence of the social order of varnas in the course of the last 50 years. Discussions of caste in the regional languages in India make less and less use of the category of varnas. If one talks to modern Indians, if one looks at the newspapers, the discussion of caste is no longer in the language of varnas as was the case until the middle of the nineteenth century. Today, the discussion of caste is in the language of jati which is the other aspect of caste.

Now, what are jatis? I said that there are four and only four varnas – Brahman, Kshatriya, Vaisya, Sudra – but the jatis are innumerable. I myself studied a village in South India in the early 1960's. In that one single village, there were as many as 35 or 36 distinct jatis. If you take the region as a whole, you might find the population divided and sub-divided and sub-sub-divided into a couple of hundred different jatis. So, they are numerous and they are ranked, but the order of ranking is not as tidy or as rigid as the order of ranking of the varnas. Not only that, the jatis are not the same in all parts of the country. They vary from one part of India to another. Each region has its own distinctive complement of jatis, and, whereas the varnas are believed to have been unchanging and immutable, we know that new jatis were being created and old jatis were dying out all the time. So, it is a much more flexible and dynamic system than the system of varnas.

Today, when one talks about caste in India, s/he is really talking about jatis rather than varnas. What does this mean in sociological terms? It simply means that when one talked about varnas, s/he talked about the hierarchy that not only existed in fact, but also had certain legitimacy in the normative order of society. Whereas, when one talks about jatis, s/he is talking about divisions of a kind which do not enjoy the legitimacy that the system had in the past. If I may use an analogy from other societies, I would say that the system of varnas corresponded to the medieval system of estates.

"The rich man in his castle, the poor man at his gate, God made them high and lowly and ordered their estate." That is a Church of England hymn, as a matter of fact. It is a system whose legitimacy is accepted and taken for granted. In contrast, the jatis operate rather like the ethnic groups in the United States do. The differences must also be noted: the varna order had far greater stability and continuity over time than the system of estates in medieval Europe did, and the system of jatis in contemporary India is far more elaborate than the system of ethnic groups in the United States.

There is a ranking of jatis but there is a difference between groups which are ranked in terms of *de facto* criteria and the social hierarchy whose basic principles are accepted generally, if not universally, in society. If one looks at the traditional order of Hindu society and of Indian society in general, I would say that it was a hierarchical social order in the sense that inequalities not only existed, but that they were accepted as right, proper and desirable. All this was considered to be part of the natural scheme of things, not just inequalities between the varnas but also between the jatis, because the varna system provided a kind of framework, a benchmark for ranking the different jatis. It was considered right, proper and desirable that they should be ranked in this way. This applied not just to the ranking of varnas and jatis, but also to the ranking of men and women. That was the traditional order, it was the most complete and the most elaborate hierarchical social order known to human history. And, the legitimacy of ranking was taken for granted by and large. It was questioned from time to time, but over a long historical period the legitimacy of this ranking of jatis and varnas was taken for granted in the classical, legal and religious literature of Hinduism. There is a whole range of classical legal texts which lay out the basic principles of the hierarchical order, but the epitome is to be found in the "Manusmriti" or the "Manavadharmashastra". In the entire literature, the logic of caste is explained and the "Manusmriti" gives the blueprint of a quintessentially hierarchical society.

Today, the Constitution of India provides a blueprint for an egalitarian society. The Constitution is not based on the premise of hierarchy, but on the premise of equality. But, of course, you do not just erase or cancel out age-old inequalities simply by adopting new principles in a Constitution. So what else has to be done in order to reduce the inequalities of the past? This is what affirmative action or positive discrimination addresses itself to. The object is to reduce the level of inequality in a society which has had a hierarchical order over a very long period of time. Affirmative action or positive discrimination was not the only major programme adopted when the country became independent and created a Constitution based on the premise of equality. For example, there was a massive programme of agrarian reform which was also designed to give greater thrust to the pursuit of equality. I would say that these were the two main programmes – agrarian reform and affirmative action – designed to improve the conditions of what came to be known as the backward classes in Indian society.

I have often been asked outside India about the insensitivity of Indians in using a term like this – the backward classes. It shows a certain kind of insensitivity and I have often been asked if I feel embarrassed to use this phrase when talking about a section of my own society. Well, yes and no. The term 'backward' has become a fighting word in India today so it is not necessarily something that one wants to sweep under the carpet. It has become a fighting word although it was not always a fighting word and this question of terminology, in fact, bedevilled the administrators of India even before independence. One major component of the backward classes consists of those who are called Dalits today or the untouchables or the Harijans as Mahatma Gandhi called them. J. H. Hutton, a distinguished anthropologist, who was also the commissioner for the 1931 census, wrote that this section of the Indian population had come to be called the 'depressed classes', which was an odious phrase to use in to reference to a whole section of society. He was very unhappy with the term and favoured 'exterior castes' in its place. Finally, the Government of India, in 1935, that is, before independence, settled for 'scheduled castes'. Thus, the policy of positive discrimination in India, which I am going to talk about, has antecedents in colonial rule. It was not created *ex nihilo* with the Constitution of India. It has antecedents in colonial rule and right from that time we see the two faces of positive discrimination, a desire to bring about greater equality, greater social justice as well as a desire to use it as an instrument for devising politics. It has also been used as an instrument of divisive politics since independence.

Successive governments in independent India have used positive discrimination as an instrument for furthering specific political ends. So, what is tantalising about positive discrimination in India is that it is not just a question of furthering social justice, it is also a question of maintaining a certain balance of power between different groups in society. This did not start with independence and the adoption of a new Constitution. In fact, it started at least 30 years before the new Constitution was adopted. So, what is this programme of positive discrimination which has such a long history in India? I will now very briefly indicate the basic features of positive discrimination before I invite questions. I am often asked, "Is positive discrimination a good thing or is it a bad thing?" I think, it is impossible to give a blanket answer to that question because the programme is so large and so elaborate and has so many different aspects that almost inevitably one sees that some parts of it are good, other parts are not so good and it is very difficult to disentangle what is good in positive discrimination from what is not. It is not easy to determine how much it has contributed to reducing inequalities and how much it has contributed to the heightening of rivalries, tensions and hostilities between groups. If one wants to examine it more closely, I think there are two distinctions that have to be kept in mind. The first relates to the beneficiaries of positive discrimination – that is to say, those groups for whose benefit the programme of positive discrimination has been constructed and elaborated over the last 80 years. So, one must get some idea of the interested beneficiaries of positive discrimination. They are not a single homogeneous block; in fact, they are very diverse and one must keep this diversity in mind in order to evaluate the success and the failure of positive discrimination. One might take the view that positive discrimination is justified in the case of some of these groups, but not in the case of others. Secondly, one has to distinguish between the different kinds of programme that come under the broad policy of positive discrimination; here, one might say that positive discrimination is justified in certain areas of public life but not in others. At least, one must have some appreciation of the wide range of the beneficiaries of positive discrimination as well as a sense of the variety of policies which come under the umbrella of positive discrimination.

Let me first say something about the intended beneficiaries of positive discrimination, who are broadly known as the backward classes. Who are the backward classes? They are not a single homogeneous block, and this must always be kept in mind. And, what must also be kept in mind is that the backward classes are not really classes in the ordinary sociological sense of the term. They are really groups of communities and not classes. These groups of communities fall into three broad divisions: firstly, there are the scheduled tribes, secondly, there are the scheduled castes and thirdly, there are the other backward classes (OBCs).

Let me very briefly give you an idea of these three divisions among the backward classes. The smallest group consists of the scheduled tribes. In a very rough way, they can be compared to the native American population of the United States but the analogy is deceptive beyond a certain point. They are the tribal population of Indian society and they are the smallest division of the backward classes. However, although they only comprise a little over 8.5 per cent of the population, that means over 85 million people. That is not a very small population by the standards of European countries or by the standards of countries anywhere in the world. The scheduled tribes are very diverse, and this is directly relevant to the discussion, because the critics of positive discrimination point out that in India, it benefits not the most disadvantaged members of the backward classes but the least disadvantaged among them.

The scheduled tribes are divided into more than 400 distinct tribes varying enormously in size, occupation, economic condition, habitat and many other things. Their general characteristic so far has been their physical isolation in the hill and forest areas either on the frontiers of the country or in the interior. But, their isolation is no longer as conspicuous as it was till the middle of the nineteenth century. So, today, it is often very difficult to decide whether a community is a tribe or a caste. The British were very keen to distinguish the tribes from the castes, but they frequently confused them. If you look at the terminology which they used in the census reports, you will find that this is a very genuine problem, and perhaps I can address this point when I answer your questions.

The scheduled tribes constitute the smallest section of the backward classes. The next consists of what are known as the scheduled castes. Whereas the scheduled tribes have been isolated in hill and forest areas, the scheduled castes have been segregated. They have been very much a part of the economy of land and grain on which Indian society was based. But they were segregated and were not allowed access to many civic amenities. They were denied access to education and the other advantages through which one could achieve success in economic and social life. They comprise over 16 per cent of the population, so around 165 million persons. But they are also highly divided. First of all, they are regionally divided. India is a country of many regions, each with its own distinctive language, and the scheduled castes are divided by language just like the rest of the population, although they come at the bottom of the hierarchy. This means that there is a distinction between the scheduled castes of Tamil Nadu who speak Tamil like the non-scheduled caste population of Tamil Nadu and the scheduled castes of Bengal who speak Bengali. Even if we confine our attention to the scheduled castes of one particular region, there also we will find a considerable amount of differentiation as well as ranking. The ranking of castes did not stop at the boundaries of untouchability, it went right down. So, the scheduled castes or the so-called untouchables were themselves also ranked. It is this that makes the problem of the scheduled castes quite different from the problem of the blacks in the United States. It is this that makes the problem of administering a policy of positive discrimination so much more difficult and so much more complex in the Indian case because the benefits of the programme tend to be gathered not by the weakest among the scheduled castes but by the strongest among them. There are analogies to this of course in the affirmative action programme in the United States. But, in India, the problem is far more complex.

Finally, there is what is called the "other backward classes". The Constitution of India was drawn up at a time when the country had been partitioned on the basis of religion so the mood was against further divisiveness. Therefore, in the Constitution of 1950, special provisions were only made for the scheduled castes and the scheduled tribes. But, it did not stop there because one of the directive principles of state policy said that some measures may also be adopted for the benefit of other backward classes without specifying what these measures should be and who the other backward classes were. So commissions were set up and as a result we have today a third section of the backward classes consisting once again of numerous castes and communities, which are even more diverse in their economic and social standing than the scheduled castes or the scheduled tribes and which are known as the other backward classes. They comprise anything between 25 to 50 per cent of the population.

One can give exact figures for the scheduled tribes and the scheduled castes, but not for the other backward classes. What the British did was to enumerate all castes and communities throughout the country. At the time of independence it was felt that the benefit of this was outweighed by the divisive implications of enumerating caste in the census. So, the enumeration of castes was discontinued in the censuses from 1951 onwards with the exception of the scheduled castes and the scheduled tribes, who have been enumerated separately. So, these are the three broad divisions, very different in their social standing. Some of the other backward classes are and have been politically dominant in their areas although their social and ritual standing in the traditional hierarchy was not very high. Whereas the scheduled castes and scheduled tribes, one would agree on the whole, have been severely disadvantaged and deprived, this is not true, or not true to the same extent, of the other backward classes.

These groups are the intended beneficiaries of positive discrimination. What are the benefits? There are three main kinds of benefits and I will just enumerate them and then stop. The first is what may be described as political reservation. This means that a certain number of seats in parliament and in the state legislatures are reserved for members of the scheduled castes and the scheduled tribes, roughly in proportion to their strength in the population. Political reservation in parliament and in the state legislatures is only for the benefit of the scheduled castes and the scheduled tribes, not for the other backward classes. Political reservations are written into the Constitution of India and the provisions reveal the ambivalence of the makers of the Constitution as well as of policy makers in contemporary India. The constitutional provisions for political reservations for the scheduled castes and scheduled tribes are mandatory. That is, the Constitution says that 'seats' shall be reserved in parliament for such and such. However, when the provisions were made mandatory in 1950, it was decided that this would apply only for ten years, so they would last for a single decade. But, since then, the Constitution has had to be amended every ten years to keep on extending political reservations for the scheduled castes and the scheduled tribes. I think the general idea is that these should not be written into the Constitution permanently, that at some future time the need for these special provisions will no longer exist. But that future seems to be moving further and further away. So that is political reservation.

The second kind of reservation, which is even more contentious than the first is known as job reservation. Job reservations apply mainly to government appointments at union and state levels and also to organisations which are substantially funded by the government. The provisions for job reservation apply not only to the scheduled castes and the scheduled tribes but also to the other backward classes. Over the years there has been an extension of job reservations for the benefit of the other backward classes. This has now become the most contentious issue, whether the wholesale extension of job reservations for the other backward classes accords with the spirit of the Constitution or not. For job reservations, unlike political reservations, the provisions are not mandatory; they are enabling provisions. The Constitution says that the state may take such measures as are necessary for the special benefit of the other backward classes.

Finally, there are what may be called reservations in education. These, again, are matters of contention, for reservation exists not only in general arts and science courses but also in medical and engineering schools. Those who are familiar with the subject will perhaps know that in the United States two of the most contentious legal cases have been over reservation; first, in law school in the case of Marco De Funis, and then in medical school in the case of Alan Bakke. In India, reservation in law schools somehow has not been a subject of such bitter contention. But reservation in medical and engineering schools is very controversial. Once again, when assessing the merits of this, one must ask whether provisions that are justified for the scheduled castes and scheduled tribes on a limited scale should be extended on such a large scale. What is the problem with extending these reservations on such a very large scale? The logic of reservations or of positive discrimination is that special opportunities should be created for some over and above the general provisions for equality of opportunity for all. Now, if you create special opportunities for some, then it does eat into the provision of equal opportunities for all.

The question is one of balance and, once again, this question came up at the time of the making of the Constitution of India. And, the man who piloted it through the constituent assembly was himself from an untouchable caste – Dr. Ambedkar, a formidable lawyer. In putting these proposals forward to the constituent assembly, Ambedkar argued that there are several conflicting aims which have to be reconciled. First, there is the aim of providing equal opportunity for all, irrespective of caste, creed and community. That is very important. The second aim is to create special opportunities for those sections of society which have been severely deprived and disadvantaged. But he went on to add that these special opportunities should not be so extensive as to 'eat up' the general provision of equality of opportunity for all. Those were the words he used. And now many people feel that the extension of reservations to the other backward classes on such a large scale has carried the policy of reservations so far that in many ways it threatens the more general principle of equality of opportunity irrespective of caste, creed and community which is also inscribed into the Constitution of India. So, very broadly speaking, this is the framework within which the problem of positive discrimination or affirmative action in India has to be assessed.

3

Caste Indignities and Subjected Personhoods

A.R. VASAVI

The intricacies of caste, as a system, as an idea, and as a form of social stratification, have been much debated and written about. But, what has been the impact of the caste system on the personhoods of those who are at the receiving end of its rules of hierarchy, pollution and untouchability? As Berreman has noted, "The human meaning of caste for those who live it is power and vulnerability, privilege and oppression, honour and denigration, plenty and want, reward and deprivation, security and anxiety" (cited in Raman 2003: 89). While descriptions and representations of such lived experiences are just beginning to be highlighted, little has been noted about how caste as a system creates in people dispositions that define not only relations between different caste members, but also their own notions of personhood, identity and self-worth.

This article indicates some ways in which caste indignities or its violence and inequities mark individuals and groups of scheduled communities, leaving them with subjected personhoods. The idea of personhood refers to the social and cultural norms by which individuals are recognised by society, and to the relational contexts and transactions by which a person's interactions and positions in the society are defined. An individual cannot be or become a person on the basis of her or his own capacities or nature. "People cannot be treated as being simply persons in themselves, they owe their personhood to others" (Shotter 2004: 7). If groups, communities and societies play a significant role in defining the personhood of individuals, then furthering this, by subjected personhoods I refer to the personalities and orientations in which there is an erosion of agency, and the sense of self-worth of individuals or groups is not individually defined or directed but is marked by the violence of persistent and pervasive humiliation, deprivation and indignities.

It is important to identify the ways and contexts in which the identities and personhoods of dalits are subjected to and marked by caste indignities, and how these subjected personhoods are manifested in the context of educational institutions and in the larger public sphere. In such a context, the role and contributions of educational institutions becomes significant as there is an urgent need to address and remove the sense of inadequacy and the deep socio-cultural and psychological marking to which many dalits have been subject.

Although not widely acknowledged by the general public, caste derived and defined indignities persist so much so that the dalit Kannada writer Devanoor Mahadeva (2001) has called untouchability and its attendant forms of segregation and separation as the "great grandfather of apartheid". In identifying it as a precursor to the institutionalised and deeply entrenched system of apartheid, Mahadeva calls attention to the ways in which caste as a system also encodes and impacts a systemic disadvantage on the low-ranked caste groups. There are several contexts, arenas and structures in which this disadvantage of caste discrimination is internalised and articulated in the formal and informal structures of the nation and its cultures. And, as Narendra Jadhav notes in his sensitive and compelling autobiography, "caste discrimination may have changed forms, but it has certainly not changed its substance" (2003: 267), and discrimination at the individual and collective level persists for many.

That this is so has been documented by several human rights groups and enquiry commissions. For example, Human Rights Watch, in its review of atrocities and violations of the human rights of dalits (1999), records the pervasive indignities which range from a high court judge cleansing his court chambers which had earlier been occupied by a dalit judge; the reintroduction of untouchability in the form of the two-tumbler system in the villages of Andhra and Tamil Nadu; to the rampant and everyday violence against dalit men, women and children. And, more tragically, the reports about caste-based discrimination during rehabilitation after the December 2004 tsunami disaster attest to the entrenchment of caste in our private and public lives.

While the above examples are an evidence of the continued public humiliation of the scheduled communities, it is important to clearly identify the more subtle, persistent and systemic forms of indignities that corrode their sense of self-worth and lead to the making of subjected personhoods. Some of these processes and forms of marking difference and instilling insecurity are evident in the ways in which children of scheduled communities are socialised into passivity, in the processes of sanskritisation, and in the representation of scheduled community members in the public sphere and their experiences in educational institutions.

Socialisation and the Acceptance of Indignities

Perhaps one of the primary sources of the internalisation of such indignities is linked to the socialisation process itself which, in turn, has led to the scarring and particular marking of dalits' subjected personhoods. The dominance of the caste system, with its prescription of a low, segregated position and status to low-ranked caste members, has led them to internalise low social status and to accordingly articulate and interact with others on terms of submission and subordination within a hierarchical system. Several autobiographical accounts make a note of this. For example, Kancha Ilaiah (1996) notes that in his own childhood, they were taught to "shake with fear" in interacting with higher castes and to be submissive, subordinate and passive students. Referring to the denial of literacy and education, he goes on to note that, "childhood formations are important for a person – female and male – to become a full human being. But our childhoods were mutilated by constant abuse and by silence, and stunning silence at that" (1996:101). Similarly, Ramaiah (1999) details how he did the homework for upper caste boys in his school just so that he could receive their share of the food served at school, which he then took home to his starving family. Viramma (cited in Racine and Racine 1997), in her oral narrative, describes how she has to curb and control her son from defying the landlord's autocratic ways, as she considers the landlord to be her master and food provider. Such caste-based subservience to the order is reinforced by the general Indian socialisation pattern in which submission to the interest of the group and to linear structures of authority are upheld and reinforced in multiple forms (Saraswathi 1999). Internalised ideas of natural and given hierarchies have been the legitimising bases for not challenging utter humiliation and degradation. Take, for instance, Bama's description of her grandmother's justification for accepting stale food from her upper caste employers: "These people are Maharajahs who feed us on rice. Without them, how will we survive? Haven't they been upper caste from generation to generation, and haven't we been lower caste? Can we change this?" (2000: 14).

Bearing the burden of a stigmatised identity persists longer than in the childhood phase and continues to mark many dalits for much of their lives. Thorat, writing about the experiences of untouchable children elaborates this: "Although [the untouchable child] would have been identified even earlier as a child of an untouchable father, this would not have affected his thinking process directly. It is when he begins to walk independently, and when the play of his own will takes him to other people and things, that he experiences a stigmatised identity personally; and this makes an impression, subtle and indirect, upon his thinking process" (cited in Raman 2003).

While such subservience and servitude were linked to and compounded by the fact that dalits had no resources of their own and were economically dependent on the upper castes, the long-term impact of it has meant that such subservience and submission have become strategies of survival and are internalised and accepted as unquestionable structures. This in turn means that such socialisation and internalisation of caste norms has led to non-defiance of established and hegemonic forms of exploitation and discrimination at individual and collective levels.

Sanskritisation and the Reproduction of Caste Norms

If dalit children are socialised into internalising subordinate and submissive identities, then at the macro cultural and social level, the processes and patterns of sanskritisation play a role in marking the personhoods of scheduled community members. This is observable in the extent to which sanskritisation and replication are widespread and have resulted in the appropriation and practice of upper caste rites and rituals. Most popular and widespread are the practices of conducting annual 'Satyanarayana vrats', secluding girls and women, adopting dowry practices instead of bride-price, vegetarianism, and most significantly, practising caste discrimination against other groups, etc.

Different theories and perspectives review the meaning and implications of sanskritisation. The replication of upper caste practices among the low-ranked caste groups indicates, as Moffat (1979) elaborates, a form of consensus which largely accounts for the reproduction of both the culture of the caste (with its norms and ideology of purity, pollution, hierarchy and differentiation) and the system (of exclusion, identification, rules and regulations) across generations and in different spaces. The implications or direct results of such a process are that even the positive characteristics of dalit culture and society are being eroded. The outstanding example of such a process is the decline of bride-price and the adoption of the practice of dowry among dalit groups and the subsequent decline in the status of women among these groups.

Barring the cases in which some low-ranked castes in Kerala have drawn on cultural, religious and political mobilisation to contest and overcome indignities, most other attempts to challenge caste-based atrocities have been only partially successful. Dube observed this among the Satnamis of north India, who even as they formed and charted new organisations which challenged untouchability, "also reproduced the significance of meaning(s) and power embedded within the ritual schemes of the caste order" (1998: 216).

Currently, many dalit activists and intellectuals deny the hold of sanskritisation over scheduled community members and assert their march towards modernity. However, not recognising the hold of sanskritisation and its implications for the reproduction of the caste system and of subjected identities is myopic. Some scholars see such emulation of upper caste norms as a reproduction or replication of the caste system and link it to the assertion of identity and to attempts towards status parity with recognised superiors (Karanth 2004). Views such as this attempt to give recognition to such social practices as the only way to gain acceptance in the dominant and hegemonic order and do not assess the implications of these practices in terms of what their significance for the constitution of caste identities and the reproduction of the system itself. As astutely pointed out by Chakravarti, "an analysis of the ideological underpinning of sanskritisation can be sharpened by arguing that hegemonic ideology works to limit the cultural imagination of the lower orders and makes it difficult to radically re-conceptualise society" (1998: 57).

Recent scholarship sees the formation of caste associations and caste political parties among the low-ranked caste groups as a form of "civil society" in India and asserts the need to understand such mobilisation as a form of "alternate modernity" (Chatterjee 1997). While such perspectives rightly challenge the simplistic dichotomisation of societies as modern and non-modern and call attention to the nuanced and varied routes to modernity, we must critically consider if caste-based mobilisation can lead to modernity (as the challenging of inherited identities and of reproductive regimes of discrimination), even if of an "alternative" type of modernity.

Caste and the Public Sphere

That the reading of caste-based mobilisation as modernity is problematic is to be seen in the results and impact of such mobilisation. While the political apparatus retains most scheduled community members as clients, without catering to the needs of their constituencies, the economic system has eroded the vast repertoire of knowledge and skills that members of the scheduled communities possessed. And, in the context of the non-absorption of a majority into a viable economic system, the members of the low-ranked caste groups, especially the labouring poor, are subject not only to processes of displacement, but also to disorientation. This is observable in the extent to which the submission to state agendas of nomenclature and identification has led many scheduled communities to appropriate such terms and to refer to and identify themselves as "scheduled castes and scheduled tribes" instead of to their jati or occupation-linked names. This process, in which official categories have become social categories (Jaffrelot 2003), compounds the problem of identity leading to the loss of ancestral links and a sense of belonging. In addition, although the term and identification as dalit is being promoted by activists, the term and identity are yet to gain widespread acceptance.

The dominance of sanskritisation as a mode of social and cultural change can be linked to the failure of the modernisation agenda and to the fact that it has not provided an alternate non-caste basis of identity formation. Pandian makes a note of this when he indicates that in the case of Tamil Nadu, among the poorest and the most marginalised of the dalit caste groups, ".... caste identity seems to compensate their marginality in other domains" (2000: 515). In this vacuum created by the failure of a genuine modernity (associated with ideas of egalitarianism, individual rights and democracy) to have taken root and the fact that the processes and structures of democracy and modernity are based on caste organisations and alliances, mean that the caste system is also being reproduced. Witness the extent to which patron-client relations of the agrarian order are replicated in the political order and in many cases members of the scheduled communities occupy political positions only in terms of being the domesticated (Kaviraj 1998) clients of the upper caste leaders. As caste-based mobilisation gains ascendancy, several questions can be posed about its implications for the reproduction of caste as a system and the reaffirmation of caste-based identities as the basis for the personhoods of low-ranked groups.

The marking of dalit youth identities by processes of erasure and amnesia must be contrasted to what is happening among upper caste youth. Based on the privileges of urbanisation and their own engagement with western modernity and globalisation, upper caste youth are re-invoking and asserting their caste cultures and identities as markers of superiority. This reinvention and reassertion, which is also linked to the growth of Hindu nationalism and its associated fundamentalism, then marks the low caste, non-sanskritised dalit as an object whose identity must be realigned and reworked. The range of re-Hinduisation and integration rituals that the Sangh Parivar has resorted to in north India highlights the extent to which dalit youth are sought to be domesticated and their emerging identity as dalit is sought to be checked (Shah 2004).

Compounding these experiences in the public institutions of the nation are popular and public images that portray dalits as inherently disabled and limited in personality. Take, for example, the popular film *Lagaan* in which the last member of the village cricket team is the handicapped Kachra, whose very name means "rubbish" and who is not given the option to join the team but is commanded by the team's *de facto* leader to do so. Such images and representations reinforce conceptions that the low-ranked are inadequate and incapable of any independent volition and thought (Anand 2002).

These negative public images and the lack of support for scheduled community members from the elite compound the isolation and continued degradation of scheduled community members. Marc Galanter (1998) and Devanoor Mahadeva (2001) have noted, unlike the whites of the US who fought both the civil war and led the civil liberties movement to help African Americans gain equality or established associations such as the National Association for the Advancement of Colored People, there is no similar support from upper caste persons in Indian society. In fact, a greater sense of caste awareness and a widespread sense of loss and deprivation have contributed to strengthening upper caste assertions about themselves. High-ranked caste groups remain embedded within their caste cultures and their ideology of varied capabilities and rights. Widespread hostility towards caste-based reservations confirms the lack of empathy for the low-ranked caste groups and the continued resentment that they experience in the public sphere.

Educational Institutions

In such contexts, the role of institutions, especially educational institutions, has also been dubious. Ranging from overt discrimination and hostility in elementary schools, to covert discriminatory practices and policies at higher education institutions, members of scheduled communities continue to be subjected to a culture of hostility and indifference.

The recent National Focus Group on Problems of Scheduled Caste and Scheduled Tribe Children (NCERT 2005) highlights this.

Teachers are observed to have low expectations of SC and ST children and girls and a condescending and downright abusive attitude to poor children from slums. Teachers also have stated and unstated assumptions of "deprived" and "deficient" cultural backgrounds, languages and inherent intellectual deficiencies of SC/ST children. They follow discriminatory pedagogic practices of labelling, classifying and teaching styles and operate on the basis of "realistic" perceptions of low caste children's limited cognitive capacities and life chances (p. 31).

Several studies of schools and the treatment of dalit children have observed the ways in which discrimination accounts for the higher dropout rates among such children (Subrahmanian 2003; Vasavi 2003). Segregating children during mid-day meals at schools, prohibiting them from drinking water from common sources, forcing them to perform menial tasks in the school, etc., are ways in which dalits' rights to education is challenged. In fact, linked to the range of incentives (such as free uniforms, texts, scholarships, etc) available to scheduled community students and as a way in which to express their resentment against the reservation system, it is not uncommon to hear government school teachers refer to children from scheduled communities as "government children" and treat them with disdain and resentment. Such treatment often leads to high dropout rates and, worse still, to an internalisation of a sense of inferiority and despondency. A case of this is graphically described by the writer and activist Bama.

Besides the usual lessons, they could have educated the dalit children in many matters, and made them aware of their situation in the world about them. But instead, everything they said to the children, everything in the manner in which they directed them suggested that this was the way it was meant to be for dalits; that there was no possibility of change. And mainly because of this, those children seemed to accept everything as their fate (2000:89). Such experiences not only challenge dalit rights to education, but also pose the problem of reinforcing notions of inadequacy and difference. This is compounded by the fact that no institution has recognised the knowledge and skills of such communities and has instead enforced a body of knowledge that is alien and unfamiliar to them. More particularly, in the larger culture in which labour itself is neither recognised as valuable nor respected as an important dimension in human capability and contribution, the work of millions of dalits continues to be overlooked. Identities and subjectivities formed on the basis of work, crafts and artisanal abilities, knowledge forms of medicine, ecology, agriculture, animal husbandry, etc., are continually eroded not merely on the basis of their non-viability in the industrial era but through their association with pollution and degradation in the forms of work itself. The non-recognition of these skills as legitimate and valid knowledge forms and their lack of integration in the formal education and training structures, has meant that dalit youth are expected to do a double bind: on the one hand, they must eschew and reject their familial and customary knowledge and skills; on the other hand, they must learn new skills and knowledge in a context in which teaching learning practices are inadequate and that in most cases does not afford them the opportunity to use these skills.

Further, teachers' insensitivity to the culture of orality and to the conditioning and orientation of first generation learners is not an issue that is either understood or addressed. Studies have noted this and indicated the extent to which this lack of recognition has led to feelings of "loss of self and self-confidence" (Aggarwal and Sibou 1994:401) and accounts for the poor performance in academia among the scheduled community students. These institutions, despite functioning under the mandate of the constitutional obligation to cater to such scheduled communities, have been particularly negligent and even resentful of the presence of scheduled communities in colleges and universities and of the government schemes made available to them. That a supportive environment would have and will help realise the objectives of the programme is noted in the suggestion that Weisskopf makes in his comparative review of positive discrimination policies in India and the US:

> In order to overcome the kinds of obstacles to good performance..., many [Positive Discrimination] beneficiaries are likely to need access to support mechanisms in their study or work environment – over and above what is routinely available to all students or employees. Thus, the average quality of performance of PD beneficiaries will surely vary positively with the extent of support for the PD beneficiaries – in the form of facilities and programmes provided by the institutions into which they are selected and special attention from the personnel under whom they are performing (2004: 70).

In fact, it would not be an exaggeration to note that the experiences of scheduled community students in universities and in institutions of higher education are the extensions of such sharp discrimination at schools. Periodic outbreaks of caste-related violence in hostels and universities are reported from various parts of the nation. The Anveshi report on caste-related violence at the Central University, Hyderabad highlights such persistent and extant discrimination where... the sense of self-worth is the first casualty of university life. Dalit students are embittered by the way they are perpetually on probation at a university that at best suffers their presence...They are ignored in the classroom, invisible in the curriculum. Try as they might, their grades never improve. They are regarded as "untouchable". They are watched while they eat, mocked at by teachers and students, suspected for their corruption, hounded for their misuse of hostel rooms for guests from the village, chastised for their inability to pay bills on time, condemned for their violence (2002: 101).

Culture of Antipathy towards Dalits

Conditions such as these have made universities the new sites for the production of casteism. Most upper caste students are insouciant about the disadvantages and differences of dalit students and form opinions about them primarily on the basis of competition, resentment and apathy towards them. Under such conditions, is it any wonder, then, that the rates of retention in education institutions remain low (Aggarwal and Sibou 1994; Weisskopf 2004) and poor academic performance or achievement levels are then seen as the indicators of the "inherent incapability" of members of the scheduled communities? Low performance and negative experiences at institutions and the subsequent attrition or elimination have reinforced stereotyped notions and images of the unworthy and incapable low-caste. Experiences such as these which result primarily from lack of empathy on the part of the dominant groups and from poorly implemented policies have, in turn, led to the low self-esteem and poor self-image of the youth of the scheduled communities, a condition compounded by the large-scale unemployment of such persons.

This also accounts, in large measure, for the failure of policies such as reservations in higher education. For despite the years it has been in implementation, the results of the policies have not been significant. As the few studies on the impact of reservations in higher institutions have indicated, the experience of stigma, social divide and even segregation account for the poor academic performance of most scheduled community students who also come from socio-economically disadvantaged families (Kirpal and Gupta 1999). The failure to address the localised, institutional contexts of reservations, the continued hostility of others to the policy, and the association of it with decline in standards, have led to making the policy itself less effective than it could have been (Weisskopf 2004). While assessments see the failure of the reservation policy in terms of its intended effects – that is of providing scheduled community members with opportunities to new occupations and social and economic status – the impact of failure in such contexts remains largely undocumented. Very few studies so far make a note of this. From their detailed observations and interviews with educated unemployed Chamar youth in Bijnor, Uttar Pradesh, Jeffrey, Jeffery and Jeffery (2004) note that these youth refer to themselves as "useless", "empty", "wandering" and "unemployed". More importantly, they note that a fallout of such large-scale unemployment has led to the new generation of parents educating their children only up to the 8th standard level and or questioning the value of higher education. In continuing her summative work on the scheduled communities of India, Marika Vicziany (2005) refers to college educated dalits as the "breakthrough generation" but also goes on to note how many of the educated unemployed have become vulnerable and submit to fundamentalist agendas. Ravinder Kaur's (2004) observations of the functioning of reservations in the IITs indicates that a lack of openness and concerted support to these students continues to be the basis of their segregation, low self-esteem and poor academic performance. In fact, the association of differential capabilities has meant that many institutions continue to allocate upper caste or general caste category students to higher-ranked sub-specialisations and allocate unpopular or low-ranked specialisations to students from the scheduled communities. Such blatant discrimination and the overall culture of antipathy towards them mean that not only is the reservation policy defied vicariously, but the ideas of public institutions addressing issues of national inequity and discrimination are bypassed.

Although most studies do not make a direct link between education experiences and the political and cultural orientation of dalit youth, there is a need to assess and understand what rejection, discouragement and negative experiences mean for their identities and orientation. One result of such reinforced marginalisation is the absorption of these people into agendas and programmes by fundamentalist associations which give them a sense of agency but only by providing another enemy and another "other". The mobilisation of large numbers of dalits into the RSS and the Bajrang Dal and the violence that they have perpetrated against Muslims are representative of this. This was singularly visible in the 2002 Gujarat riots against Muslims (Breman 2002). What energy and agency should and could have gone into reclaiming their own rights and contesting upper caste and class hegemony has now been diverted into fundamentalist pogroms in which their role itself is that of being a perpetrator of violence.

In instances where scheduled community members seek to mainstream into the dominant society, they also face opposition and violence. Much of this violence stems from upper caste resistance and resentment against the socio-political changes that are taking place in rural society and culture. New forms of mobilisation and political rights for the low-ranked caste groups, and their resistance against the ritual, economic and social forms of discrimination, have led to various forms of retaliation by upper caste leading to the emergence of the new and more violent forms of caste discrimination. Documents from Navsarjan, the Gujarat-based organisation that works for dalit human rights, provide a summative purview of the forms of intransigence that provoke violence against dalits: when dalits are elected and attempt to sit on a chair in the local government office; when they do not give up their seats to non-dalits in the bus; when they dress well or ride their scooters in the village or if a dalit falls in love with an upper caste girl (Macwan 2002).

The end result of such persistent and widespread humiliation and indignities is that a majority of scheduled communities' persons experience what Shotter identifies as "the lack of opportunity for being" (1989: 162). Such process or marking highlights the combination of a cultural and political economic ethos in which scheduled community members are constantly in a state of contest with others for the "very nature of (their) being, for the kind of person (they) would feel (they) would like to be" (Shotter 1989: 162). Given these trends and conditions it is urgent that the further erosion of the personhood of dalit youth be halted and dalits be scaffolded into an agenda in which their agency and sense of self-worth is asserted. The importance of personhood as "a status conferred upon one by others, and if others do not take one's expressions of self seriously, if they do not respond to your utterances and other expressions as you intend, then you are being denied your opportunity to be a person - you are being degraded and humiliated" (Shotter 2004:7), needs to given due recognition. Challenges to subjected personhoods should lead to the possibility of enabling all scheduled community members to craft their identities in order to realise their abilities and interests. Yet, this cannot be an individualised endeavour, and it must be recognised that the formation of personhoods is a dynamic and relational *process* (Giovanola 2005), and it is the larger society and its institutions that must scaffold this process.

Some forms of resistance to the system, alternative identities and political mobilisation among dalits are now on the horizon (Clarke 1998; Raj 2001). A long overdue recognition of Ambedkar as an icon of the community and his message of "educate, organise and agitate" are now being recognised as a clarion call to emancipation. And, enunciations and calls for recognising their rights have become most strident. But, the challenge remains as to how dalits can craft identities and personhoods that will draw on their own defiance of inequality, retain the strength and advantages of their own culture and mould this with the ideals of modernity so as to generate a culture that is oppositional to caste culture. It is to enable such possibilities and in understanding and seeking to address these multiple forms of indignities and their impact on the subjected personhoods of dalit youth that institutions must strive towards. Continuing to support this until these subjected personhoods are challenged and a sense of independent identity and personhood for every student has emerged will be the basis of breaking the cycle of reproduction of indignities. This will also ensure the establishment of a genuine modern society that breaks from its past of placing a significant number of people in an oppressive and total institution, that of caste.

References

Aggarwal, Y. and Sarika Sibou (1994): *Educating Scheduled Castes: A Study of Inter-District and Intra-Caste Differentials,* NIEPA, New Delhi.

Anand, S. (2002): *Brahmans and Cricket: Lagaan's Millennial Puranaand Other Myths,* Navayana, Chennai.

Anveshi (2002): 'Caste and the Metropolitan University', *Economic and Political Weekly,* Anveshi Law Committee, Vol. 37 (12).

Bama (2000): *Kurrukku: Trans Lakshmi Holmstrom,* MacMillan, Chennai.

Breman, Jan (2002): 'Upheaval as Resurgence of Social Darwinism', *Economic and Political Weekly,* Vol. 37 (16).

Chakravarti, Uma (1998): *Rewriting History: The Life and Times of Pandita Ramabai,* Kali for Women, New Delhi.

Chatterjee, Partha (1997): 'Beyond the Nation? Or Within?' *Economic and Political Weekly,* Vol. 52 (1 and 2).

Clarke, Sathianathan (1998): *Dalits and Christianity: Subaltern Religion and Liberation Theology in India,* Oxford University Press, New Delhi.

Dube, Saurabh (1998): *Untouchable Pasts: Religion, Identity and Power among a Central Indian Community, 1780-1950,* Vistaar Publications, New Delhi.

Galanter, Marc (1998): 'The Abolition of Disabilities: Untouchability and the Law' in J. Michael Mahar (ed.), *The Untouchables in Contemporary India,* Rawat Publications, Jaipur.

Giovanola, Benedella (2005): 'Personhood and Human Richness: Good and Well-Being in the Capability Approach and Beyond', *Review of Social Economy,* Vol. LXIII, No. 2, June.

Human Rights Watch (1999): *Broken People: Caste Violence against India's Untouchables,* Books for Change, Bangalore.

Ilaiah, Kancha(1996): 'Why I Am Not a Hindu: A Sudra Critique of Hindutva Philosopy', *Culture and Political Economy,* Samya, Calcutta.

Jeffrey, Craig, Roger Jeffery and Patricia Jeffery (2004): 'Broken Trajectories: Dalit Young Men and Formal Education' in *Educational Regimes in Contemporary India* (eds.) Radhika Chopra and Patricia Jeffery in collaboration with Helmut Reifeld, Sage, New Delhi.

Jadhav, Narendra (2003): *Outcaste: A Memoir,* Viking Books, New Delhi.

Jaffrelot, Christophe (2003): *India's Silent Revolution: The Rise of Low Castes in North Indian Politics,* Permanent Black, New Delhi.

Karanth, G.K. (2004): 'Replication or Dissent: Culture and Institutions among 'Untouchable' Scheduled Castes in Karnataka', *Contributions to Indian Sociology,* Vol. 38(3), September-December.

Kaur, Ravinder (2004): *The State and Social Equality: Deconstructing Reservations in Institutes of Technology,* MS, New Delhi.

Kaviraj, Sudipta (1998): 'The Culture of Representative Democracy' in Partha Chatterjee (ed.), *Wages of Freedom: India at Fifty,* Oxford University Press, New Delhi.

Kirpal, V. and Meenakshi Gupta (1999): *Equality through Reservations,* Rawat Publications, Jaipur.

Macwan, Martin (2002): 'Dalit Rights: Migration in Search of Labour and Other Experiences of Dalits' proceedings of the Round Table Workshop on Human Rights Education in Indian Universities, KWIRC, Bangalore.

Mahadeva, Devanoor (2001): 'Untouchability: Great Grandfather of Apartheid', MS, NLSIU, Bangalore.

Moffat, Michael (1979): *An Untouchable Community in South India,* Princeton University Press, Princeton.

Nambissan, G. and M. Sedwal (2002): 'Education for All: The Situation of Dalit Children in India' in R. Govinda (ed.), *India Education Report*, Oxford University Press, New Delhi.

NCERT (2005): 'National Focus Group on Scheduled Caste and Scheduled Tribe Children', MS.

Pandian, M.S.S. (2000): 'Dalit Assertion in Tamil Nadu: An Exploratory Note', *Journal of Political Economy*, Vol. XII, Nos. 3 and 4.

Raj, M.C. (2001): *Dalitology: The Book of the Indian People*, Ambedkar Resource Centre, Tumkur.

Raman, Vasanthi (2003): 'The Diverse Life-Worlds of Indian Childhood' in Margrit Pernau, Imtiaz Ahmad, Helmut Reifield (eds.), *Family and Gender: Changing Values in Germany and India*, Sage, New Delhi.

Ramaiah, T. (1999): *Manegara: Ondu Atmakathe* (Manegara: An Autobiography) (in Kannada), Bodhishree Prakashan, Tumkur.

Saraswathi, T.S. (1999): 'Adult-Child Continuity in India: Is Adolescence a Myth or an Emerging Reality?' in T.S. Saraswathi (ed.), *Culture, Socialisation, and Human Development: Theory, Research and Applications in India*, Sage Publications, New Delhi.

Shah, Ghanshyam (2004): 'Underprivileged and Communal Carnage: A Case of Gujarat', Manuscript.

Shotter, John (1989): 'Rhetoric and the Recovery of Civil Society', *Economy and Society*, Vol. 18(2).

— (2004): 'The Manufacture of Personhood, and the Institutionalisation of Mutual Humiliation', *Concepts and Transformation*, Vol. 9(1).

Subrahmanian, Ramya (2003): 'Exploring Processes of Marginalisation and Inclusion in Education, in Education Inclusion and Exclusion: India and South Africa Perspectives', *IDS Bulletin*, Vol. 34(1), January.

Vasavi, A.R. (2003): 'Schooling for a New Society? The Social and Political Bases of Education Deprivation in India', *IDS Bulletin*, Vol. 34, No. 1.

Vicziany, Marika (2005): 'Dalit Response to Unemployment in Contemporary India', *South Asia: Journal of South Asian Studies*, Vol. XXVIII, No. 1, April.

Viramma Racine, Josiane and Jean-Luc Racine (1997): *Viramma: Life of an Untouchable* (translated by Will Hobson), Verso, London.

Weisskopf, Thomas (2004): Affirmative Action in the United States and India: A Comparative Perspective, Routledge, London.

4

The Eternal Debate

ASHWINI DESHPANDE

The debate over reservations – the Indian version of affirmative action – is in the foreground once again. Since this time, the debate, at least ostensibly, is about the other backward classes (OBCs), one of the first stumbling blocks in any informed intervention is the paucity of data. Most of what has appeared in newspapers and television commentaries are a set of pre-conceived notions intertwined with a virulent opposition to affirmative action. Prima facie, this could be attributed to the lack of data: reservations for OBCs could possibly be the first instance of affirmative action for a category that even the national census does not enumerate. The National Commission for Backward Classes only lists the jatis that comprise OBCs without any demographic data about these jatis. Also, there are no firm estimates of the distribution of OBCs in jobs and institutes of higher education.

It is entirely true that the government, whether in 1990 or now, ought to have preceded this major move with building a comprehensive case for this particular component of affirmative action, with adequate backing of data that could be released to the public. Also, while this move is supposed to be coupled with an increase in the non-reserved seats, very little thought seems to have been given to the logistics and practicality of increasing seats. Most departments and colleges already face huge constraints in the form of inadequate infrastructure and high student-teacher ratios and have very little scope for increasing student intake, without the concomitant structural changes that would be needed to sustain a higher intake. If the government is indeed serious about alleviating the condition of OBCs via increasing their share in public sector jobs and institutions of higher education, then, this lack of preparation not only worsens its case but actually casts a doubt over the degree of its commitment to the reduction of caste-based barriers.

Having said that, it would be a mistake to believe that the opposition to this move is only or mainly because of lack of data and/or preparedness. The domination of an upper caste mindset in the media, the academia and the wider public, is evident in most of the anti-reservation commentaries. Concerns about merit declining because "they", rather than "us", will swamp educational institutions; the completely mythical nightmare of "we" or "our children" being reduced to demeaning jobs like shining shoes and sweeping, whereas it is only fair that "they" continue to do so, etc., are only some of the indicators of a latent casteism that constitutes the reality of the supposedly caste-neutral contemporary urban India. Thus, the status quo, in which the share of the upper castes in both good jobs (in the public and the private sectors) and seats in higher educational institutions is far in excess of its share of population, is seen as essentially fair. While state-imposed reservations are seen as a murder of merit, the much more widespread "natural reservations" that come from birth in business (upper caste) families which ensure that no outsiders are ever considered for the top jobs in family-owned businesses; other manifestations of caste-class privilege being expressed via donations, capitation fees, etc., are never seen as threatening merit. Thus, the operation of caste barriers and a belief in caste hierarchies as natural underlies the dominant thinking so completely that, ironically, these beliefs are not seen as casteist, but their questioning is. Indeed, this mindset asserts that caste was virtually extinct before it was resurrected by V.P. Singh or Mandal or Arjun Singh. The possibility that the invisibility of caste from "our" lives is a privilege that "we" enjoy because "we" belong to a small minority of urban, upper caste elite that has the luxury of leading a casteless existence, something that the majority is far from attaining, are issues that are virtually never discussed. However, distinct from this mainstream is the relatively small body of opinion that recognises the reality of caste-based barriers and disadvantages and has been engaged with the question of the combination of instruments that would be needed to break this.

Is Caste Past or Present?

One of the key issues in this debate is whether caste is an indicator of disadvantage at all, in the present. There is now a growing volume of literature that establishes empirically the reality that all indicators of advantage/disadvantage (monthly per capita expenditure, landholding, occupational attainment, educational attainment, ownership of consumer assets, type of housing, poverty ratios and so forth) are very clearly stratified by caste. Thus, while reasonably accurate income data are hard to come by, all these indicators suggest the distribution of both income and wealth are skewed along caste lines. This is not a trivial finding as it challenges the notion that disadvantage or advantage is randomly distributed between castes and, thus, establishes a case for focusing on groups, rather than individuals, as targets for policy making. Of course, this does not deny intra-group inequality, but any group-based programme can be fine-tuned to take that into account, if necessary.

Since the current debate is about OBCs in particular, it is true that the census does not count OBCs as a separate category. However, there are some other data sources that give a fairly instructive glimpse into the state of the OBCs. I am familiar with two large all-India data sets: the National Sample Survey (NSS) and the National Family Health Survey (NFHS) that have added the OBC category to their surveys after the late 1990s. Both of these indicate a clear disparity between OBCs and "others" (the non-SC-ST-OBC residual: an approximation for upper castes). According to the second round of the NFHS, caste disparities in occupational attainment are clear. Sixty-eight per cent of SCs and 75 per cent of STs are agricultural and manual labourers, with the proportions among OBCs being 61 per cent and the upper castes, 47 per cent. At the other end of the spectrum, among the professional, managerial and high-level administrative jobs, the proportion of OBCs is 8 per cent with that of upper castes over 13 per cent. As a part of my research, using the NFHS data, I have created and calculated a "Caste Development Index" (CDI) that is based on five indicators: landholding, occupational attainment, educational attainment, consumer durable ownership and asset ownership. It is only the second round of the NFHS data set that allows for the OBC category and it turns out that both in rural and in urban India, in 1998-99, the CDI for the OBCs was less than that for "others" in virtually all states of India, as the following chart shows:

Chart

Caste Development Index, India, 1998-99

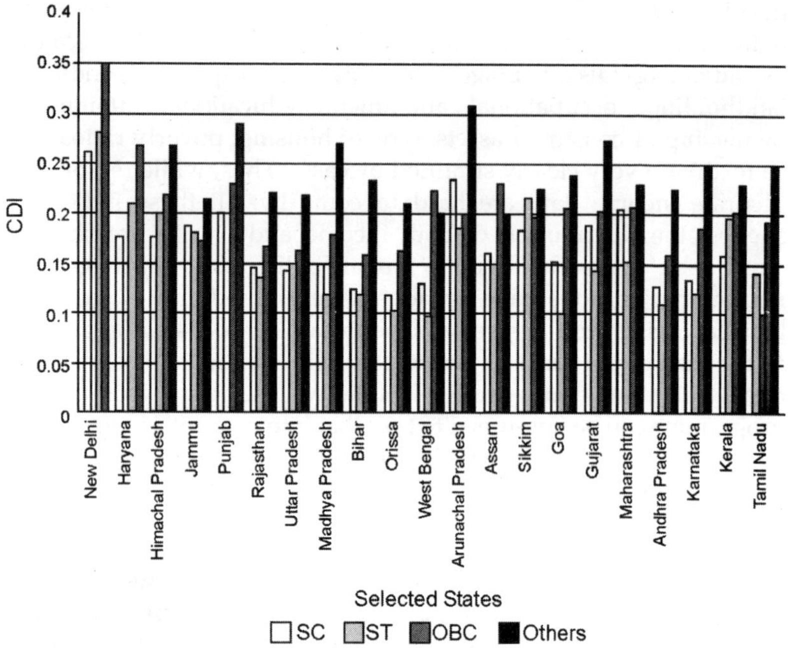

These results are striking for several reasons. First, they challenge the notion of OBCs as the new elite or as the new dominant castes that have presumably displaced the dominance of upper castes. As an economist, I am not competent to comment on the nature of the political change; however, there seems to be no indication of a reversal in the relative economic position between upper castes and OBCs.

Second, these results are based on the OBCs as a whole without any distinction between the "creamy layer" and the more disadvantaged OBCs. It follows then, that if we exclude the creamy layer, the disparities would be even sharper. The National Commission for Backward Classes (http://ncbc.nic.in) has several criteria (economic, social and educational) to define the creamy layer among OBCs that ought to be excluded from the proposed reservations.

Third, there is a view that the preparation of the OBC list, despite very detailed objective indicators of backwardness listed in the Mandal Commission Report, has been influenced by lobbying such that fairly prosperous and dominant jatis have managed to get themselves labelled as "backward". Again, I am not competent to comment on the validity of these claims. However, assuming such errors have occurred, these would bias the standard of living indicators for the OBCs upwards. It follows then that the gap between the truly disadvantaged OBCs and the upper castes would only be larger than what our estimates indicate. Finally, my limited experience with field work in rural UP indicates that not only is the dividing line between purity and pollution critical, but that the distinction between "dwija" and "non-dwija" jatis matters too. Recently, at a small workshop in Delhi, Yogendra Yadav circulated tables based on his election survey data that provided broader empirical evidence in support of this.

Of course, this still begs the question – whether these disparities are a hangover from the past or whether they are being perpetuated in contemporary India. The literature on dalits indicates that mechanisms for perpetuating inter-caste inequality are strong and alive in contemporary India. Indeed, comparing changes in monthly per capita expenditure (MPCE) between SCs and "others" over the last two decades does not indicate a closing of the gap; there is evidence of wide regional variation, with disparities increasing in several states, particularly since the late 1980s. A similar analysis with OBCs would require more data points.

Discrimination in Labour Markets

In addition to disparities that are group-based, most labour markets in the world display evidence of discrimination, viz., that average wages of groups differ more than what a skill or merit differential would warrant. This discrimination is over and above what economists call "pre-market" discrimination that individuals are subjected to before they enter the job market. So, while pre-market discrimination would lead to differences in access and quality of education between, say dalits and upper castes, job market discrimination would lead them towards different kinds of jobs (job discrimination) or different wages for similar jobs (wage discrimination), after controlling for merit.

Indeed, India is no exception to this nearly universal tendency for labour markets to discriminate on the basis of group identity. Thus, a common misconception is that the only reason dalits fare badly in labour markets is because they are less educated or are less meritorious. This argument assumes an absence of discrimination or caste prejudice: if dalits managed to acquire better education and were similarly qualified, then this argument assumes that their occupational profile would be similar to that of high castes. A corollary of this argument is that, therefore, all policy efforts should be directed towards equalising educational opportunity and educational attainment and this would eventually equalise labour market outcomes. Without doubt educational opportunities and attainment need to be equalised with urgency, given huge disparities in quality of and access to basic education. However, studies of the formal sector have shown that there are differences in average wages of SCs and non-SCs that cannot be accounted for by education differences alone. In other words, controlling for skill or human capital characteristics (indeed, for all possible measurable characteristics that explain wages), a part of the wage gap between SCs and non-SCs can be attributed to labour market discrimination. Admittedly, similar studies for OBCs have not been undertaken, partly because data availability has been a problem. Also, as a field of research, while this is now very common in the developed world, particularly North America, it is still in its infancy in India. It would be instructive to see what a similar exercise for OBCs would reveal. Additionally, while the role of caste in the allocation of more traditional rural jobs is documented and accepted, it needs to be noted that the job search process in urban labour markets is marked with a complete lack of transparency: most jobs are never advertised and networks/connections of families and friends play a very important role in how jobs are allocated. This puts the whole question of "merit" in a different perspective: to quote from a study on the US job markets, often "who you know" is more important than "what you know". One of the studies that I am involved with suggests that even for highly qualified university graduates, there are big differences between dalits and others in the job search process, eventual placements and salaries, time taken to find jobs, and the gap between ideal jobs and the jobs they eventually find.

Growth or Affirmative Action? For Whom?

My calculations with the NFHS and the NSS indicate that it is not possible to draw a neat relationship between the per capita State Domestic Product (SDP), the rate of growth of SDP on the one hand,

and the absolute level of development of, say SCs, and the SC-others disparity, on the other. In other words, one sees all kinds of patterns: rich states with low disparity, rich states with high disparity, rich states with higher development of the SCs and rich states with relatively lower development of the SCs (and similarly for poor states). There is a similar confounding of patterns when we look at rates of growth (faster growing states and slower growing states). This suggests that while rate of growth and levels of SDP are matters of concern, these do not provide an easy solution to tackle caste disparities that need to be targeted independently. Indeed, this confirms the international experience where both highly developed and poorly developed countries find themselves grappling with the problem of inter-group disparity. One is, thus, led to conclude that caste may not wither away with development but, in fact, some form of affirmative action might be imperative to tackle caste-based disparity and discrimination.

Of course, affirmative action need not be synonymous with quotas and different sections warrant different kinds of affirmative action. Dealing with the complexity of issues inherent in the method and form of affirmative action would require a separate article; suffice it to say that one of the results of the Indian quota system has been social mobility, evident in the growth of a dalit middle class, conspicuously missing from the neighbouring Nepal that has a similar social structure but virtually no social mobility among the dalits. However, it is equally true that the programme is mechanically implemented, in that the announcement of quotas is seen as the beginning and the end of affirmative action and typically, no other form of support or remedial teaching is ever provided to help the "quota" students cope with the pressures of higher education, leading to large dropouts. In recruitment and promotions, a lack of will ensures that efforts are made to undermine quotas. Institutions can get away with the minimal or sometimes no regard to the quota system, since there is never any effort to monitor and assess the functioning of the quotas and no penalties for exploiting loopholes in the system. More importantly, since the debate is only centred around quotas, a variety of other powerful instruments, particularly relevant to improving the lives of the mass of rural dalits, are never discussed.

One is, therefore, wary of a similar mechanical approach to the problems of the OBCs. Also, the greater heterogeneity among the

OBCs and the lack of a stigma associated with untouchability, suggest that not only should the "creamy layer" be excluded from a blanket provision of reservations but that alternative proposals being suggested by scholars, such as a combination of academic qualifications with points to redress various forms of disadvantage, must be considered. Also, we might go much further in bridging the gap in education if equal and immediate attention is given to the dropouts at the primary and middle school levels and to improving both the quality and access to education in rural areas. This need not be an "either-or" choice: both affirmative action and attention to the larger structural problems can complement each other in a virtuous cycle. This would necessarily require thinking outside the box. What the government urgently needs to do is to set concrete goals and monitor outcomes very strictly, rather than paying lip service to only one possible instrument with no regard to the outcomes.

5

Reservation and Social Justice

AMBROSE PINTO

I
The Reservation Debate

It is unfortunate that the issue of reservation has become a topic for debate among pro- and anti-reservation groups. In debates, the stronger and the most articulate win, though facts may be very different. The issue of reservation is not a matter for debate but a concern that has to be addressed. There is much more at stake for the country here than the honour of being the sharpest wit, or the most persuasive tongue, or of having the greatest influence and power. And yet, the manner in which the merit versus quota controversy has generated arguments, it looks as if the socio-economic reality is totally overlooked. *The reservation policies are not for settling scores among our academicians, political leaders and policy makers,* but to address the issue of socio-economic equality and justice.

Unequal Society

The Indian society continues to be a caste society. Such a society is premised on inequality and discrimination. For centuries, those at the top of the caste hierarchy did not permit those at the lowest rungs the SCs, STs and other marginalised groups to own property, enter institutions of learning or even be present in the public space. The situation has not changed much even today. There are several communities across the country who are treated as untouchables, impure, polluted and low. And, what is most shocking is that the system is legitimised by religion.

When India became independent, the framers of the Constitution promised to all citizens equality, fraternity and justice. The system of reservation was set up to provide justice and equality to those who never enjoyed them. Dr. Ambedkar was right when he said that, with the independence, we would enter a world of contradictions. At the political level, there would be "one person, one vote with one value". However, at the social level, the untouchables will continue to be treated as untouchables, without experiencing the freedom of political independence. In fact, political freedom has no meaning apart from social equality. *It is to provide social equality through representation in all the institutions of the state that the reservation system was introduced.*

The Purpose of Reservation

Reservation is provided to include the excluded in the socio-economic and political system of our country by creating opportunities for their development. The objective is to usher in a society of equality. The question debated in the public space is merit versus reservation. Reservation undermines merit and efficiency and is thus unfair, argue a section of the elite who have benefited from the institutions of the state for centuries. I consider the question wrongly posed. *The debate is in reality a battle between elitism and massification, in which democracy can become a casualty.*

The idea of excellence by which the proponents of merit so vehemently swear, is a one-dimensional measure. But, there is no pure merit anywhere. Besides, merit cannot be measured only in terms of the highest marks obtained in an examination. *Merit should also include qualities of mind and heart so very essential for public and national service.* The so-called merit of the upper castes and classes comes from the exploitative nature of socio-economic relations, where the upper castes for centuries have oppressed the lower castes in the name of caste and religion and excluded them from all institutional entries. *To accept such a definition of merit is to damage the polity and society.*

Reservation and Democratisation

Besides, we have mystified the idea of intelligence as well. Intelligence can only be determined in a concrete socio-economic and cultural context. Once we accept that premise, it becomes clear that customs and traditions have not equipped certain people to gain entry into the mainstream form of education. Their absence or exclusion from the mainstream society has deprived them from the mainstream education also. In the Indian context, merit then becomes an alibi for preserving the Brahminical *status quo* where access to and control over knowledge and institutions is restricted to an elite minority. The challenge is to make knowledge itself more inclusive without permitting it to be the exclusive preserve of a class. The objective of reservation is to create opportunities for the unequals who have suffered for no fault of theirs. *Reservation enhances and widens the access to education, thus democratising institutions and knowledge.* It is aimed at the massification of education and knowledge, and representation in all the institutions of the state, in proportionate measure.

Massification may not be democratisation. But it is an important step towards democratisation. If massification does not take place for lack of critical state interventions, democracy is likely to be undermined. *The policy of caste-based reservations in India has made our institutions more representative and democratic.* Some excluded groups now have a legitimate place in them. It is a principle of democracy that representative institutions in social life are even more important than efficient institutions. Hence, reservations – the only direct tool to dismantle the structural impediments to making the public and private sector institutions really representative – need to be used with full force and without guilt and even an iota of concern for efficiency.

Furthermore, the *argument that reservations bring about inefficiency is not true*. Even, in 2006, people prefer state rather than private educational institutions in Karnataka. Among all the engineering colleges, for instance, the government-run Viswesvarayya Institute of Technology, Bangalore and the National Institute of Technology, Surathkal are rated more qualitative in spite of being representative of all castes and communities. Similarly, the top students in the common entrance examinations prefer the medical colleges run by the state. *Democracy does not mean sub-standard services.* Reservation has in fact protected the basic quality of our institutions, bringing into them a quality of its own. The implementation of reservations in central and state government jobs and educational institutions is to transform and integrate the country's oppressive traditional structure into the institutional framework of modern India.

Democratisation of the Knowledge System

It is also expected that reservations will democratise the knowledge system, though this may not have yet taken place in India. When more and more groups enter the educational institutions, they will bring into them their concerns and knowledge systems and challenge the elite perceptions on society and its functioning. *Widening the access to higher learning through reservation can thus make knowledge more democratic.*

Initially, the new 'entrants' may lack the political wherewithal to change the contours of institutionalised knowledge, so as to dialogically transform and assimilate the excluded experiences and skills into valid and valued forms of knowledge. But this is bound to take place gradually. In this context, we would do well to remember how studies on Ambedkar and subaltern movements have made established knowledge systems more inclusive. These unleashed new currents of thought, which reorganised existing disciplines, especially in human sciences, and created new approaches and discourses that sought to expand the frontiers of the economy, society and humanity itself.

Conclusion

Thanks to the system of reservation, we have a more democratic and humane society. *If the process is carried on* – from schools, colleges, institutions of higher learning, state and central governments, and the private sector – *we are sure to have a new society, more egalitarian and just.* To implement the system of quotas, there is a need for a strong political will. *We must absolutely end the traditional divide between the 'well-educated' and the 'uneducated' that has perpetuated the elitist system of hierarchies.* In our struggle, we have to accept that there will be, for quite some time, a marked difference in the academic performance of the traditional recipients and the newcomers. It is therefore clear that positive discrimination cannot be abandoned. *For, it can effect the convergence of democratisation and social cohesion, transforming the structures of our economy and society so that a more inclusive system of values is put in place.*

II
Relevance of Reservation for the Backward Classes

Indian society is premised on inequality because of the age-old caste system. Between the upper castes and the outcastes (the SCs and STs), hundreds of other castes are condemned to educational, cultural, social and economic backwardness. Any discussion on the caste system reveals its firm links with the economic life. The OBCs (Other Backward Classes) had no right to education and could only practise occupational skills. As a result, they ranked way below the upper castes in the economic ladder.

Democracy cannot become meaningful to all the citizens of our land as long as we accept, from their birth, some people as 'pure' or 'high' and others as 'backward' or 'low'. In the name of caste and by using religion, the 'upper' castes have committed wrongs and continue to perpetuate injustice on the OBCs, Dalits and minorities. We therefore need mechanisms to intervene on behalf of the discriminated and bring them equality and justice. There cannot be social democracy without proper representation. To correct the wrongs done to social groups in the name of caste and religion, the Constitution of India introduced Articles 15 and 16. Article 15(4) permits the state to make "any special provision for the advancement of any socially and educationally backward classes of citizens", while Article 16(4) permits the state to make "any provision for the reservation of appointments or posts in favour of any backward class of citizens which, in the opinion of the State, is not adequately represented in the services under the State".

The Rationale for OBC Reservation

There has not been much opposition to the reservation system for the SCs and STs, though the implementation has been sluggish. Even 60 years after independence, *the position of the SCs/STs has not greatly improved. This is party due to the caste mindset of our bureaucrats, administrators and officials*. If the country had drawn a large number of bureaucrats from the weaker sections in 1947, things might have been different. As far as the OBCs are concerned, their situation has further deteriorated since independence. This has not been sufficiently highlighted in the public space. And yet, *because of political reasons, reservations for the OBCs arouse much more opposition than for the SCs/STs.*

Table 1

Representation of SCs, STs, OBCs & Upper Castes in the Indian Embassies (%)

Category	SCs	STs	OBCs	Upper Castes
Group A	8.0	1.0	0.0	91.0
Group B	4.2	0.6	5.0	90.2
Group C	4.3	1.2	1.5	93.0
Group D	7.0	1.0	0.2	91.8

Source: 4th Report of the National Commission for SCs/STs, Government of India, Volume 1, p. 15.

Any talk of reservation for the backward classes or the socially and educationally backwards raises immediate social conflicts. We have seen it across the state and country. For instance, every time, the Government of Karnataka decided to implement the reports of the Backward Classes Commissions, the state has experienced violence. At the national level, it was the government order on the implementation of the Mandal Commission that created bloodshed, burning and violence across the country in 1990. Right now, in May 2006, protests are mounting against an OBC quota in institutions of higher learning. The opposition is mainly from the upper castes. *This kind of protest and violence,* in spite of the Preamble of the Constitution that assures to all citizens social, economic and political justice, *is anti-national.* Given the principles of social justice and the nature of our Constitution, it is the responsibility of the 'upper' classes to part with some of their privileges and thus contribute to the emergence of an egalitarian society. We already mentioned the contents of Articles. 15(4) and 16(4). And Articles 38 to 46 emphasise the obligation of the state to the weaker sections of the people, to prevent their exploitation and to eliminate various forms of inequality and injustice The reality presented in Table 2 is tragic, to say the least. In Class I services, there was a better distribution of jobs among different social groups during the colonial period in 1935 than after independence in 1989. While the 69 per cent of SCs, STs and OBCs had a mere 8 per cent of the jobs in 1989, the 5.20 per cent of Brahmins had pocketed as much as 70.20 per cent. *One gets the impression that the state is more and more Brahminised.* The other castes seem unable to challenge the hegemony of the priestly caste, which is gaining a greater hold on society. *There is no meaning in social justice and democracy when the privileged few pocket all the resources and jobs under the pretext of merit and efficiency*. This situation cannot be permitted to go on.

Table 2

Communities in Class I Government Services in 1935 & 1989 (%)

Communities	*1935*		*1989*	
	Population in percentage	*Share in services*	*Population in percentage*	*Share in services*
Kayasth	0.85	40.00	1.03	7.00
Muslim	21.00	35.00	10.13	3.20
Christian	4.00	15.00	2.08	1.00
Brahmin	3.50	3.00	5.20	70.20
Rajput	2.50	2.00	3.80	1.70
Baniya	1.20	1.00	1.78	3.50
Sikh	1.40	1.60	1.60	1.90
Other	1.60	0.90	5.50	2.50
SC, ST & OBC	64.00	1.00	68.85	8.00

Source: Verma, P.S.: *Dalit Peeda*, Vimukt Jati Trading Pvt. Ltd., Delhi 1992. The 1935 data refer to the then united India, comprising Pakistan and Bangladesh.

Articles 15(4) and 16(4) are constitutional mandates and there is no need to offer any apology for reservation. It is high time that the state becomes representative of all castes and classes. There cannot be any genuine democracy when the 5.20 per cent of a single caste hold 70 per cent of the jobs in the government and administration. What the SCs, STs and OBCs are seeking through the reservation process is equality and justice. *The provisions of the Constitution are not concessions, favours or philanthropy, but matters of right and justice*.

Obviously, the reservation provisions will not pull all the weaker sections out of poverty and bring them to the level of equality. Only a few benefit from the reservation system in terms of government jobs and seats in medical and engineering colleges. That too might soon disappear with the privatisation of the state, which is vigorously pursued by the ruling elite. A much broader programme is required if the weaker sections are to experience equality and justice *most important device for this is quality education for the people from the weaker sections*. All the same, reservation remains essential and no social group can any more be permitted to have a monopoly over the state.

The Issue of Merit and Efficiency

It is sometimes asked why the present upper castes should be made to pay for the sins of their ancestors by negating them their legitimate place in terms of merit. The answer is simple. Since they inherited so many unjust benefits and advantages from their ancestors, they should be made to pay for social justice at present.

What about the question of merit then? Merit is the surplus product of the labour of millions of 'unmerited'. *It is the classes of the unmerited who have contributed to the creation of the intellectual class in the country*. Without their sweat and blood, the upper castes would never have enjoyed their wealth and education. The fact that the unmerited were kept out for centuries from all learning through a set of beliefs and dogmas manipulated by the merited in their own favour has produced an intellectual class that is often bereft of any moral character. Having been accustomed to grab everything for themselves, they are reluctant for any change in the socio-economic order.

It is therefore important to clearly state that the kind of merit the upper castes are talking about is high marks in public examinations, *which has nothing to do with rectitude, social concern and feeling for others*. Besides, administration is not about merit. To the extent that the upper castes do not possess the qualities of concern and compassion, they cannot be in administration and serve India. *What the country needs to pull millions out of poverty and penury is compassionate hearts, concerned spirits and sensitive consciences*. The country needs morally superior persons more than an intellectually brilliant class.

Efficiency is the other argument against reservation. But, in the last 60 years, we have witnessed so much large-scale corruption, administrative inefficiency and non-performance from those who have been appointed on the basis of merit! In fact, the attacks against reservation in the name of efficiency only project the contempt of the upper castes for the OBCs. Ever since the OBCs started claiming their legitimate share in the cake of resources, the upper castes have begun to use the slogan of efficiency to keep them away. The mere securing of high marks in an examination does not make an individual efficient!

An efficient administrator is a person who has tilled and ploughed, cultivated and produced, a person who possesses the skills of conscientising and organising the poor. Only such people will be able to tackle the problems of poverty, unemployment and injustices in our country. We therefore need to reconsider the whole question of recruitment to administrative offices. Those who merely possess some intellectual knowledge may be the least suited for administration. Thus, the OBCs cannot anymore be denied their rights by using the argument of efficiency.

In our corrupt administrative system, those who are in power did not always acquire their position through merit either! Several have been appointed through the manipulation of rules and regulations. Many others owe their posts to marks card scandals, partiality and favouritism in interviews and a host of other crooked means. The powerful have acquired special skills to operate the system in their favour and they thus succeed to appoint their kith and kin to important positions.

The need of the hour is unity among all the subaltern classes. With the globalisation and privatisation of the economy, there are more threats to the livelihoods of the marginalised. Unless all the discriminated come together to fight the hegemony of the upper castes, we will be fighting a losing battle. In recent years, the biggest enemies of the SCs and STs have been the OBCs. Most of the violence against the Dalits has been from the OBCs, though its religious ideology is provided by the upper castes. *Rigorous attempts have to be made to unite all the subaltern communities under one platform.* It is the divisive ideology of the upper castes that has kept our country fragmented and divided. Groups fight among themselves on who is higher and who is lower, and in the process the upper castes continue to enjoy all the benefits of power. *It is high time that all those who believe in the oneness of humanity come together under one banner for the cause of democracy and rights.* We must reject the exploitative religious ideology that has divided this country into high and low, pure and polluted, sacred and profane. What we need is a common economic programme that can ensure the basic needs of one and all so that we may live as members of one human family.

III
Should Dalit Christians be Included Among Dalits?

B.R. Ambedkar was a social visionary. He was fully aware that the system of reservation would not be the answer to the exploitative status of the Dalits. Though he advocated reservation in educational institutions, legislatures and state employment, *he was fully aware that reservation could not be the final answer for Dalit empowerment.* He wanted the Dalits to understand the root causes of their social exploitation and mobilise themselves through education, agitation and organisation for their rightful place in society. The three words of his campaign that have impacted the Dalit movements across the country were: educate, agitate and organise. If the Dalit scene is different today, the nation should thank Ambedkar, the ideologue of the Dalit world.

Ambedkar and Conversions

Conversion was one of the weapons that Ambedkar advocated to escape from the clutches of the caste masters. Conversion for him was a social and political protest against the caste system. Through conversion, Dalits were moving out from a community of hierarchy with the notions of high and low, pure and impure, to a community of equality. Renouncing one community to join another may not change the socio-economic situation of the converts. Yet, *the converts change internally by adopting another set of beliefs and values that foster in them the sense of community and equality.* In fact, in 1956, Ambedkar along with his followers embraced Buddhism, a religion of brotherhood and community. While inviting other Dalits to convert, he was convinced that Dalits should remain united as Dalits, irrespective of their religious affiliations, and fight against the caste structure. Only a united struggle will provide the Dalits their final victory.

Ambedkar's dream has not been realised. Both state and society have managed to keep the Dalit flock divided. *Instead of rising against their oppressors, Dalits fight among themselves on the basis of sub-castes, religion and even class.* This has weakened the Dalit movement. A section of the educated Dalits has further played into the hands of political leaders by demanding reservation for sub-groups. Political parties too have set up Dalit leaders one against the other to improve their bargaining powers with the community. *As a result, no single Dalit leader is acceptable to all Dalits in politics today.* These leaders are more and more associated with their sub-castes representing particular parties, rather than with the entire Dalit world.

Further fragmentation has taken place on religious lines – the converted and the non-converted. While the socially conscious among Dalits claim that Dalits are indigenous people, the Hindutvavadis have enrolled them in their political Hinduism for the purpose of vote-banks without any desire to include them in their social community. Those who were converted to Buddhism and Sikhism and those who call themselves Hindu SCs have benefited from the reservation policy of the state. But those who were converted to Islam and Christianity have been kept out from the Dalit fold by the state. *The purpose is to weaken the Dalit movement,* say the awakened and the enlightened among Dalits.

Religion as Accidental

Religion is an 'accidental' identity for people. In fact, many Western countries have not included religion even in their census enumeration. Being a personal matter, religion's place is in one's heart. Individual beliefs cannot be imposed and forced on others, though they can be practised in common and proposed to others, if they do not affect public order and morality.

However, *the struggle for the inclusion of Dalits who profess a religion other than Hinduism has been hard and difficult.* While they do remain Dalits even after embracing a different faith, the state more than society looks at them with communal eyes. The idea seems to be to keep the Dalits as untouchables, and bonded and cheap labourers, by compelling them to internalise the beliefs of the caste system. It looks as if the state would like to reward the SCs as long as they remain within a social and religious system of inequality and exploitation for slavery and cheap labour. *The day Dalits decide to quit social and religious oppression, the majoritarian state would not like them to come under any special provision of state protection and empowerment.*

Yet, the Dalits who have embraced Buddhism and Sikhism have succeeded in their struggle to be included in the special provisions of the Constitution, while those who are Christians and Muslims are told that they cannot be Dalits once they convert. In truth, this is an attack on Dalit identity and on their right to choose a religion of their choice. *The identity of any social group does not primarily depend on religion.* It emerges from the relationship of the people to the productive processes; it is influenced by social, economic and cultural factors and religion is only a peripheral issue. There are Buddhists, Sikhs and Christians among Brahmins, Reddys, Gowdas and various other communities. While those belong to their social groups in terms of identity, at the religious level they adhere to different faiths. *How does their adherence to a different faith change their belonging to their social group?*

The Opposition to Inclusion

Including Christians in the Dalit list has become highly controversial and political, especially on account of the politics of the extreme right. The Union Social Justice Minister Satya Narain Jatiya in the NDA government stated in 2003 that the attempts to include Dalit Christians are an international conspiracy. Jatiya also said that the Registrar General of India and the Chairman of the National Commission for SCs and STs had advised against giving any reservation rights to Dalit Christians. Since both were appointees of the NDA, their opposition was very understandable. The All India Christian Council then denounced the Union Minister for misleading the parliament. They observed that Jatiya had committed a breach of privilege by withholding vital information and concocting half-truths to hide the real motives of the NDA government.

Inclusion as Natural Justice

The campaign for the inclusion of the Dalits of different faiths in the Dalit list has national and international support as a matter of natural justice. The issue was debated at the UN – sponsored World Conference against Racism and Discrimination at Durban, South Africa, in 2001, and Dalit forums all over the world have been making similar demands. *All egalitarian religions like Buddhism, Sikhism, Christianity and Islam denounce any system that discriminates between human beings because of their origins of birth.* Of course, Dalits have not found total liberation as a result of being included in egalitarian faiths. This is bound to be so, since religions are only a part of the larger system. Since they live in the societal environment after conversion, the way society perceives and treats them does not change. They continue to suffer social discrimination because of their origins.

Worse, the existing laws are coercive and punish the converts to Islam and Christianity by robbing them of their reservation rights. This is to keep the converts poor, jobless and landless. In fact, the socio-economic situation of the Muslims is worse than that of the Dalits in several parts of the country. And yet many refuse to understand the state bias against Dalits embracing other religions. How do the Dalits see religion-based discrimination? *They look at it as an assault on their freedom of faith and a ploy to keep them in the social and religious captivity of one religion under the threat of losing their civil and economic rights*. Though some Dalits have been converted, they still maintain their records as SCs, both to express their belonging to their social group and to benefit from the opportunities provided by the state.

While denying the Dalit tag to converted Dalits, the state machinery dominated by the extreme right has been misleading the 'Hindu' Dalits that their rights will be eaten away by Christian and Muslim Dalits if the latter are included in the Dalit list. It is only the National Commission for Minorities that has repeatedly urged the Indian government to restore equality and give all Dalits their rights and privileges irrespective of religion. In fact, the Central Government once moved a bill to give Dalit Christians their reservation rights. The bill was moved by the then Welfare Minister Sitaram Kesri after being cleared by the Union Cabinet, but was not passed due to deliberate political blunders.

Conclusion

The Supreme Court is now examining a PIL case to provide an equal treatment to Dalit Christians (cf. below, pp. 41-45). The Court has asked the Union Government the reasons for keeping out the Christian Dalits from the Dalit list. The fact that the UPA is not opposing the move in the Court is a gesture of the Alliance that could give an impetus to the strengthening of the Dalit movement in the country. In recent years, the contribution of Dalit Christians to the Dalit cause, especially in terms of lobbying and advocacy, both at the national and international levels, has been significant. If they can fight for their social and political space as a united group with the ideology of Ambedkar, aligning themselves with the progressive forces, Dalits are bound to have a better future.

The only lurking fear is whether the vested interests within the Dalit community and the extreme rightist forces will allow the Dalits to emerge as an autonomous and united force. *They are not likely to permit it and that is exactly the challenge faced by the Dalits and those who are concerned about their plight today*. The Dalit issue is not merely a Dalit concern; it is a human right issue. *All progressive and concerned citizens must therefore contribute their mite to the Dalit cause by assisting them in the process mapped out by Ambedkar* – educate, agitate and organise. *That would be the right kind of tribute we could all pay to Ambedkar*.

6

Positive Discrimination

A Political Analysis

PARTHA S. GHOSH

Any democratic society faces the challenge of harmonising two essentially contradictory political concepts – one, equality before the law irrespective of religion, caste, creed, race, and gender, and the other, social justice at the cost of the same commitment for equality before the law. Even a developed democracy like the United States is no exception to the rule and has taken recourse to affirmative action to ensure justice for the less privileged sections of the society at the cost of individual merit and equality of all citizens before the law. In India large numbers of people have experienced social discrimination through centuries on account of its peculiar institution called the caste system, efforts have been made to provide redress for these underprivileged sections, through the policy of reservations or quotas for them in jobs, seats in educational institutions and legislatures, and in governmental aid, loans and other developmental assistance.

In all, four underprivileged categories have either received benefits under the scheme or have been seeking such benefits, namely, the Scheduled Castes (SCs) and the Scheduled Tribes (STs), the Other Backward Classes (OBCs), the religious minorities or sections thereof, and lately, the women. This chapter discusses these categories from a political perspective. Its scope, however, is limited to assessing the schemes both under operation as well as under consideration, only at the national level. The experiences of different states have been referred to only occasionally to provide an example or to make a particular point.

Scheduled Castes and Scheduled Tribes

The need to discriminate positively in favour of the socially underprivileged was felt for the first time during the nationalist movement. It was Mahatma Gandhi, himself a devout Hindu and a staunch believer in the caste system, who was the first leader to realise the importance of the subject and to invoke the conscience of the upper castes to this age-old social malady of relegating whole communities to the degrading position of "untouchables". He also understood the political logic of inducting this large body of people into the political mainstream in order to make the freedom movement more broad based. By renaming these untouchables as "Harijans" (people of God) he tried to give this policy a religious sanction so as not to disturb the traditional sensitivities of the caste Hindus more than was really necessary.[1]

Gandhi's logic was not greeted with enthusiasm by all sections of the untouchables, most notably by their leader B.R. Ambedkar, who felt that it represented an extension of the patronising attitude of the upper castes, and no more than that. Against the background of the political conflict between the Congress and the Muslim League Ambedkar found the situation conducive to ask for separate electorates for the untouchables on the lines of the Muslim League. The British government had obvious reasons to support the demand and on 17 August 1932 it announced the Communal Award granting separate electorates for the depressed classes by treating them as a minority. Gandhi protested against it and went on a fast unto death if it was not withdrawn. His contention was that the caste Hindus would react violently to the scheme and in rural areas, which were dominated by upper castes, the lives of the depressed classes would become even more miserable. Behind this argument of course was Gandhi's political understanding that it would weaken the freedom movement. Whether Gandhi was actually interested in bringing the depressed classes into the social mainstream of Hinduism or was just indulging in a political ploy to gain the support of these classes for the freedom movement without tampering too much with the Hindu caste structure has been a long debate which has become extremely acrimonious of late. The political crisis that Gandhi's hunger strike had triggered was resolved by the Poona Pact of 24 September 1932 signed between the non-Harijan Hindu leaders and Ambedkar. The pact was a compromise which provided for 148 reserved seats instead of the 78 separately elected members provided for by the Communal Award. It also granted certain privileges to the Harijans, such as educational opportunities, representation in services, and the franchise.[2]

It had become necessary to list the depressed castes for purposes of representation at the national and state levels. This schedule was prepared in 1936 after considerable difficulty following the passage of the Government of India Act, 1935. It covered 43.6 million people in all, which meant 28.5 per cent of the Hindu population and 19 per cent of the total population of British India.[3] By the time of the census of 1941 the number had raised to 48.8 million. It was this list which the Constituent Assembly later adopted. At the 1991 census there were about 135 million SC people in India consisting of 15.75 per cent of the population.

So far as the enumeration of tribes was concerned it was relatively easy because of their cultural and spatial specificities. Moreover, the British had already treated them separately for administrative purposes. Since the 1935 Act provided for the separate representation for the Scheduled Castes, separate representation for the "Backward Tribes" was a logical extension of the principle. Accordingly, a schedule of these tribes was also prepared.[4] At the 1991 census they were about 66 million making up 7.75 per cent of India's population.

An Assessment

The assessment of implementation of reservation policy tells that there has been only marginal improvement in the lot of the SCs and STs. Social discrimination still persists even sixty years after independence and so does the stigma attached to persons belonging to such castes. The quotas earmarked for the SCs and STs are often not filled on account of the indifference of the heads of departments. According to the Chairman of the National Commission for Scheduled Castes and Scheduled Tribes, this is done systematically through a variety of subterfuges – from destroying application forms from such persons, to filling up posts through *ad hoc* recruitment on the ground that there is a ban on new recruitment on a permanent basis. He is particularly critical of institutions of excellence in this regard: "These institutions are particularly resistant to SC reservation. Not one of them has filled the quota, including the Indian Institutes of Technology."[5] They are also not filled owing to the non-availability of qualified people even at the standards specifically lowered for these groups. For example, in 1980, the upper caste Hindus who made up 25 per cent of the population held 89.63 per cent of the Central Government jobs while the SCs and STs who made up for almost the same percentage of population (23%) accounted for only 5.6 per cent of the jobs.

The primary reason for this depressing situation is that caste feelings still persist in Indian society which does not permit an egalitarian approach to develop roots whatever the state might direct. Surprisingly, while the intermediate castes fight for their rights *vis-à-vis* the upper castes yet when it comes to castes lower than theirs they show the same disregard to these lower castes which they themselves are subjected to by the upper castes. The noted social anthropologist M.N. Srinivas sums up this attitude as: "I am equal to those who think of themselves as my betters, I am better than those who regard themselves as my equals, and how dare my inferiors claim equality with me?"[6]

As a natural corollary to this, politics is also caste-oriented and does not allow public policies to be oriented to the upliftment of the SCs and STs. The landlessness of these groups keeps them perpetually poor which also prohibits them from learning new skills which the present liberalisation process demands. The cumulative effect of all this is a lack of effort on their own part to improve their lot. It has been seen that the Dalits in predominantly Dalit villages are the worst off.[7] There is of course the obvious political reason for this as well – no political voice is articulated on their behalf.

There are, in addition, certain inherent flaws in the policies of the government. The unprecedented growth of private English-medium schools, which are far better than the state-funded schools and where it is not necessary to reserve seats for the SCs and STs, has totally undermined the policy meant to educate the latter and make them employable in a highly competitive job market.[8] Insofar as the job quota is concerned, the fact that they are not category-specific permits most of the offices to fulfil the statutory requirement by filling the posts at lower levels thus leaving the leadership levels largely upper caste dominated. It is, however, a double-edged weapon. If the situation is altered in favour of the SCs and STs for each category of jobs the allegation against the policy of positive discrimination that it has benefited mostly the élites amongst the SCs and STs would become even sharper and would become more easily verifiable.

Dalit Ascendancy

Whatever may be said in criticism against the policy of positive discrimination it has served at least one purpose. It has made the Dalits conscious of their rights and they have learnt that in a democratic milieu these rights have to be extracted through agitational and electoral politics and not to be expected as charity doled out by the privileged classes.[9] the old theoretical controversy between Gandhi and Ambedkar seems to be coming to the fore once again. That this conflict would generate increasingly high levels of violence is a foregone conclusion and there is considerable evidence of this. Reflecting on the situation Rajni Kothari writes:

> It poses the question of what to emphasize more: Western hegemony or caste domination within India, reflecting the issue posed much earlier during the independence movement as to what was more important: social emancipation or political autonomy. What is more important: autonomy (and agitational politics) of the community or autonomy of the nation in the international order? If it is both, how to reconcile the two? We seem to be back to the Ambedkar-Gandhi controversy.[10]

There is visible evidence of organised violence directed against the Dalits the result of which is an equally visible evidence of Dalit anger. One saw this in Maharashtra, particularly in Mumbai, in July 1997, when the statue of Ambedkar was defiled by some miscreants. That act of vandalism was obviously not accidental. Behind the outburst of violence on the part of the Dalits were pent up frustrations and anger rooted in deep social maladies.[11] There is no evidence to support the contention that wherever the Dalits are present in large numbers conflicts between them and others inevitably follow. An analysis of the violence, and indeed the atrocities, committed against the Dalits during the period 1977-85 would show that these incidents are largely concentrated in the Hindi-speaking states of Bihar, Madhya Pradesh (MP), Rajasthan and Uttar Pradesh (UP) where agriculture and the land tenure system are still highly feudalistic. Recent reports show the same pattern.

According to data available with the National Crime Record Bureau (NCRB), UP accounted for 47.7 per cent of the total recorded violence countrywide against the SCs in 1994. The corresponding figures for Rajasthan and MP were 14.2 and 11 per cent respectively. Atrocities against the STs were most rampant in MP with 35.3 per cent of the total national figure, followed by Rajasthan, Maharashtra and Gujarat with 28.8, 8.9 and 8.6 per cent respectively. The data also showed that violence against both SCs and STs, considered together, rose from 24,992 cases in 1992 to 33,908 in 1994, registering a rise of 89.03 per cent. It may be noted that the violence against the SCs/STs, which had been witnessed ever since independence and before, increased measurably after 1970 when the political and economic influence of the OBCs increased and the OBCs began asserting their dominance over the SCs and STs, particularly in the rural areas.[12]

Against this background the political rise of the Dalits, through their most vociferous voice, the Bahujan Samaj Party, can be easily explained. In UP the party has emerged as a force to reckon with and has not only ruled the state twice through political alignments with other parties, but is also ruling it now on its own. It would not be surprising if in the near future it develops a stake in other states and national politics as well, with Dalit politics increasingly enlarging its area of operation.

Other Backward Classes

Unlike the SCs/STs there was no clear thinking about the backward classes in the pre-independence period. Yet in provinces such as Bombay, Madras and Mysore there was some reservation of jobs and seats for them in the field of education.[13] After independence, Articles 15(4) and 16(4) of the Constitution did make some reference to them but no special provision was made for their upliftment. In 1953, the First Backward Classes Commission was set up by the Government of India under the chairmanship of Kaka Kalelkar. In its report submitted in 1955 the Commission expressed doubts about using caste as the sole criterion to identify the backward classes. Nevertheless, it identified 2,399 caste groups as socially and educationally backward. The recommendations of the Commission, however, were not accepted by the government on the ground that objective tests had not been applied in making the selections.[14]

In some of the states, however, reservation for the OBCs (Other Backward Classes) was introduced. For example, in 1970, on the basis of recommendations of the Manohar Pershad Commission,

Andhra Pradesh reserved 25 per cent of seats in colleges for them. This protective discrimination was extended to the level of Lecturers (Assistant Professors) in 1976 and to that of Readers (Associate Professors) in 1983. These policies, however, largely remained on paper; as for example, in the Osmania University during the period 1977-83, the number of teachers belonging to the. BC, SC and ST categories all put together did not constitute even 10 per cent of the selected candidates although 43 per cent of the jobs had been reserved for them. The periodic reports submitted by the Andhra Pradesh Backward Classes Legislative Committee constantly drew attention to this non-implementation of the rules.[15]

In the 1970s and 1980s, however, the backward caste movements picked up momentum in several parts of India and a number of castes such as the Yadav, Kurmi and Koiri and Vokkaliga, emerged as important political forces. Arguing that their lot was even worse than that of the SCs/STs for they constituted 52 per cent of the population while they accounted for only 4.69 per cent of the Central Government jobs, they launched political agitation in the name of the OBCs. The Janata Party which came to power in 1977 represented many of there forces.[16] It was against this background that the Second Backward Classes Commission was set up in 1978 under the chairmanship of B.P. Mandal. Popularly known as the Mandal Commission its report was submitted on 31 December 1980.

By using eleven indicators for determining social and educational backwardness[17] and by basing its caste data on the 1931 census (the last census in which caste affiliations of Hindus were recorded) the Mandal Commission Report came out with a list of 3,248 castes or communities as OBCs accounting for 52.4 per cent of India's population, which meant roughly 350 million people then.[18] The report pinpointed social disabilities they confronted and their economic, social and educational backwardness (see Table 1).

Table 1

Caste Composition of Class I Officers in the Central Government (%)

Class Category	*Share*	*Population*
Upper Castes	89.63	25.34
Backward Castes	4.69	52.10
SC/ST	5.68	22.60

Source: Mandal Report, Part 1, p. 92, cited in O.P. Mehra, "Backward Classes: Some Issues," *Vacham* (Bhopal), 3(1), January 1992, p. 40.

For the upliftment of the OBCs the Mandal Commission recommended a number of reforms including structural changes in oppressive production relations. But, its most important and controversial recommendation was that 27 per cent of jobs in government and public enterprises should be reserved for the OBCs. The report also specified the exact scheme and procedures to be followed to implement this recommendation:

1. Candidates belonging to OBCs recruited on the basis of merit in an open competition should not be adjusted against their reservation quota of 27 per cent.
2. The above reservation should also be made applicable to promotion quota at all levels.
3. Reserved quota remaining unfulfilled should be carried forward for a period of three years and de-reserved thereafter.
4. Relaxation in the upper age limit for direct recruitment should be extended to the candidates of OBCs in the same manner as for SC and ST members.
5. A roster system should be maintained for the OBCs in the same manner as for SC and ST candidates.[19]

The rationale behind the 27 per cent formula was that since 22.5 per cent reservation had already been made in favour of the SCs/STs (in direct proportion to their number) and since Supreme Court rulings had prescribed that the reservations should remain below 50 per cent it was not possible to reserve 52 per cent of seats for the OBCs in direct proportion to their number. "In view of this," the report said, "the proposed reservation for OBCs would have to be pegged at a figure which, when added to 22.5 per cent for SCs and STs remains below 50 per cent. In view of this legal constraint, the Commission is obliged to recommend a reservation of 27 per cent only, even though their population is almost twice this figure".[20]

By the time the Mandal Commission Report was submitted the Janata Party had split and the Congress was all set to return to power. The recommendations of the Mandal Commission remained in cold storage for about a decade. It was in 1990 that Prime Minister V.P. Singh, partly for the purposes of refurbishing the social base of his ruling coalition and partly to blunt the *Hindutva* edge of the Bharatiya Janata Party (BJP), decided to implement them.[21] With this a new chapter opened in Indian politics and along with it an acrimonious debate over the issue of social justice started.

The government promulgation provided for a 27 per cent quota in government jobs for people belonging to the OBC category. Implementation of the report led to violent protests from the upper castes and eventually resulted in the fall of the V.P. Singh government. But, the movement has continued and at present no political party finds it possible to dissociate itself from the recommendations of the Mandal Commission. The arithmetic of numbers at the hustings has made the OBC phenomenon almost a permanent fixture in India's politics. Some of the South Indian states breached the ceiling of 50 per cent laid down by the Supreme Court for reservations.[22] In Tamil Nadu there is a reservation of 69 per cent; in Karnataka it is as much as 73 per cent. Even such a strong critic of the OBC quota system such as Orissa's late strong-man Biju Patnaik also gave in to pressure. Announcing the introduction of the OBC quota (within the legal norms) in his state in September 1994, he said, "I must admit we should have tried to follow the path enunciated for the backward classes in states like Tamil Nadu, Kerala and Karnataka."[23] In Bihar reservations have reached 76 per cent. The pressure for similar policies has reached North India as well.

Reservations for Minorities

Lately, a new controversy has been added to the reservations debate with demands from sections of the minorities for their inclusion in the category of affirmative action beneficiaries. The issue is politically sensitive and particularly so because the Hindu chauvinistic BJP, the principal opposition party in parliament, regards it as another ploy to pamper the minorities. Its position on the issue may be viewed against the background of several conflicting realities, namely, that the party claims that the Muslims are pampered while the social indicators tell a different story, that the Muslims are growing in numbers disproportionately compared to the national and Hindu averages which is a fact, and lastly, that while the BJP stands for reservations of SCs, STs and OBCs and also economically depressed classes it is strongly opposed to affirmative action for the Muslims (including Dalit Muslims) and Dalit Christians.[24]

While the policy of reservation for SCs and STs is enshrined in the Constitution and reservations for the OBCs have gained political support over the years, the question of reservations on the basis of religious identity remains very controversial and generally leads to acrimony. As a self-proclaimed secular state India shows equal respect to all religions, or, maintains an equal distance from all religions. But, there is some ambiguity in the case of India's policy of affirmative action meant for the upliftment of SCs and STs.[25] Hinduism as understood in India's constitutional parlance includes Sikhs, Buddhists and Jains. Therefore, the SCs belonging to these communities should have been granted the quota benefits as was done in respect of Hindu SCs. But it was not the case to start with. In 1950 a Presidential Order made under Article 341 of the Constitution had declared that "no person who professes a religion different from Hinduism shall be deemed to be a member of a Scheduled Caste". In 1956 the Sikh religion was included with Hinduism as part of this order. Thus came the Sikh SCs (Mazhabi and Ramdasias Sikhs). So far as the Buddhist SCs were concerned they were granted limited benefits, that too in UP and Maharashtra only, till 1990 when this anomaly was rectified and they were brought on par with the Hindu SCs. So far as the Jain SCs are concerned they are either non-existent or are too minuscule to make any political demand in their favour.[26]

It may be noted that all the three religions – Sikhism, Buddhism and Jainism – emerged as protest movements against the evils of Hinduism, most importantly, the institution of caste. If so, the existence of SCs among them is a contradiction in terms. That many early adherents to these religions would be from the depressed classes is also understandable. Did not the same situation prevail in regard to converts to Christianity and Islam at a later date? The argument advanced by adherents of the *status quo* is that since Christianity and Islam were opposed to the recognition of caste, then depressed caste converts to these faiths should not be allowed to think in terms of affirmative action. The same argument could be used against affirmative action benefits for Sikh, Buddhist and Jain SCs.

The confusion is further confounded if one raises the issue of conversion and compares the SCs with the STs. If an SC converts to Christianity or Islam such a person is automatically deprived of his SC benefits.[27] But if the convert is an ST he continues to take the advantage of the ST benefits because those benefits, as the argument goes, are ethnicity-based and not religion-centric. In short, when the Dalit Muslims or the Dalit Christians are demanding quotas for themselves, their claims are advanced on the basis that in reality, India's Islamic and Christian societies are as much socially stratified as the Hindu society, the difference being only one of scale.[28]

The current official position is that "no scheme for minorities below the poverty line is being implemented in the country."[29] Still, there is a standing instruction of the Government of India "to all the Ministries/Departments of Government of India that whenever a Selection Committee/Board exists or has to be constituted for making recruitment to 10 or more vacancies in Group C or Group D posts/services, it shall be mandatory to have one member belonging to SC/ST and *one member belonging to minority community* in such Committees/Boards. Where, however, the number of vacancies against which selection is to be made is less than 10, no effort should be spared in finding a Scheduled Caste/Scheduled Tribes officer and *a minority community officer* for inclusion in such Committees/ Boards."[30]

The Issue of a Muslim Quota

In several states either the Muslims in general or the Muslim OBCs as part of the general OBCs are on the positive discrimination list. For example, in Kerala, 12 per cent of the jobs are reserved for the Muslims. In August 1994, the Andhra Pradesh government included the Qureshi (butcher) Muslims in the OBC list.[31] In September 1994 the Manipur government announced the inclusion of Meitei Pangal (Muslims) in the state OBC list.[32] In early 1995, the Government of Karnataka announced a 75 per cent enhancement in the OBC quota of which 6 per cent was assured for the Muslims. In July 1995, the UP government decided to issue caste certificates to Muslim sub-castes so as to enable them to benefit from the 8.44 per cent reservations under the OBC category.[33]

In national politics too political parties compete with each other in demonstrating their concern for the Muslims. The issue of reservations figures largely in this. In July 1995, when preparations for the 1996 Lok Sabha elections had already started the Welfare Minister in the Narasimha Rao government, Sitaram Kesari, advised his party not to ignore the Muslims. He said, "In the Assembly elections of Uttar Pradesh, Bihar, Andhra Pradesh, Maharashtra, state party leaders hailing from the upper castes did not highlight the fact that we gave 27 per cent reservation to the backwards which included 110 Muslim sub-castes. This led to the poor showing."[34] Kesari's successor in the H.D. Deve Gowda-led United Front government, B.S. Ramoowalia, repeated the same promise and announced several schemes for the benefit of Muslim OBCs.[35]

However, the current controversies do not relate to the Muslim OBCs, but are over reservations for the entire Muslim community as one social unit and also over the question of quota benefits for the so-called Muslim Dalits. The first demand for reservations for the Muslim community was mooted in West Bengal during the regime of the Congress Chief Minister Siddhartha Shankar Ray, during the days of the Emergency (1975-77). A delegation led by Zainul Abedin, a minister in Ray's cabinet, met Prime Minister Indira Gandhi and demanded reservation for Muslims. In 1980, the Muslims of the state made the same demand before the Gopal Singh Committee. The committee recommended inclusion of Muslims under the reservation scheme.[36]

As the issue of quota matters electorally many of the state governments where the Muslim community figures politically would like to make commitments in their favour however cosmetic they may eventually prove to be. For example, in Bihar, the Janata Dal leader Laloo Prasad Yadav had promised 10 per cent reservations for Muslims before the assembly elections of 1995. In Assam, Hiteshwar Saikia of the Congress tried to ward off attacks on his government's inability to stop the killing of Muslims in Bodoland by promising the community 24 per cent reservations. In West Bengal, the Congress and the Muslim League leaders launched agitations to remind Jyoti Basu of his 1977 poll pledge to provide quotas for Muslims in jobs and educational institutions.[37] In UP the Samajwadi leader Mulayam Singh Yadav wants to make a dent in the growing popular bases of the BJP and the Bahujan Samaj Party (BSP) by advocating reservation for the Muslims in the state.[38]

Following the increasing communalisation of politics in the late 1980s and particularly after the demolition of the Babri mosque on 6 December 1992 the demand has been picked up by the Muslims in several parts of the country. In Bihar two organisations – the Bihar Backward Muslim Morcha (BBMM) and the Muslim Reservation Front (MRF) – surfaced, demanding 20 per cent reservations for the community.[39] In April 1995, about 100 representatives of the Muslim community met in Delhi under the leadership of Syed Ahmed Bukhari, the Naib Imam of the Jama Masjid, and demanded reservation for Muslims on a proportionate basis in all fields as the minority community was backward educationally, economically and socially.[40] In September, the 95-member strong Jama Masjid Action Committee adopted a 10-point charter of demands which included reservation for Muslims.[41]

Of late, even the National Commission for Minorities, a statutory body, has appealed to the Government of India to do away with the proviso in the 1950 Presidential Order for SCs and STs which uses religion as the criterion for deciding the SC status. According to Tahir Mahmood, the Chairman of the Commission, there must be the recognition of absolute equality of all religions and, religious communities under the constitution and laws. He believes that the 15-year-old Gopal Singh Committee's report on problems of minorities has outlived its utility and there should be a fresh and comprehensive study of the problems faced by the religious minorities.[42]

One of the arguments levelled against the demand for quota for the entire Muslim community runs along the predictable line that if the quota is granted to the community as a whole the beneficiaries would be upper caste Muslims such as the Saiyads, Shekhs and other Ashrafs at the cost of the really needy classes.[43] Dalit Muslims tend to subscribe to this logic and ask for a quota not for the community *per se* but only for themselves.[44] To this the Muslim leaders like Syed Shahabuddin have strong objections. They argue that the Muslim community as such is depressed and therefore deserves affirmative action and, so far as the criticism that benefits under reservations would be cornered by the socially and economically privileged group among them is concerned, they argue, that it is equally applicable to the entire question of quota for the SCs, STs and the OBCs.[45]

Dalit Christians

The question of Dalit Christians is different from the issue of reservation for the Muslim community or the Muslim OBCs. Dalit Christians are those who were originally untouchables and who converted to Christianity. But conversion did not improve their social status and upper caste converts continued to look down upon them. As a result, casteism continued to exist in the Church in India. In 1929 a delegation of depressed class Christians stated in a deposition before the Simon Commission: "We remain today what we were before we became Christians-untouchables degraded by the laws of social position in the land, rejected by caste Christians, despised by caste Hindus, and excluded by our own Hindu depressed class brethren."[46] According to social activist-cum-lawyer Flavia Agnes, "For all its homogenous appearance the Christian community is very caste-ridden. Especially, the recent converts. The converts, largely from the backward communities, now find that they are losing out on both fronts. They continue to be sub-castes without the benefit that would have accrued to them if they hadn't converted."[47]

There are about 16 million Dalit Christians in India and they form over 60 per cent of the total Christian population of 25 million. Economically, it is a depressed lot. A study undertaken by the Jesuits in Tamil Nadu reveals that 79.6 per cent of the Dalit Christians are landless, with their average annual income put at Rs 903; 54 per cent live under single-layer thatched roofs. The illiteracy rate is 65 per cent. Nearly 35 per cent of households manage with one set of clothes. Though Dalit Christians constitute 70 per cent of the Roman Catholics in Tamil Nadu, there is only one Dalit bishop and a mere 3.8 per cent Dalit priests. Several reports submitted by various committees such as Kumara Pillai (1965), Santhnam (1970) and Chidambaram (1975), apart from the two Backward Class Commissions reports of Kalelkar (1955) and Mandal (1980) of the Central Government, as well as the several BCC reports of the states including Andhra Pradesh (1970), Tamil Nadu (1970 and 1975) as also the Third and the Fourth Annual Reports of the Minorities Commission of the Central Government (1980 and 1981/82) and the SC-ST Commissioner's reports, have recognised this fact and recommended remedial measures. The Mandal Commission affirmed that "there is no doubt that social and educational backwardness among non-Hindu communities is more or less of the same order as among Hindu communities. Thus, both from within and without, caste amongst non-Hindu communities receive continuous sustenance and stimulus."[48]

The Dalit Christians made their demand for inclusion into the list of the Scheduled Castes as early as in 1950. It was not heeded.[49] But a contemporary letter dated 7 November 1950 from Pandit Jawaharlal Nehru written from the Prime Minister's Office in reply to C.X. Francis (President of the Catholic Regional Committee of Nagpur) who had pointed out the injustice done to the Dalit Christians by the Presidential Order, said that "all state aid and facilities are to be given not only to the Hindu scheduled castes but also to all other educationally and socially backward classes whether they profess Hinduism, Christianity or any other religion. Only in the matter of reservation of legislative bodies and Parliament, no person who professes a religion other than Hinduism shall be deemed to be a member of scheduled castes."[50]

Lately, the demand has been renewed. In 1994, the All India Christian Federation in its memorandum to the Prime Minister, demanded that "there should be an end to discrimination by the state against Christian Dalits only on the ground of religion ignoring other evidences of their social and educational backwardness and, to grant them SC status... on par with the Scheduled Castes belonging to the Hindu, Sikh and Buddhist religions."[51] On 21 November 1995, the Christian educational institutions in most parts of the country went on a day's strike in support of the demand for reservations for the Dalit Christians. In March 1996, the All India United Christians Movement for Equal Rights and the National Coordination Committee for SC Christians advised the community to vote for those political parties which would include Dalit Christian issues in their election manifestos in the forthcoming eleventh general election.

Such efforts did not go waste and in the 1996 parliamentary elections, all the major political parties barring the BJP, included in their election manifestos the demand that the Christian Dalits be treated as Scheduled Castes. The Common Minimum Programme of the United Front also included it. When a 14-member delegation of the All India Christian People's Forum met the then Prime Minister Deve Gowda on 14 June 1996 the latter promised the delegation that a bill would soon be introduced to extend the SC status to the Dalit Christians.[52] But nothing happened, for the reason that the ruling United Front coalition did not have enough confidence to secure its passage in the teeth of a determined BJP opposition.

The BJP is opposed to reservations for the Muslim community as a whole and the Dalit Muslims, as well as to granting SC status to the Dalit Christians. So far as the Muslims are concerned, it is not opposed to the idea of the backward caste Muslims asking for reservation under the OBC quota scheme[53] but it is vehemently against introducing any quota for the entire community for it would have "a serious repercussion" for the nation. It is also against individual states deciding on quotas in general. It endorses in principle the Supreme Court verdict that total reservation should not exceed 50 per cent with the exception of Tamil Nadu and Karnataka.[54]

The BJP's opposition is probably based on its *Hindutva* considerations. Its premise is two-fold. If the Dalits of other communities, namely, the Muslim and Christian, are granted SC status, then it would, on the one hand, make the Hindu SCs feel insecure for there would be more claimants on the quota and on the other, it would discourage "de-Christianisation" of the Dalits, a phenomenon which is otherwise expected in the given situation.[55] The party hopes that the more the Dalit Christians would be denied the SC status the greater would be their compulsion to reconvert to Hinduism. In March 1994 many Dalit Christians of Tamil Nadu did indeed re-convert to Hinduism for getting the SC status.[56] Gopal Sardesai of the Vishwa Hindu Parishad (VHP) argues: "Scheduled Caste Christians should return to the Hindu fold and then claim the benefits of reservation."[57]

Reservations for Women

Though oppressed and underprivileged through centuries of male domination, women as a whole have not received the attention of the Indian state in terms of compensatory discrimination. One reason for this neglect could be that there were many leading women in India's freedom struggle and they always regarded themselves as equals of their male counterparts. As emancipated women themselves they felt they would serve as role models for women's liberation in general. Moreover, against the background of such a great cause as national independence they felt that emphasising group interests such as women's rights would serve to weaken the larger struggle.

Even after independence it took many years for the demand for women's rights to crystallise. It actually happened under the UN pressure. In the early 1960s the United Nations had asked its member-nations to "prepare reports on women's status". India procrastinated for years. It responded only in the early 1970s, when the UN decided to observe 1975 as the International Year of Women. Prime Minister Indira Gandhi nominated the veteran freedom fighter from West Bengal Phulrenu Guha to prepare a report on the Status of Women in India. The report, *Toward Equality,* which ran into 480 pages and is frequently termed as the "founding text" in feminist circles was tabled in parliament in 1975.[58] Its recommendations, however, were not for positive discrimination in favour of women but against discrimination of women for which the state should be vigilant.

Neither the Kalelkar Commission nor the Mandal Commission had a female member. Had there been one or some female members a demand for reservation for women as an underprivileged social category may have emerged. For the last couple of decades, primarily on account of the activities of women's organisations, considerable social consciousness has developed in favour of feminist demands. Sensitivity to the issue is manifest in the way cabinets or the working committees of different political parties are composed. A recent opinion poll showed that 75 per cent men and 79 per cent women were in favour of an active role of women in politics. They also favoured reservation for women in the legislatures.[59]

The United Front government, elected in 1996, in keeping with its Common Minimum Programme and in line with the resolution adapted by the 10th Lok Sabha, has tabled the Constitution (81st Amendment) Bill (popularly known as Women's Reservation Bill) providing for reservation of one-third of the seats in the Lok Sabha and state assemblies for women. Already at the panchayat level 33 per cent of seats are reserved for them. The bill has raised a huge controversy in Indian politics. While, on the one hand, the women activists themselves are divided about its efficacy it has vertically split the movement between depressed class women and those champions of the bill who see it primarily as one for gender justice.[60] To add to the controversy is the opposition of the OBC leaders to the bill. They apprehend that the bill would deprive them of their hard-earned gains made through years of agitation. They fear that since their womenfolk are much more backward compared to their upper caste counterparts all seats would be taken by the upper castes tilting the political balance once again in favour of the upper castes.

As a *via media* it has been suggested that the proposed women's quota in the parliament be reduced from 33 per cent to 20 per cent or 25 per cent and also that states like Arunachal Pradesh, Manipur, Meghalaya, Mizoram, Nagaland and Tripura in the North-East, which send fewer than three MPs each, be excluded from the purview of the bill. But, the women's organisations which considered this suggestion put forward by the Lok Sabha Speaker, P.A. Sangma, unanimously rejected it on the ground that the 33 per cent formula had been recommended by the Joint Select Committee of Parliament and there was no reason to dilute the position.[61] Mulayam Singh Yadav's suggestion is to amend the Representation of the People Act to make it mandatory for all political parties to reserve a reasonable percentage of the contested seats for women.[62]

The catch in this suggestion that while parties may consider putting up women candidates they could relegate them to constituencies where the chances of its victory are little. Naturally, therefore, there is no scramble for party tickets.

Double-Member Constituency Formula

It may probably be true that once the bill is passed it would dilute the backward classes movements. In all probability, therefore, the MPs belonging to the OBCs would not vote for the bill in parliament. But, as it has been questioned, would not such a move amount to throwing the baby along with the bath water? As a compromise it has been suggested that the women's constituencies, reserved for some categories or the other, the OBCs for instance, be allowed with due safeguards to the democratic rights for all citizens as enshrined in the Preamble and Article 15 of the Constitution. This may be done through the expedience of double-member or multi-member constituencies.

The idea of a double or multi-member constituency formula has been mooted by Justice E.S. Venkataramiah, the former Chief Justice of India. In such constituencies, while one seat may be reserved for a woman or a member of the SC or ST categories, the other seat or seats may be contested by men or women not belonging to any of the said categories. Since the introduction of such constituencies could lead to a considerable expansion of the size of parliament, which may be prohibitive in terms of costs, it has been suggested that the same can be effected by better delimitation of constituencies. If the present size of the parliament consisting of 543 members is not to be disturbed, the double-member constituency formula may look something like the following:

1. 15 single-member constituencies: all adult citizens, men or women, belonging to SC/ST or not, are free to contest;
2. 147 double-member constituencies: one seat for women and one for men, with everybody, whether SC/ST, are free to contest;
3. 79 double-member constituencies: one general seat in each constituency can be contested by men and women, SC/ST or not; the other seats (79) reserved for SC – 23 for women, 23 for men, 33 for SC open to both men and women;
4. 38 double-member constituencies: one general seat in each constituency can be contested by men and women, SC/ST or

not; the other seats (38) reserved for STs – 11 for women, 11 for men and 16 for ST open to both women and men.[63]

Some Perspectives

Merit versus Social Justice

The most common criticism raised against the policy of reservations is that it is at the cost of meritocracy and that it promotes mediocrity which a developing society like India can ill-afford. While apparently and theoretically the argument seems well-founded, there is neither evidence to support the fear nor is it true to say that meritocracy would be the norm once reservation is lifted. All kinds of undocumented reservations operate in India through kinship connections, caste connections and professional connections. For instance, the Delhi University Teachers Association (DUTA) is generally opposed to the OBC reservation but does not mind asking for reservations for the wards of the teachers or for weightage in their favour for university enrolment. Commenting on the impact of reservations on the educational standard, noted sociologist André Béteille writes:

> Everybody says that the standards have fallen in the Indian universities. However, I find it difficult to judge, firstly, whether standards have in fact fallen, and secondly, if they have fallen, whether the fall has been due to affirmative action. At the bottom end of the scale, a very large proportion of the present crop of graduates would not have graduated in the 1950s. On the other hand, the number of good students is probably higher – so at the top end of the scale, standards are maintained. I would attribute the lowering of standards in this particular sense to the massive and sometimes reckless expansion of higher education under political pressure.[64]

It is probably not correct that the weightage system would perpetually introduce bad students to the university. From the record of the South Indian states it appears that the more the backward classes enter the system, the more their standards improve on account of competition amongst themselves (see Table 2). (This must be read together with the facts that many upper caste students have migrated to northern universities and also there are allegations that marks of SC students are inflated by the SC examiners.)

Table 2

Selection to Professional Courses (1990):
Cut-off Points (%) ***(Some South Indian Universities)***

Course	*Open Competition*	*Backward*	*Most Backward*	*SC*
Computer	97.98	96.58	93.25	84.38
Electronics	97.74	96.08	92.16	82.22
Electrical	95.84	95.42	91.48	81.98
Mechanical	95.78	94.10	90.66	79.21
Medical	95.22	93.18	89.62	83.98
Agriculture (B.Sc.)	90.90	90.08	86.10	78.04
Agriculture (B.E.)	92.66	91.96	87.46	76.14
Veterinary	94.90	93.48	91.18	85.24
BF.Sc.	96.96	95.58	95.02	93.02

Source: Madhu Limaye, "A Democratic Weapon", *Seminar* (New Delhi), No. 375, November 1990, p. 63.

Inherent Contradictions

The more fundamental question, however, is how far have the quotas and other privileges helped the target groups. As we have seen above, the progress in this regard has at best been marginal. Whatever progress has been registered by the depressed classes, it is more or less proportionate to the overall progress achieved by the nation. As target groups, they should have shown a visibly better record, but this has not happened. In a country like India, where poverty, illiteracy and deprivation are so widespread, it is a questionable proposition to think in terms of upliftment for particular social groups, that too by emphasising reservations alone. A report on the state of primary education in India brought out by the *India Today* portrays a depressing picture of the Indian state's failure in this regard.[65] The problem as such is much larger and mere targetting particular sections of society would not do. It is surmised that since reservations are the least expensive and politically most rewarding the political parties find them the easiest policy options available to them.

A related question is whether the privileges are being cornered by the élites amongst the target groups. One common criticism against the reservation policy is that it has benefited only a small section of them. According to estimates, only 6 per cent of the SC families have benefited from the policy. It must, however, be admitted that even this small number has thrown up leadership for the community to bargain for the larger interests of the community at large.[66] Moreover, it is a fact of life that in any community within a competitive polity the initial beneficiaries are invariably the élites.

This criticism, however, is largely valid in respect of the OBCs where some of the backward castes are way above others amongst them.[67] As such, any reservation policy meant for the OBC, as a whole, is bound to end in ineffectiveness in the long run by this internal contradiction alone. As most of the underprivileged amongst the OBCs would ask for their rights there would be cleavages in the OBC identity as is now being seen in Bihar. There, the Kurmis and the Koiris are opposing the Yadavs, both belonging to the OBC category. Moreover, with other demands being raised for quota allocations by women, professional groups, the poor from the upper caste Hindus, and so on, there is a possibility that the entire system of OBC reservation would collapse as a result of these divisions.

Persistence of Caste Prejudice

One other issue which needs to be discussed here is whether there can ever be any real improvement in the lot of the underprivileged sections of the society, whether they belong to the SCs/STs or the OBCs, without attacking the caste system itself, this being the essence of the debate between Gandhi and Ambedkar. Can the elimination of the stigma experienced by the underprivileged be achieved through the philanthropy and grace of the upper caste Hindus or has it to be earned or wrested by the under-privileged themselves through their struggles, even violent struggles. If violence is inherent in the circumstances, would it not perpetuate the caste cleavages at the cost of social harmony? In any event it has been noticed that the quota system has eliminated whatever goodwill the upper castes had for the lower castes. As one non-Indian scholar wrote in 1979, "In the course of my visits to India over two decades I have noticed an erosion and virtual disappearance of a liberal-minded public opinion supporting private efforts to improve opportunities for the SC."[68]

This lack of concern is manifest in the record of private sector employment. "The pervasive over-estimation of the amount and effectiveness of preferential treatment reinforces the notion that enough (or too much) is already being done and nothing more is called for."[69] A recent study based on interviews of 500 Punjab government employees stationed in Chandigarh reveals the deep-seated prejudice among the non-SCs against the quota privileges meant for the SCs. Particularly prejudiced are the Class II and III categories of the employees.[70] Caste conflicts are rampant as a reading of the Annual Reports of the Home Ministry reveals. During 1996 there were 672 caste-related incidents involving all the three broad caste categories, namely, the Forward Castes, the OBCs and the SCs.[71]

A Spectre of Two Indias

In the current context the most critical question is whether two Indias are being created by two diametrically opposite socio-political forces – the demand for modernisation on the one hand bolstered by the opening up of the economy and its integration into the techno-intensive global economy – and on the other, the demand for social justice undermining the core of that theory. One calls for the withdrawal of the state and the other assigns to the state the role of the greatest dispenser of equity. Against this background it would be increasingly difficult for the state to implement its policy of reservations, especially where the OBCs are concerned. On the one hand, the number of government jobs is shrinking while on the other pressure for more jobs is mounting.[72]

There is yet another related issue. Greater liberalisation of the economy means more modernisation of trade and industry. The traditional vocations of the backward classes such as cleaning, hair-cutting, fishing and tanning are under threat of being controlled by the upper castes, particularly in the urban areas. With the growing use of technology in these trades, they are no longer looked down upon as occupations. Therefore, the backwards cannot depend any more upon the state; they would have to respond to the market as well.[73] This brings into question the broader recommendation of the Mandal Commission (structural changes in the oppressive production relations). But, no OBC leader seems to be much concerned about that. Of course, the market has its own logic and the OBCs are getting drawn into them.

Conclusion

The debate over positive discrimination in India is acrimonious and is increasingly finding expression in violence. On the one hand, the policy is defended as ethically correct as it is meant to compensate for centuries of injustice perpetrated against large sections of people on account of their social origin, while on the other it is assailed as something echoing the inherently incorrect logic of robbing Peter to pay Paul. But a democracy which is essentially a social contraption is neither dictated by logic nor by ethics. At the root of democratic success is social engineering which is effected through political bargaining. In India, the process is on and only the future would tell whether its experiments were in the right direction or not.

Social categories are neither static nor monolithic. But, in India, the hierarchical stratifications have by and large survived for centuries and they continue to be politically relevant. In the given situation the policy of reservations seems to continue for an indefinite period, at least for the SCs/STs. But this is the easiest thing that the state could think of. The real challenge for the state should be to make the disadvantaged groups competitive through raising their standards so as to let them be on par with the traditionally successful upper classes. That is cost-intensive and for that there has to be a shift in the dynamics of power. The disadvantage would have to come to the fore of politics. The present Dalit movement seems to be straws in the wind indicating this penchant for transformation which is bound to be violent.[74]

The same may not, however, be said about the OBCs. Unlike the SCs and STs the so-called OBCs have held political power in different historical periods in different regions of India. They are neither as socially stigmatised nor at the bottom of the economic hierarchy as the SCs. In short they are not such an ostracised lot as the SCs have been. Given this situation the demand for OBC reservation is indeed politically motivated, the logic behind which is largely indefensible.

In any case, increasingly, the role of the state would be in question. The assumption here is that the Indian society is traditionally violent and vertically and horizontally disintegrative. It is the enormous military power in the hands of the central government, both during the Mughals and the British, that actually contained it. The apologists for state power argue in favour of a militaristic role of the state to maintain societal order while the champions of civil society put the blame squarely on the state for the growing violence in the society. The debate warrants a closer scrutiny against the background of the social acrimony that the policy of reservation has accentuated.

Acknowledgement

The author thanks Professors Suma Chitnis and Imtiaz Ahmad for their valuable comments on the original draft. The responsibility for the views expressed in this article lies with the author alone.

Notes

1. Gandhi accepted the rationale behind the caste system and its ideal. He was, however, unhappy about its reality. In fact he was ambivalent about its continuity. The origin of the word "untouchables" is not clear. The four-tier Hindu *varnashram* system does not include them. Obviously they were the fifth category in the social hierarchy. The original inventor of the word "Harijan" was not Gandhi. It was Narsi Mehta who used it to refer to the children of *Devadasis* (temple dancers). See T.K. Oommen, "Panchamas to Dalits: The Context and Content of Identity," *Times of India*, New Delhi, 11 May 1994. Lately, the term "Harijans" has been rejected by the Harijans themselves.
2. There were fundamental theoretical differences between Gandhi and Ambedkar on which there is a volume of literature. For a brief analysis of Ambedkar's thought, see Uma Shankar, "Political Thought of B.R. Ambedkar," *Jigyansa*, New Delhi, 1 (1), October 1996, pp. 32-39; B.K. Roy Burman, "The Problem," *Seminar*, New Delhi, No. 177, 1974, pp. 10-15; Michael Mahar (ed.), *The Untouchables in Contemporary India, Phoenix*, The University of Arizona Press, 1972. A recent study argues that Ambedkar's one-point programme was to oppose Gandhi to promote his own political interest. See Arun Shourie's, *Worshipping False Gods*, New Delhi, ASA Publications, 1997. For a representative sample of the type of debate that Shourie's book has triggered off, see Praful Bidwai, "Attacking Ambedkar: The Dwija's Last War-Cry," *Times of India*, 13 August 1997; Kancha Ilaiah, "Attacks on Ambedkar," *The Hindu*, New Delhi, 30 August 1997; Anirudha Gupta's review of Shourie's book in *Mainstream*, New Delhi, 22 November 1997, pp. 25-26.
3. These figures were according to the Indian Statutory (Simon) Commission, 1930. See Marc Galanter, *Competing Equalities: Law and the Backward Classes in India*, Delhi, OUP, 1984, p. 124.
4. Suma Chitnis, "Definition of the Terms Scheduled Castes and Scheduled Tribes: A Crisis of Ambivalence," in V.A. Pai Panandiker

(ed.), *The Politics of Backwardness: Reservation Policy in India,* New Delhi, Konark, 1997, p. 104.

5. Vidya Subrahmaniam, "Reality of Dalit Power: Condemned Before," *Times of India,* 9 August 1997.
6. M.N. Srinivas, *Social Change in Modern India,* New Delhi, Orient Longman, 1977, p. 92, quoted by M.V. Nadkarni, "Broadbasing Process in India and Dalits," *Economic and Political Weekly,* Mumbai, 16-23 August 1997, p. 2164.
7. Nadkarni, *ibid.,* p. 2167.
8. Given equal opportunity the SC children may do as well as their upper caste counterparts. A comparative analysis of the personality traits of students belonging to SC and other categories tends to prove this. See S.B. Kakkar, "The Personality Characteristic and Educational Problems of Scheduled Caste Students", A Pilot Study Report submitted to the Indian Council of Social Science Research, New Delhi, 1990.
9. A study conducted in the late 1970s revealed that most of the SC respondents to a questionnaire favoured continuation of the policy of reservation. See Suma Chitnis, "A Long Way to Go (Report on a Survey of Scheduled Caste High School and College Students in Fifteen States of India)", mimeo, Centre for Social Studies, Surat, 1977, pp. 293-95.
10. Rajni Kothari, "Rise of the Dalits and the Renewed Debate on Caste" in Partha Chatterjee (ed.), *State and Politics in India,* Delhi, OUP, 1997, p. 449. See also, Dipankar Gupta, "Positive Discrimination and the Question of Fraternity: Contrasting Ambedkar and Mandal on Reservations," *Economic and Political Weekly,* 2 August 1997, pp. 1971-78.
11. Gopal Guru, "Why are the Dalits Angry?", *The Hindu,* 29 July 1997; J.V. Deshpande, "Behind Dalit Anger," *Economic and Political Weekly,* 16-23 August 1997, pp. 2090-91.
11. *The Hindu,* 3 July 1997.
12. Professor Parmaji, *Caste Reservations and Performance: Research Findings,* Warangal, Mamata, 1985, pp. 174 -75.
13. Paul R Brass, *The Politics of India since Independence,* Cambridge, Cambridge University Press, 1990, pp. 210-11.
14. Parmaji, *op.cit.*
15. See Ravinder Kumar, "Resurgence in the Ganga Valley", *The Hindu,* 11, 12 and 13 July 1995 (in three parts).

16. Social anthropologist Roy Burman who was the Chairman of the Research Planning Team and a member of the Technical Sub committee of the Mandal Commission and who dissociated himself from the Commission's findings, argues that the criteria adopted were faulty, and suggests what should have been done by the Commission. See B.K. Roy Burman, "Formula for Identification of OBC," *Vacham*, Bhopal, 3(1) January 1992, pp. 23-25. See also André Béteille, "Is Job Reservation a Good Policy," *Seminar*, No. 375, November 1990, pp. 41-42.
17. Brass, *op.cit.*, p. 211.
18. Veena Das, "The Mandal Commission Report: A Critical Appraisal," *Vacham*, 3(1), January 1992, pp. 8-9.
19. Quoted by Ashish Bose, "Mandal Commission Estimate of O.B.C. -Demographic Pitfalls," *Vacham*, 3 (1), January, 1992, pp. 19,55.
20. According to Bose's estimation the number of Hindu OBCs would be about 43 per cent.
21. By this time the BJP had emerged as an important political force, and riding on the band wagon of a pan-Hindu movement triggered off by the Babri Mosque-Ram Janmabhoomi controversy it was making a bid to emerge as the leading political party of India.
22. This ruling was reconfirmed in the Supreme Court verdict of 16 November 1992 in the case of Indira Sawhney vs The Union of India. It, however, specified that candidates selected for reserved posts must satisfy certain conditions of eligibility to meet the requirement of 'efficiency' in administration. It also exempted from reservation appointment to certain positions like defense personnel, research scientists, medical specialists, university professors, airline pilots, etc. For details, see M.J. Antony, *Dalit Rights: Landmark Judgments on SC/ST/Backward Classes*, New Delhi, Indian Social Institute, 1997, pp. 116-19.
23. *Times of India*, 22 September 1994.
24. It may be noted that the BJP was originally not in favour of any caste-based reservation for any community. It was in favour of reservations for only the economically depressed classes irrespective of caste and community. See P. Satyanarayana, "Reservations and Attitudes of Political Parties," in B.A.V. Sharma and K. Madhusudan Reddy (eds.), *Reservation Policy in India*, New Delhi, Light and Life, 1982.
25. T.K. Oommen, "Religious Minorities: Inconsistency in Affirmative Action", *Times of India*, 4 April 1994.

26. The Jain community, however, has been included in the list of minority communities by the National Commission for Minorities.
27. In 1986, in Soosai vs The Union of India, the Supreme Court ruled that SC members converting to Christianity were not eligible for benefits granted to SCs as their disabilities did not continue after conversion as per the meaning of the 1950 Presidential Order. For the details of the case, see Antony, *op.cit.*, pp. 63-64.
28. See Pervaiz Nazir, "Social Structure, Ideology and Language: Caste among Muslims", *Economic and Political Weekly*, 25 December 1993, pp. 2897-900.
29. Government's clarification in the Lok Sabha on 11 March 1997. *Times of India*, 12 March 1997.
30. Government statement in reply to Lok Sabha Unstarred Question No.5379 dated 28 April 1994 by S.M.L.J. Basha. See *Muslim India*, New Delhi, No. 141, September 1994, p. 413. Emphasis added.
31. Masood Ali Khan, "Reservations for Muslims," *Mainstream*, New Delhi, 20 May 1995, pp. 21-23.
32. *The Hindu*, 7 September 1994. The All Manipur Muslim Organisations Coordinating Committee feels that in spite of this the 10 per cent Muslims of the state are elbowed out by more assertive OBCs. The committee has demanded a separate quota for the Muslims as a community. *Times of India*, 2 November 1997.
33. *Ibid.*, 12 July 1995.
34. *Asian Age*, 10 July 1995.
35. *The Hindu*, 30 August 1996.
36. Masood Ali Khan, *op.cit.*, p. 22.
37. *India Today*, New Delhi, 30 November 1994, p. 83.
38. *Asian Age*, 18 August 1997.
39. *India Today*, 30 November 1994, p. 83.
40. *The Hindu*, 30 April 1995.
41. *Ibid.*, 12 September 1995.
42. *Ibid.*, 25 August 1997.
43. D.L. Sheth, "Muslim Reservations: No Provision for Community Quotas," *Times of India*, 20 September 1997.
44. A letter to Editor in *ibid.*, 30 September 1997, with reference to Sheth's article.
45. Syed Shahabuddin's rejoinder to Sheth's article in *ibid.*
46. James Massey, *Dalits in India: Religion as a Source of Bondage or Liberation with Special Reference to Christians*, New Delhi, Manohar, 1995.

Quoted by S.M. Michael in his review of the book in *Economic and Political Weekly,* 14 December 1996, pp. 342-44. See also, P. Radhakrishnan, "The Dalit Controversy," *The Hindu,* 9 and 10 January 1996 (in two parts).

47. *Asian Age,* 17 July 1995.
48. Quoted by Massey, *op.cit.*
49. A champion of the Dalit Christian rights argues that the Presidential Order was wrong as it was biased in favour of the Hindus when the social malady in India was not religion specific. See Saturnino Dias, "Dalit Christians: Constitution Grants Privileges," *The Statesman,* Calcutta, 22 August 1996.
50. George Menezes, "Dalit Christians Expect Promises to be Honoured," *Times of India,* 12 December 1995.
51. The text of the Memorandum in *Muslim India,* No.141, September 1994, pp. 426-28.
52. Brindvan C. Moses, "Christian Dalits: Victims of Discrimination", *The Hindu,* 8 April 1997.
53. In July 1995, the Shiv Sena-BJP government in Maharashtra committed itself to extend quota facility to 15 Muslim castes on par with those provided for other backward classes in the State. Entitlements for these communities would not be additional but within the 27 per cent quota for OBCs. *The Hindu,* 12 July 1995.
54. *Ibid.,* 1 September 1994.
55. The fear was expressed in a BJP National Executive resolution. See *Asian Age,* 24 June 1996.
56. S.M. Michael, "Dalit Christians in India," *Economic and Political Weekly,* 14 December 1996, p. 3244.
57. *Times of India,* 22 November 1995. See also, P. Radhakrishnan, "The Dalit Controversy", *The Hindu,* 9 January 1996.
58. Nilanjan Mukhopadhyay, "In the Eye of the Storm", *Hindustan Times Sunday Magazine,* New Delhi, 25 May 1997. For a summary of the Report, see Indian Council of Social Science Research, *Status of Women in India: A Synopsis of the Report of the National Committee on the Status of Women (1971-1974),* New Delhi, 1975, reprint 1988.
59. Madhu Kishwar, "Not a Gender War", *Hindustan Times,* 3 June 1997.
60. For two representative views see Brinda Karat, "Gender Justice is Above Caste," and Bhagwati Devi, "Elite Women Will Benefit", *India Today,* 9 June 1997, pp. 50-51.
61. *Sunday Times of India,* 3 August 1997.

62. Garimella Subramanium, "The Women's Bill," *The Hindu*, 30 August 1997.
63. This detailed formula has been provided by M.S. Dayal, "Double-Member Constituency for Political Justice to All," *The Hindu*, 22 July 1997. See also S. Shukla, "Reservation for Women and Multi-member Constituencies," *Mainstream*, 14 June 1997, pp. 13-17.
64. Beteille, *op.cit.*, p. 13.
65. *India Today*, 17 October 1997, pp. 68-73.
66. Marc Galanter, *Law and Society in Modern India*, Delhi, OUP, 1989, pp. 192-93. See also, Victor S. D'Souza, *Development Planning and Structural Inequalities: The Response of the Under Privileged*, New Delhi, Sage, 1990, pp. 196-97.
67. See D.R. Nagaraj, "Correcting Mandal's Flaws," *Indian Express*, New Delhi, 3 June 1995.
68. Lelah Dushkin, "Backward Class Benefits and Social Class in India, 1920-1970," *Economic and Political Weekly*, 14, 1979, p. 666; quoted by Galanter, *Competing Equalities*, p. 550.
69. Marc Galanter, *op.cit.*, p. 195.
70. Ravinder Singh Bains, *Reservation Policy and Anti-Reservationists*, Delhi, B.R. Publishing, 1994, pp. 178-81.
71. Government of India, Ministry of Home Affairs, *Annual Report 1996-97*, p. 6.
72. For more on this point see I.Z. Bhatty, "Implications for Government," *Seminar*, No. 375, November 1990, pp. 43-47.
73. T.K. Oommen, "Helping the Backwards: Role of State and Market," *Times of India*, 18 October 1994. For a different perspective as to how the globalisation is further affecting the depressed classes, see Kancha Ilaiah, "Dalits and Globalisation," *The Hindu*, 17 November 1997.
74. For an analysis of the Dalit politics, see Rajni Kothari, "Rise of the Dalits and the Renewed Debate on Caste," in Partha Chatterjee (ed.), *State and Politics in India*, New Delhi, OUP, 1997, pp. 439-58.

II

Size of OBCs

7

On Backwardness and Fair Access to Higher Education

K. SUNDARAM

This paper, written against the backdrop of the proposal to reserve 27 per cent of seats in institutions for higher education for the Other Backward Castes (OBCs in short), seeks to address two interrelated yet distinct issues. These are: (i) criteria for assessing the backwardness of different social groups; and, (ii) assessment of fairness of access to higher education of a "backward" caste group. Accordingly, the paper is organised in two parts.

In the first part, we review briefly the evidence, across (essentially) caste-based social groups, on poverty, livelihood categories, occupational diversification, and, educational attainments – elements in economic criteria of backwardness. It is shown that, for all households (poor and non-poor taken together) there is a clear hierarchy within the Scheduled Castes (in urban India) and the Scheduled Tribes (in rural India) at the bottom, the OBCs in the middle, the Others (non-SCs/STs) at the top. However, for the poor among them, there is more of a continuum with surprisingly small differences between the OBCs and the Others.

In the second part, we argue that evidence of "backwardness" of a social group – even one pertaining to educational attainments –

does not automatically establish the presence of "unfair" access to higher education in terms of enrolments. They are of even less help in measuring the extent of underrepresentation which is so essential to assess the appropriateness of a 'X' per cent reservation for a social group. Apart from drawing attention to the burden of history embedded in measures defined over open-ended age intervals and the crucial distinction between enrolments and attainments, we focus on a critical facet of higher education: the fact that beyond the elementary stage, entry at each step of the educational pyramid is conditional on the successful completion of the preceding stage of education.

I
Caste, Poverty and Backwardness

A substantially higher than average prevalence, depth and severity of poverty is a defining economic characteristic of the two constitutionally recognised disadvantaged groups: the Scheduled Tribes (STs, in short) and the Scheduled Castes (SCs, in short). How do the OBCs fare relative to the SCs and the STs on the one hand and the residual category of Others on the other?

Three measures, viz., the Head Count Ratio, the Poverty Gap Ratio and the Squared Poverty Gap, are widely used to capture, respectively, the prevalence, depth and severity of poverty. Table 2 presents estimates of these three measures for the four social groups – the STs, the SCs, the OBCs and the Others, separately for the rural (Panel A) and the urban (Panel B) populations at the all-India level. Also presented are the estimates of the mean per capita expenditure (PCTE) of the poor (column 5) and the mean of the poverty gaps among the poor (column 6). These estimates for 1999-2000 are based on the NSS 55th Round Consumer Expenditure Survey.

As can be readily seen, in both population segments and on all the three measures, poverty is less marked for the OBCs relative to both the STs and the SCs. However, relative to the residual category of Others, they are worse-off. This is more so in terms of depth and severity of poverty and in urban India. As between the STs and the SCs, the former are distinctly worse-off in rural India but are slightly better-off in urban India.

Table 1

Share of Social Groups in All-India Rural and Urban Population, 1999-2000: Alternative Estimates from Consumer Expenditure and Employment-Unemployment Surveys

Social Group	Rural		Urban	
	From CES	From EUS	From CES	From EUS
Scheduled Tribes	10.5	10.9	3.4	3.9
Scheduled Castes	20.5	21.6	14.4	14.2
Other Backward Castes	37.6	37.0	30.4	30.9
Others	31.5	30.6	51.8	51.1
All	100.0	100.0	100.0	100.0

Source: Computed from Unit Record Data, NSS 55th Round Consumer Expenditure and Employment-Unemployment Surveys, 1999-2000.

Table 2

Poverty Across Social-Groups in Rural and Urban Areas of India: All-India, 1999-2000

Panel A: Rural India Poverty Line: Rs 335.46

Social Groups	Head Count Rations	Poverty Gap	Squared Poverty Group	Mean PCTE Among Poor	Mean Poverty Gap Among Poor
(1)	(2)	(3)	(4)	(5)	(6)
	Percentage			(Rs. 0.00)	(Rs. 0.00)
Scheduled Tribes	48.02	11.45	3.84	255.47	79.99
Scheduled Castes	38.38	7.92	2.41	266.23	69.23
Other Backward Castes	29.04	5.48	1.56	272.22	63.24
Others	16.29	2.89	0.79	275.88	59.59

Panel B: Urban India Poverty Line: Rs 451.19

Social Groups	*Head Count Rations*	*Poverty Gap*	*Squared Poverty Group*	*Mean PCTE Among Poor*	*Mean Poverty Gap Among Poor*
(1)	*(2)*	*(3)*	*(4)*	*(5)*	*(6)*
		Percentage		*(Rs. 0.00)*	*(Rs. 0.00)*
Scheduled Tribes	35.15	8.98	3.35	335.93	115.27
Scheduled Castes	37.84	8.77	2.89	346.67	104.52
Other Backward					
Castes	28.99	6.25	1.95	353.98	97.21
Others	23.09	5.04	1.60	352.78	98.42

Source: Computed from Unit Record Data of the NSS 55th Round Consumer Expenditure Survey.

Even though the OBCs are clearly worse-off relative to the non-SC/ST group of Others on all the three measures of poverty, if we focus on the sub-set of the poor in each social group we have a striking result. In terms of differences in the mean per capita expenditure (PCTE) of the poor households taken as a group, there is very little gap between the two social groups – a little over one per cent. With similarly small gaps between the OBCs and the SCs, and the SCs and the STs, even the difference in mean PCTE of the poor separating the worst-off (the STs) and the best-off (the Others), at 6-7 per cent is still fairly small. Even in terms of the difference in the mean of poverty gaps among the poor, the gap between the OBCs and the Others (Rs.3.7 in rural India and Rs.4.6 in urban India) is quite small. The differences are sharper as between the OBCs and the SCs and as between the SCs and the STs.

This absence of sharp differences between the poor among the OBCs and the poor in the Others is also seen in the distribution of population by Means of Livelihood (MoL for short) categories, occupational structure of workers on the usual (principal plus subsidiary) status and in the proportion of population with "secondary and above" level of education.

Thus, in rural India, the proportion of the poor among the OBCs located in the MoL category with the lowest level of poverty – the self-employed in agriculture – is just one percentage point lower than the corresponding proportion for the poor among the others. However, the difference in the proportion of the poor of the two social groups located in agricultural labour households (the MoL category with the highest level of poverty) is higher at 4.6 percentage points (see Table 3). This absence of sharp divergence in the distribution of the poor population of the two social groups across MoL categories is clearer still in urban India: while 46 per cent of the OBC-poor are self-employed, for the poor among the Others, this proportion was 45.6 per cent. The difference between the two social groups in terms of the proportion of their poor population located in households with the earnings from regular wage/salary earners as the principal source of income (RWS households for short) is a little over 2 percentage points.

Table 3

Distribution of Social Group Population by means of Livelihood Categories for all Households and Poor households in Rural and Urban India: All-India, 1999- 2000

Panel A: Rural India, Percentage Shares

Group/MoL Categories	*All Households*					*Poor Households Social Group/*				
	ST	*SC*	*OBC*	*Others*	*All*	*ST*	*SC*	*OBC*	*Others*	*All*
SE Ag	39.5	19.3	39.4	45.8	37.1	33.4	15.1	30.7	31.9	27.2
SE Non-Ag	5.3	12.5	15.9	15.4	13.9	4.6	9.1	14.4	16.2	11.8
Ag. Labour	38.5	49.5	26.6	17.7	30.0	50.5	61.9	40.9	36.3	47.2
Other Labour	9.3	9.8	7.2	5.8	7.5	7.5	8.7	6.5	6.9	7.3
Others	7.4	8.9	10.9	15.2	11.4	3.9	4.7	7.5	8.7	6.4
All	100.0	100.0	100.0	100.0	100.0	100.0	100.0	100.0	100.0	100.0

Panel B: Urban India, Percentage Shares

MoL Categories	All Households					Poor Households				
	ST	SC	OBC	Others	All	ST	SC	OBC	Others	All
SE Ag	25.3	29.7	43.1	40.9	39.4	23.1	34.4	46.4	45.6	42.1
RWS-Workers	37.9	38.7	34.5	40.6	40.3	14.9	14.9	22.3	24.6	22.1
Casual Labour	27.5	26.5	16.5	7.8	14.0	51.3	51.3	26.6	24.2	30.5
Others	9.2	5.0	5.8	6.7	6.3	10.6	10.6	4.7	5.5	5.2
All	100.0	100.0	100.0	100.0	100.0	100.0	100.0	100.0	100.0	100.0

Source: Computed from Unit Record Data, NSS 55th Round Employment-Unemployment Survey.

Notes: SE AG: Self-Employed in Agriculture; SE Non-Ag: Self-Employed in Non-Agriculture; Ag Labour: Agricultural Labour; RWS-Worker: Regular Wage/Salary Workers

To see these numbers in perspective, in rural India, taking both the poor and the non-poor households together, the proportion of the population of the self-employed in agriculture for Others (45.8%) is over 6 percentage points higher than that for the OBCs (39.4%). Similarly, in urban India, the proportion located in RWS households was 10 percentage points higher for the Others (44.6%) relative to the OBCs (34.5%).

This fairly close correspondence between the distribution by MoL categories of the poor among the OBCs and the Others is also in evidence when we examine the occupational structure of the usual (principal plus subsidiary) status workers (see Table 4R for rural India and 4U for urban India) located in poor households.

In rural India, ranked by the share of each occupation group in the total workforce in poor households of each social group, the list of top five occupation groups has three or more common categories in any pair of the four social groups.

In urban India, which has a more diversified occupational structure, Table 4U lists the top 10 occupational groups for each of the four social groups, again ranked by the share of each occupation group in the total workforce in poor household of each social group. As between the OBCs and the Others, there are eight common categories. Across any pairing of the four social groups, there are at least six common occupational categories.

Table 4R

List of Top Five Occupations of UPSS Workforce in Poor Households Across Social Groups: All-India, Rural, 1999-2000
Top Five Occupations Ranked by Share in Work Force

Social Group/Rank of Occupation	*Scheduled Tribes*	*Scheduled Castes*	*Other Backward Castes*	*Others*
1	Agricultural Labourers	Agricultural Labourers	Agricultural Labourers	Resident Farmers, Fishermen, Hunters etc.
2	Resident Farmers, Fishermen, Hunters etc.	Resident Farmers, Fishermen, Hunters etc.	Resident Farmers, Fishermen, Hunters etc.	Agricultural Labourers
3	Labourers not elsewhere classified	Labourers not elsewhere classified	Sales Workers	Residual Direct Production Workers
4	Bricklayers and Other Construction Workers	Bricklayers and Other Construction Workers	Residual Services Ancilliary to Production Process	Sales Workers
5	Sales Workers	Residual Services Ancilliary to Production Process	Labourers not elsewhere classified	Labourers not elsewhere classified

Source: Based on Detailed Tabulation from Unit Record Data, NSS 55th Round Employment-Unemployment Survey, 1999-2000.

Table 4U

List of Top Ten Occupations of UPSS Work Force in Poor Households Across Social Groups: All-India, Urban, 1999-2000
Top Ten Occupations Ranked by Share in Work Force

Social Group	*Scheduled Tribes*	*Scheduled Castes*	*Other Backward Castes*	*Other Castes*
1.	Agricultural Labourers	Agricultural Labourers	Sales Workers	Sales Workers
2.	Labourers not else where classified	Labourers not else where classified	Resident Farmers, Fishermen, Hunters etc.	Residual Direct Production Process Workers
3.	Resident Farmers, Fishermen, Hunters etc.	Resident Farmers, Fishermen, Hunters etc.	Residual Services mostly to Households	Transport Equipment Operators
4.	Sales Workers	Bricklayers and Other Construction Workers	Agricultural Labourers	Labourers not else where classified
5.	Bricklayers and Other Construction Workers	Sales Workers	Labourers not else where classified	Residual Services mostly to Households
6.	Residual Services Ancillary to Production Process	Transport Equipment Operators	Residual Direct Production Process Workers	Resident Farmers, Fishermen, Hunters etc.
7.	Residual Services mostly to Households	Residual Universal Services Associate with production Process	Bricklayers and Other Construction Workers	Spinners, Weaves, Knitters, Dyers and Related Workers
8.	Transport Equipment Operators	Resident Farmers, Fishermen, Hunters etc.	Transport Equipment Operators	Bricklayers and Other Construction Workers
9.	Maids & Other Housekeeping Service Workers	Residual Production Process Workers	Residual Universal Service Associate with Production Process	Machinery Fitters, Machine Assemblers & Precision instrument makers
10.	Material Handling & Related Equipment Operator	Maids & Other Housekeeping Service Workers	Spinners, Weavers Knitters, Dyers and Related Workers	Agricultural Labourers

This broad correspondence in the occupational structure of the workers in poor households is also seen in the educational attainments of the population in poor households across social groups. Thus, in rural India, the proportion of poor population in OBC households having a "secondary and above" level of education (4.3%) is lower than that for the poor among the (non-SC/ST) Others (5.7%) by less than 1.5 percentage point. In urban India, the proportion of population in poor households with the same level of education, at 12.4 per cent for the Others, is higher than the corresponding proportion for the OBCs (9.7%) by less than 3 percentage points, with just one percentage point separating the two groups in terms of the proportion of "graduates and above" among them.

Again, to judge the scale of these differences, let us note that, for the total (poor plus non-poor) population, in urban India, close to 44 per cent of those in the social group "Others" had a "secondary and above" level of education, whereas for the OBCs, the corresponding proportion was a little under 25 per cent. More significantly, the bulk of this difference is in the proportion of population with a "graduate and above" level of education (5.6% for the OBCs and 16.4% for the Others). In rural India too, the contrasts in educational attainments as between the OBCs and the Others is sharper when we focus on the total as opposed to the poor population. In the social group "Others", 16.9 per cent had a "secondary and above" level of education. For the OBCs, this proportion was just 9.2 per cent.

Our discussion above suggests that while there is a clear hierarchy of the four social groups in terms of differences in levels of living, poverty, educational attainments and means of livelihood with the OBCs sandwiched between the SCs/STs at the lower end of the scale and the Others at the top, for the poor among them, there is more of a continuum across the caste groups with strikingly small differences as between the OBCs and the Others. Having already recognised the SCs and the STs as clearly disadvantaged social groups, it would be more appropriate to club the poor among the OBCs and the Others as a backward class rather than divide them further along caste lines.

We had noted above that when we compare the educational attainments of the total (poor plus non-poor) population across the four social groups, we find a fairly sizeable difference in the proportion having a "graduate and above" level of education as between the OBCs and the Others – especially in urban India. Does this form an adequate basis for the proposed 27 per cent reservation of seats in institutions of higher education? We examine this issue in the rest of this paper.

II
OBCs and Fair Access to Higher Education

In the context of the proposal for reservation of 27 per cent of seats in higher education for the OBCs, the key question is whether the OBCs of college-going age with the qualifying level of education are underrepresented in enrolments to higher education to the extent of 27 per cent or more of the total enrolments.

In seeking an answer to this question, three issues embedded within this question need to be sorted out. These are: age cut-off; the distinction between enrolments and completed level of education; and, crucially, the caste composition of the population with the qualifying level of education for entry into a given (next higher) level of education.

Consider first the issue of age cut-off

The estimates of proportion of the population of each social group who have a "graduate and above" level of completed education noted in the previous section relates to the total, all-age population. In the absence of a lower age cut-off, the denominator includes a sizeable population of those below 20 years who, individual exceptions apart, cannot have obtained a graduate degree and this depresses the resulting proportions artificially. Depending on the demographic history, the share of the 0-19 population could also vary across the four social groups.

Specifying an upper age bound is equally necessary for the chosen indicator to reflect the situation in the more immediate past without the burden of history embedded in the educational structure of the older population captured in an indicator for population in the open-ended age interval "20 and above".

Secondly, from the perspective of the policy focus on reservation of seats, indicators relating to completed levels of education, even when more narrowly restricted to population in, say, the 20-30 age group (for "graduate and above" level of education) are inappropriate. For, differences in failure/drop-out rates across social groups would convert even an initial "fair" allocation at the enrolment stage into an "unfair" outcome in terms of proportions with a given level of completed education.

Fortunately, in the NSS Employment-Unemployment Survey, a closer approximation to the structure of enrolments is available in terms of the population reporting current attendance in educational institutions (further classified by course of study) as their Usual Activity Status.

This shift of focus to attendance in educational institutions also helps specify the age limits more realistically. An analysis by age of the sample population reporting attendance in institutions for graduate (and postgraduate) studies shows that the age group 17-25 accounts for nearly 90 per cent. This would suggest the age group 20-30 as appropriate for the population with "graduate and above" level of completed education.

Finally, and even more importantly, assessments of fairness of access to higher education need to bear in mind that entry at each step in the educational pyramid is conditional on the successful completion of the preceding stage of education. Thus, holding a graduate degree is a must for entry into a postgraduate programme and a higher secondary or equivalent qualification is necessary for entry into an undergraduate programme, and so on down the line. It is only at the elementary or primary school stage that we are free of this consideration.

For all the three reasons noted above, a simple comparison of the share of a given social group in the population in the open-ended age interval of "20 and above" with their share in the population (in the same open-ended age interval) with a "graduate and above" level of completed education (see Deshpande and Yadav, 2006), can be extremely misleading.

In view of the above, to assess whether the OBCs (or, any other social group) have had a fair share in enrolments to undergraduate programmes, we need to know their share among those with a higher secondary certificate or an equivalent qualification. This will involve, in the case of enrolments or rather attendance in institutions for undergraduate studies, a comparison of the share of a social group in the population with a higher secondary certificate in the 17-25 age group with their share among those in the 17-25 attending these institutions and reporting higher secondary as their highest level of completed education.

Let us elaborate

The codes used in the survey to describe the level of education for which persons are attending educational institutions cover broad categories such as "secondary and higher secondary" and "graduate and above". In terms of completed level of education, however, secondary and higher secondary are coded as separate levels of education.

Now, those attending institutions for "graduate and above" level of education will include both the undergraduate students and the postgraduate students. While the former, i.e., the undergraduate students will have higher secondary as the highest level of completed education, the postgraduate students will have a "graduate and above" level of completed education.

For examining the question of fair access to undergraduate enrolments, we focus on the social group composition of the population in the 17-25 age group attending institutions for "graduate and above" level of education with higher secondary as their highest level of completed education. Similarly, for access to postgraduate enrolments we focus on the population in the 20-30 age group who are also attending institutions for "graduate and above" level of education but with "graduate and above" level of completed education.

It needs to be stressed that, as defined by us, the eligible population for entry into, say, an undergraduate programme, consists of all those who have passed the Higher Secondary School Certificate (or equivalent) examination, without any reference whatever to percentage of marks obtained or any other rank-ordering indicators.

Let us now turn to a discussion of our empirical results based on an analysis of the Unit Record Data of the 55th Round Employment-Unemployment Survey.

Tables 5 and 6, respectively, present our estimates of the percentage shares of the social groups in population in the 17-25 age group – both total and those with a higher secondary certificate or equivalent level of education – and among those attending institutions for graduate (or, rather, undergraduate) studies. In each table, Panel A presents the results for all households, while the results for the non-poor (above poverty line) and the poor households are presented in Panels B and C. Both for the total and the non-poor households, separate estimates are presented for those attending (under-) graduate programmes in Technical Subjects (agriculture, engineering and medicine, taken together for reasons of sample size); the other subjects; and, all subjects. However, for poor households, sample size considerations have led us to present the estimates only for all subjects taken together.

Table 5

Percentage Shares of Social Groups in the Population in 17-25 age group (Total and With Higher Secondary Certificate) and Among Those Attending Institutions for Graduate Studies in Rural India by Poverty-Status of Households: All- India, 1999-2000

Panel A: Rural All- Households Percentage Shares of Social Groups

Social Group	*Total Population*	*Population with Hr. Sec. Certificate*	*Attending Institutions for Graduates Studies*		
			*Tech. Subjects**	*Other Subjects*	*All Subjects*
ST	10.4	9.0	4.6	12.9	11.8
SC	21.4	13.8	8.4	13.0	12.5
OBC	36.6	31.1	33.0	26.8	27.6
Others	31.6	46.2	54.0	47.3	48.1
All	100.0	100.0	100.0	100.0	100.0

Panel B: Rural Non-poor Households Percentage Shares of Social Groups

Social Group	*Total Population*	*Population with Hr. Sec. Certificate*	*Attending Institutions for Graduates Studies*		
			*Tech. Subjects**	*Other Subjects*	*All Subjects*
ST	8.5	9.1	4.9	13.1	12.1
SC	19.9	12.6	7.8	12.2	11.7
OBC	36.7	30.3	33.0	26.8	27.5
Others	35.0	48.8	54.2	47.9	48.7
All	100.0	100.0	100.0	100.0	100.0

Panel C: Rural Poor Households Percentage Shares of Social Groups

Social Group	Total Population	Population with Hr. Sec. Certificate	Attending Institutions for Graduates Studies, All Subjects
ST	7.8	7.8	4.5
SC	28.9	28.9	33.5
OBC	41.0	41.0	29.8
Others	22.3	22.3	32.3
All	100.0	100.0	100.0

*Covers agriculture, engineering and medicine.

Table 6

Percentage Shares of Social Groups in Population in 17-25 age group (total and with Higher Secondary Certificate) and Among those Attending Institutions for Graduate Studies in Urban India by Poverty-Status of households: All-India, 1999-2000.

Panel A: All Households Percentage Shares of Social Groups

Social Group	Total Population	Population with Hr. Sec. Certificate	Attending Institutions for Graduates Studies		
			Tech. Subjects*	Other Subjects	All Subjects
ST	3.7	2.7	3.4	2.5	2.7
SC	14.6	8.6	7.2	8.5	8.3
OBC	32.1	26.5	22.6	25.9	25.2
Others	49.7	62.2	66.9	63.2	63.9
All	100.0	100.0	100.0	100.0	100.0

Panel B: Non-Poor Households Percentage Shares of Social Groups

Social Group	Total Population	Population with Hr. Sec. Certificate	Attending Institutions for Graduates Studies		
			Tech. Subjects*	Other Subjects	All Subjects
ST	3.3	2.7	3.3	2.5	2.6
SC	12.8	8.3	6.5	8.2	7.9
OBC	30.2	24.9	22.8	24.9	24.5
Others	53.7	64.2	67.4	64.5	65.0
All	100.0	100.0	100.0	100.0	100.0

Panel C: Poor Households Percentage Shares of Social Groups

Social Group	*Total Population*	*Population with Hr. Sec. Certificate*	*Attending Institutions for Graduates Studies, All Subjects*
ST	5.7	3.3	3.0
SC	22.0	12.5	16.0
OBC	39.9	46.9	40.9
Others	32.4	37.3	40.1
All	100.0	100.0	100.0

*Technical Subjects: Agriculture, Engineering and Medicine.

Consider first, the results for rural India. Both for all households and the non-poor households, the STs, the SCs and the OBCs have a smaller-than-average proportion of their population in the 17-25 age group who have a higher secondary certificate (or equivalent) level of education. This reduces the share of each and all of the three groups in the population with a higher secondary certificate – the eligible set for entry into an undergraduate programme – below their respective shares in the total population in the 17-25 age group. Focusing on the OBCs, their share in the eligible set (31.1%) is lower than their share in the total 17-25 population (36.6%) by 5.50 percentage points.

In relation to their share among those having a higher secondary certificate or equivalent qualification (31.1%), in 1999-2000, the OBCs in rural India had a 27.6 per cent share among those attending an undergraduate programme. So that, they are underrepresented by 3.50 percentage points. With a 33 per cent share among those attending an undergraduate programme in technical subjects, the OBCs are marginally overrepresented in this set.

The extent of OBC underrepresentation is even smaller (0.9%) for the over 70 per cent of those households who have an "above poverty line" level of living. Poor households by contrast have a much greater degree of OBC underrepresentation among those attending educational institutions for undergraduate studies – by a little over 12 percentage points.

In urban India, parallel results in Table 6 shows that, relative to their share in the population with a higher secondary certificate in the 17-25 age group (26.5%), the OBCs had a 22.6 per cent share among those attending undergraduate studies in technical subjects and a 25.2 per cent share among those attending undergraduate studies in all subjects taken together. This will translate to an OBC underrepresentation of a shade under four percentage points for technical subjects and a little over one percentage point (1.3 percentage points, to be exact) overall.

In respect to the urban non-poor households (those above the poverty line), the difference between the share of OBCs in the population with a higher secondary certificate (24.9%) and their share among those attending institutions for graduate studies (24.5%), at 0.4 percentage point could just reflect the margin of error surrounding these estimates.

For enrolments for postgraduate studies, the relevant comparison is between the percentage share of a social group in the population in the age group 20-30 who have a graduate degree and their share among those attending institutions for postgraduate studies. The relevant estimates are presented in Table 7. They are presented separately for the rural (Panel A) and the urban (Panel B) populations. For each population segment, results are presented separately for all households, the non-poor households and the poor households.

Again, focusing on the OBCs and taking the poor and the non-poor households together, we find that in rural India, their share among those attending institutions for postgraduate studies (26.4%) is lower than their share in the population in the 20-30 age group with a graduate degree (27.9%) by just 1.5 percentage points.

In urban India, the OBCs, with a 19.6 per cent share among those attending institutions for postgraduate studies, compared to their 19.3 per cent share among those with a graduate degree in the 20-30 age group, are marginally overrepresented. The gap or the extent of OBC underrepresentation for the poor among them is close to 5 percentage points.

To summarise our results in this section, for the OBC population as a whole, and, especially for the over 70 per cent of the OBCs who are above the poverty line, the extent of OBC underrepresentation in higher education is less than 5 per cent.

Before drawing policy inferences from the above results, it is necessary to resolve two issues.

First, what would be the impact of any possible misclassification of the OBCs as belonging to the residual category of Others either because of misdeclaration by the respondents or,

Table 7

Percentage Shares of Social Groups in Population in the 20-30 age group (total and with Graduate and above degree) and Among Those Attending Institutions for Postgraduate Studies in India by Poverty Status of Households: All- India, 1999-2000

Panel A: Rural India Percentage Share of Social Groups

Social Group	Total Population in 20-30 age group			Population in 20-30 with Graduate and Above Degree			Attending Postgraduate School in 20-30 age group		
	All Households	Non-Poor Households	Poor Households	All Households	Non-Poor Households	Poor Households	All Households	Non-Poor Households	Poor Households
ST	11.0	8.6	17.4	3.9	3.8	5.6	6.9	6.5	15.9
SC	21.5	19.4	26.9	13.2	11.8	29.2	11.9	11.7	16.5
OBC	36.7	37.0	36.0	27.9	27.3	34.7	26.4	25.1	55.0
Others	30.8	35.0	19.6	55.0	57.1	30.4	54.8	56.7	12.6
All	100.0	100.0	100.0	100.0	100.0	100.0	100.0	100.0	100.0

Panel B: Urban India Percentage Share of Social Groups

Social Group	Total Population in 20-30 age group			Population in 20-30 with Graduate and Above Degree			Attending Postgraduate School in 20-30 age group		
	All Households	Non-Poor Households	Poor Households	All Households	Non-Poor Households	Poor Households	All Households	Non-Poor Households	Poor Households
ST	3.7	3.2	5.7	2.2	2.2	3.4	2.5	2.5	4.3
SC	14.3	12.3	22.2	5.2	4.9	14.4	6.6	6.4	12.1
OBC	31.5	29.8	38.2	19.3	18.9	29.3	19.6	19.4	23.4
Others	50.6	54.7	34.2	73.3	74.1	52.9	71.4	71.1	60.3
All	100.0	100.0	100.0	100.0	100.0	100.0	100.0	100.0	100.0

In relation for share to the 20-30 population OBC underrepresented less than 13 percent because of incompleteness of OBC lists used when the respondents were not sure? Quite obviously, any correction for such a misclassification would raise the share of OBCs in the total population. However, as would be equally obvious, any transfer of the sample population from the category of "Others" who are overrepresented in enrolments for higher education relative to their share in the eligible population, would narrow down, and possibly eliminate totally, the small gap between the share of OBCs in the eligible population and their share in those among them who are attending institutions for higher education.

In this perspective, therefore, the estimates of the extent of OBC underrepresentation revealed by the estimates presented in Tables 5, 6 and 7 should be treated as upper-bound values of such underrepresentation.

The second question is: are we getting these results because of the inclusion of Karnataka and Tamil Nadu which have a long history of reservations for OBCs in higher education? Briefly, the answer is no.

As can be seen from the estimates presented in Tables 8 and 9 respectively for the rural and urban populations, for India excluding Karnataka and Tamil Nadu, the exclusion of these two southern states does indeed lower the OBC representation among those attending institutions for (under-) graduate studies. For all subjects, in rural India, their share falls from 27.6 per cent to 24.5 per cent when we exclude Karnataka and Tamil Nadu. In urban India, the exclusion of these two states results in a decline in the share of OBCs among those attending educational institutions for undergraduate studies in the 17-25 age groups (all subjects) from 25.2 per cent to 22.1 per cent.

The exclusion of the two southern states, however, also reduces the share of OBCs in the population eligible for entry into higher education – for undergraduate studies, those with a higher secondary certificate or equivalent level of completed education. Thus, in rural India, the share of OBCs in the eligible set goes down from 31.1 per cent to 27.6 per cent and in urban India from 26.5 per cent to 22.6 per cent.

Table 8

Percentage Shares of Social Groups in the Population in 17-25 age group (Total and With Higher Secondary Certificate) and Among Those Attending Institutions for Graduate Studies in Rural India by Poverty-Status of Households in 1999-2000: All- India excluding Karnataka and Tamil Nadu.

Panel A: All Rural Households Percentage Shares of Social Groups

Social Group	Total Population	Population with Hr. Sec. Certificate	Attending Institutions for Graduates Studies		
			Tech. Subjects*	Other Subjects	All Subjects
ST	11.0	9.9	5.0	14.0	12.8
SC	20.7	12.7	8.9	12.0	11.6
OBC	34.7	27.4	28.6	23.9	24.5
Others	33.0	50.0	57.6	50.2	51.1
All	100.0	100.0	100.0	100.0	100.0

Panel B: Rural Non-Poor Households Percentage Shares of Social Groups

Social Group	Total Population	Population with Hr. Sec. Certificate	Attending Institutions for Graduates Studies		
			Tech. Subjects*	Other Subjects	All Subjects
ST	9.0	10.0	5.4	14.2	13.1
SC	19.3	11.8	8.2	11.2	10.9
OBC	34.6	26.5	28.7	23.8	24.4
Others	37.2	51.7	57.8	50.7	51.6
All	100.0	100.0	100.0	100.0	100.0

Panel C: Rural Poor Household Percentage Shares of Social Groups

Social Group	Total Population	Population with Hr. Sec. Certificate	Attending Institutions for Graduates Studies, All Subjects
ST	17.8	8.4	5.2
SC	25.2	26.1	31.0
OBC	35.3	40.1	26.5
Others	21.7	25.4	37.3
All	100.0	100.0	100.0

*Covers agriculture, engineering and medicine.

Table 9

Percentage Shares of Social Groups in Population in 17-25 age groups (total and with Higher Secondary Certificate) and among those Attending Institutions for Graduate Studies in Urban India by Poverty-Status of households in 1999-2000: All-India, Excluding Karnataka and Tamil Nadu

Panel A: All Households Percentage Shares of Social Groups

Social Group	Total Population	Population with Hr. Sec. Certificate	Attending Institutions for Graduates Studies		
			Tech. Subjects*	Other Subjects	All Subjects
ST	3.9	3.0	3.9	2.7	2.9
SC	14.9	8.6	7.6	8.4	8.2
OBC	28.0	22.6	17.0	23.2	22.1
Others	53.2	65.9	71.6	65.7	66.8
All	100.0	100.0	100.0	100.0	100.0

Panel B: Urban Non-Poor Households Percentage Shares of Social Groups

Social Group	Total Population	Population with Hr. Sec. Certificate	Attending Institutions for Graduates Studies		
			Tech. Subjects*	Other Subjects	All Subjects
ST	3.5	3.0	3.8	2.7	2.9
SC	13.2	8.3	7.0	8.1	7.9
OBC	25.9	21.0	17.0	22.3	21.3
Others	57.5	67.7	72.2	67.0	67.9
All	100.0	100.0	100.0	100.0	100.0

Panel C: Urban Poor Households Percentage Shares of Social Groups

Social Group	Total Population	Population with Hr. Sec. Certificate	Attending Institutions for Graduates Studies, All Subjects
ST	5.6	3.2	3.6
SC	22.2	11.4	15.5
OBC	36.9	42.8	38.0
Others	35.3	42.7	
All	100.0	100.0	100.0

*Technical Subjects: Agriculture, Engineering and Medicine.

With a larger reduction in the share of OBCs in the eligible population (relative to the reduction in their share among those attending undergraduate programmes, for all subjects taken together, the extent of OBC underrepresentation is reduced rather than raised by the exclusion of Karnataka and Tamil Nadu: from 3.5 percentage points to 3.1 percentage points in rural India, and from 1.3 percentage points to 0.6 percentage points in urban India. For technical subjects, in rural India, the OBCs in all households and in non-poor households, continue to be marginally overrepresented, but for the poor households, the extent of underrepresentation is greater: up from 11.8 to 13.6 percentage points. In urban India, also, the OBC underrepresentation for technical subjects is larger at 5.6 percentage points. But, for undergraduate studies for other subjects, the OBCs are marginally overrepresented.

Table 10 presents the results for postgraduate studies for India excluding Karnataka and Tamil Nadu. In both rural and urban segments, the extent of OBC underrepresentation is increased by the exclusion of the two southern states. While in rural India the gap widens to 5 per cent, in urban India a marginal overrepresentation gets converted to a 1.5 point deficit.

Our broad results stand: except for the 29 per cent poor among the OBCs who have a greater degree of underrepresentation (a little over 12 percentage points in rural India), the extent of OBC underrepresentation in higher education is less than 5 per cent. For the over 70 per cent of the OBCs, and not just for the so-called "creamy layer", the extent of OBC underrepresentation is even smaller. As noted above, the exclusion of Karnataka and Tamil Nadu or, for that matter, the exclusion of all the four southern states alters these results only fractionally if at all.

The Hasan-Mehta Paper

Before summarising our results, a few comments on the most recent paper on the subject that came to my notice after this paper was finalised (Hasan and Mehta, *EPW*, September 2, 2006).

In one key respect, the Hasan-Mehta approach to the assessment of underrepresentation of disadvantaged social groups in higher education, namely, the setting-up of a comparison of their share in the eligible set against their share in the "college availing population" parallels the approach adopted in this paper. There are, however, important differences.

Table 10

Percentage Shares of Social Groups in Population in the 20-30 age group (total and with Graduate and above degree) and Among Those Attending Institutions for Post -Graduate Studies in India by Poverty Status of Households in 1999-2000: All-India Excluding Karnataka & Tamil Nadu

Panel A: Rural India Percentage Share of Social Groups

Social Group	Total Population in 20-30 age group			Population in 20-30 with Graduate and Above Degree			Attending Postgraduate School in 20-30 age group		
	All Households	Non-Poor Households	Poor Households	All Households	Non-Poor Households	Poor Households	All Households	Non-Poor Households	Poor Households
ST	11.7	9.2	18.6	4.2	4.0	6.5	7.7	7.3	15.9
SC	20.8	19.0	25.7	12.3	11.1	27.2	10.9	10.7	16.5
OBC	35.0	34.9	35.2	25.5	24.6	35.9	20.5	18.7	55.0
Others	32.6	37.0	20.6	58.1	60.3	30.3	60.9	63.3	12.6
All	100.0	100.0	100.0	100.0	100.0	100.0	100.0	100.0	100.0

Panel B: Urban India Percentage Share of Social Groups

Social Group	*Total Population in 20-30 age group*			*Population in 20-30 with Graduate and Above Degree*			*Attending Postgraduate School in 20-30 age group*		
	All Households	*Non-Poor Households*	*Poor Households*	*All Households*	*Non-Poor Households*	*Poor Households*	*All Households*	*Non-Poor Households*	*Poor Households*
ST	3.9	3.3	5.9	2.3	2.8	2.8	2.8	2.5	2.5
SC	14.7	12.8	22.0	4.9	12.5	6.1	5.9	9.2	9.2
OBC	27.1	25.2	34.7	15.4	28.3	14.4	14.1	23.9	23.9
Others	54.3	58.7	37.5	77.5	56.4	76.7	77.1	64.4	64.4
All	100.0	100.0	100.0	100.0	100.0	100.0	100.0	100.0	100.0

In relation for share to the 20-30 population OBC underrepresented less than 13 per cent

The key difference lies in how the eligible set and the college availing population are defined.

Formally, Hasan and Mehta define the eligible set or the minimally qualified as follows: "a student is minimally qualified to enter college only if he has completed Higher Secondary (HS) School" (p. 3792). At first sight, this would appear to correspond exactly with what we have called "Population with a Higher Secondary Certificate".

However, in empirically implementing this definition – as reflected in the estimates of sample size and what they call imputed sub-population size in Table 1 of their paper (p. 3792) – they would appear to have included in the set of "minimally qualified population", not only those who report Higher Secondary as their highest level of completed education but, crucially, also those who report "graduate and above" as their highest level of completed education. Thus, for "Minimally Qualified Males Aged 17-30" in rural areas, Hasan and Mehta report a sample size of 7,062 and an imputed sub-population size of 10,612,781. Computations by us from Unit Record Data reveals a sample size of 4,625 and an estimated population of 7,185,416 for rural males with Higher Secondary as their highest level of completed education in the 17-30 age group. It is only when you add to this the number of those who have "graduate and above" as their completed level of education (sample size: 2,426, estimated population: 3,391,937), which will yield a combined sample size of 7,051 and an estimated population total of 10,577,083, that we have a close match with their figures.

So that, *de facto*, the Hasan-Mehta eligible set is the sum of those (in the 17-30 age group) who report Higher Secondary and of those who report "graduate and above" as their highest level of education.

As regards the college availing population, Hasan and Mehta have defined the same as those in the 17-30 age group "who are either currently enrolled in college courses or who report having completed a college course" (p.3793). In the absence of any mention to the contrary the set of those "currently enrolled in college courses" would include all those with a Graduate degree who are pursuing postgraduate studies. So that, this sub-set of graduates who are pursuing postgraduate courses would be counted twice in the college availing population: once as part of those who "report having completed a college course" and again as part of those "currently enrolled in college courses".

The Hasan-Mehta definitions of the eligible set (de facto) and of the college availing population has several implications.

Firstly, the combining of those currently enrolled and those who have completed college courses obliterates the distinction between enrolment and successful completion and eliminates the role of differential drop-out/failure rates in understanding inter-group differences in educational outcomes. This also prevents a clearer focus on the issue of access to enrolments that is at the heart of the debate on quotas for the OBCs.

Secondly, a one-for-one counting of those with a completed graduate degree both in the eligible set and in the college availing population (with the sub-set of graduates pursuing postgraduate studies getting counted twice in the college availing population) would, ceteris paribus, tend to narrow the gap between the share of a social group in the eligible set and its share in the college availing population. More importantly, it robs this gap of any operational significance.

Thus, for OBC urban males, the difference between their share in the eligible set (24.55%) and their share in the college availing population (23.03%) does not imply that their number in college enrolments need to be raised by 1.52 per cent of 10 million – the number of "minimally qualified" urban males in the 17-30 age group. For included in this 10 million are about 4.5 million who have a "graduate and above" level of completed education.

Thirdly, because of the lumping together of all those attending institutions for "graduate and above" level of education, we have a blurring of the key distinction between enrolments for undergraduate and postgraduate studies. For undergraduate studies, the relevant age group would be 17-25 and enrolments would be conditional on a Higher Secondary Certificate. For postgraduate enrolments, on the other hand, the appropriate age group would be 20-30 and would require a graduate degree as the minimum qualification. This distinction is not merely academic: as our results show, while the OBCs are underrepresented in the former, at least in urban India, in postgraduate enrolments, the OBCs are marginally overrepresented. Finally, their conclusion that the 27 per cent quota for the OBCs would only raise the fraction of minimally qualified OBCs availing of college education from 50.2 per cent to 53.0 per cent is conditional on their assumption that "the 27 per cent reservation for OBC students would include all those OBC students who would have otherwise secured an educational seat to the general category (i.e., on basis of open competition) but choose instead to apply through the reserved category in order to maximise their likelihood of securing a seat" (footnote 13, p.3795).

This is not how the reservation system works. Students do not apply separately for a "quota" seat. They all apply for a given course of study. And, all those who make it to the admission list on their own merit, in this case, all the OBC students who are currently availing of education without any quota provisions are mandated to be part of the open or general list. The quota seats will need to be filled-in additionally. So that, in a scenario where the total number of seats remains unchanged as it is in their numerical example, a 27 per cent quota for the OBCs would raise their share in college availing population to over 50 per cent – well above their share of the minimally qualified.

Summary and Conclusions

Let us begin by summarising the key results to emerge from the paper.

First, on a range of economic criteria – poverty, means of livelihood, occupational structure and educational attainments – there is a clear hierarchy among the four social groups studied in this paper, namely, the Scheduled Castes (SCs) the Scheduled Tribes (STs), the Other Backward Castes (OBCs) and, the residual category of Others. The OBCs are sandwiched between the SC/STs at the lower end of the scale and the Others (non-SC/ST) at the top.

Second, separating the poor households within each social group, we find that for the poor among them, there is more of a continuum across the caste groups with strikingly small differences between the OBCs and the Others.

This would suggest that, with SC/STs already recognised as disadvantaged groups, the poor among the OBCs and the Others should be treated together as a single backward class rather than divided them further along caste lines.

Third, on the issue of fair access to higher education, since entry into it is conditional on completion of the preceding stage of education, we argue that the extent of under- (or, over-) representation of a social group can only be judged by the comparison of a group's share in enrolments in a given level of education with their share in the population eligible for entry into that level of education.

Setting-up such comparisons on the basis of our analysis of Unit Record Data from the NSS 55th Round Employment-Unemployment Survey 1999-2000, we show that for the OBCs as, a group, and especially for the over 70 per cent of them, who are above the poverty line and not just for the so-called "creamy layer", the extent of underrepresentation is less than 5 per cent. We have also shown that these results are not affected even when we exclude Karnataka and Tamil Nadu, or for that matter, when we exclude all the four major southern states: Andhra Pradesh, Karnataka, Kerala and Tamil Nadu. What conclusions follow from the above?

First, at least on grounds of fair access, the proposed 27 per cent reservation of seats in institutions for higher education are totally unjustified. To see this clearly, note that all quota seats are mandated to be over and above those that students from any beneficiary group (whether SCs, STs or, in this case the OBCs) obtain on their own merit, i.e., in a non-quota regime. So that, a 27 per cent quota for the OBCs would have the effect of raising the share of OBCs among those enrolled in (attending) institutions for undergraduate studies to a little over 54 per cent in rural India and over 52 per cent in urban India. This is to be compared to their share in the eligible population (those with a Higher Secondary Certificate) of, respectively, 30.7 per cent and 26.5 per cent. (see Tables 5 and 6). For enrolments in postgraduate studies, the quota would raise the OBC share to 52.5 per cent in rural India and 45.6 per cent in urban India relative to their shares in the population in the 20-30 age group with a graduate degree, of 27.5 per cent in rural India and 19.1 per cent in urban India. A much simpler and vastly more cost-effective solution would be to work with slightly lower cut-offs for the OBCs to enable them to make-up for the very small deficit in their share in enrolments relative to their share among those having the basic qualification for entry into higher education (see, Somanathan 2006).

Second, as regards the poor among the OBCs and the Others, as also for the SCs and the STs, the real solution to their small share in enrolments even relative to their share in the eligible set lies in tackling their poverty.

It may be argued that the purpose of the quota is to raise the proportion of OBCs having higher education. Undeniably, there is a need for raising the proportion of population with higher education and employable skills to meet the skilled manpower needs of our fast growing economy and the global trends towards outsourcing.

However, this is true for all social groups and not just the OBCs. More importantly, the solution, lies not in prescriptive quotas in higher education for this or that social group. It is at the school stage that we need to provide more resources to raise the proportion of the population acquiring the basic qualification for entry into higher education – across the board. Quotas in higher education merely divert social attention and resources from the more difficult tasks lower down in the education pyramid.

References

Deshpande, S. and Y. Yadav (2006): "Redesigning Affirmative Actions: Castes and Benefits of Higher Education", *Economic and Political Weekly*, June 17, 2006.

Hasan, Rana and Aashish Mehta, "Underrepresentation of Disadvantaged Classes in Colleges: What Do The Data Tell Us", *Economic and Political Weekly*, September 2, 2006.

Somanathan, Rohini (2006): " Assumptions and Arithmetic of Caste-Based Reservations", *Economic and Political Weekly*, June 17, 2006.

8

Identifying Other Backward Classes

A. RAMAIAH

Transforming India into an egalitarian society and strengthening its unity and integrity will remain a myth as long as the widening gap between the attitude of the rich and the poor, the high castes and the low castes, and the religious and ethnic majorities and the minorities towards each other is not changed significantly for the better. Such change in the people's attitude cannot be brought about overnight. Centuries old caste and religious practices, which have got ingrained in their social-cultural milieu, cannot be uprooted so easily. It is a long-term process, but it is imperative.

To bring all those who are considered the socially and economically backward on par with the rest of the society, it is a must that they should be assisted in all possible ways. Education, which can accelerate amongst them the process not only of conscientisation but also of becoming economically independent, should be made accessible to everybody. But given the heterogeneity in the existing socio-economic status, only some are able to climb the socio-economic ladder while the rest either remain at the same position or find their position declining. The practice of untouchability, which is very much part of the tradition that we have inherited, is prevalent even today. Hence, the existing protective and welfare measures provided in the Constitution of

India for the untouchables, officially known as the scheduled castes. However, besides the untouchables, there exists a huge proportion of people who are identified as socially and educationally backward classes. Talk of implementing similar welfare measures to this section (OBCs) has ignited resentment especially among the high castes. However, it is the constitutional obligation of the government under Articles 340(1) 340(2), 15(4) and 16(4) to promote the welfare of the OBCs.

Article 340(1)

The President of India may by order appoint a commission, consisting of such persons as he thinks, fit to investigate the conditions of socially and educationally backward classes within the territory of India and the difficulties under which they labour and to make recommendations as to the steps that should be taken by the union or any state to remove such difficulties and as to improve their condition and as to the grants that should be made, and the order appointing such commission shall define the procedure to be followed by the commission.

Article 340(2)

A commission so appointed shall investigate the matters referred to them and present to the President a report setting out the facts as found by them and making such recommendations as they think proper.

Article 15(4)

Nothing in this Article or in clause 2 of Article 29 (protection of minorities) shall prevent the state from making any special provision for the advancement of any socially and educationally backward classes.

Article 16(4)

Nothing in this article shall prevent the state from making any provision for the reservation of appointments or posts in favour of any backward class citizens which, in the opinion of the state, is not adequately represented in the services under the state.

Despite the fact that the term 'backward class' has appeared more than once in the Constitution, it has not been defined clearly. Thus, there was a need to determine backwardness by means of adopting suitable criteria and identify all those who come under the backward classes category.

First Backward Classes Commission

Adhering to Article 340, the First Backward Classes Commission was set up by a presidential order on January 29, 1953 under the chairmanship of Kaka Kalelkar. Its terms of references were to:

1. determine the criteria to be adopted in considering whether any sections of the people in the territory of India in addition to the SCs and STs as socially and educationally backward classes, using such criteria it was to prepare a list of such classes setting out also their approximate members and their territorial distribution;
2. investigate the conditions of all such socially and educationally backward classes and the differences under which they labour and make recommendations (i) as to the steps that should be taken by the union or any state to remove such difficulties or to improve their economic condition, and (ii) as to the grants that should be made for the purpose by the union or any state and the conditions subject to which such grants should be made;
3. investigate such other matters as the president may hereafter refer to them; and
4. present to the president a report setting out the facts as found by them and making such recommendations as they think proper.

For identifying socially and educationally backward classes, the Commission adopted the following criteria:

1. Low social position in the traditional caste hierarchy of Hindu society.
2. Lack of general educational advancement among the major section of a caste or community.
3. Inadequate or no representation in government services.
4. Inadequate representation in the field of trade, commerce and industry.

The Commission submitted its report on March 30, 1955. It had prepared a list of 2,399 backward castes or communities for the entire country and of which 837 had been classified as the 'most backward'. Some of the most noteworthy recommendations of the Commission were:

1. undertaking caste-wise enumeration of population in the census of 1961;
2. relating social backwardness of a class to its low position in the traditional caste hierarchy of Hindu society;
3. treating all women as a class as 'backward';
4. reservation of 70 per cent seats in all technical and professional institutions for qualified students of backward classes; and
5. minimum reservation of vacancies in all government services and local bodies for other backward classes on the following scale: class I = 25 per cent; class II = 33.50 per cent; class III and IV = 40 per cent.

There was considerable divergence of opinion among the members of the Commission as to what should be the criteria of backwardness. However, the Commission in its final report recommended caste as the criteria to determine backwardness. But this report was not accepted by the government as it feared that the backward classes excluded from the caste and communities selected by the Commission may not be considered and the really needy would be swamped by the multitude and would hardly receive special attention. Thus, there was a need of a Second Backward Classes Commission.

Mandal Commission

The decision to set up a Second Backward Classes Commission was made official by the president on January 1, 1979. The Commission, popularly known as the Mandal Commission, its chairman being B.P. Mandal, submitted its report in December 1980. The terms of reference for the Commission were:

1. to determine the criteria for defining the socially and educationally backward classes;
2. to recommend the steps to be taken for their advancement;
3. to examine the desirability or otherwise for making any provision for the reservation of appointments or posts in their favour; and
4. to present a report setting out the facts found by the Commission.

The Mandal Commission adopted various methods and techniques to collect the necessary data and evidence to fulfil the above objectives.

The Commission prepared three questionnaires: one for the state government, another for the central ministries and yet another for the general public besides its extensive tours in the country to collect the necessary evidence. A socio-educational field survey was conducted under the panel of experts with M. N. Srinivas as chairman. This study also included caste studies, analyses of data, village monographs and study of legal and constitutional issues. To identify the socially and educationally backward classes, the Commission adopted 11 criteria, which could be grouped under three major headings: social, educational and economic. These are as follows:

Social

1. Castes/classes considered as socially backward by others.
2. Castes/classes which mainly depend on manual labour for their livelihood.
3. Castes/classes where at least 25 per cent females and 10 per cent males above the state average get married at an age below 17 years in rural areas and at least 10 per cent females and 5 per cent males do so in urban areas.
4. Castes/classes where participation of females in work is at least 2 per cent above the state average.

Educational

5. Castes/classes where the number of children in the age group of 5-15 years who never attended school is at least 25 per cent above the state average.
6. Castes/classes where the rate of student drop-out in the age group of 5-15 years is at least 25 per cent above the state average.
7. Castes/classes amongst whom the proportion of matriculates is at least 25 per cent below the state average.

Economic

8. Castes/classes where the average value of family assets is at least 25 per cent below the state average.
9. Castes/classes where the number of families living in *kuccha* houses is at least 25 per cent above the state average.
10. Castes/classes where the source of drinking water is beyond half a kilometre for more than 50 per cent of the households.

11. Castes/classes where the number of households having taken consumption loans is at least 25 per cent above the state average.

Of these three groups, separate weightage was given to indicators of each group. A weightage of three points each was given to all the social indicators. Educational indicators were given two points each. And economic indicators were given one point each. In addition to social and educational, economic indicators were considered important as they directly flowed from social and educational backwardness mainly to highlight the fact that socially and educationally backward classes are economically backward also.

It can be understood from the values given to each indicator that the total adds up to 22. All these 11 indicators were applied to all the castes covered by the survey for a particular state. All castes which had a score of 50 per cent (i.e., 11 points) or above while applying the said score were listed as socially and educationally backward and the rest were treated as 'advanced'. Using the above-mentioned criteria, the Commission identified 3,743 caste groups as other backward classes.

Figures of caste-wise population are not available beyond 1931. So, the Commission used 1931 census data to calculate the number of OBCs. The population of Hindu OBCs was derived by subtracting from the total population of Hindus, the population of SCs and STs and that of forward Hindu castes and communities, and it worked out to be 52 per cent. Assuming that roughly the proportion of OBCs amongst non-Hindus was of the same order as amongst the Hindus, population of non-Hindu OBCs was also considered as 52 per cent of actual proportion of their population of 16.16 per cent or 8.40 per cent. The total population of Hindu and non-Hindu OBCs therefore naturally added up to nearly 52 per cent of the country's population. However, only 27 per cent reservation was recommended owing to the legal constraint that the total quantum of reservation should not exceed 50 per cent. The already existing reservation for SCs and STs is in tune with their proportion to total population, i.e., 15 per cent for SCs and 7.2 per cent for STs and together amounts to 22.5 per cent is to be taken into account, while counting the total percentage of reservation. States which have already introduced reservation for OBCs exceeding 27 per cent will not be affected by this recommendation. With this general recommendation, the Commission proposed the following overall scheme of reservation for OBCs:

1. Candidates belonging to OBCs recruited on the basis of merit in an open competition should not be adjusted against their reservation quota of 27 per cent.
2. The above reservation should also be made applicable to promotion quota at all levels.
3. Reserved quota remaining unfilled should be carried forward for a period of three years and de-reserved thereafter.
4. Relaxation in the upper age limit for direct recruitment should be extended to the candidates of OBCs in the same manner as done in the case of SCs and STs.
5. A roster system for each category of posts should be adopted by the concerned authorities in the same manner as presently done in respect of SC and ST candidates.

These recommendations in total are applicable to all recruitment to public sector undertakings both under the Central and state governments, as also to nationalised banks.

All private sector undertakings, which have received financial assistance from the government in one form or other, should also be obliged to recruit personnel on the aforesaid basis.

All universities and affiliated colleges should also be covered by the above scheme of reservation.

Although education is considered an important factor to bring a desired social change, 'educational reform' was not within the terms of reference of this Commission. The Commission was expected to suggest palliative measures within the existing framework.

The Commission suggested that there should be additional funds and framing of integrated scheme for creating proper environment and incentives for services and purposeful studies.

To promote literacy the following measures were suggested: (i) An intensive time-bound programme for adult education should be launched in selected pockets with high concentration of OBC population. (ii) Residential schools should be set up in these areas for backward class students to provide a climate specially conducive to serious studies. All facilities in these schools, including boarding and lodging, should be provided free of cost to attract students from poor and backward homes. (iii) Separate hostels for OBC students with above facilities will have to be provided. (iv) Vocational training was considered imperative.

It was recommended that seats should be reserved for OBC students in all scientific, technical and professional institutions run by the Central as well as state governments. The quantum of reservation should be the same as in the government services, i.e., 27 per cent. These states, which have already reserved more than 27 per cent seats for OBC students, will remain unaffected by these recommendations. Students of OBCs selected in reserved quota should be given special coaching assistance.

Members of village vocational communities, who want to set up small-scale industries on their own should be given suitable institutional finance and technical assistance. A similar assistance should also be extended to those promising OBC candidates who have undergone special vocational training. In this regard, separate financial institutions should also be established. It was also considered imperative that all state governments should create a separate network of financial and technical institutions to foster business and industrial enterprises among OBCs as a part of its overall strategy to uplift them.

The Commission felt that a radical transformation of the existing production relations is the most important single step that can be carried out for this welfare and upliftment of all backward classes. The Commission recommended that all state governments should be directed to enact and implement progressive legislation. It also suggested that a part of surplus land, as a result of the operation of ceiling laws, should be allotted not only to SC and ST but also to OBC landless labourers.

The Mandal Commission recommended that all development programmes at the state level especially designed for OBCs should be financed by the central government in the same manner and to the same extent as is done in the case of SCs and STs. The Commission suggested that the entire operations of its recommendations should be reviewed only after 20 years.

Although all these recommendations and suggestions are acceptable to many, there are differences of opinion in supporting them fully. There are two major reasons for it, of which one arises out of total ignorance of the objectives behind such recommendations and also due to lack of understanding of the real cause for the escalating problem of unemployment.

Reserving 27 per cent of government jobs to those who have been identified as socially and educationally backward classes by the Mandal Commission besides the existing 22.5 per cent for SCs/STs has caused a sense of fear among non-SC/ST and OBC students that their future is doomed, all their efforts to achieve higher education will become meaningless, and all their job opportunities are going to be usurped by SCs/STs and OBCs. It is to be remembered that even if we leave all the job opportunities in open competition, the unemployment problem is not going to be solved.

Ignoring or being ignorant of the reality, students went berserk during the anti-reservation agitation. Unfortunately, some of them went to the extent of self-immolation. The media and some of the political leaders eulogised and glorified such incidents instead of condemning and discouraging them. Such incidents were portrayed as protest against casteism and communalism. As a result, many students tried to immolate themselves. While extending my heartfelt sympathy to those parents who lost their children in the anti-reservation agitation, I also question the inhuman way in which some of the innocent students and even a few school children have been forcefully burnt by the agitating students and named them all as acts of self-immolation against Mandal Commission recommendations. These 'conscious and patriotic' students never protested when innocent Sikhs and Muslims were ruthlessly murdered, when Harijan women were raped and murdered, when a few Harijans were forced to eat human excreta, when Harijans were killed *en masse* in rural areas and when a Harijan cop was stoned to death just for taking shelter for a few minutes on the steps of Hanuman Temple.

The other reason arises out of a critical approach and understanding of the justification attributed and criteria adopted to the recommendations of the Mandal Commission. It is represented by some of the intellectuals and critics of the Mandal Commission. Social scientists and intellectuals have opposed the Mandal Commission's recommendations on the ground that there are many technical errors in the methodology adopted for identifying the educationally and socially backward people. They oppose it also on the ground that the justification advanced for reserving 27 per cent government jobs for OBCs is not valid. First of all, let us see what are the criteria that the Mandal Commission adopted to come to the conclusion that the representation of OBC employees in government services is lesser than that of SC and ST employees.

Following are the criteria furnished to Central government offices for identifying OBC employees for both Hindu and non-Hindu communities:

1. *In respect of employees belonging to the Hindu communities:*
   (i) an employee will be deemed to be socially backward if he does not belong to any of the three twice born (*Dvij*) 'varnas', i.e., he is neither a Brahmin, nor a Kshatriya, nor a Vaishya; and
   (ii) he will be deemed to be educationally backward if neither his father nor his grandfather had studied beyond the primary level.
2. *For non-Hindu communities:*
   (i) an employee will be deemed to be socially backward if either (1) he is a convert from those Hindu communities which have been defined as socially backward as per para (a) (i) above, and (2) in case he is not such a convert, his parental income is below the prevalent poverty line, i.e., Rs 71 per head per month; and
   (ii) he will be deemed to be educationally backward if neither his father nor his grandfather had studied beyond the primary level.

It may be noted, an employee will qualify for membership of an OBC only if, both socially and educationally, he is found to be backward according to the above criteria.

Of the various criteria adopted to identify the number of OBC employees in government services, let us see criteria (a)(i) and (a)(ii) which may be called the first set of criteria and compare them with all those three criteria (v, vi and vii) adopted to identify the educationally backward people which may be called the second set of criteria.

While looking at these two sets of criteria, there seems to be some technical errors in the nature of criteria adopted for the purpose. The Commission instead of finalising the list of OBCs first and then identifying among them the number of those employed in government services, using some criteria arbitrarily, had already finalised the list of the so-called OBC employees in government services who may or may not fall in the category of OBCs according to the criteria adopted later by it. Second, when a particular set of criteria was adopted to decide whether or not an employee in government service is socially and educationally backward, the same set of criteria should have been adopted to decide whether or not an individual is socially and educationally backward. Had the Commission adopted the same set of criteria the population of OBCs would not have accounted for 52 per cent. As the proportion of OBC employees in government service is found to be less, the proportion of OBC population would have also been less. The 11 criteria model adopted later by the Mandal Commission to identify the OBCs has in fact included a huge proportion of population into OBC category which according to the first set of criteria was not part of OBCs. This can be understood if we look at the first set of criteria to identify the proportion of OBC employees in government services. The emphasis has been placed on the educational achievements of the employees' fathers and grandfathers instead of emphasising on the employees themselves. This is needed because the employment achievement of an individual depends directly on his/her educational achievement and not on his/her father's or grandfather's educational achievement although it may contribute indirectly in the longer run.

Representation of SC/ST and OBC Employees in Government Services

Category of Employees	*Total Number of Employees*	*Percentage of SCs/STs*	*Percentage of OBCs*
Class I	174043	05.68	04.69
Class II	912786	18.81	10.63
Class III & IV	484646	24.40	24.40

Source: Report of the Backward Classes Commission (1980), First Part, p. 42.

Let us now see how far the conclusion that the representation of OBC employees in government services is less than that of SC/ST employees. Table giving the details of representation of OBC and SC/ST employees in government services indicates that the percentage of OBC employees in Class I and Class II services accounts for 04.69 and 10.63 respectively whereas the same of SCs/STs employees accounts for 05.68 and 18.81 respectively. It is rather unbelievable. The OBCs who had the access to start their educational career next to Brahmins but much before the SCs and STs would definitely be having more number of educated fathers and grandfathers than that of the SCs and STs. In that case the number of OBC employees in government services is bound to be much more than that of the SCs and STs. B.K. Roy Burman aptly questions, "Can any one with intimate knowledge of the social scene in India say that even among the scheduled castes and scheduled tribes there would be many persons in Class I jobs and, whose fathers or grandfathers would not have read upto primary level" (*Mainstream,* September 29, 1990). Then what could be the reason?

Let us see criterion number a(ii) of the first set of criteria which declares that an employee will be deemed to be educationally backward if neither his father nor his grandfather had studied beyond the primary level. It is clear that the Commission while counting the number of OBC employees in government services has taken into consideration only those employees whose fathers or grandfathers had not studied beyond primary level and it has left all other employees whose fathers or grandfathers had studied beyond primary level. This is perhaps an important reason why the proportion of OBC employees in government services is seen to be lesser than that of SC/ST employees.

Let us also see the criteria adopted to determine the educational backwardness of OBCs. While in the first set of criteria to decide whether or not an employee comes under OBC, the educational achievement of employees' fathers or grandfathers has been considered an important criteria, and in the second set of criteria to decide whether or not the OBC community as a whole is educationally backward or advanced the emphasis has been laid only on the children's educational achievement ignoring the educational status of their parents and grandparents. The educational status of their parents and grandparents should be given the main consideration as only such criteria can reveal the historical reasons behind their present educational status.

The Mandal Commission's recommendations have been opposed on the ground that the term 'backward classes' enshrined in the Constitution under Article 340 does not imply those whom the Commission has identified as the other backward classes. So, a clear understanding of the meaning of the term is imperative.

The meaning attached to the term 'backward classes' as understood in recent days, seems to contradict the meaning attached to it during pre-independence period. For many, during pre-independence period, the term backward classes was a synonym for untouchables. Over a period of time the term has come to mean different things in different places.

The term 'backward classes' first acquired a technical meaning in the princely state of Mysore. Preferential recruitment of backward communities was instituted in 1921 and they were defined as "all communities other than Brahmins, who are not adequately represented in the public service". In 1928, the Hartog Committee defined backward classes in their glossary as castes or classes which are educationally backward. They include the depressed classes, aboriginals, hill tribes, and criminal tribes. The Indian Central Committee not only excludes from backward classes the word 'depressed classes' but includes in addition to tribal, some strata of the caste population. The State Committee in Bombay proposed in 1924 that a wider group should be called backward classes which should be divided into depressed classes (untouchables); aboriginals, and hill tribes; other backward classes (including wandering tribes). They also noted, it should be renamed 'intermediate caste'. According to the Simon Commission, the term backward classes refers to 'intermediate castes'.

The United Provinces Hindu Backward Classes League founded in 1929 was of the view that the term 'depressed' carried a connotation of untouchability in the sense of causing pollution by touch as in the case of Madras and Bombay and that many communities were reluctant to identify themselves as 'depressed'. The League suggested the term 'Hindu backward' as a more suitable nomenclature. The list of 115 castes submitted included all candidates for the untouchable category as well as a stratum above. They were described as low socially, educationally and economically. In 1937 Travancore discarded the nomenclature depressed classes and substituted the term 'backward communities' to include all educationally and economically backward communities. The term backward classes was used in Madras to refer the strata above the untouchables. In 1934, the Madras Provincial Backward Classes League was founded for the purpose of securing separate treatment from the 'forward non-Brahmin communities'. In November 1947 separate reservations were provided for these backward Hindus in the Madras service.

It is apparent now that there was no definite meaning attached to the term 'backward classes' at the all-India level. Although the meaning of backward classes varied from state to state, representatives from Madras, Mysore and Bombay by the time of Constituent Assembly were of the opinion that the term 'backward classes' was a distinct term with technical meaning. For example, in Mysore, the backward classes were all but Brahmins, in Madras the backward classes were referred to a stratum of non-untouchable Hindu castes, and in Bombay the backward classes were not only SCs and STs but also others who were economically, educationally and socially backward.

Although, there was no nationwide accepted definition for the term 'backward class', the term has been used in the Indian Constitution. However, as stated earlier, nowhere in the Constitution, the term 'socially and educationally backward' has been defined. Ambedkar, the chairman of the drafting committee of the Constitution, when asked about the criteria to be followed to determine the social and educational backwardness, explained, "we have left it to be determined by each local government. A backward community is a community which is backward in the opinion of the government. As a result, social scientists have come out with varying definition of who should be and who should not be called OBC. There is no consensus even among different state governments in this matter. While some have favoured the definition given by the Mandal Commission, some others have rejected it altogether.

I have earlier expressed the view that the term 'socially and educationally backward classes' (SEBCs) as it appears in the Indian Constitution under Article 340 is the same as the SCs and STs and it only reflects their low position in the caste hierarchy and their educational backwardness. I have also expressed that the OBCs in practice do not like to be identified as socially backward although they claim to be so just for some government benefits (*Mainstream*, August 18, 1990, p. 19). This judgement becomes more and more true in the light of the increasing number of atrocities meted out on SCs by the high castes most of whom come under OBC category. André Béteille and M.N. Srinivas have also expressed almost similar opinion on this issue. Béteille has rightly said "reservation to SC and ST are for all their limitation directed basically towards the goal of greater equality over all. Reservation for OBCs and for religious minorities, whatever advantages they may have are directed basically towards balance of power" (*The Times of India*, September 11, 1990).

But it does not mean that all those who have been identified as SEBCs are not so. There are castes among OBCs which also suffer from caste discrimination like the SCs and STs. These caste groups should not be in the list of OBCs instead they should be incorporated in the list of SCs and according to the increase in the total SC population arising out of such inclusion of new castes in the list of SCs, the percentage of reservation available for SCs should be increased.

There is another aspect in the Mandal Commission's analysis of 'socially and educationally backward classes' which needs some modification. To understand the meaning of the term 'socially and educationally backward classes' better, it may be bifurcated into two: (i) socially backward classes, and (ii) educationally backward classes. These terms are applicable for both Hindu and non-Hindu communities. According to the Mandal Commission, people belonging to socially backward classes among Hindus are those who fall below the high castes in the caste hierarchy, who are also known as the middle castes or intermediate castes and whose economic condition needs to be improved. Obviously, the main emphasis here has been laid first on identifying those castes which are considered socially backward and then among them the economically backward classes have been identified. By and large, caste has been considered the important criterion to determine an individual's social backwardness. If this is taken as valid, then how can we call the Muslims, Christians, Buddhists and other religious minorities which do not or which are not supposed to believe in caste system. Is it because they are numerically minority? or, is it because they believe in altogether different religious faith, values and customs? or does it mean that all the non-Hindu religions are inferior to Hindu religion? However, the Mandal Commission treated all those among non-Hindu religions who were educationally and economically backward as socially backward. This certainly needs modification. The term 'socially backward' is applicable only for those Hindus who, compared to the high castes, are considered low castes. It cannot be applicable to people belonging to non-Hindu religions. Thus, all those caste Hindus who are both educationally and economically backward according to the Mandal's criteria may be called 'socially, educationally and economically backward castes' (SEBCt) and all those among non-Hindu religions who are both educationally and economically backward may be called 'other backward classes' (OBCl). Identifying among the SEBCt and OBCl the really deserving individuals as M.N. Srinivas suggested, may not be an easy task in a country like ours. It is relatively easy to identify the deserving families among SEBCt and OBCl. Identifying deserving families instead of deserving individuals may help avoid problems like many individuals in the same family trying to avail all the existing provisions instead of one or two individuals in every family making use of such provisions.

There is yet another aspect of the Mandal Commission's recommendations which needs modification, i.e., recognising caste identities in non-Hindu religions which do not believe in caste system. Most Christians and Buddhists in India were untouchables in the Hindu fold. They embraced non-Hindu religions mainly to get rid of the humiliating practices of caste discrimination meted out to them by the high caste people. If this is the main cause of embracing non-Hindu religions, then, why should the government insist on caste identities in non-Hindu religions. We can take the case of neo-Buddhists. Most of them are those who were once untouchables. They need to identify themselves as SCs to take advantage of any government assistance although they have embraced Buddhism. We can refer the criterion number (b)(i) of those criteria adopted by Mandal to identify the OBC employees in government services. This seems to defeat the very purpose of untouchables renouncing Hinduism and embracing non-Hindu religions. The better way of helping them all will be that they all should be treated as part of the religious minorities, and among them we should identify the educationally and economically backward families. As most of the converts (low caste people) are economically poor and educationally backward, all of them are bound to become the beneficiaries of those provisions extended to the non-Hindu religions/religious minorities/OBCl.

The SEBCt and OBCl should be further divided into three categories: (1) those who are economically backward but educationally advanced; (2) those who are educationally backward but economically advanced; and (3) those who are both economically and educationally backward. All these three categories should be measured taking into account their present educational and economic status.

For those families in which most of the members are educationally advanced but economically backward, there should be less or no percentage of reservation for admission in educational institutions but maximum percentage of job reservation in government services. For those families in which the per capita income of most members is very high but their educational advancement is very low, there should be less or no job reservation but maximum reservation for admission in educational institutions. And, for those families which are both educationally and economically backward, there should be maximum reservation for both education and employment. The quantum of reservation should be decided taking into consideration the overall socio-economic development of the various castes and religious communities.

Conclusion

The government should make a national level survey immediately and list out all the caste groups including that of the forward castes, and their socio-economic and educational status. The survey should take note of all the technical errors found in the various criteria adopted by the Mandal Commission and formulate more rational criteria and scientific approach towards identifying the really deserving people within the castes and communities of each stratum of our society.

The survey should not mix the socially, educationally and economically backward castes (SEBCt) with the other backward classes of non-Hindu religions, i.e., the religious minorities (OBCl). After finalising the list of SEBCt and OBCl, we should find out the proportion of SEBCt and OBCl employees in government services. The quantum of reservation should be finalised only after undertaking this exercise and understanding the magnitude of the problem of each caste and communities. For those who are economically well-off but educationally backward, there should be reservation for education. For those who are educationally advanced but economically backward there should be reservation for employment. And for those who are both educationally and economically backward there should be reservation for both education and employment.

Pointing out the various technical errors and limitations of the recommendations of the Mandal Commission, as we have discussed so far, is not an effort to oppose the move directed towards uplifting the OBCs, instead it is an attempt to make such efforts more rational, just and logical which in turn could avoid all possible criticism against such a move in future.

Whatever be the criticism advanced against the recommendations of the Mandal Commission, none can question its objective of uplifting those sections which are really backward – backward in terms of their educational and economic achievements. It is difficult obviously to accept the logic of giving admission in educational institutions and jobs in government services to students/candidates who are relatively less qualified in terms of required marks/experience, and not doing the same to students/candidates who are relatively more qualified. To understand the meaning of this logic, we should go beyond merely looking at the marks, experience of the concerned students or candidates. We should not ask a sweeper's son to compete with a professor's son to judge the competence of these two students. "There is equality only among equals. To equate unequals is to perpetuate inequality."

9

Underrepresentation in Colleges

What do the Data Tell us?

RANA HASAN AND AASHISH MEHTA

The government's decision to reserve 27 per cent of positions in institutions of higher education managed by the central government for other backward classes (OBCs) has prompted a fierce debate on the role of reservations in addressing inequities in educational attainment across social groups. Many proponents of the decision believe that caste-based discrimination denies educational opportunities to the disadvantaged and that reservations are a useful tool in addressing this. Opponents, however, see things very differently. Even if they accept the existence of discrimination, they point to a variety of flaws with reservation policies including: (i) a dilution of academic standards as some meritorious students are displaced by reservations; (ii) an unhealthy rise in caste consciousness among students; (iii) the capture of reserved seats by the elite amongst disadvantaged castes – elites who may be better off, at least economically, than low income groups among higher castes; and (iv) serious implementation problems, particularly in verifying the caste of those seeking to avail of quotas.

An interesting but disturbing feature of the various debates is the limited and weak database upon which positions have been taken. For example, arguments that reservations for OBCs would seriously dilute academic standards seem to often rely on anecdotal evidence. Similarly, the 52 per cent share of the OBCs in India's population, cited by the 1979 Mandal Commission and used extensively in shaping both debate and policy on reservation, has drawn upon caste data from the 1931 census. Concerns regarding the accuracy of this share have been raised by various analysts (see, for example, the discussion in Ghosh 1997) and along with the very different estimate derived from 1999-2000 National Sample Survey (NSS) data, point to the phenomenon of data lagging policy decisions.

In this note, we take what we believe to be a small but important step in confronting reservation-related issues with hard data. In particular, we use data from the employment-unemployment survey of the 55th round of the NSS canvassed in 1999-2000 to examine whether certain social classes and religious groups are underrepresented in higher education.[1] We find that relative to the national average, scheduled castes and Muslims are significantly underrepresented in higher education. Of course, this does not automatically imply that discrimination – defined as the rejection of a college application based on the applicant's social or religious identity – is at work. Underrepresentation may also exist for a variety of other factors unrelated to pure discrimination, including economic ones (for example, the inability to afford college education) and cultural ones (for example, a preference for a religious education over a secular education or a preference for occupations which do not require a secular education). Another possibility is that members of disadvantaged groups are less likely to possess the prerequisite education to enter college.

Although the NSS data do not allow us to distinguish between all the different factors that might lie behind underrepresentation, they do allow us to dig deeper into the issues in a way that brings some clarity to the current debates. We focus on three questions. First, are particular social or religious groups underrepresented in college relative to the overall population? Second, are they underrepresented relative to the slice of the population that is minimally qualified to enter college? Third, can inter-group disparities in economic status explain underrepresentation in college, relative to the minimally qualified population? Our findings suggest strongly that underrepresentation is not, at heart, a function of the college admissions process, as it mostly originates at lower rungs on the educational ladder. Further, the low economic status of disadvantaged groups explains much of their underrepresentation in college relative to the minimally qualified population. Finally, even correcting for qualification and income, there is still evidence, although it is substantially weaker, of underrepresentation.

Of course, whether reservation is the right policy instrument at any level of the educational system – either for addressing inter-group variations in basic educational attainment, or for dealing with the non-economic factors responsible for the underrepresentation in higher education – is another matter entirely, and beyond the scope of this paper. In what follows, we first describe our analysis of underrepresentation of particular groups in higher education, including the role of economic status. This is followed by a discussion of the implications of our findings for the current debate on education-related reservations.

Analysis

Underrepresentation in Higher Education

As noted above, we draw upon the employment-unemployment survey of the 55th round of the NSS. We limit our sample to only those persons between the ages of 17 and 30, inclusive, as persons reported to be enrolled in graduate level studies or higher fall exactly in this age range. In addition, we further limit our sample to males. Educational attainment, community and gender are deeply intertwined variables in India for several reasons, some of which may have little to do with government policy or discrimination. Focusing on males allows us to avoid the added complications that gender-related issues bring to the interpretation of our statistical results. In the following discussion all statistical results are calculated and presented for the rural and urban population separately.[2]

The NSS permits respondents to classify themselves as belonging to one of four social groups,[3] according to the definitions utilised by the state in which the household resides. For ease of exposition, we allocated reported religions to three groups: Hindu, Muslim and other. The non-responsive categories capture those who did not supply their caste/class or religious identity.

The first two columns of Table 1 present the estimated distributions of the urban and rural sub-populations across social (class/caste) and religious groupings. Because sample weights are utilised throughout this paper,[4] two sample sizes are provided – the actual number of sample observations, and the number of persons in the population this sample represents, given the sampling scheme. The data show that the existing centrally required quotas for scheduled castes (SCs) – 15 per cent of college seats, and scheduled tribes (STs) – 7.5 per cent, slightly exceed their shares in the urban male population of this age group, but are substantially less than their shares in the rural population. Meanwhile, the 27 per cent reservation proposed for OBCs is less than their population share in either environ. The 52 per cent share of OBCs in the general population cited by the Mandal Commission Report, and others since, is not consistent with the NSS data.[5] These columns also show that the SC, ST and OBC population is disproportionately rural, while Muslims are more likely to reside in urban areas.

Many definitions of "underrepresentation" are possible. Under the simplest and most common definition, a community is said to be underrepresented if its share of the population availing of college is less than its share in the overall population. Another definition would consider a community underrepresented if its share of the population availing of college is less than its share in the population that is actually "qualified" to enter college. Definitions of qualification may vary. We adopt the least controversial of these – that a student is minimally qualified to enter college only if he has completed higher secondary (HS) school. This definition is reasonable because completing a course of HS education and passing the associated board examinations are just about universally required to enter college[6] in India.

Columns (3) and (4) of Table 1 provide the distribution across caste and religious groups of the college male population that have obtained the minimal qualification for entry into college for HS education. Comparison with columns (1) and (2) provides compelling evidence that SCs and Muslims are substantially underrepresented amongst HS graduates relative to their population shares. There is also evidence of underrepresentation of OBCs and STs amongst HS graduates. Conversely, Hindus and forward classes (FCs) are substantially overrepresented.

Table 1

Distributions of Social and Religious Groups in Relevant Sub-Populations

	Distribution of Males Aged 17-30 (per cent of sub-population)		Distribution of Minimally Qualified Males, Aged 17-30 (per cent of sub-population)		Distribution of College Availing Male Sub-population, (per cent of sub-population)	
	Urban(1)	Rural (2)	Urban(3)	Rural (4)	Urban(5)	Rural (6)
Class/Caste						
Scheduled Tribes	3.63	10.49	2.69	6.89	2.45	5.72
Scheduled Castes	14.68	21.56	7.89	14.72	6.93	14.30
Other Backward Classes	31.70	36.63	24.55	31.78	23.03	28.49
Forward Classes	49.98	31.32	64.87	46.61	67.59	51.49
Non- responsive	0.00	0.00	0.00	0.00	0.00	0.00
	100.00	100.00	100.00	100.00	100.00	100.00
Religion						
Hindu	76.97	84.56	83.05	88.38	84.57	88.41
Muslim	16.62	10.03	8.25	6.06	6.90	6.89
Others	6.40	5.41	8.68	5.56	8.50	4.69
Non responsive	0.01	0.00	0.02	0.00	0.02	0.00
	100.00	100.00	100.00	100.00	100.00	100.00
Sample Size	32,129	46,015	10,237	7,062	6,537	3,572
Imputed Sub-population size	33,233,529	82,642,251	9,984,536	10,612,781	6,341,213	5,125,667

We present the HS completion rates by community in columns (1) and (2) of Table 2. These figures are implicit in the comparison of columns (1) and (2) to columns (3) and (4) in Table 1,[7] but are useful to consider explicitly. Two features of these completion rates are noteworthy. First, they are low – averaging 30 per cent in urban areas, and 12.8 per cent in rural areas, for a combined national average of only 17.8 per cent. UNESCO Institute for Statistics (2005), which uses different sources to our own, arrives at a slightly higher completion rate of 22 per cent amongst Indian males, which compares poorly with results from China (33%), Thailand (44%), Indonesia (41%) and the Philippines (56%). There is certainly anecdotal evidence that this situation is improving in line with rising demand for skills, and this issue should be revisited as soon as the 2004 NSS data are released. Second, HS completion rates vary tremendously across communities,[8] with SCs and Muslims around half[9] as likely as FCs and Hindus to be minimally qualified to enter college. The completion rates amongst STs are roughly three-fourths the national average. The OBC rate of HS completion in urban (rural) areas is 77 per cent (87%) of the national average.

With this background in hand, columns (5) and (6) of Table 1 show how males who are availing of or have recently availed of college, are distributed across caste and religious groups. Specifically, we look at the rural and urban sub-samples of males between the ages of 17 and 30 who are either currently enrolled in college courses, or who report having completed a college course. Columns (3) and (4) of Table 2 present the percentages of HS graduates from each group that avail of college. These can be calculated from the figures in Table 1.[10]

These columns throw up five sets of results. First, from Table 1, we find that amongst the college age population 19.1 per cent[11] of urban (6.2% of rural) males avail of college. However, columns (3) and (4) of Table 2 show that of those actually minimally qualified, a rather high 63.5 per cent urban (48.3% of qualified rural) males enroll in college.

Second, despite reservations of 15 per cent and 7.5 per cent of college seats respectively, STs and SCs make up only 10.2 per cent and 3.9 per cent of the national college attending population. This suggests that any analysis of the impact of reservations will need to consider carefully the implementation arrangements.

Third, taking a population weighted average of rural and urban shares OBCs comprise 25.5 per cent of the national male college-availing population. This compares with 27 per cent of college seats that the government has proposed reserving for OBCs. Assuming, for illustration's sake, that the gender composition of OBC college attendees is unaffected by reservation, it follows that if the 25.5 per cent figure is representative of all colleges that would be brought under the policy, the fraction of minimally qualified OBC entering college would only rise from 50.2 to 53 per cent.[12, 13] However, it should be noted that some colleges may currently be fielding more than 27 per cent OBC candidates and others less. As a consequence, while these calculations are crudely indicative of the magnitude of the impact of the policy on the college attending OBC population, the outcome of the policy cannot be precisely determined from these data.

Fourth, comparisons of the caste and religious breakdowns of the college-availing population (Table 1, columns 5 and 6) with those of the college-age population uncorrected for minimal qualification (Table 1, columns 1 and 2), reveal high underrepresentation amongst SCs, STs and Muslims, and significant underrepresentation amongst OBCs.[14] Urban persons of other religions are over represented, while their rural counterparts are not. Filling the arithmetic gaps left, the large Hindus and FC populations are mildly over represented in college.

Fifth, most (though not all[15]), of the evidence presented above of distorted representation of social groups in the college-availing population (columns 5 and 6), disappears when it is compared to the minimally qualified population (columns 3 and 4). While SCs, STs, OBCs, other religions and urban Muslims are underrepresented in college compared to the minimally qualified population, the margins of underrepresentation under this comparison are much, much smaller than before. For example, SCs make up 14.7 per cent of the urban group, but only 6.9 per cent of the college-availing. However, they also make up only 7.9 per cent of the minimally qualified group. Thus, the share discrepancy falls from 7.8 per cent to 1 per cent when the minimally qualified group is considered as the appropriate comparator.

Columns (3) and (4) of Table 2 present this last result from a different angle. They show that the proportion of HS graduates availing of college does not vary dramatically across social groups. For example, 55.8 per cent of SC urban male HS graduates avail of college – a figure that, while still indicative of underrepresentation, is not too far off the 63.5 per cent of all urban male HS graduates who do. In other words, once qualified, persons of various social groups have comparable proclivities to avail of college.

Table 2

Higher Secondary Completion Rates amongst College-Age Persons, by Social and Religious Group

	Per cent of Males Aged 17-30 Completing HS, by Group		*Per cent of Male HS Graduate Aged 17-30 Availing of College*	
	Urban(1)	*Rural(2)*	*Urban(3)*	*Rural(4)*
Class/Caste				
Scheduled Tribe	22.32	8.44	57.80	40.09
Scheduled Castes	16.14	8.77	55.82	46.91
Other Backward Classes	23.26	11.14	59.82	43.31
Forward Classes	38.99	19.11	66.17	53.35
Non-responsive	1.33	0.00	50.00	Na
Whole sub-population				
Average	30.04	12.84	63.51	48.30
Religion				
Hindu	32.42	13.42	64.68	48.32
Muslim	14.92	7.75	53.13	54.94
Others	40.76	13.20	62.17	40.77
Non-responsive	46.90	19.32	71.16	Na
Whole sub-population				
Average	30.04	12.84	63.51	48.30
Sample size	32,129	46.015	10,2379,	7,062
Imputed sub-population size	33,233,529	82,642,251	984,536	10,612,781

The above comparisons therefore show that evidence of disproportionate representation of social and religious groups in the college-availing population is largely, though not totally, eliminated when the comparator population is limited to those completing higher secondary education. This is serious and important evidence that underrepresentation of disadvantaged groups in college relative to their population shares has much more to do with factors in operation at the level of higher secondary school and below, than with the process of college admission. Disadvantaged groups are simply far less likely to receive the prerequisite education.

Accounting for Economic Status

The comparisons just described can be further refined by considering the role of economic status. We take the mean per capita expenditure level (MPCE) of the person's household[16] to capture economic status. Table 3 presents the mean and standard deviation of MPCE by caste and religious group, for the minimally qualified sub-population.[17, 18] The results show significant levels of inter-caste economic disparity. For example, MPCE among minimally qualified urban SCs is only 78 per cent of the national average, while among similar FCs it is 108 per cent of the average. Muslims and SCs are the least economically well-off groups.

Table 3

MPCE of Social and Religious Groups in the Minimally Qualified (Rs/person per month)

	Mean	*Std. Dev.*	*Mean*	*Std. Dev.*
Class/Caste				
Scheduled Tribes	1010.26	672.02	678.64	473.78
Scheduled Castes	852.83	610.40	552.82	373.76
Other Backward Classes	955.87	651.27	579.53	375.18
Forward Classes	1185.00	815.57	710.96	445.19
Non-responsive	1283.50	632.59	na	na
Religion				
Hindu	1084.42	715.16	635.65	418.70
Muslim	905.49	634.11	605.86	330.01
Others	1410.43	1187.78	814.68	512.94
Non-responsive	1070.54	61.20	na	na
Sub population average	1097.92	769.45	643.6536	421.704
Overall sample size	10,206	7,032		
Imputed Sub-population size	9,964,432		10,591,522	

The fact that the groups which are underrepresented in college are also poorer suggests that what few distortions remain in the representation of caste and religious groups in college (once obviously unqualified persons are dropped) might be explained by these income disparities. To examine this, we restrict the sample to the minimally qualified population, and estimate a probit model on whether the respondent is college-availing. The explanatory variables considered are caste and religious identity, as well as MPCE and MPCE-squared. FC Hindus are the base case. Table 4 presents the results, with coefficients that are statistically significant at the 5 per cent level presented in italics.[19]

The regression coefficients on MPCE and MPCE-squared indicate, as expected that over the expenditure range actually observed, higher economic status increases the propensity to avail of college. However, the regression results indicate that even after correcting for economic status, and restricting the sub-population whose enrolment rate is considered to the minimally qualified, FC Hindus are more likely than any other group to avail of college.[20]

The regression coefficients therefore show that both economic status and social identity play a role. Policymakers wishing to promote equity in the probability of college admission might, therefore, choose to target their policy instruments (of which there are many available, in addition to reservations, most obviously – scholarships and preparatory schools), on the basis of social group, or economic status. It would therefore be useful to know whether low economic status or membership of a disadvantaged social/religious group is a better predictor that a student is at risk of not enrolling. The answer is not obvious from the regression results presented.

To investigate this question further, we tested two restrictions on the above probit regression. First, against the unrestricted model presented in Table 4, we restricted MPCE and MPCE – squared to have no effect on enrolment. This restriction is associated, in the urban sample, with a test statistic of F2,4074 = 45.86. Second, again, against the unrestricted model in Table 4, we test the null? that college attendance is invariant to the five identifiers of social and religious group. The resulting test statistic in the urban sample is F5,4071= 4.53. Both restrictions carry p-values of zero.

This procedure can be viewed as a non-nested test of two theories of college enrolment (Kennedy 2003:100-01). The first holds that only identity is relevant and economic status is irrelevant; and the second that identity is irrelevant and only economic status matters. The test statistics imply that neither theory suffices. Both identity and economic status are relevant.

This said, the much larger test statistic associated with the restriction on economic status does indicate that economics are a better predictor of college enrolment than identity in the urban population.[21] Interestingly, in the rural population, the F statistics on the two restrictions are: $F_{2,5966} = 4.23$ (economic status is irrelevant), and $F_{5,5963} = 6.11$ (identity is irrelevant). In contrast to the situation in urban areas, these results provide no indication that economic status is a better predictor of college enrolment than identity in rural areas.

These results on the relative importance of economics and identity will bear further investigation for two reasons: (i) they could be sensitive to the measures of economic status and choice of social groupings; and (ii) the results of the comparison could be "local" – i.e., economic status could be a better predictor for some groups than for others.

Discussion and Concluding Remarks

To recapitulate our main findings: First, SCs and Muslims are massively underrepresented in college, relative to their shares in the wider college-age population. OBCs and STs are also underrepresented, although less so. There is therefore an urgent prima facie case for working on improving the representation of backward castes and Muslims in college.

Table 4

Probit Results: Determination of College Attendance amongst Minimally Qualified Males, Aged 17-30

Independent Variables	*(1)Urban*		*(2)Rural*	
	Coeff	*Std. Err*	*Coeff*	*Std. Err*
MPCE(in thousand of Rs)	0.5850	0.0795	0.4524	0.1626
MPCE-squared (in 000's of Rs squared)	– 0.0648	0.0165	– 0.1431	0.0538
Scheduled Tribes	– 0.1448	0.1064	– 0.2909	0.1219
Scheduled Castes	– 0.1644	0.0699	– 0.1098	0.0707
Other Backward Classes	– 0.1079	0.0565	– 0.2247	0.0544
Muslim	– 0.2499	0.0702	– 0.1085	0.0910
Other religion	– 0.1341	0.0732	– 0.2329	0.0973
Constant	– 0.0907	0.0696	– 0.1358	0.0953
Number of observation	10,206		7,032	
Imputed sub-population size	9,964,432		10,591.522	

Second, most of this distorted representation is explained by the abysmal higher secondary completion rates of these groups. This finding corroborates those of reports like the Probe Team's, emphasising the importance of improving access to and the quality of public schools. Reservation of college seats for OBCs is an instrument that will marginally improve access[22] to college for only the 14.3 per cent of the OBC population that completes higher secondary school. Given this, and the expense of college education relative to schooling, it follows that amelioration of distorted representation in college might well be better pursued through concerted and courageous reforms of the pre-college education system. Such an approach, if successful, would improve the upward mobility of most OBCs, both by improving their representation in college, and by serving the vast majority of OBCs who do not pursue college education.

Third, our probit analysis shows that group identity is statistically important for predicting college enrolment, even once we control for economic status (by introducing MPCE as an explanatory variable) and higher secondary completion (by focusing on a sample of the minimally qualified). As noted in the introduction, this does not imply discrimination. Further, in urban areas, economic status is a better predictor of college enrolment than identity, implying that much of the remaining underrepresentation of social groups relative to the minimally qualified population is explained by the lower economic status of these groups. This suggests that it would be useful to consider whether policies to boost educational equality in urban areas might be targeted on the basis of economic status, rather than social group. On the other hand, in rural areas, there is no evidence that economic status predicts the risks of non-enrolment better than group identity. These results suggest the importance of considering different targeting mechanisms in urban and rural environments, and of paying due attention to the empirics of rural-urban migration by students.

Fourth, SCs and STs make up a smaller share of the college population than their quota dictates.

In light of this evidence, it is useful to re-examine the arguments of Thorat (2005), who points out that discrimination is a form of economic inefficiency because it results in poor allocations of human resources. As such, he argues that reservation of college seats or jobs corrects the primary distortion (respectively, discrimination in college admissions or hiring practices) and should unambiguously increase economic efficiency. Our results are direct evidence that it is incorrect to apply this argument to college admissions in India. Because the vast majority of underrepresentation in college is explained by lower higher secondary graduation rates, reservation of college seats cannot be seen as fixing the primary distortion. The primary distortion(s) occur at lower rungs on the educational ladder. The bulk of the inefficiency is associated with the pre-college education system. Therefore, there is no obvious reason to believe that fixing the underrepresentation problems at the college level will enhance economic efficiency.[23]

Policy therefore needs to focus on tackling the distortions that prevent children from accessing and completing lower levels of education. And to do this, it is essential that we have a good understanding of the precise nature of the distortions, and where exactly they apply in terms of both the level of education (for example, primary versus secondary schooling) as well as location (for example, rural versus urban India). More concretely, efforts at data collection like that made for the Probe report, which paid careful attention to the factors which influence both the supply and demand for primary education, need to be undertaken in more parts of the country and for higher levels of education. Such efforts are urgently required in order to design appropriate policy interventions for addressing inefficiencies and inequities in the education system.

Acknowledgement

This paper represents the views of the authors and does not necessarily represent those of the organisation to which they belong. We are grateful to Paolo Hernando for his assistance with cleaning the NSS data. Shiela Camingue and Susan Torres provided valuable research assistance. We were greatly aided by discussions with Ifzal Ali, Linda de la Fuente, Frank Harrigan, Dalisay Maligalig, Vivek Rao, Vaskar Saha, Janmejay Singh and Ajay Tandon. [All errors are our own.]

Notes

1. Because caste may not be the only basis for discrimination and/or underrepresentation of communities in terms of educational attainments, we carry out our analysis by religious groups along with caste/class groupings.

2. Persons may be allocated to the rural sector if their household is based (and therefore sampled) in a rural area, even if they are currently residing in an urban area (and vice versa).
3. The four social groups are: scheduled tribe, scheduled caste, other backward class, and other. We have used the term "forward class" in lieu of "other". Social and religious groups are orthogonal, in the sense that households can, and do, identify themselves as belonging to any of these castes irrespective of their religious grouping.
4. The sample weights were constructed in accordance with the instructions accompanying the NSS unit level data and verified against the implied population estimates reported in *Employment and Unemployment in India, 1999-2000: Key Results* (NSSO 2000).
5. The share of OBCs in the overall population nationwide is 35.8 per cent according to the 1999 employment-unemployment NSS data. A weighted average (using the imputed sub-population sizes in Table 1 puts the share of OBCs in the population aged 17-30 at 35.2%).
6. The definition of "graduate or postgraduate" education (which we use interchangeably with "college") adopted by the NSS, excludes diploma courses, some of which may not require higher secondary education.
7. For example, from Table 1, out of 33.2 million urban males in our age group, roughly 10.0 million are qualified, yielding the 30.04 per cent figure in Table 2, column (1). Similarly, from Table 1, there are (14.68% × 33.2) million urban SC males, of whom (7.89% × 10) million are qualified. Thus the HS completion rate for urban SCs is 16.14 per cent.
8. Four Pearson chi-squared tests of the null that completion rates are the same across groups were rejected with p-values of zero. There are four tests because we have two cuts of the population (by religion and social group) and two sub-populations (urban and rural).
9. Compare the Muslim HS completion rate of 16.14 per cent with the national average of 30.04 per cent.
10. These figures are implicit in the comparison of columns (3) and (4) with (5) and (6) of Table 1. See footnote 7.
11. From the sub-population sizes in columns 1 and 5 of Table 1 (6.34 million/33.23 million) = 19.1 per cent.
12. From Table 1, it is straightforward to calculate that nationwide there are roughly 5.82 million college-age, minimally qualified male OBCs, of whom 2.92 million (or 50.15%) are college availing. Raising the share of OBCs to 27 per cent, given the total college – availing

male population of 11.47 million, would imply 3.10 million OBCs in college (or 53.016 per cent of qualified, male, college-aged OBCs).

13. This assumes that the 27 per cent reservation for OBC students would include all those OBC students who would have otherwise secured an educational seat to the general category (i.e., on the basis of open competition) but choose instead to apply through the reserved category in order to maximise their likelihood of securing a seat.
14. Pearson chi-squared tests of the null – that propensity of the college-age population to avail of college is the same across groups – were rejected with p-values of zero in the urban and rural samples and across religious and social groups.
15. Again, Pearson chi-squared tests indicate that inter-group variation in propensity to attend college is statistically significant, even after restricting the sub-sample to males, aged 17-30, that are minimally qualified to attend.
16. Readers should note that the MPCE data used here, obtained from block nine of the employment-unemployment survey, are not directly comparable with MPCE data from the Round 55 consumer expenditure survey. This is because in contrast with earlier rounds, the employment-unemployment and consumer expenditure surveys were administered to entirely different households, and the questions concerning expenditure were posed differently.
17. The sample has been trimmed. Observations reporting MPCE in the highest and lowest 0.1 percentile were dropped.
18. The reader is reminded that the restriction to the minimally qualified population means that these figures are not representative of the distribution of economic status in the overall population. The restriction eliminates less educated, typically poorer, households. As indicated above, more of these come from lower castes or are Muslims.
19. We used sample weights, and standard errors corrected for the stratified and clustered sampling design. The NSS stratification scheme involves a complex mix of state, district and rural/urban identifiers, as well as population. For simplicity we assume stratification by state only for estimating standard errors.
20. The only (statistically insignificant) exceptions are rural Muslims, who are more likely to avail of college than rural Hindus.
21. This comparison of F-tests is intuitively analogous to comparing the R2 statistics for each of the restricted regressions to see which fits the

data best. However, because probit regression with survey weights involves a pseudo log-likelihood, R2 statistics cannot be computed.

22. See footnote 8 for assumptions leading to this conclusion.

23. Others with whom we have shared these results have pointed out that the patterns we discern in the data could, in theory, be driven by discrimination at college entry, as this would dissuade disadvantaged groups from completing higher secondary education. After all, 63 per cent of urban higher secondary graduates go on to attend college, suggesting that higher secondary education is pursued specifically in order to secure entry into college. However, there are at least two good reasons to believe that this theory is not empirically relevant to India. First, the Probe team has shown that dropout rates in basic education are driven largely by the poor quality of education provided and its cost. Second, in further cuts of the NSS data (not included for reasons of brevity), we find that solid underrepresentation at the primary level, which becomes progressively worse at higher levels of education. Secondary school completion rates look almost as distorted as higher secondary completion rates. This suggests that evening the odds of different groups obtaining entry into college will not do much to alter higher secondary completion rates.

References

Ghosh, Partha (1997): *Positive Discrimination in India: A Political Analysis*, Ethnic Studies Report, Volume XV, Number 2, July.

Kennedy, Peter (2003): *A Guide to Econometrics*, Blackwell Publishing, Massachusetts.

National Sample Survey Organisation (2000): *Employment and Unemployment in India, 1999-2000: Key Results*, Ministry of Statistics and Programme Implementation, Government of India.

The Probe Team (1999): *The Public Report on Basic Education in India*, Oxford University Press, New Delhi.

Thorat, Sukhadeo (2005): 'Reservation and Efficiency: Myth and Reality', *Economic and Political Weekly*, February 26, pp. 808-10.

UNESCO Institute for Statistics (2005): *Global Education Digest 2005: Comparing Education Statistics across the World*, UIS, Montreal, Canada.

10

Assumptions and Arithmetic of Caste-Based Reservations

ROHINI SOMANATHAN

The group-based reservation policies that are currently being proposed for other backward classes (OBCs) in higher education have their rationale in three basic premises. The first is that the groups concerned are socially disadvantaged relative to other unreserved groups in the population. Second, that disadvantage is most effectively addressed by directing benefits towards groups rather than directly to disadvantaged individuals and households. Lastly, that among available group-based affirmative action policies, reservations are the right choice. It is instructive to examine the validity of these assumptions in the Indian context, using theoretical arguments and the limited empirical evidence available on group outcomes and public policy. Throughout the discussion that follows, I will stay clear of the tangled debate on the acceptability of differential treatment to the socially disadvantaged and focus instead on the relative efficiency of alternative policies that can be used for such transfers. How great is the OBC disadvantage relative to unreserved groups in the population? This question has remained controversial because there are no contemporaneous census data that can be used to link caste to social outcomes. The last detailed caste enumeration was undertaken by the colonial administration in 1941. These data were only partially tabulated due to the world war and the political unrest of the last few years of British rule. Most social historians therefore resort to the more complete data from 1931. The 1931 data provide a detailed district-level enumeration of caste that could potentially be used to link the numbers in groups or 'jatis' that are now classified as OBCs to educational outcomes from the time. For rural districts which have had relatively slow changes in social composition, historical caste shares could also be analysed together with social and economic indicators that are available at the district level for later years. We could, for example, examine whether districts with large shares of groups that are now classified as OBCs had systematically different rates of literacy and educational attainment than areas with concentrations of other categories. These historical data are currently unexploited and their study could provide valuable insight into the historical, and perhaps the contemporary, position of groups that are now classified as the backward classes.

There are some recent surveys that contain data on both caste and household demographics and allow some comparisons of OBCs with other groups. The 55th round of the National Sample Survey (NSS) administered in 1999-2000 collected self-reported caste data on OBCs and the post-election surveys that are regularly conducted by the Centre for Study of Developing Societies (CSDS) include data on jatis that can be aggregated to arrive at averages for the OBCs and other categories. Satish Deshpande of Delhi University finds, based on the NSS data, that OBCs as a group lie somewhere between the scheduled castes (SCs) and scheduled tribes (STs) and the unreserved Hindu castes in terms of average years of schooling. The CSDS post-election survey of 2004 suggests a similar ranking. Very little is known about the relative position of the OBCs when compared with the religious minorities because survey data using representative samples does not yield large enough numbers for each of the minority groups to make meaningful statistical comparisons.

Simple Model

Turning to the second question, if we assume that average social and economic outcomes for OBCs are lower than those for upper caste Hindus, how effective are group-based policies in addressing these inequalities? This depends critically on the extent of heterogeneity among the OBCs and the existence of other disadvantaged groups that are not covered by reservations. The importance of these factors can be illustrated with a simple model and some stylised examples. Suppose that there are two equal-sized groups, A and B ("advanced" and "backward" if you like) who would like to enter institutions of higher education and a test is used to ration available seats. Test performance depends on a variety of other household characteristics which we call "social advantage". This term is meant to capture economic resources, parental education, social status and networks, all of which influence the schools attended by these students and learning that takes place within and outside these schools. As a benchmark case, suppose that only those in group B are socially disadvantaged, that the scores for groups A and B are clustered around their medians *t*A and *t*B respectively (*t*A>*t*B), and that the extent of social disadvantage is well captured by the difference *t*A-*t*B. If half of all applicants are admitted and the qualifying scores for both groups are the same, group B will be underrepresented. Any affirmative action policy that leaves the score distribution unchanged but seeks to restore the balance in the shares of the two groups admitted must necessarily drive a wedge between their qualifying scores. In this case, using *t*A and *t*B as the qualifying scores for the two groups ensures half of each group gets admitted. Controlling for social disadvantage in this case leads to equal representation of both groups because disadvantage fully accounts for the differences in their medians. Stated more generally, for any population shares of the two groups, group B will be underrepresented in the absence of affirmative action policies if the test score distribution for group A first-order stochastically dominates that for B. Setting group-specific qualifying thresholds will lead to equal representation if differences in the distributions of scores across groups arise only because of social disadvantage. It is also worth noting that a variety of affirmative action policies could be used to achieve identical results: Instead of giving group B students a point advantage of *t*A-*t*B, quotas for the two groups based on their population shares could be used. Any case for one type of policy over the other can only arise when one or more of the assumptions of this special case do not hold. We will come back to this.

In the above example, affirmative action policies are very effective in bringing about equal opportunity since disadvantage and group B membership are perfectly correlated and all those within group B are equally disadvantaged. If there are sub-groups within groups A and B with varying degrees of disadvantage, group-based policies become a much blunter instrument for equalising access to higher education. As long as these policies do not separately address each sub-group, the relatively privileged within group B would benefit disproportionately. This is the basis of the "cream-skimming" argument that is often made in the media. Also, for a given level of disadvantage, admission would be more likely for group B individuals than for those in group A and, with enough social heterogeneity within each group, there would be a set of aspirants from group A who would be admitted without affirmative action, but are now left out.

Another stylised example can help clarify the mechanism at work here. Suppose, in this case, that the test scores for groups A and B are uniformly distributed on [50, 80] and [20,50] respectively and that differences in scores reflect only the relative social advantage of the test-takers. As in the benchmark case, the two groups are equal sized and there are half as many seats as aspirants. In the absence of affirmative action, the qualifying score will be set at 50, all group A students will be admitted and no group B students will be admitted. Suppose now that group B students are set a lower qualifying threshold, based on the mean difference in social disadvantage between the two groups. With qualifying thresholds of 35 and 65 for the two groups, half of each group is admitted. Once again, quotas requiring equal representation of the two groups and lowering the qualification threshold for group B yield identical results. Now if instead group A scores are distributed on [40, 80] and group B on [20,60], equal representation can be had by giving group B a 20- point advantage (set $tA = 60$ and $tB = 40$). The group of applicants with scores between 40 and 60 are now admitted if they belong to group B but not if they are from group A. This is the sense in which affirmative action policies can be interpreted as discriminating against disadvantaged individuals in unreserved groups. Several recent court orders against affirmative action in specific US universities have adopted this line of argument.

Critical Factor of Heterogeneity

Can we still make a case for group-based affirmative action policies in cases when groups are internally heterogeneous in the manner described above? The answer to this question depends on whether the errors of targeting that accompany these policies are greater than those that would result from any attempt to directly measure the disadvantage of applicants. For high enough levels of social heterogeneity in the reserved and unreserved groups, it is unlikely that affirmative action policies are effective in bringing about equal opportunity. The nature of the most appropriate policies to achieve social justice in the Indian context therefore depends critically on how much social heterogeneity there is among the groups that receive or seek to receive benefits through reservations. While we do not have systematic data on the relative disadvantage of sub-groups within the SCs, STs, OBCs and general categories, there is some research on caste and political representation and anthropological studies on social relations within rural communities that can throw some light on the heterogeneity issue. Christophe Jaffrelot (2003) considers the representation of jatis and religious minorities in politics and finds considerable heterogeneity within the OBCs in both membership in major political parties and in seats in parliament. There is substantial evidence (Deliege 1999 and Mendelson and Vicziany 2000) of differentiation within SC communities. Some of this shows that the populations of "dalit Hindu" castes which received the benefits of reservations are comparable to those who converted to Christianity and were not therefore covered by the reservations of the post-independence period. In joint work with Abhijit Banerjee I have looked at access to primary and high schools as well as other public amenities in rural India during the two decades between 1971 and 1991 (Banerjee and Somanathan, forthcoming). We mapped census data on the location of public goods and population shares of different communities to parliamentary constituencies and found that constituencies with SC and ST concentrations had lower access to primary and high schools in 1971 relative to other areas, with the STs especially disadvantaged. By 1991, SC access to primary schools was very similar to that for other groups and there was also considerable convergence for the STs. For high schools and other public goods, we found that SCs did far better than STs, reflecting perhaps their much more successful political mobilisation. We also find that Muslims and Christians benefited relatively little from the growing availability of public goods during this period. Based on this literature, there is reason to be cautious in the use of affirmative action policies to achieve equality in access to higher education. There appears to be considerable heterogeneity within the broad social groupings that are currently used and differences in the extent to which groups that were traditionally disadvantaged have managed to extract benefits from the state.

Let us turn finally to the choice between alternative affirmative action policies. In the examples considered above we saw an equivalence between quotas based on population shares and lower test score thresholds for the disadvantaged group. The assumption, however, was that the test score distribution was independent of the type of policy chosen. In practice, quotas will influence incentives differently from score thresholds since the set of students admitted will depend only on their relative rankings and not their scores. Quotas are therefore consistent with both large and small differences between the scores of the reserved and unreserved groups. Those writing on the potential effects of quotas as a tool for affirmative action in the US have often emphasised their disincentive effects on minority effort. It is also possible, however, that those at the margin in both reserved and unreserved groups will work harder under quotas as they compete with each other for admission. Given the scarcity of seats relative to applicants to elite institutions of higher education in India, these tournament-like effects are quite plausible.

Based on the three premises for effective reservation policies that this article began with, is there a case for OBC reservations in higher education? The limited available evidence on average outcomes of OBCs relative to other groups suggests some disadvantage relative to unreserved Hindus, but these differences are small in comparison to those of the SCs and STs. The large number of groups in a complex social hierarchy implies a great deal of heterogeneity among the broad categories such as the OBCs. This, together with the fact that some communities have, through effective political mobilisation, been able to corner a disproportionate share of state resources suggests that affirmative action policies that target broad social groups are not going to act as powerful tools of social justice – too many of the disadvantaged will be excluded in favour of the more privileged. Lastly, alternative affirmative action policies might have different effects on the effort levels of reserved and unreserved groups and these differences are likely to have implications for the extent to which students who enter through reservations successfully complete their higher degrees

References

Banerjee, Abhijit and Rohini Somanathan: 'The Political Economy of Public Goods: Some Evidence from India', *Journal of Development Economics*, forthcoming.

Coate, Stephen and Glenn Loury (1993): 'Will Affirmative Action Eliminate Negative Stereotype', *American Economic Review*, December, pp. 1220-40.

Deliege, Robert (1999): *The Untouchables of India*, Berg Publishers, Oxford.

Jaffrelot, Christophe (2003): *India's Silent Revolution: The Rise of the Lower Castes in North India*, Columbia University Press, New York.

Mendelson, Oliver and Marika Vicziany (2000): *The Untouchables: Subordination, Poverty and the State in Modern India*, Cambridge University Press, Chapter 1.

III

Alternative Equal Opportunity Policies

11

Redesigning Affirmative Action

SATISH DESHPANDE AND YOGENDRA YADAV

It is often claimed that India's affirmative action policy is among the largest, longest running, most elaborate and successful initiatives of its kind in the world. There is some truth to these claims. At the same time, it is surely true that sustained attention to the design of such policy has not been among our strengths. In fact, the republic of India adopted a pre-designed and pre-positioned affirmative action policy at birth. Since the adoption of the Constitution in 1950, there have been no substantive changes in the basic affirmative action prescription of reserving proportional quotas in selected fields (legislatures, government jobs, education) for designated castes and communities.

As is well known, targeted quotas of this sort have many virtues. They encourage political solidarities and loyalty; they are easy to administer and monitor; and they are relatively resistant to appropriation by unentitled groups. However, quotas are not necessarily the best solution to all affirmative action problems. But they seem to have become the default option in contemporary India. This applies not just to the recent debate on extension of affirmative action to groups other than the scheduled castes (SCs) and the scheduled tribes (STs) in the educational sector; it is equally true of affirmative action to bring more women into our legislatures or to alter the social profile of job holders in the private sector.

The limitations of caste quotas were first foregrounded by the 1950s attempts to extended them beyond the STs and SCs to the other backward classes (OBCs). Of course, all affirmative action is inherently contentious because it seeks to alter the status quo of inter-group power equations. Issues like this form the very stuff of politics, and better policy design alone will not make these contestations vanish. On the other hand, bad policy design will certainly make things much worse, because it will ensure that political costs are much higher than they need to be and that the social benefits are either too meagre, or badly targeted, or both. Thus, apart from its primary objective of enabling the attainment of social objectives (such as equality of opportunity or elimination of unjust inequalities), policy design also has the important responsibility of ensuring efficiency in the sense of minimising unavoidable costs and maximising potential benefits.

We believe that this secondary objective has not received adequate attention, and that shortcomings on this front may even affect the ability to achieve the primary goal. In this paper, we try to provide an illustrative example of a feasible alternative to the basic model of caste quotas. The emphasis is on indicating the broad direction in which we believe policy design in this field should be moving – the specific details of our scheme are tentative and are intended only as a concrete example. The next section briefly discusses the specificity of the OBCs and the challenges they pose to policy design. This is followed by a section discussing the recent decision by the Government of India to implement OBC reservations in elite institutions of professional education. Since our emphasis is on an evidence-based and multidimensional approach, the third section considers examples of available macro-statistical evidence on which an alternative design can be based. The fourth section spells out the basic features of our model in an attempt to demonstrate how both group and individual disadvantage can be addressed. A brief concluding section outlines the specificities and potential advantages of the model proposed.

Affirmative Action and the Other Backward Classes

From its earliest days, the OBC category proved to be a contentious one. This was because it formed the terrain on which the vexed questions of the precise relationship between caste and backwardness – and between both these and special treatment from the state – had to be decided. The backwardness of the SCs rested on the idea of untouchability, which, despite wide variations in its practice (specially across south and north), was too stark and compelling to permit quibbling. So too with the STs – their usually sharp spatial (if not always social) separation from mainstream Hindu society and/or their undisputed poverty ensured definitional stability. Moreover, the entitlement of both the scheduled groups to compensatory discrimination from the state – though grudgingly conceded initially – had never seriously been questioned until the Mandal conflagration of 1990. It was otherwise with the OBC category – its definition (who should be included and why?) as well as its implications (what should be the nature and extent of the entitlements it confers?) have been vigorously contested. The anti-reservation "movement" of May 2006 is only the most recent instance of this contest.

The OBCs embody a more complex relationship between caste and privilege or disprivilege, and thus present affirmative action policy with challenges as well as opportunities. Whereas caste is seen as conferring only privilege on the forward castes and only disprivilege on the SCs/STs, it can potentially confer both on the OBCs. Policy design thus needs to be more sophisticated to capture the nature and extent of the relative disadvantages suffered by the OBCs. Instead of exploiting this opportunity to expand policy horizons, the general response has been to split the OBC category into sub-groups to which the same quota logic is re-applied. An alternative approach would be to move towards a more nuanced policy design that seeks to capture degrees of disadvantage as well as multiple kinds of disadvantage. The OBC category may thus enable the transition to a more integrated policy framework where caste is only one among many parameters of affirmative action.

Mandal II: The Roads Not Taken

While it cannot be accused of thoughtfulness or sophistication, the government's move to introduce OBC reservations in elite institutions of higher and professional education is likely to improve OBC access to higher education and middle class jobs. The available evidence on educational inequalities in contemporary India (examined later in this paper) shows that the OBCs as a whole are certainly disadvantaged compared to the upper castes as a whole. Therefore, even the caste-bloc approach adopted by the government will help reduce some of these inequalities. It should also help expand the pool from within the OBCs that can take advantage of the existing scheme of reservation in government jobs. Thus, even a crude caste quota is better than none.

But an appreciation of the positives should not blind us to the long-term costs. A one-dimensional caste-bloc quota cannot but result in an inefficient targeting of this scheme. The relatively better off families from the "upper" OBCs will be able to corner most of the benefits. In regional terms, students from South India and other states with a long history of affirmative action and a strong backward caste movement are much better placed to take advantage of this scheme. Needless to say, most of these opportunities will be cornered by men, for the gender gap in education is higher among the OBCs than among upper caste Hindus. This failure to target the scheme precisely is bound to give rise to deep resentment. Many non-OBC students and their families may rightly feel that they are more disadvantaged than the OBC students gaining admission due to the new reservations. The evidence of multiple disadvantages presented in this paper strengthens some of these apprehensions.

Is it still possible to remedy the situation and reduce some of these costs within the parameters of the scheme? The announced policy closes one of these possibilities, namely, that of addressing disadvantaged groups other than the OBCs. But, the Veerappa Moily Oversight Committee on implementation of reservations in higher education can at least try to ensure that the reservation for the OBCs is targeted more efficiently. One, it can recommend that the "creamy layer" within the OBCs be made the last claimant on the benefits of the new reservation. The exclusion of the "creamy layer", as per the definition evolved by the National Commission for Backward Classes (NCBC), is already in operation for job reservations. This could be applied to professional education, with the proviso that only the unfilled seats in the OBC quota will be offered to the "creamy layer" OBC candidates (rather than being transferred to the general category). Secondly, the committee can recommend that the 27 per cent quota be sub-divided among "upper" and "lower" OBCs. Such sub-divisions already exist in many states and a statutory body like the NCBC can be requested to prepare lists of upper and lower OBCs for the remaining states. This would guard against the bulk of the benefits being cornered by a handful of landed OBC communities that are much better placed than the rest to take advantage of caste-bloc based benefits. This would also ensure that the lower OBC communities, mainly artisan and service communities, whose educational condition is often worse than the upper crust of the SCs, will gain something from the new scheme. Again, the unfilled seats in the lower OBC quota could be filled by the upper OBCs. Thirdly, the committee can suggest some special provision to ensure that OBC women have adequate opportunity to access this quota. Finally, the committee can specify a minimum threshold of eligibility (say, two-thirds of the score of the last candidate admitted in the general category) for OBC candidates seeking admission into "super speciality" professional courses.

More long-term measures also need to be thought about. The government must ensure the generation of reliable data on caste and other sources of disadvantage. The National Sample Survey Organisation (NSSO) or other independent organisation can be requested to conduct a nationwide survey of the social profile of higher educational institutions and job holders in the organised sector – public as well as private. Lack of such data is the biggest obstacle blocking the transition towards more robust and fine-tuned policy making in the future. Second, it is time the government thought about the setting up of something like a diversity and disadvantage commission as a permanent statutory body to regularly monitor the diversity profile of public institutions and to advise the government on improving it.

Towards a Better Policy Design

Our basic argument is that better affirmative action policies can be designed by trying to cultivate the following features: (a) an evidence-based approach; (b) sensitivity to multiple dimensions of disadvantage including but not limited to caste; (c) sensitivity to the interaction effects of the different dimensions of disadvantage; and (d) sensitivity to degrees of relative disadvantage.

By an evidence-based approach we mean a policy framework that is explicitly linked to empirical information relating to disadvantage, usually but not necessarily of a macro-statistical kind. The major advantage of such an approach is that it highlights the fundamental reasons why affirmative action is being undertaken – namely, various sorts of social and economic disadvantage. This helps to deessentialise identity markers like caste or religion – i.e., it provides a rational explanation why specific castes or communities are entitled to compensatory discrimination and under-mines attitudes that treat such entitlements as a "birthright". A second important advantage is that evidence-based approaches have a built-in flexibility – they can adjust to and reflect changes in patterns of relative disadvantage. The downside is that such approaches become data-dependent, and is vulnerable to the failings of the data sources, and to the reification of data. However, the advantages far outweigh the disadvantages at present.

Sensitivity to multiple sources of disadvantage, to interaction effects and to degrees of disadvantage – all of these features are also data-dependent in practice if not in theory. Such sensitivity can only be developed if there is some stable method of measuring things like interaction effects and relative intensity of disadvantage. The virtues of these features are self-evident a more nuanced and comprehensive framework will lead to more precise targeting and, other things being equal, will produce faster and better results. In short, such approaches are not only more robust in ethical-moral terms but also in terms of practical efficiency, i.e., minimising costs and maximising benefits. The disadvantage is that policy design becomes much more complicated and the institutional mechanisms involved can become fragile. Such policies are also more difficult to monitor. But, once again, the benefits exceed the costs.

We provide below some examples of the kind of evidence that can be used to design policy. While we have used data from the NSSO and the Centre for Study of Developing Societies' (CSDS) National Election Study, 2004, this is for purposes of illustration. Similar or related data from other sources (such as the census or the National Family Health Survey) can also be used. Conventions and procedures need to be established for this purpose. Above all, we need a more pro-active attitude towards social statistics that breaks out of an excessive and irrational fear of collecting identity-related information.

Table 1 shows the percentage of graduates in the population aged 20 years or above in different castes and communities in rural and urban India. Only a little more than 1 per cent of STs, SCs and Muslims are graduates in rural India, while the figure for Hindu upper castes is four to five times higher at over 5 per cent. The real inequalities are in urban India, where not only the SCs in particular, but also Muslims, OBCs and STs, are way behind the forward

Table 1
Inequalities in Higher Education, 1999-2000

Caste/Communities	*Rural India*	*Urban India*
ST	1.1	10.9
SC	1.2	4.7
Muslim	1.3	6.1
Hindu-OBC	2.1	8.6
Sikh	2.8	25.0
Christian	4.7	23.7
Hindu-Upper Caste	5.3	25.3
Other Religions	5.4	31.5
All-India Average	**2.6**	**15.5**

Cell shows percentage of graduates in population aged 20 years and above.

Source: Computed from NSSO 55th Round Survey, 1999-2000.

communities and castes with a quarter or more of their population being graduates. Another way of looking at it is that STs, SCs, Muslims and OBCs are always below the national average while the other communities and especially Hindu upper castes are well above this average in both rural and urban India.

Table 2 shows the share of different castes and communities in the national pool of graduates as compared to their share of the total population aged 20 years or more. In other words, the table tells us which groups have a higher than proportionate (or lower than proportionate) share of graduates. Once again, with the exception of rural Hindu OBCs and urban STs (who are underrepresented, but less severely so), the same groups are severely underrepresented while the Hindu upper castes, other religions (Jains, Parsis, Buddhists, etc.) and Christians are significantly overrepresented among graduates. Thus, the Hindu upper castes' share of graduates is twice and one-and-a-half times their share in the above 20 population of rural and urban India respectively. Compare this, for example, to the urban SCs and Muslims, whose share of graduates is only 30 per cent and 39 per cent respectively of their share in the above 20 population. It should be emphasised that these data refer to all graduates from all kinds of institutions nationwide – if we were to look at the elite professional institutions, the relative dominance of the upper castes and forward communities is likely to be much

Table 2

Overrepresented and Underrepresented Groups, 1999-2000

Caste/Communities	*Rural India*	*Urban India*
ST	43	71
SC	47	30
Muslim	52	39
Hindu-OBC	82	56
Sikh	107	164
Christian	200	154
Hindu-Upper Caste	205	164
Other Religions	**200**	**400**

Cell shows group share of all graduate as a percentage of group shares of 20+ populations. Numbers bellow 100 indicates underrepresentation; above 100 indicate overrepresentation.

Source: Computed from NSSO 55th Round Survey, 1999-2000.

stronger, though such institutions refuse to publish the data that could prove or disprove such claims. The above tables show the simplest and most straightforward type of information that can feed into the design of an affirmative action programme. Relative under-representation or proportion of graduates significantly below the national average can constitute valid and transparent grounds for targeting affirmative action at specific castes, communities or groups of other kinds. Degree of relative disadvantage can also be estimated from such data and used to calibrate policy.

Table 3 illustrates the interaction effects among different types or sources of disadvantage, in this case those of caste and community, class and gender. It is drawn from the National Election Study of the CSDS done in 2004 and shows the percentage of postgraduate and professional degree holders among men and women from different caste-community groups belonging to different economic strata. The first three rows for "all castes-communities" show us the operation of gender and class. The figures for men and women for all communities and all classes make the obvious point that there is a big gender gap in educational attainment. Among men the highly educated are 3.4 per cent, compared to only 1.4 per cent for women. Figures for different classes for all communities make a similar point about the operation of economic inequalities. As we go down the economic strata, the proportion of highly educated goes down sharply, especially among the bottom three strata. This is true both for men and women.

Table 3

Postgraduates and Professional Degree Holders by Caste/Community, Class and Gender: Data from the National Election Study 2004(%)

		All Classes	*Rich*	*Middle*	*Lower Middle*	*Poor*	*Very Poor*	*N*
All castes communities	All	2.5	8.1	6.8	1.6	0.8	0.6	26829
	Men	3.4	9.8	9.1	2.2	1.2	1.0	14345
	Women	1.4	5.8	3.9	0.8	0.4	0.1	12484
Hindu dwija upper caste	All	5.6	13.6	8.8	2.7	1.7	0.5	4148
	Men	7.4	17.8	10.3	3.9	2.7	1.0	2230
	Women	3.5	8.3	7.3	1.4	0.3	0.0	1918
Hindu and Sikh intermediary caste (non-OBC)	All	2.8	6.2	4.6	0.7	1.2	0.8	2521
	Men	3.5	7.3	5.8	1.2	0.9	1.7	1361
	Women	2.0	4.8	3.4	0.0	2.2	0.0	1160
OBC (Hindu and Sikh)	All	1.8	5.8	6.6	1.1	0.7	0.7	9505
	Men	2.7	6.2	10.1	1.6	1.3	1.3	5020
	Women	0.8	5.2	1.9	0.4	0.1	0.1	4485
SC (any religion)	All	1.4	4.2	8.0	1.6	0.5	0.4	4278
	Men	2.1	2.3	11.0	2.8	0.7	0.8	2287
	Women	0.6	5.0	2.6	0.2	0.2	0.1	1991
ST (any religion)	All	0.9	1.9	6.1	1.4	0.6	0.4	2181
	Men	1.3	3.3	10.1	1.6	0.3	0.7	1185
	Women	0.5	0.0	1.8	1.1	0.5	0.2	996
Muslim	All	1.8	7.1	4.0	1.5	0.3	0.0	2963
	Men	2.5	10.1	6.0	1.2	0.5	0.0	1638
	Women	0.9	1.7	1.6	2.0	0.0	0.0	1327
Christian	All	3.3	13.2	7.8	1.8	0.8	0.0	630
	Men	3.0	(11.1)	5.7	3.3	1.5	0.0	302
	Women	3.7	15.0	9.5	0.0	0.0	0.0	328

Note: All figures are for per cent of respondents belonging to a category who report having a postgraduate professional degree. Figures based on less than 50 cases have been put within parentheses. Class categories are based on a combination of self-reported data on income and observed data on possession of assets.

Source: National Education Study 2004, CSDS Data Unit. Data is weighted by state population

A look at the first column for "all classes" shows that the traditional hierarchy of the Hindu caste order still matters in higher education. At 5.8 per cent the Hindu dwijas (Brahmin, Kshatriya, Vaishya and Kayasthas including equivalent jatis like Bhumihars and Tyagis of North India, Boddis of Bengal and Khatris of north-west India) are still way ahead of every other social group in higher educational attainments. As we go down the hierarchy, the figures come down to 2.8 per cent for intermediary castes (non-dwija and non-OBC castes like Jat Sikh, Maratha, Reddy, Nair, Patidar, etc.), 1.8 per cent for all the OBCs (excluding Muslim and Christians) and still lower for the SCs and STs. The share of highly educated among the Muslims as a whole is about the same as the Hindu and Sikh OBCs. The Christians have done much better and are next only to Hindu dwijas in their educational attainments.

This table also maps the interaction of these three variables. We have already seen that gender matters within each economic stratum. The gender gap increases as we go from the rich to the poorest: among the very poor, a man is 10 times more likely than a woman to have a higher educational degree; however, among the rich, a man is only 1.7 times more likely than a woman to have a similar degree. Gender also matters within each caste-community, with the exception of the Christians among whom women do marginally better than men. Here again, the gender gap is wider at the lower end of social hierarchy: SC, ST, OBC and Muslim women are more disadvantaged vis-à-vis the men of their communities than upper caste Hindu women are vis-à-vis the men of their community.

Table 3 offers a useful picture of the interaction between caste-community and class as factors that make a difference to educational opportunities at the upper end. It shows that class matters within each caste-community – a point that is not sufficiently recognised by proponents of caste-based reservations. By and large, the level of educational attainment goes down as we go down to lower economic strata within each caste-community. The only exception to this rule is that among OBCs, SCs and STs the rich tend to do a little worse than the middle class in educational terms, suggesting a possible disjunction of economic resources and educational opportunities at that level. Once we go below the middle class, we find a pattern similar to all other caste-communities. Within each caste-community group people belonging to lower-middle, or poor or very poor economic strata have considerably lower chances of accessing higher education compared to those from the top two categories in their own caste-community group. Table 3 also shows that caste matters within each class – a point often overlooked by enthusiasts of economic criteria. This point is more valid at the upper end of the caste and class hierarchy than at the lower end. Within the same economic stratum, Hindu dwijas are much more likely to be highly educated than any other caste-community. Similarly, among the rich, educational attainment falls as we go down the caste-community hierarchy. This relationship is much weaker at the lower end: among the lower-middle, poor and the poorest economic strata, there are no systematic differences among the OBC, SC and ST communities. At this end the class effect seems to dominate the caste effect in conditioning access to higher education.

It should now be amply clear as to what an evidence-based approach is and how it will seek to first identify and then reflect interaction effects as well as gradations of intensity in relative disadvantage. Obviously, different data sources will have different strengths and weaknesses, and these should be analysed carefully. (For instance, the NSSO survey offers nationwide coverage and very stable methodology, but is unable to provide information beyond very broad caste blocs. The NES survey provides such information, but has only limited coverage.) While available sources of information can and should be used for this purpose, it would be ideal if dedicated social surveys could be conducted periodically to provide an affirmative action database.

An Alternative Model

In this section we attempt to provide a concrete illustration of what a scheme for regulating admission to institutions of higher and professional education might look like. In keeping with the discussion above, our model is evidence-based and envisages using the kinds of data shown in the previous section. It addresses four main dimensions of group disadvantage, namely, caste/community, gender, region and sector of residence (i.e., rural/urban residence). There is separate evaluation of urban and rural candidates based on the location of the school where the 10th class examination was taken. Regions are divided into three zones based on common indicators of backwardness such as those used in the Jawaharlal Nehru University scheme. Castes and communities are awarded disadvantage points based on agreed empirical indicators of relative backwardness in the context of higher education. Needless to say, all group disadvantage evaluations are made on the basis of empirical evidence and not on mere group membership.

Besides group disadvantages, this scheme also considers individual disadvantages. While a large number of factors determine individual disadvantages (e.g., family history, generational depth of literacy, sibling education, economic resources, etc.), we believe that there are two robust indicators of individual disadvantage that can be operationally used in the system of admission to public institutions: parental occupation and the type of school where a person passed the high school examination. These two variables allow us to capture the effect of most of the individual disadvantages including the family's educational history and economic circumstances.

In the tables below we illustrate how this scheme could be operationalised. It needs to be underlined that the weightages proposed here are tentative, based on limited information, and meant only to show how the scheme works. The exact weights to be allotted to academic performance and social disadvantage is a key issue which can only be decided after examining more evidence; it could be 90:10, 70:30 or some other ratio. Purely for purposes of illustration, we are assuming an 80:20 ratio here, i. e., the academic score would be converted to a standardised score on a scale of 0-80, while the social disadvantage score would range from 0-20. (Note that the social disadvantage score is being capped at a maximum of 20 even though it is theoretically possible for candidates to obtain a higher score as per Tables A1, A2, B and C.)

Table A1

Group Disadvantage for Rural Students: Caste-community, Region and Gender

Community/Zones		*Zone I Most Backward*	*Zone II*	*Zone III*
Lower OBC/MBC/Muslim OBC	Female	20	18	16
	Male	16	14	12
Upper OBC/Non-OBC Muslim	Female	18	16	14
	Male	15	13	11
All Others	Female	12	10	8
	Male	10	8	6

Table A2

Group Disadvantage for Urban Students: Caste-community, Size of city and Gender

Community/Zones		*Up to 1,00,000*	*Up to 5,00,000*	*Up to 10,00,000*	*Million plus Cities*
Lower OBC/MBC/Muslim OBC	Female	14	12	10	8
	Male	11	9	7	5
Upper OBC/Non-OBC Muslim	Female	12	10	8	6
	Male	10	8	6	4
All Others	Female	4	3	2	1
	Male	2	1	0	0

Notes:
1. If a candidate's parents fall within the category of 'creamy layer' (as defined by the NCBC). The group disadvantage points of the candidate will be half of those indicated in the table A1 or A2.
2. List of lower and upper OBC to be prepared by the NCBC.
3. Zones are to be classified by the districts. A candidate will be assumed to belong to the district in which the candidate's school is located. JNU's classified of districts could be accepted as the starting point.
4. The points presented here are only indicative. When the scheme is operationlised, these points should be derived from and linked to data on educational disadvantage of each of the social groups and categories mentioned in the cells for each table.

Tables A1 and A2 show how the group disadvantages points can be awarded to rural and urban residents respectively. (As already mentioned, residence will be determined by the location of the school from where the 10th standard examination was taken. This information is typically already available from most application forms.) There are three axes of group disadvantage considered here: the relative backwardness of the region one comes from one's caste and community (only non-SC/ST groups are considered here), and one's gender. The zones in the top row refer to a classification of regions – this can be at state, sub-state region, or even district level – based on commonly used indicator of backwardness. Thus, zone I is the most backward region while zone III is the most developed region. The disadvantage points would thus decrease from left to right for each caste group and gender. The castes and communities identified here are clubbed according to broadly similar levels of poverty and education indicators (once again the details of this can be agreed upon). The lower OBCs and most backward castes (as determined by state lists or by NCBC criteria) along with OBC Muslims are considered most disadvantaged or least represented among the educated, affluent, etc., while upper caste Hindus, Sikhs (non-SC, non-OBC), Christians (non-ST, non-OBC), Jains, Parsis, etc., are considered to be the most "forward" communities. Disadvantage points thus decrease from top to bottom. Gender is built into this matrix, with women being given disadvantage points depending on their other attributes, i.e., caste and region. Thus, the hypothetical numbers in these tables indicate different degrees of relative disadvantage based on all four criteria – i.e., caste/community, gender and region considered separately for rural and urban sector. Most important, the tables also try to capture the interaction effects among these variables. Thus, a woman from the most backward region, who belongs to the lower OBC, MBC or Muslim OBC, groups gets the maximum score of 20 if she is from a rural area and 14 if she is from a town with less than one lakh population. At the other extreme, a male from the forward community from the most developed region gets no disadvantage points at all if he is from a rural area.

Table B

Individual Disadvantage: Type of Schooling

	Village/Town up to 20,000	*Town up to 1,00,000*	*City up to 10,00,000*	*Million-plus Cities*
Ordinary Government School	6	5	4	3
Private School (non-English Medium)	3	2	1	0
Private School (English medium)	2	1	0	0
Special Residential Government School (Navodaya/Sainik)	1	1	0	0
Exclusive/Residential "Public" School	0	0	0	0

Table C

Individual Disadvantage: Family Background

Mother's Occupation	*Father's Occupation*		
	Managerial/Pro-fessional/Big Business/ Class I and II	*Clerical Lower/Professional/ Medium Business/ Class III and IV*	*All Others*
Managerial/Professional/Big Business/Class I and II	0	0	0
Clerical Lower/Professional/Medium Business/Class III and IV	0	1	2
All Others (non-Income Tax Paying)	0	2	4

Tables B and C work in a similar manner for determining individual disadvantage. For these tables, all group variables are excluded. Table B looks at the type of school the person passed his/her secondary examination from and the size of the village, town or city where this school was located. Anyone going to an ordinary government school in a village of small town gets the maximum of six points in this matrix. The gradation of schools is done according to observed quality of education and implied family resources, and this could also be refined. A student from an exclusive English medium public school in a large metro gets no disadvantage points.

Table C looks at parental occupation as a proxy for family resources (i.e., income, wealth, etc., which are notoriously difficult to ascertain directly). We have limited the maximum points awarded here to three, but this could be changed based on experience. Children of parents who are outside the organised sector and are below the taxable level of income get the maximum points, and the occupation of both parents is considered. Those with either parent in class I or II jobs of the government, or in managerial or professional jobs get no points at all. Intermediate jobs in the organised sector, including class III and IV jobs in the government, are reckoned to be better placed than those in the unorganised, low-pay sector.

Combining the scores in the three matrices will give the total disadvantage score, which can then be added to the standardised academic merit score to give each candidate's final score.

Admissions for all non- SC/ST candidates, i.e., for 77.5 per cent of all seats, can then be based on this total score.

Specificities and Advantages

While both the caste-bloc quota (adopted by default by the government as well as proposals like ours share a commitment to affirmative action and the desire to extend it to educational opportunities, our scheme differs in many ways. The government's method will create a bloc of "reserved" seats. Our proposal applies to all the seats not covered by the existing reservation for the SC/ST and other categories. The government proposal recognises only group disadvantages and uses caste as the sole criterion of group disadvantage in educational inequalities. We too acknowledge the significance of group disadvantages and that of caste as the single most important predictor of educational inequalities. But our scheme seeks to fine-tune the identification by recognising other group disadvantages like region and gender. Moreover, our scheme is also able to address the interaction effects between different axes of disadvantage (such as region, caste and gender, or type of school and type of location, etc.). While recognising group disadvantages, our scheme provides some weightage to individual disadvantages relating to family background and type of schooling. Our scheme also recognises that people of all castes may suffer from individual disadvantages, and offers redressal for such disadvantages to the upper castes as well. While the government proposal is based on an all-or-nothing approach to recognising disadvantage (either you are an OBC or you are not), our proposal allows for flexibility in dealing with variations in degrees of disadvantage.

In its essence, the scheme we propose here is not new – ideas of this kind have been around for some time. We were ourselves involved in designing and implementing such a scheme for the selection process of a well-known international fellowship programme for higher education, where it was successful for some years. A similar scheme has been in use at the Jawaharlal Nehru University for regulating admissions, and a related but some-what different one has been suggested by Purshottam Agrawal of JNU.[1] In short, ideas of this sort have wide acceptability and have been arrived at independently by different scholars and administrators in varied contexts. Despite their greater complexity relative to the simplest possible option of the caste quota, it is perfectly possible to implement such schemes in practice, despite the vast expansion in scale that some contexts might involve. In the final analysis, the most critical advantage of a scheme such as the one we are proposing is that it helps to push thinking on social justice along constructive and rational lines. One of the inescapable dilemmas of caste-based affirmative action policies is that they cannot but help intensifying caste identities. The debate then gets vitiated because it concentrates on the identities rather than on the valid social reasons why those identities are used as indicators of disadvantage. Our scheme clearly links caste identities to measurable empirical indicators of disadvantage. It thus helps to deessentialise caste and to focus attention on the relative progress made by these communities. Transparent indicators justifying the position allotted to particular groups allow room for necessary scrutiny and oversight as well as legitimate debate. The scheme also allows policies to be flexibly calibrated according to the changing relative positions of different groups. It also automatically addresses prickly issues like the legitimate claims of poor or disadvantaged upper castes, or the restraining of the "creamy layer" among lower castes, etc. In short, it allows us to demonstrate in an open and accountable fashion that affirmative action is not about the "appeasement" of particular castes or communities but about abolishing continuing sources of tangible disadvantage in our unequal and unjust society.

Acknowledgement

The scheme outlined here has benefited from the comments and criticisms of many friends, colleagues and interlocutors. We thank Peter D'Souza, Gopal Guru, Mary E. John, Suhas Palshikar, Udit Raj, Mahesh Rangarajan, Ghanshyam Shah, Mihir Shah, Syed Shahabuddin, Abusaleh Shariff and Dhirubhai Sheth. Parts or earlier versions were presented at events hosted by the Programme for the Study of Discrimination and Exclusion, JNU (April 27); the Centre for the Study of Developing Societies (April 28) and Sahmat (May 19); we thank the organisers and participants for their inputs and to the CSDS Data Unit for analysing the NSES Data. A different and much shorter version of this scheme was published in *The Hindu* (May 22 and 23; later translated into Hindi in *Amar Ujala* and Marathi in *Loksatta*) and discussed in programmes on CNN-IBN (May 18) and DD News (May 28). The section 'Mandal II: The Roads Not Taken' uses material that has appeared in the *Times of India* (May 31). We also thank scores of email respondents, both named and "pen-named", most of whom disagreed strongly and sometimes abusively.

Notes

1. The JNU admissions policy provides for reservations for SC and ST students but implements a system of deprivation points on the basis of caste, gender and region for other disadvantaged groups. A candidate seeking admission can get up to a maximum of 10 deprivation points (which are added on to the merit score) as follows: five points for OBCs (10 for OBC women); five points for most backward regions (three for less backward regions); and five points for other groups (Kashmiri migrants and dependants of armed forces personnel killed in action). Our understanding is that the academic merit score is out of a maximum of 100 points, to which the deprivation points (maximum of 10) are added to give the final score.

   Purshottam Agrawal suggests a modified version of this in what he calls 'Multiple Index Related Affirmative Action' (MIRAA). Under this a maximum of 30 deprivation points are awarded (the scheme is intended to cover the SC and ST students as well) as follows: up to five points each for caste, tribe, gender, region and type of schooling; up to six points for economic status; and up to four points for level of parental education. While we have not studied these schemes in detail, initial impressions suggest the following points of difference: Both schemes are additive and do not consider the interaction effects among different axes of disadvantage; this does however have the advantage of simplicity. The JNU scheme does not make a distinction between rural and urban sectors when considering regional backwardness; it also does not differentiate between upper and lower OBCs; finally, the deprivation weightage – a maximum of 10 points out of a total of 110 – appears to be too low to make much difference, specially to lower OBCs. Agrawal's scheme does distinguish between most backward and others among OBCs, but the relative points it awards for the SC/ST categories – five compared to two for upper OBCs – appear to be too low. Also, while parental education is a valid and good indicator, the problem is that lack of education is difficult to document. Moreover, the pitfalls involved in direct self-reporting of income are also well known.

12

Three Myths about Reservations

NEERA CHANDHOKE

Indians, suggests Amartya Sen, possess a long tradition of public debate and reasoned argument. But it is precisely this tradition of reasoned public debate that has been hijacked by the current imbroglio about reservations for the other backward classes (OBCs). Today, our public debate is marked by acrimony, hateful stereotyping, caste determinism, and pathological anxiety. It becomes difficult to engage with this debate from the perspective of public reason. However, it is necessary to do so, simply because too much is at stake. At stake is our entire future as a society that works through contentious issues in a spirit of deliberation, rather than spiteful confrontation. For this it is essential to sort out three myths that continue to dodge the entire dispute about reservations.

The main frame of the confrontation is set by the allegation that reservations contravene the principle of equality. Basically, formal equality is based on the principle of anonymity and substitutability. Every individual has the equal right to access structures of opportunity, as well as participate in the decision-making processes, irrespective of caste, creed, gender, or class. Each, in other words, counts for one. This is best exemplified in the basic precept of democracy – one person one vote. It does not matter whether x is richer than y, when it comes to voting x's vote is as good or as bad as y's vote. 'y' can easily substitute for x. However, not every individual in a highly unequal society like India can profit from opportunities, or participate in decision-making processes equally. A person who lacks the basic necessities of life, i.e., nutrition, clothing, shelter, and as assured income is simply not equal to a rich and often overfed person. This purely empirical fact should be more than visible in India, where poor children are not only non-literate, they are also malnourished and prone to disease, homeless, and who are for these reasons subjected to every indignity that humankind is capable of inflicting on its own. In order to neutralise inequality, the state must provide resources to the underprivileged on non-market principles of free education, assured incomes, nutritious food, and health. This is the minimum that a good society owes to the underprivileged, because every individual has the right to live with dignity. It is not that this argument does not respect what is euphemistically called merit; all it asks for is that every child should be given the chance of translating her or his natural skills into merit, through the provision of basic needs. This will allow him or her to compete with other more privileged children. This version of equality is termed 'egalitarianism'.

Distinguishing Egalitarianism from Humanitarianism

Egalitarianism, it is important to note, is not humanitarianism, which calls for a transfer of resources from the rich to the poor. Humanitarians are concerned with well-being, but egalitarians are concerned with much more. Transfer of resources from the rich to the poor might alleviate harsh deprivation, but it does not make society egalitarian, for the rich will still possess far more resources than the poor. Society will still remain unequal. Egalitarians are concerned with deeper equality. Each individual has an equal pre-political stake in the collective resources of his or her society. If society is organised unequally, then, this right should be met through remedial action: land reform, income generating schemes, equalisation of assets, and provision of resources through collective action. Humanitarians are not concerned with equalising resources; egalitarians are, simply because for them society is a relational entity. No one should command many more resources than his or her share, and no one should command less. This is what distinguishes humanitarianism from egalitarianism. The Left in India, which is presumably well versed in the works of the grand old German, Karl Marx, should be more than aware of this.

But there is another kind of inequality in our society, that of caste. Historically, the dalits have been unable to access education and professions, because of the sickening and inhuman system of purity and pollution, which remains embedded in religious communities across India. Reservations were meant to assure the former "untouchables" a place in the educational system, and in the public professions, not only to counter economic deprivation. The scheduled tribes were granted reservations on another ground that of being far removed from the mainstream of Indian society. In the process, India took a step beyond egalitarianism, even as it provided for these two communities. This has been the unique Indian contribution to the equality debate; it progresses from basic tenets of formal equality, to egalitarianism, to protective discrimination. Of course, there is the phenomenon of the triply disprivileged – a landless dalit woman who suffers from caste, class and gender discrimination and measures should address this phenomenon. The important point is that the founders of the Indian political system grounded their defence of reservations on sound public reason, and on incontrovertible historical facts. Sociologists will have to tell us whether some of the OBCs suffer from the same troubling discrimination on the basis of pollution and purity, if so these castes should be given the benefit of reservations. But castes who suffer only from economic deprivation should be made the recipient of other ameliorative measures, which belong to egalitarianism.

To phrase the point differently, reservations were meant to benefit the doubly disprivileged those who were disprivileged on grounds of caste and class. Denial of education and access to professions had practically ensured that dalits were denied access to income or to dignity. Reservations were meant to amend this double disprivilege. For others who have been historically denied access to structures of opportunity, egalitarianism should ensure a social minimum. In order to counter social and economic disprivilege we need to grant resources. In order to counter caste disprivilege, which bars certain castes from entering education and professions, we need to fortify reservations. In recent debate, however, reservations are being put forth as counters to poverty, and it is precisely here that we have gone wrong. I am particularly puzzled by the stance of the Left in India. Our friends on the Left seem to have abandoned class, and fulsomely adopted caste as their political strategy. In the process they have discarded the basic precepts of egalitarianism and adopted humanitarianism, which might be a good stance but perhaps not a politically sound one for reasons enumerated above.

Confusing Protective Discrimination with Affirmative Action

Secondly, we find an unfortunate tendency to confuse protective discrimination with affirmative action. This is plain silly, because affirmative action in the US is neither based upon quotas, nor on lower eligibility criterion. All things being equal, in the sense of equal qualifications of the candidates, firms that cohere to the affirmative action platform give preference to women and to Afro-Americans. It is the combination of quotas and lower eligibility criterion that marks protective discrimination in India, and this is what gives to the measure a particular clout. Let us not confuse concepts and practices, this makes for bad theory and even worse practice. Finally, reservations are not meant to introduce respect for diversity. This is another theme that pro-reservationists have adopted uncritically from the US and Canada, both of which are immigrant societies and which has only recently discovered that communities of the indigenous people deserve to be recognised. Caste is about inequality, hierarchy, and powerlessness within a religious community, whether Hindu, Sikh or Muslim, and the only concept that can tackle this is that of egalitarianism, and protective discrimination. Diversity is meant to ensure toleration and respect for the other between communities, egalitarianism is meant to ensure a rough and equal access to structures of opportunity within communities.

Reservations are important, but they should be taken seriously and employed sparingly. The dominant perspective of redressing inequality should be egalitarianism, or the provision of a social mini- mum to all that require it. But reservations, which should have formed one component of egalitarianism, have come to substitute for egalitarianism. The victims of history have been compensated in the most minimal of fashion possible. In the process, the realm of egalitarianism has narrowed down rather than expanded. Whereas issues of land reform have been consigned to the dustbin of history, reservations have expanded to rather absurd proportions. For reservations have proved a soft option for political elites, who reluctant to carry out deep-rooted changes in society, would rather opt to enlarge the constituency for reservations in a shrinking state sector and in a declining educational system, than transform ownership of resources in the country. And unfortunately reservations have limited the political imagination of those who fight for social justice. Protective discrimination policies are being defended today for the wrong reasons. At best they amount to humanitarian caring and at worst they belong to vote-gathering devices. Secondly, because the political defences for protective discrimination have become wafer thin, they have aroused hostility. This has exacerbated rather than diminished the problems of caste discrimination that bedevils our society.

13

Affirmative Action

Experiments in the Former Soviet Union, Japan and America

DIPAK BASU

> "If our political progress is to be real, the underdogs of our society must be helped to become men".
>
> — Rabindranath Tagore, *Letters from Russia*

The debate on affirmative action in India tends to drag and is not always geared to the desired objective: creation of equality of opportunity. As with secularism, the reservation system in India has a different political aim – to make the system more unequal than what it is. Secularism, far from making the state independent of religion, is intended to provide special privileges to certain religious groups. Similarly, the affirmative system is politically designed to provide restricted, not equal, rights to some chosen people.

The policy was perhaps started in India by Lord Curzon in 1905 by banning the employment of Hindu Bengalis in government services. The official argument was that they were too advanced and others, particularly Muslims, would be deprived of job opportunities. Later, it was extended to the military services by giving preferential treatment to Muslims and Sikhs who were branded as martial races.

Divide Population

Reservations in government jobs were introduced in 1918 in Mysore in favour of a number of castes and communities that had little representation in the administration. In 1909 and in 1919 the system was introduced for the Muslims in British India. In 1935, political reasons prompted the government to provide job reservation for the backward castes.

The real idea was to divide the population of India into several warring groups along religious, ethnic and caste lines by granting special rights so that India of the future would be divided and weak. A number of prominent politicians had acted as agents of the British Raj to implement that line of action. Among them was B.R. Ambedkar. Although today he is regarded as a founding father of the nation, the writer of the Constitution and the cult figure of the backward castes with four universities named after him, he took no part in the freedom movement. Instead, like E.V.R. Periyarer of Tamil Nadu, C.P. Ramaswamy Aiyar of Kerala, Jinnah and Mohammed Iqbal, he was a staunch loyalist of the empire, hand-in-glove with the British to divide India along caste, religion and tribal lines. The followers of the same person today include the Communists who, forgetting the essentials of the Marx-Lenin ideology, are supporting job reservation along caste and religious lines.

Equality of opportunity is the basis of a true democracy and as such affirmative action is required to equalise opportunities among people who are endowed differently. Even in the USA, affirmative action was promoted first by President Lyndon Johnson in 1974 to promote American blacks, who were deprived of most opportunities. However, it was not a success. The countries where it was most successful are Japan, the former Soviet Union and other former socialist countries of East Europe along with Cuba and Vietnam. India should take a lesson from them to implement a proper policy on affirmative action.

The success of the Soviet society regarding affirmative action was observed by Rabindranath Tagore, who wrote: "Throughout the ages, civilised communities have contained groups of nameless people. They toil most, yet theirs is the largest measure of indignity. They are deprived of everything that makes life worth living. I had often thought about them, but came to the conclusion that there was no help for them.... In Russia at last. Whichever way I look I am filled with wonder. From top to bottom they are rousing everyone up without distinction."

Immediately after the revolution, Lenin proclaimed the affirmative action known as *korenizatsiia* to provide affirmative preferences for non-Russians, backward ethnic groups and poor Russians. To gain the support of the non-Russians, who were largely illiterate except in Georgia and Armenia, a Sovietisation in three phases was developed. In the first phase, the respective cultures were promoted. This aroused their national conscience. This eventually led to the second phase which was rapprochement and finally to the third phase which was merger. Non-Russians were awarded their own administrative territories and accorded preference in educational and promotion policies. This policy led to the creation of massive educational facilities in the republics of the backward people, employment for the representatives of the ethnic intelligentsia, foundation of republican academies of science and research centres supporting ethnic unions of writers, painters and film-makers. The policy was applied uniformly to create elites, which, like their culture, would be national in form, but with the same content in all units of the union.

However, there was no fixed quota in admissions to the educational establishments or in jobs. Instead, education was made free at all stages and compulsory up to certain ages depending on their ethnic background. Every qualified student was entitled to scholarship to cover his or her costs of maintenance. Education was taken to the people where they lived. Even mobile schools and libraries were established for the nomadic populations of Central Asia. A certain number of students from the backward areas of the Soviet Union were taken to the very best universities and institutes of higher learning. They got separate training so that they could compete effectively with the more advanced Russian students.

Due to this social engineering, within two decades, the Soviet Union had eradicated illiteracy and had the best educated population in the world. It was not a reservation system for the backward people, but completely free education and massive extension of education. Both the Soviet Union and Japan improved the lot of the totally uneducated without any formal reservation or quota system but through compulsory free education on a massive scale.

Japanese System

The guiding principle of the Japanese system of education is uniformity, conformity and integration. There is no room for special rights or reservations in that regimented system, which is available equally for everyone.

In the USA, the term 'affirmative action' was first used in the Executive Order 11246, issued by President Johnson. The order called on federal government contractors to "take affirmative action to ensure that applicants are employed, and that employees are treated during employment, without regard to their race, creed, colour, or national origin". However, those who were already educated or advanced financially among the blacks or Hispanics, equivalent to the creamy layers in India, got the benefits. Thus, the affirmative action could not change the basic nature of the most unequal society. There was considerable opposition to the system in the days of Reagan. Today, nearly 26 per cent of the population is functionally illiterate. Social mobility is on the decline. There is widespread homelessness and poverty among the blacks and Hispanics. In a word, affirmative action has not changed the characteristics of American society.

The Policy Comes a Cropper in India

As the reservation system India is based on caste, the government has not been able to improve the lot of the backward or the poor as they may not belong to the castes or tribes entitled to receive aid from the state. This is the major reason why Muslims and Christians are demanding reservation. The reservation system has also led to inter-caste conflict as they have to compete for the limited social and economic benefits.

The failure of the reservation system is all too palpable. Quotas for Scheduled Castes (SCs) in schools and government posts remain largely unfilled, whereas reservations for OBCs are generally filled to capacity. A 1997 study indicates that nationally preferential policies only benefit six per cent of Dalit families. It also reported that "none of India's elite universities and engineering institutes had filled its quota for members of the Scheduled Castes".

The listed classes are largely unrepresented in white collar positions. For the country, as a whole, members of the SCs and STs combined did not receive even 3 per cent of the degrees in engineering or medicine, though together they add up to nearly one-fourth of the population, according to a study by Sowell (2004).

Not Enough

The government provides scholarships to SC students to attend school, but that is not enough. Even when the government provides primary schooling free of charge, the cost of books and supplies may not be affordable to the very poor. For secondary education, rural students may not always find a school nearby. Parents, who cannot afford the cost of commuting or relocating, often find it difficult to send their children to school despite preferential admission policies.

Some SC candidates do better than others, raising the demand in certain quarters for "quotas within the quota". A particular case in point are the Chamars. In Maharashtra, they are the most prosperous among the SCs. A study revealed that they formed 17 per cent of the state's population and represented 35 per cent of its medical students. In Haryana, the Chamars received 65 per cent of the scholarships for the SCs at the graduate level and 80 per cent at the undergraduate level. But 18 of the 37 untouchable groups in Haryana failed to get any preferential scholarship. In Madhya Pradesh, Chamars represent 53 per cent of the total number of SC students in schools. In Bihar, just two of the 12 SCs in the state one being the Chamars accounted for 61 per cent of the SC students in schools and 74 per cent in colleges.

It is time for the government to acknowledge that the policy of affirmative action, based on such unscientific criteria as caste or tribe, introduced by Ambedkar and reinforced by V.P. Singh has failed. However, the government and the political parties, including the Communists, want to preserve this failed system and also extend it by including religion as a parameter.

Writing in *People's Democracy*, the organ of the CPI-M, Teesta Setalvad has pleaded that as Muslims are also backward, they too deserve the benefit of reservations. The Communists seem to have forgotten that class rather than caste, tribe or religion, should be the criteria for affirmative action. They have also forgotten the lesson derived from the former Soviet Union that free education on a mass scale can remove social and economic backwardness. The experience of Japan, Korea, Taiwan and Vietnam also demonstrate that what India could not achieve in 60 years can be achieved within

10 years if the policy framework is designed to remove inequality of opportunity.

To solve the problem, India should introduce reservation based on poverty and physical disability irrespective of religion, tribe or caste. As in Europe, education must be free at all levels, including universities and specialised institutes of higher learning. All students should get automatic grants. Villages should either be consolidated or mobile schools set up in remote areas. As in the former Soviet Union, villages should be equipped with public libraries and reading room to ensure that poor students get space to study. To remove linguistic discrimination and to maintain proper representation of all states, an informal system of fair representation or quota can be introduced for jobs in both the public and private sectors. The caste system must be abolished by law.

Disparities in income and wealth are central to unequal opportunities. Large sections of the rural population still depend on 'mahajans' or moneylenders. The nationalisation of banks in 1969 was aimed at removing the moneylenders from the rural economy. But, since 1991, the government has reversed the system, aggravating poverty among farmers and increasing their dependence on the money-lenders. It is essential for the government to set up a rural banking network to remove the moneylenders and extend educational and business loans to those who might be refused such facilities by private banks.

Affirmative action is not just quota and reservation. It also envisages incentives for the poor. Such incentives cannot be provided without public banking. When job opportunities are rare, reservations for chosen sections can only lead to resentment among the unemployed in the general category who will be deprived just because of their birth.

To quote Albert Einstein, "Unlimited competition leads to huge waste of labour. A planned economy, which adjusts production to the needs of the community, would distribute the work to be done among all those able to work and would guarantee a livelihood to every man, woman, and child."

Unethical System

Economic reform has intensified the mismatch between the availability of jobs and the number of people unemployed. This problem cannot be solved in a market economy that depends increasingly on external forces beyond the control of the national government. Affirmative action is needed to create equal opportunities and remove discrimination. A reservation system based on castes and tribes cannot provide money to the poor students of the backward castes to travel to schools or colleges or to buy books or to have a space to study. Severe poverty exists even among the higher castes and among those who are not qualified to receive the benefits. There are Brahmins among porters and rickshawallas. There is no reason why their children will not receive any benefits. But relatives of Jagjivan Ram, Lalu Prasad, Paswan, Shibu Soren or Mayawati are entitled to reserved vacancies in higher education and jobs. The system that exists in India is unethical in the extreme. However, both the Congress and the CPI-M want to perpetuate and enhance this system of injustice.

14

Indian Toiler Should Reject the Framework of Reservation

KRANTI KUMARA AND KEITH JONES

The plans of India's United Progressive Alliance (UPA) government to expand caste-based reservations in central government-funded universities, including a series of elite professional schools, have provoked widespread student protests and an outcry from the corporate media and big business. Doctors in Delhi, Mumbai and many other cities have mounted walkouts in support of the students and the Indian Medical Association has lent its voice to the protests.

In early April, Human Resource Development Minister Arjun Singh announced that the Congress Party-led UPA intends to set aside 27 per cent of all student entry-places at the All India Institute of Medical Sciences (AIIMS), Indian Institutes of Technology (IITs), Indian Institutes of Management (IIMs), and other centrally-funded universities exclusively for applicants from the Other Backward Classes (OBCs).

The OBCs are a state-defined agglomeration of caste groupings or *jati* who have traditionally been perceived to be socially inferior by the Hindu "twice-born" or upper castes and were found in the 1970s to be socio-economically backward. They constitute about 52 per cent of India's 1.1 billion people.

The designation "Other" distinguishes them from the Scheduled Castes (SCs – the former untouchables or Dalits) and the Scheduled Tribes (STs), who together represent about a quarter of India's total population. Close to sixty years after the Indian state formally decreed the legal equality of the SCs and STs, most continue to live in abject poverty, and they form a grossly disproportionate share of India's landless and illiterate.

The proposed 27 per cent reservation for the OBCs would be in addition to the long existing 22.5 per cent quota of entry-places dedicated to qualified SC and ST applicants. Should it be implemented, 49.5 per cent of all student places at centrally-government universities – those considered to be the country's best – will be subject to "reservations" the Indian term for mandatory affirmative action programmes.

In an attempt to mollify opposition to the expansion of reservations, the UPA government announced that it will increase the total number of student-entry places so as to ensure that the number of "open admissions" – those in the general or non-reserved category – does not fall. This will necessitate an increase in the total number of entry-places of about 50 per cent.

Despite its own repeated claims of serious fiscal pressures, the government says it can find the money to fund this expansion – an estimated initial expenditure of Rs 7,800 crore ($1.7 billion) and a recurring annual expenditure of Rs 2,200 crore ($500 million.) University administrators are largely against the expansion, however. They claim that even with the additional funding they will not be able to find the trained personnel and develop the requisite infrastructure (hostels, laboratories, etc.) to deal with such a sudden and large influx of new students.

The government also announced that legislation sanctioning the expansion of reservations will be brought before the next session of parliament and that the 27 per cent OBC admission quota will take effect as of June 2007.

According to news reports, the Communist Party of India (Marxist)-led Left Front played a major role in convincing the UPA government not to back down in the face of the protests and move forward expeditiously with the introduction of OBC reservations at Central government-funded universities. The government announcements came at the conclusion of a lengthy meeting of the UPA-Left Coordination Committee. Although formally outside the

Congress-led UPA, the Left Front has propped up the UPA government in the parliament for the past two years.

A Populist Cover for Pursuing Neo-liberal Reforms

The government and Left Front claim that the extension of reservations in central government-funded universities to OBC applicants is a blow for social justice and against caste privilege. This is a cynical fraud.

In truth the extension of reservations is meant to provide a populist covering for the government's continued pursuit of neo-liberal socio-economic reforms – reforms that have had a catastrophic impact on hundred of millions of Indians, including the vast majority of the so-called OBCs.

While Indian business and the most privileged layers of the middle class have benefited from India's emergence as a site of cheap-labour production, research and business processing for global markets, India's toilers have seen their livelihoods ravaged by privatisation, deregulation, and the slashing of public services and agricultural price supports. Of late, the government admitted that more than 1,11,000 peasants were driven to suicide by poverty and debt between 1993 and 2003.

Moreover, the extensions of reservations serves to further entrench caste divisions and, as the growing spectacle of pro- and anti-reservation protests demonstrate, threatens to divert anger over the lack of jobs and mounting economic insecurity and social inequality into the dead-end of caste conflict.

That the OBCs face discrimination and are disproportionately represented among the socially disadvantaged is incontestable. The proposed new reservations, however, will benefit only an infinitesimal minority. At issue in the current controversy are no more than 25,000 university-entry places a year.

The "Meritocracy" Fraud

The claims made by those leading the agitation against the government's plans to extend reservation – that they oppose casteism and are the votaries of merit – are no less bogus and reactionary.

Although a smattering of Bharatiya Janata Party (BJP) legislators have associated themselves with the student protests, the Hindu supremacist official opposition has, at least to date, given the government muted support on the reservation issue. Rather than opposition politicians, it is the corporate media and big business that have led the anti-reservation charge.

India's business elite instinctively identifies with the protesting students, who generally come from the most privileged sections of Indian society, and resent government measures that could affect the educational institutes that provide them with much of their professional staff. But their principal motivation in egging on the student protesters is to ensure that the government does not act on its threats to extend reservations to the private sector should business fail to speedily implement voluntary, caste-based affirmative action programmes.

Speaking at a press conference, the president of the Confederation of Indian Industry (CII), R. Seshasayee declared, "Mandatory reservation in any form is not conducive to competitiveness of industry. It is not acceptable."

Business does not want to be saddled with the additional costs of implementing reservations, but just as importantly it opposes any and all state intervention in what it considers to be the prerogatives of proprietorship.

While big business claims to champion the merit principle, what it really is upholding is the grossly unequal and socially regressive outcomes of Indian capitalism – a capitalism that couples the injustices of the freemarket with the legacy of imperialist and caste oppression. The horrendous inequalities of the present social order – an order that denies proper shelter, clean water and three-square meals, let alone equal opportunity, to the majority of Indians – are graphically demonstrated by India's education system. Six decades after Indian independence, a public education system cannot be said to exist, so woeful is the education provided by the state schools. At great sacrifice, even workers and peasants send their children, whenever possible, to private schools.

As a result of poverty and the lack of decent public schools, millions never complete even their primary education. According to the government's own figures, in 2001, close to 35 per cent of all Indians and 50 per cent of all Indian women were illiterate.

Less than 1 per cent of India's population – 10 million people – is currently enrolled in post-secondary colleges and institutes. But, the quality of education that these institutions provide varies enormously. Many are poorly funded and lack the requisite infrastructure. Many graduates, except from the elite universities, fail to find decent jobs. Hence, the desperation even among youth coming from the upper echelons of the middle class to get into the best schools and the intensity of the current protests.

Much is made about the merit of the students who secure places in the top institutions. Given that just 1 to 3 per cent of the hundreds of thousands who sit the entrance examinations each year get admission, they clearly are a talented group. But, even the *Times of India,* which has been strongly supportive of the anti-reservation protests, concedes that few pass without receiving extensive tutoring, and that the cost of such special instruction makes it impossible for those who do not hail from well-to-do families.

While big business now presents itself as an opponent of caste, it has been quite ready to promote India as the world's most populous democracy despite routine caste violence against Dalits in much of rural India, as well as the continuing relegation of the majority of Dalits and tribals and large numbers of other Indians to a subsistence existence. Moreover, the Indian ruling class has patronised and continues to promote casteist and communal parties, including the Hindu supremacist BJP, and has incorporated caste categories into its forms of rule.

Reservations: A Pillar of the Bourgeois Order

Reservations were pioneered by the British colonial state as part of its attempts to cultivate various petty bourgeois elites so as to buttress its rule against the emerging nationalist movement.

Although the bourgeois Indian National Congress mounted controlled mass movements against the British, it ultimately struck a deal with the India's colonial overlords and aborted the anti-imperialist struggle. As part of this abortion, it adopted reservations in parliamentary seats, government jobs and universities for the Dalits and tribals, while instituting a modest land reform that stripped the landlords of their political privileges, but left the roots of caste oppression in the historic inequity of India's land relations essentially untouched.

Six decades of post-independence reservations have done nothing to lift the overwhelming majority of Dalits and tribals from poverty, yet they have nourished a small petty bourgeois layer that zealously promotes caste identities and politics, while at the same time defending the capitalist social order.

A similar process has taken place with the OBCs, although pressure for the defining of such a caste grouping came much later and was fuelled by the growing crisis of the post-independence Congress project of national economic development, on the one hand, and the emergence of a relatively small, but politically influential, layer of prosperous erstwhile peasant farmers, on the other.

It was the Janata Party government – a coalition that united dissident elements of Congress, social democrats, and the Hindu supremacist right and which came to power after Indira Gandhi sought to contain mounting social discontent through her authoritarian Emergency – that struck a commission to investigate what measures should be taken to ameliorate the condition of the "socially and educationally backward classes", a grouping it defined first and foremost by *jati* and *varna* castes.

Basing itself on the 1931 census (since the purportedly secular Indian state had ceased to compile information on caste affiliation), the Mandal Commission identified 3,743 *jati* as belonging to the socially and educationally backward classes, a grouping that has become known in popular parlance as the OBCs. Subsequently, the government set up a permanent bureaucracy named the National Commission for Backward Classes (NCBC) with a mandate to periodically update this caste catalogue.

The Janata government fell from power before the Mandal Commission had filed its final report. But, in 1989, under conditions where India's nationally regulated and protected economy was mired in crisis, the National Front government of Congress-renegade V.P. Singh seized on one of Mandal's proposals – the reservation of 27 per cent of Central government jobs for OBCs – to try to burnish his government's claims to be a people's, even socialist, alternative to the Congress.

The reservation issue quickly became a *cause célèbre* with the Stalinist Communist Parties, which joined forces with V.P. Singh and various parties that claim to represent the lower castes in pressing for the implementation of the OBC reservation. Meanwhile, university students, supported by sections of the media, staged noisy anti-reservation protests.

Within this context, the Hindu supremacist BJP came forward to exploit the fears and prejudices of the middle class, as well as those whose families have traditionally been defined as upper caste, to agitate in the name of Hindu/national unity for the building of a temple to the Hindu god Ram on the site of a famous mosque in Ayodhya. This agitation culminated in the razing of the Babri Masjid in December 1992 and the worst anti-Muslim communal violence since the partition of the sub-continent in 1947.

Official politics in the early 1990s were dominated by the caste and communal effervescence promoted by the agitations over the Mandal Report and Babri Masjid. During this time, the Indian ruling class, with the connivance of the Stalinists, successfully escaped the potentially revolutionary consequences of the collapse of its national development strategy and carried through a major strategic reorientation – India's full integration of into the world capitalist economy, so as transform it into a cheap labour haven for global capital.

Likewise, the UPA government is bringing forward the reservation issue at a time of acute social crisis, with the aim of giving itself a populist guise and so as to be assist it in pursuing a socio-economic programme with incendiary consequences for the vast majority of India's population.

And, once again, there is a grave danger that the Stalinists will enable the Indian ruling class to divert the mass social discontent of India's toilers into mobilisations focussed on the rationing of education places and jobs – that is the rationing of capitalist misery – on caste lines. Such politics leaves the programme of big business and the capitalist social order unchallenged and reinforces caste divisions, thereby allowing the bourgeoisie to press forward with the implementation of its neo-liberal policies and opening the door for the BJP and other ultra-right forces to falsely present themselves to the rural and urban middle class as their defenders.

The *World Socialist Website* urges India's toilers not to fall into this trap. A genuine struggle against caste oppression is possible only through a movement led by the working class that mobilises all sections of the oppressed, irrespective of caste, religion or ethnicity, against the UPA government and the capitalist social order.

IV

Why Reservation for OBCs?

15

Case for Caste-Based Quotas in Higher Education

JAYATI GHOSH

Reservation in public sector education and employment is a particularly (but not uniquely) Indian practice enshrined in the Constitution, a legal form of affirmative action designed to provide greater opportunities to communities and social groups that have been traditionally deprived and excluded. While the quotas in public sector employment and education that are allocated for scheduled castes (SCs) and scheduled tribes (STs) are now taken for granted in most discussions, the current debate is around the recent decision of the Union Ministry of Human Resource Development to provide quotas for backward castes in all institutions of higher learning funded by the Central government. There is no question that this is a highly emotive subject; the current protests leave no doubt about the passions that are aroused by what may appear to be one of the less significant of government policies in terms of the number of people it directly affects. Indeed, it is interesting to find that so much very strong reaction has been generated among people who otherwise would automatically condemn public action such as strikes, demonstrations, etc., and are hardly ever involved in them, or aroused by "public" issues. Not only that, but the (relatively few) strikes and street protests by those who are against reservation have received disproportionate attention and coverage in both electronic and print media. The role of the mainstream media in covering both the policy decisions and the subsequent anti-reservation reactions deserves further commentary. It is quite remarkable that, even in the past year, very large demonstrations involving tens of thousands of people, and sometimes even hundreds of thousands of people, involving crucial issues of survival and livelihood (such as direct job losses, or the impact of displacement and the lack of rehabilitation) or concern about national policies that affect the entire citizenry (such as signing international treaties with possibly adverse conditions), have received desultory treatment in the mainstream media. They have been largely ignored by television and obtained minuscule coverage on the inside pages of newspapers. In sharp contrast, when even a few hundred students – and mostly even less – have gathered in protest against reservations or engaged in any other form of protest, there has been almost continuous and prime time coverage on all the national television news channels and front page banner headlines have graced the major newspapers. The nature of the coverage also has had little pretension to objectivity and leaves no doubt as to the biases and prejudices of most of the media, who – like so much of the other elites in India – "just happen" to be upper caste.

Reaction of Media

In fact, the reaction of the media, along with the response of others in privileged positions, throws a lot of light on the undercurrents of social discrimination that are still so pervasive amongst us. Indian society is probably unique in the complex, subtle and yet deep and widespread forms of social discrimination that have developed historically, and which have withstood the many challenges posed by the modernisation process. These peculiarly Indian forms of social stratification have combined with other more structural forms of inequality such as property ownership and access to economic opportunities. So caste divisions have not really been eroded by other economic and political changes, but have been made more complex and subterranean, and have sometimes even been reinforced by such changes.

It would be a mistake to blame this on cynical politicians who manipulate caste sentiment for their own ends, or on government policies that use caste identities for differential treatment, since these essentially recognise an existing reality and do not create it. The rise of political parties based on caste identity – which in itself should be a cause for distress, since it serves to distract from so many other critical issues – also reflects this underlying reality, rather than creating it. The truly extraordinary thing about Indian society is the degree to which it has been resistant to all the various attempts by governments and civil society to dislodge caste perceptions (which are often unacknowledged, but no less powerful for that) from determining patterns of discrimination and social exclusion, and how new forms of "caste" have come up in the midst of all this. This is evident from the very composition of the elites. It is not common in public discussion to inquire into the caste composition of any group that "matters" in the establishment in general – in terms of material wealth, the exercise of power, involvement in skilled professions, or even the ability to influence policies and opinion. In fact, such a question would be considered not merely impolite but also revanchist and backward-looking. But, despite this squeamishness in public discourse, it is unfortunately still the case that any examination of caste origins is likely to reveal that all such elite groups "just happen" to be dominated by upper castes and social groups that account for no more than 20 per cent of the population.

Of course, in the case of the SCs and STs, discrimination is more evident since it has been historically compounded by oppression, which still continues in blatant and often vicious form in many parts of the country. This has persisted despite the official policy of reservations for these communities in government employment and public institutions of higher education, but it does not reflect the "failure" of reservation policy so much as inadequate implementation of it in both letter and spirit. It also shows that exclusion is not something that social institutions stop doing in "voluntary" fashion, in response to a more general social pressure for affirmative action, since the exclusion of SCs and STs is particularly marked in private sector education and employment.

The case of "Other Backward Classes" (OBCs) is more complicated, since there is no similar history of overt oppression. Rather, it is the simple exclusion of what turns out to be the majority of the population, and effective "cornering" of the privileges offered by both public and private establishments by a relatively small proportion of the population. This is almost inevitably the case unless there has been an overt concern with diversity and including others from different backgrounds, or where there has actually been (as in Tamil Nadu, for example) a tradition of the same quota systems that are being resisted in North India today. So, it is hardly surprising that there is so much resentment among the vast majority of the population, which have been so excluded from various forms of privilege.

Indeed, few people would deny the reality of continued discrimination and exclusion, and certainly even the opponents of reservation, such as the protesting students and medicos, accept this reality. Therefore, the debate appears to hinge more on the precise form that affirmative action should take, and whether there should be a quota-based system rather than a more complex and voluntary system based on several different indicators of deprivation. Those who oppose the policy of reservation operate primarily with the following arguments:

- It does not address the basic problem of inadequate expansion and poor quality of public education at elementary and secondary levels.
- It militates against "merit" and allows degrees and qualifications to be awarded with less than deserving aptitude and performance.
- It is "inefficient" compared with openly competitive and therefore implicitly "market-based" systems.
- It creates perceptions of "victimhood" and democratically undesirable identity politics.
- Inequalities within the specified communities allow a "creamy layer" to take advantage of the reservations and benefit unduly while depriving the rest of the community.
- The rigid and inflexible nature of the instrument of reservation does not allow for more creative modes of affirmative action.
- It privileges caste-based discrimination and therefore ignores other and possibly more undesirable forms of exclusion.
- It compresses the notion of social justice into only reservation, instead of encompassing broader socio-economic policies such as land reform and other asset redistribution, strategies of income generation, etc. There is certainly some relevance to each of these points. Certainly no one would deny that the system that has operated in India thus far has been inadequate

not only in addressing these issues, but even in achieving the goals set in terms of filling the allocated quotas for SCs and STs in public education and employment. It is also true that caste-based quotas are relatively crude and blunt instruments to address a very complex socio-economic reality. But all of the arguments against them are also flawed. I will consider several of the more prominent arguments in turn, and finally conclude that quotas currently remain the most effective instrument among the many imperfect instruments available to us in dealing with this issue.

Education for All

A peculiar feature of the current debate is that anti-reservationists (many of whom have rarely bothered about issues of mass education before this, and are also resistant to other education policy proposals such as common schooling based on neighbourhoods) present the problem as a choice between reservations, on the one hand, and better primary and secondary education for all, on the other. But, the two are not alternative choices at all.

Of course, it is true that the quota issue has become so prominent mainly because poor performance in education is among the major failures of the development project in India thus far. And, there can be no debate on the need to provide universal good quality education up to secondary level for all of our population. There are huge inadequacies in government school infrastructure (with an inadequate number of schools, nearly one-fifth of rural schools operating without any building at all and another one-fifth functioning with only one classroom and one teacher for up to five classes).[1] Across India in the government school system, there are massive problems in terms of too few teachers, uneven quality of teachers and other staff and lack of prior or continuous training for school teachers. But this requires really massive increases in spending on education by the government, which are not immediately forthcoming, and for which there has been no concerted campaign even by those who now raise this as the main issue.

This is certainly a priority matter, and there must be public pressure to ensure that the government goes even part of the way in this, for example by meeting its commitments made in the national common minimum programme and in the right to education bill. But this is still a different issue from the need to address and reduce social discrimination, which requires – in addition to more and better public schooling – different measures. Note that this is not about economic inequality but social exclusion. Nearly 60 years after independence, it is not possible to ask the majority of the population, which has been excluded so far from elite institutions, to wait until the promised increases in quantity and quality of public education finally come about, while a small elite continues to garner all the benefits of the public investment that have been made so far. What quotas seek to do is to ensure that a wider set of social groups get access to the higher education institutions that do exist, than occurs at present.

Issues of "Merit" and Efficiency

The most common argument against reservations is that they will affect quality and undermine "merit". But, the supposed contradiction between reservations on the one hand, and merit and efficiency on the other, is a false one. First of all, there are many reasons to believe that drawing upon a wider social base increases the diversity and, therefore, the quality of institutions of higher education. Secondly, there are good reasons to be sceptical regarding the extent to which current systems of selection are genuinely "merit" based. Internationally, there is substantial theoretical literature on the co-existence of markets and discrimination (whether in terms of caste, community or gender), and on how such discrimination reduces the efficiency of the economy – in which case affirmative action to reduce such discrimination can only increase efficiency.[2] It is well known that the Indian private sector employs wide-ranging discriminatory practices (such as inheritance determining managerial control, preferential employment based on social networks, and so on) which are inherently inefficient. It is now widely accepted across the world that diversity makes economies more, rather than less, competitive. The example of countries like Malaysia, which combined a very severe and restrictive form of reservation and other affirmative action with remarkable economic growth for several decades, points to this.

But how truly competitive is the current system of selection that operates for the elite higher education institutions in India? We are all agreed that there is huge excess demand for higher education in the country, and that good quality higher education is extremely under-provided. Therefore, there is severe rationing for places, especially in the best institutions. The question is therefore not whether we should have rationing or not, but, which form of rationing is the best in the prevailing social circumstances.

It is currently believed that the current system is based on "merit", that is, ranking of performance in all-India entrance examinations or such similar criteria. Yet any teacher or administrator at some of these top institutions (such as IITs or IIMs) will agree that there are typically several hundred candidates of equally good quality at the top, and they are able to admit only a small fraction of them, so that there is a large element of luck and randomness in the process of selection.

For example, at the national entrance examination to the IITs every year, there are more than 3,00,000 entrants, yet only around 3,000 gain admittance to the various IITs. Yet it is quite likely that the top 20,000 are equally good if not better than those few who are fortunate enough to get selected, since performance at one single examination is rarely a complete indicator of actual aptitude or quality. In any case it is also well known that these entrance tests typically test not intelligence or ability in the subject per se, but a certain aptitude for answering such tests. This is itself a skill that can be learnt, and there are now training institutes all over the country, especially in certain cities for this purpose. Such training in turn costs time and money, which effectively excludes most potential candidates. So, the flourishing "coaching" industry for these competitive examinations amounts to another form of exclusion, or "reservation" for those who can afford to spend enough time and resources to ensure this prior coaching.

A further reservation effectively exists for those who can come in through "NRI quotas" which are now to be found in many institutions, or in institutions which require capitation fees or charge very large annual fees from students. This is a system of reservation of seats in higher education based on wealth, parental income or access to credit in the expectation of future incomes – all of which exclude the majority of the population. It is interesting that the sudden and apparent concern about merit has not touched on the implications of such admissions based on fees and whether students who get in through this means are "deserving" or not, although such processes have been going on for years.

If we accept that intelligence and talent are not the monopoly of any particular social group but are normally distributed across society, then this means that the current system is inefficient since it is effectively picking up candidates from only a small section of society instead of the whole population. It is elementary logic that this would give sub-optimal results for society. This is an argument on social efficiency grounds, which is quite separate from other arguments about creating a more democratic and inclusive education process in general.

The most convincing empirical argument against the idea that reservations will inevitably lead to inferior quality comes from the actual experience in several southern states, where there have been large quotas on seats in higher education in operation for several decades. In Tamil Nadu, for example, reservations account for around two-thirds of such seats, even in private institutions, and in Karnataka they are close to half. Yet there is no evidence of inferior quality among the graduates of such institutions; instead, it is widely acknowledged that graduates from the medical and professional colleges in the south are among the best in India. Surely, no one would contest that Vellore Medical College, for example, is one of the best medical colleges in India; yet, it has consistently operated with an extensive system of reservations accounting for more than half of the seats. It is notable that even in the north, elite "minority institutions" such as St. Stephens' College in Delhi University have functioned for decades by reserving around half the students' seats for different categories, and still maintained their reputation of being among the best in the country.

Economic Inequalities and Creamy Layers

It is true that reservations do not address the most fundamental problems of economic inequality or access to opportunities in India. There is no question that asset inequalities and related income inequalities are at the heart of the issue of unequal access in our country. So it is clear that reservations can in no sense be seen as any kind of substitute for the more serious and still necessary strategies of change with respect to land reform and other asset redistribution.

In turn, the lack of asset ownership among deprived communities is critical in determining other forms of discrimination. Deprivation in terms of early access to quality education is increasingly becoming the most crucial determinant of subsequent life achievement for many socially and economically marginalised groups. The emergence of professional activities and "knowledge-based" employment as a major source of not just income but also privilege has meant that ownership of physical property is not the only means to material comfort and economic enhancement. Higher education, especially in certain areas and in certain professional courses, has become the most obvious means to mobility and access to both material wealth and social privilege. Inequality of access to this increasingly important source of economic and social mobility compounds the structural inequalities created by asset ownership. This is precisely the reason why it has emerged as an area of social contestation and why the apparent monopolisation of even such access by a relatively small number of upper castes is seen as so unfair by the majority of the population. This is why the demand for reservation in higher education for deprived social groups has such strong political resonance.

However, there are some complications in this matter. The first is the issue that is frequently raised, about the relative significance of economic inequality and social deprivation. It is argued that the main divide in India is economic, and that economically speaking, many of the so-called "backward castes" are not at all deprived, either in terms of property ownership or control over resources stemming from political power. The system of reservations would allow these relatively better off groups within the OBCs as generally defined to corner all the benefits, excluding those who are more genuinely in need of special concessions. Meanwhile, the poor and needy among upper caste students would not only receive no benefit in terms of scholarships, etc., but would also be deprived of access despite being more "deserving".

Economic inequality, while important, requires a separate set of measures which must operate in addition to others that are devoted to rectifying social discrimination. The most important way to deal with this in higher education is a system of needs-blind admission in all institutions combined with very extensive provision of scholarships, so that no student is prevented from access to higher education because of lack of resources. This is something that should be implemented across public institutions with immediate effect, and rules need to be framed for ensuring similar systems in privately-run institutions as well. This would actually be in contrast to recent trends in higher education, where the proportion of scholarships provided to students in higher education has been declining, even as costs of higher and professional education have been rising steadily, thereby imposing a significant burden not only on poor families but even on the middle classes. So, there is certainly a strong case for reducing disparities in access to higher education resulting from income differentials. But, this is different from the impact of social discrimination, which, as pointed out above, requires specific and separate measures. The second issue relates to the fact that some "OBCs" are not really socially, politically or economically backward and have been included in the list mainly because of political pressure and because the original list in the famous report of the Mandal Commission was derived in a somewhat haphazard way. Clearly, there is a case for a systematic survey and assessment of the current social context, which would allow for a more systematic listing of OBCs, avoiding as far as possible the errors of unjustified inclusion or unfair exclusion. So, the government should undertake a more careful assessment of "backwardness" to enable the proposed reservations to be implemented in the most socially desirable way. This is an urgent task for social scientists, many of whom are unfortunately more occupied in railing against the proposed reservations than in thinking of ways to make them truly effective.

The third issue relates to differences within deprived communities and castes, whereby an elite within the caste group that has benefited from past systems of reservation, or which has disproportionate political/economic power, can grab the benefits and leave the majority still deprived. This is the problem of the "creamy layer", which is currently receiving much attention. Once again, this is not a trivial issue, and clearly something that needs to be addressed, even though it could be argued that centuries of exclusion and deprivation cannot be corrected in one generation alone. Several methods of dealing with the creamy layer have been proposed: for example, an economic cut-off, above which there would be no eligibility for a reserved seat; or allowing a maximum of two or three generations of any particular family to benefit from reservations. These have their merits, especially as they are not so difficult to administer, and could be considered as part of the package to ensure that the system is as just and fair as possible.

Reservations versus Other Forms of Affirmative Action

Caste-based reservations are often critiqued on more sophisticated grounds as well. One criticism is that they promote unhealthy forms of identity politics that distract from more substantive and critical social issues. However, this argument tends to mistake cause for effect in social analysis, assuming that caste consciousness is a creation of the government's policies rather than a historical tendency that has permeated our society and meshes in complex ways with other more current social attributes. The very fact that so many people who constitute the elite can claim to be without caste consciousness, even while they "just happen" to come from certain castes (as noted above), testifies to the extensive discrimination that runs so deep in Indian society that it can even appear to be invisible. While such innocence may be excused to some extent among the elites in general, it is indefensible in social scientists who should know better. Caste-based identity politics has emerged as such a powerful force not because it has been generated by public policy, but because public policy has for too long swept it under the carpet, and thereby allowed patterns of discrimination to replicate and become more entrenched. (Similarly, the greater demands for more gender equality and women's empowerment that are being made both socially and politically are certainly not the result of public policy promoting gender differences, but rather emerge from past and present gender oppression and discrimination against women.)

A more persuasive argument against reservations is that they do not allow for more flexible and creative forms of affirmative action that would incorporate more complex criteria of deprivation. In particular, a case is made for a more comprehensive "deprivation index" that would incorporate a range of criteria where differences in access are known to exist. For example, such an index could take account of rural or urban residence, gender differences, income differences, and so on – since in all of these, there is strong evidence of differential access to higher education. Such a system certainly appears attractive, especially as it would be a more apparently just and efficient way of ensuring diversity as well. The problem with such schemes is two-fold: they are very complex to administer, and indeed impossible on a national scale; and because they incorporate a number of different criteria, with unclear impact, they can end up not actually ensuring a more diverse student intake as desired.

Thus, such schemes can work in those institutions for which there is a national entrance examination, but that is the case in only relatively few institutions. Even in these cases, there is already evidence of strong regional bias, with applicants from some metros and certain cities where there is a proliferation of "coaching institutes" dominating the examination results. Further, if a deprivation index involves simply adding numbers onto existing examination marks rather than quotas, it does not necessarily ensure that the final student intake will actually be diverse. The most telling argument, however, is a practical one: the larger the number of criteria that are evoked, the greater are the administrative costs of such a system, and the greater the pressure on individual students to procure the necessary certificates, etc. For most institutions, the costs of administering such a system, with uncertain effects in terms of resulting student diversity, will become an excessive burden compared to the greater simplicity of a quota system. So, while reservations have been inadequate and relatively rigid instruments of affirmative action, they do have certain advantages which explain why they have been preferred. They are transparent, inexpensive to implement and monitor and therefore easily enforceable. Any other system of affirmative action must have these attributes in order to be practical.

Another proposal that has been made is a voluntary system of affirmative action to be enforced by the higher education institutions themselves, which would then be periodically monitored to ensure that it fulfils certain criteria of diversity. Once again, this is an attractive idea, especially because it would allow for flexibility and recognition of the particular features of different institutions. The problem with systems based on the periodic audit of institutions to check on their "diversity" is that they do not have the transparency and enforceability of quotas. Also, unfortunately in India, the experience with voluntary action is thus far dismal. We have too many examples of this not only with respect to caste but also in other areas where we are still relying on voluntary action, and where inevitably those chosen "just happen" to be the already privileged. Even in areas where there are legally binding commitments, such as in the case of private hospitals and medical clinics that have benefited from public land and other government subsidies on the promise of providing a certain number of free beds and cheaper medical care to poor patients, there has been an appalling lack of adherence to these promises or even responses to Supreme Court strictures. So hoping for a sudden change of culture whereby individual institutions of higher education will themselves enforce effective systems of affirmative action is probably too idealistic: if they wanted to do so, they could and would have done so already. If they do not want to do so, there are too many ways of avoiding it in the absence of some compulsion.

One of the problems of the current system of reservation in the public sector is that there has been no institutional mechanism of incentives and disincentives to ensure effective affirmative action. At the moment, there are "legal" requirements for filling certain quotas, but there are no penalties for public institutions that do not fill them, or rewards for those that more than fulfil them. That is at least part of the reason why so many quotas remain unfulfilled. So this may be one of the issues that deserve greater attention: how to ensure that quotas do actually get filled.

The basic issue, of course, is that the roots of discrimination go so deep that social and economic disparities are deeply intertwined, although in increasingly complex ways. In this imperfect world, none of the proposed solutions is perfect either: the choice is between imperfect instruments with different degrees of effectiveness. That is why we still need reservations for different groups in higher education – not because they are the perfect instruments to rectify long-standing discrimination, but because they are still the most workable method to move in this direction. And most of all, because the nature of Indian society ensures that without such measures, social discrimination and exclusion will only persist and be strengthened.

Notes

1. As indicated by the NSSO, *Report on Education Infrastructure*, 1996-97.
2. Some of this literature is surveyed in Thorat et.al., (eds.) 2005.

Reference

Sukhadeo Thorat, Aryama and Prashant Negi (eds.) (2005): *Reservation and Private Sector: Quest for Equal Opportunity and Growth,* Indian Institute of Dalit Studies and Rawat Publications, New Delhi.

16

Reservation without Reservation

T. PRADEEP

Suddenly, we are into another storm. As usual, we have shown that our interests and solutions are only peripheral. I have been concerned about the issue, but hesitated to write, as in our developed society, disagreement often damages career and personal well-being. As John Ralston Saul says it is normal not to react. Yet, to be alive, it is necessary to be sensitive to the world around. May be in the era of opportunistic politics, your reactions may not lead to much apparent benefit; nevertheless they may make certain individuals think differently. The bottom line is that people largely are good, although those governing them may be the opposite. Let us not, however, forget that we have a functioning democracy, its defects notwithstanding, with several well-meaning individuals at responsible positions, which makes it possible to discuss issues.

In this small piece, I plan to look at the reservation issue in totality and not to comment on the various aspects of its OBC avtar.

I have been fortunate to study in the best institutions in the country and abroad and had opportunities to work with the best minds in my chosen area of science, although born in a village where electric bulbs glowed when I was in the Masters. I have not forgotten the days of the kerosene lamp and the weeks spent tilling the land and tending to the vegetables grown in the paddy fields during summers. During my school days, over 25 years ago, the Dalits, who worked in the fields, were given rice porridge in banana leaves placed in pits dug in the courtyard, several metres away from the house. The quality of food and the way it is served have improved these days, but still done outside the house, in the verandah, in the back or in the front. At least some of us eat with the workers, but there is some hidden separation. This is the situation today in one of the forward-looking, pro-Left houses of Kerala, the most literate state of India. This may be contrasted with the situation where I teach, in an IIT, where in some houses, the cookware, washed by a servant from the lower caste, are re-washed before use. Extreme situations of untouchability prevail in certain parts of India.

Discussing caste in public is not considered a welcome social behaviour, although it is deeply rooted in the society. In the six decades of independence, we have only increased caste-based divides. In fact, every form of inequality is on the rise. Look at the rise of the wedding extravaganza, dowry and sex mafia: women have not been liberated. Look at the landholdings in metros, positions of importance in public service, respectable jobs with reasonable income and any number of parameters you take: the marginalised communities do not have adequate representation. Those who do not have money are not listened to; their dignity is robbed in police stations, hospitals and offices. They can give birth in the open and their nudity does not arouse media attention. Black is still not an accepted colour of skin when it comes to beauty, aristocracy, wealth, prosperity, etc.

Yet, it is the black (well, in the international sense, the black side of the brown) who produce grains on which this country lives. It is the underprivileged whose sweat makes the roads and the buildings; the development you see out there is due to their muscle. It is true that a majority of the Dalits, even today, are manual labourers. Some of us, fortunate to be here in these rooms to discuss (or read) the issue of reservation will burn out in one day, if subjected to the torture they go through day after day, year after year. Yet, in the ultimate analysis, their work may have produced far better social good than ours. They too have to live in this 'developing' and 'goggling' India, which they contribute in building. Of course, we owe something to them, because this country is built on their generations of suffering. In fact, on this point, no one disagrees.

But charity is not the way as it has not served any social purpose in any nation. It has not lifted people from the drudgery of day-to-day life. It has not removed child labour and violence in impoverished societies. We need something better. Caste-based reservation, as an option for removing social inequality, has failed in the past several decades. Those with better vote banks, more control over them and with better pressure tactics gained and got themselves included in the reserved list. Now every community is trying hard to be reserved in some category or the other as being 'reserved' brings security for the next generation. For getting themselves reserved, parties are born. We wanted to remove social inequality, but instead more divisions appeared. In fact, the present growth of pressure groups would make the whole population reserved in some class or the other in the foreseeable future. The policies we frame, work against the very objective for which they were created!

What has reservation produced?

A privileged group among the reserved has been created, who compete against their brethren to enjoy the benefits. This competition goes on and on and as a result, a 'creamy layer' or super-caste within caste, has evolved. Its members are similar to the privileged of the unreserved class, except for the apparent biological manifestations, which unfortunately the years of reservation could not erase. The reserved who enjoyed the benefits refused to acknowledge the fact that they were recipients of social support and considered the two-three letter acronym a curse and tried to hide it as much as possible, except when it came to admissions, recruitment, jobs and promotions. Mind you, I do not blame them as these acronyms are treated with contempt, even decades after the word 'Harijan' was coined. The fortunate among the reserved, who got admissions for better courses, did their best within their ability; got jobs, promotions, accommodation, social benefits, contacts, etc., and this continued for decades. It is natural that once the benefits of reservation are available to an individual, those continue along his/her family tree, forcing others in the community to compete with them.

The majority, who does not enjoy the comforts, become further marginalised. As the size of the reservation pie is not increasing, the benefits of reservation do not reach the other sections of the less privileged. This goes on and the results of this are seen in all institutions. The first generation reserved will decrease in number (or has it started already?) as time goes on. In the house of the officer, who enjoyed the reservation benefits, a maid servant from the reserved caste is most often not allowed to share the dining table. The class-based tambra has replaced the caste-based one. It is unlikely that marriages happen between widely separated social hierarchies. The new rulers among the class evolved get economic, political and intellectual superiority. Another animal farm got institutionalised.

So, where do we go?

Let us understand the objectives of reservation policies. Ideally, we want to create a system in which the less privileged gets an opportunity to compete and excel. The structure of such a policy should be such that it removes the very need to have it erased over a finite period. The statement, although simple, is hard to implement in practice. A successful application would imply concerted efforts of all, in various spheres of activity. It must remove social/religious/caste/creed-based imbalances in all spheres, and if it happens, it would be our second freedom struggle. It is only natural that we, who do not have the might of the Mahatma, looked at softer options.

Enough of the argumentative Indianness. What are the solutions? But, before that let us be clear of the facts: The caste system evolved over a very long period and it continues to thrive in our midst. It needs only common sense to see that any caste-based policy will divide us further. You cannot negate one by using the very same yardstick. Obviously, a solution to this problem requires the wisdom of the whole country, since all of us have contributed to create this in the first place.

Let us also be clear of the following. Caste, in a larger sense of human inequality, exists in every country and fundamentally it is impossible to get rid of this mindset. What is possible to create by any social system, however, is equality in terms of opportunities. Rest of the imbalances have to be removed by the competence of the humans themselves, by mechanisms such as education. By the practice of a proper policy, the Nair, Namboodiri and Iyengar suffixes may shrink to mere last names, but they are unlikely to disappear. I recall that some of the suffixes we have are centuries old.

I make the following suggestions in the time frame of 25 years:

1. Every child, at the time of registration in a school, should be given an electronic identity, which will be nationally linked. This will be the identity of the person, connected to every transaction.
2. Provide free and compulsory education to all children till high school (Class 10). That is, no child can be found on the streets or match factories, for whatever reason.
3. Free senior secondary high school education for the deserving of the marginalised.
4. The deserving, reserved category students after senior high school are given one option to choose their course of interest among the possibilities they are eligible for (in the 12-year period, from the point of implementation of this policy, it is assumed that college admission in the country will be e-linked). This will be the last and final option. Education for that course, till its successful completion, under certain established norms, will be supported by the government.
5. Those who did not qualify for point 4 above, will have the opportunity to appear against the reserved quota in government jobs till they get one.
6. Those who enjoyed the benefits of reservation will acknowledge this fact and it will be known to public.
7. There will not be reservation or quota for promotions.
8. The benefits outlined here will start from 10th and 12th year of implementation and the existing quota will be systematically reduced in a fixed time frame.
9. Implement this policy for 25 years (with periodic review and modifications), through a separate mission, undisturbed by politics.
10. Implement it in such a way that the structure created for this can be fragmented and made part of other ministries and institutions after its intended purpose.

Notes

'Reserved' and 'marginalised' in the points above mean those without means.

'Free' in points 2 and 3 means, with financial assistance, not waiving tuition fee.

Point 4: Various aspects of 'deserved' and 'successful completion' need discussion. Quantum and eligibility of support will depend on income levels and the generation of reservation benefit enjoyed.

Questions

Where to find resources? I say, the answer is: the Great Indian Will. As a teacher, let me also add, it is the young in this country who are going to pay for it and let them decide which India they want to live in. From what I know of the young Indians, I am sure, there will be enough and more to pay for it. Is the timescale enough? Indians living abroad in developed (in the conventional sense) nations have a message for us. Regardless of their educational, cultural or economic background, their second generation is as good as, or better than the natives. They earned their position through competition, in a system of equal opportunities. If we fail to realise the magnitude of the problem and do not implement the right solution with our collective wisdom, India will be the only society in which caste, class and knowledge based divisions co-exist even in 2100. It will truly be a madhouse, this time the whole country, not only Kerala – what a pitiful remembrance of Swami Vivekananda's disgusted remark!

17

Equality with Social Justice

R. ARUN KUMAR

"You do not take a person who, for years, has been hobbled by chains, bring him to the starting line in a race and then say, 'you are free to compete with all others'. It is not enough just to open the gates of opportunity. All our citizens must have the ability to walk through those gates", says Lyndon Johnson, former US President (in a famous speech in 1965 that laid the foundations for the affirmative action in America). These days, the papers are full of the word 'equality', a term otherwise of not much credence to them. The 'youth for equality' by stating that they are for 'equality' and against reservations, have made clear their intentions on the reservation policy as one that breeds inequality and thus is unjust. Like Bush, they are branding all those who are opposed to the stand taken by the 'youth for equality' as being against equality. The question that arises and needs to be examined is whether it is possible to achieve equality without caring for social justice.

In Indian society, whether we like it or not, caste is a reality. Any interested reader can see scores of literate, professional persons advertising in matrimonial columns of newspapers seeking marriage from the opposite sex belonging to the same caste. In spite of the dramatic displays of blood and asking its caste by our upholders of 'equality', the reality is that many of the premier institutes breed caste and are places of caste discrimination. Even in the recent agitation against reservations, some of the dominant upper caste members among the faculty warned the students coming from the OBC, SC and ST families not to speak out in favour of reservations. Their entire argument that merit does not exist in these sections and they become professionals sans quality also speaks volumes of their caste prejudice. The incidents of coloured answer sheets given to SC and ST students to identify them in the examinations or the upper caste students calling SC/ST students as 'shuddus' are too recent to be forgotten. What is surprising is the belated reaction of the judiciary, which is otherwise overzealous in taking *suo moto* cognizance of many issues and in intervening to stop or curb the protests. The not-so-surprising reaction came from the media.

Reality of Caste Discrimination

Together with caste, discrimination based on caste too is a reality. The bias on the basis of caste has a huge influence on our society with its pangs not leaving even the education system. It starts from the entry level and shadows you till you leave it. A position paper by the NCERT's 'National Focus Group on Problems of Scheduled Caste and Scheduled Tribe Children' notes that "several studies have affirmed that educational inequality (of access and achievement) has multiple bases in the contemporary structures of caste, class, gender and ethnicity evolving in interaction with political economy". It asserts that "poverty and caste act as fundamental deterrents to education".

Dealing extensively on the subject, it focusses on myriad ways in which caste plays a role in affecting and shaping the lives of the children. The paper notes that the physical positioning of the school too is based on caste lines. "School provisioning in predominantly scheduled caste habitations is much less as compared to general rural habitations.... On the whole, higher caste habitations within larger villages are better provided." Thus, at the entry level itself, the children from these sections confront the problem of discrimination. The problems for the eager students from the SC families compound if they intend to study in the schools located in the upper caste villages or at least in multi-caste villages and the paper notes "hierarchical norms still govern social relations". This means that SC/ST children are simply not welcome to these schools in many villages in our country even today. The incident where a girl from Orissa was to be provided with police protection for going to a school on a bicycle is still fresh in our memory.

The paper also states the condition of the schools that exist in the SC and ST locations and the role of the teachers who are the sculptors shaping the "destiny of our country in the classrooms". It states that the "teacher's social background (caste, religion, language) affect their interactions with the students". Middle class, higher caste teachers are very unhappy with the environments of schools for the poor and are poorly motivated to teach children of the poor, particularly of SC/ST background, who are derogatorily categorised as 'uneducable'. An appalling body of evidence exists which suggests that teacher's preconceptions, bias and behaviour, subtle or overt, conscious or unconscious, operate to discriminate against children of SC/ST background. Teachers are observed to have low expectations of SC/ST children and girls and generally have a condescending and downright abusive attitude to poor children from slums. Levels of hostility and indifference to dalit/tribal cultural traits and value systems are high. They perceive dalit and adivasi children in a negative light, see them as unclean, dishonest, lazy, ill-mannered etc. The children could be criticised for their clothes, the dialect they speak, the abhorment of uncouth habits of meat eating, the ignorance of their parents and even the colour of their skin. They are punished and shouted at in efforts to 'discipline' and 'civilise' them. The paper also points out several examples to substantiate these findings. Children are assigned a range of menial tasks – from cleaning and sweeping the school to fetching 'paan' and cigarettes for the teacher. They assign SC/ST children menial jobs and shift the onus of low learning on children and their families. The curriculum also upholds symbols of the traditional, male-dominated feudal society and its obsolete cultural values and norms. The necessity for these arguments arose because the movement that has started against the intended reservations for OBCs has taken a position that reservations are against equality.

Case for OBCs' Reservation

It is a fact that the OBCs do not suffer to the extent as the SCs. But we should not forget the fact that the present-day OBCs are the Shudras of yesteryears and they too were down the social ladder in our hierarchical caste system. This made the Supreme Court observe in the Indra Sawhney case: "Social backwardness – it may be reiterated – leads to educational and economic backwardness." Majority of the OBCs are artisans. In spite of the changing generations, many occupations even to this day are 'reserved' for particular castes only. This is true in the case of fishermen, washermen, potters, barbers, weavers, stone cutters, shepherds and many of their like. Some sections among them have secured possession of land and are well off and this should not confuse us with the vast multitudes who are still poor. Whatever occupational mobility has taken place is very limited. The socio-economic 'progress' of our country ensured that the majority of the artisans did not go up the graph but took the downward trajectory. Thus, we do find that many of them are living in conditions of utter deprivation and some are even forced to commit suicides. The once famed weavers of our country are next only to the peasants in the number of suicides that we have seen in the recent days because of the deteriorating economic conditions. It is but natural for the economic factors to add to the social factors and impede their educational ambitions. It is after struggling against all such heavily placed odds few from these sections are coming to higher education. It is the duty of any liberal and democratic society to provide helping hand to these sections of the society.

This reality and naked truth is unfortunately not known to those students who are protesting against reservations. The socio-economic conditions in which they are brought up and the education system did not acquaint them with these facts. Neither do the corporate 'sponsors' for their protest want them to know these facts. The arguments that the reservations intended for these sections will be eaten away by the well-to-do sections should not be made with the intention of denying the benefits even to the needy amongst them. It is also necessary here to understand what criteria the Second Backward Classes (Mandal) Commission has adopted to determine the OBCs. The Commission worked out 11 indicators to determine social backwardness. These indicators are social, educational and economic, and as the major controversy revolves around the caste criteria allegedly adopted by the Commission, it would be relevant to reproduce the actual criteria used by the Commission. These are:

Social

- Castes/classes considered as socially backward by others.

- Castes/classes which mainly depend on manual labour for their livelihood.
- Castes/classes where the percentage of married women below 17 is 25 per cent above the state average in rural areas and 10 per cent in urban areas; and that of married men is 10 per cent and 5 per cent above the state average in rural and urban areas respectively.
- Castes/classes where participation of females in work is at least 25 per cent above the state average.

Educational

- Castes/classes where the number of children in the age group of 5-15 years who never attended school is at least 25 per cent above the state average.
- Castes/classes where the rate of student drop-out in the age group of 5-15 years is at least 25 per cent above the state average.
- Castes/classes amongst whom the proportion of matriculates is at least 25 per cent below the state average

Economic

- Castes/classes where the average value of family assets is at least 25 per cent below the state average.
- Castes/classes where the number of families living in *kachcha* houses is at least 25 per cent above the state average.
- Castes/classes where the source of drinking water is beyond half a kilometre for more than 50 per cent of the households.
- Castes/classes where the number of the households having taken a consumption loan is at least 25 per cent above the state average.

Definition of Creamy Layer

In the Supreme Court judgment on creamy layer, it has been explicitly stated in paragraph 85: "No objection can be taken to the validity and relevancy of the criteria adopted by the Mandal Commission." It has directed the government to identify creamy layer among the OBCs and ensure that they do not garner all the benefits of reservation. The Commission defined the 'creamy layer' as when a person has been able to shed off the attributes of social and educational backwardness and has secured employment or has engaged himself in some trade/profession of high status and at which stage he is normally in no need of reservation. Thus, according to this definition, children of (i) persons holding constitutional posts; (ii) of persons in service category Group A/Class I, Group B/Class II officials and employees holding equivalent posts in PSUs, banks, insurance, organisations, universities and private employment; (iii) personnel from armed forces and para-military forces above the rank of colonel including navy and air force; (iv) persons in professional class, trade business and industry (v) persons holding irrigated agricultural land more than 85 per cent of the statutory ceiling area; (vi) plantation owners; (vii) holders of vacant land and/or buildings in urban areas and urban agglomerations; and (viii) persons having an annual income of above Rs 2.5 lakh or possessing wealth above the exemption limit prescribed in the Wealth Act are excluded from the purview of reservations. If the opponents of reservation still feel that only the better off will somehow avail the reservation opportunities, then, they should suggest means to stop this and not cry hoarse over reservations *per se*. If they believe that reservations are against equality, then, they should propose an alternate system to replace them. The failure to do so will certainly raise doubts about their notions of equality, which is certainly bereft of social justice.

Only a Partial Remedy

We have been arguing time and again, reservations alone will not solve the whole problem of backwardness. The Mandal Commission Report itself recognises this basic truth and notes: "unless the production relations are radically altered through structural changes and progressive land reforms implemented rigorously all over the country, OBCs will never become truly independent. In view of this, highest priority should be given to radical land reforms by all the states". The class bias of the government too can be understood when it refuses to implement the land reforms agenda in the report and confines itself just to the provision of reservations. The government wants reservations to create an empowered middle class among these sections that lends its voice to the ruling class neo-liberal policies, while it is afraid of land reforms as they weaken the feudal basis of the Indian State. We in the Left support reservations even though we look at them as a partial remedy because they provide a minimum solace to the deprived sections of our society.

The people who avail of reservations and benefit from them should use their knowledge and resources for the interests of the class and sections from which they come and not become the stooges of the ruling classes.

In the era of neo-liberal globalisation, a united fight has to be waged against the policies that are curtailing both educational and employment opportunities. This struggle should demand not only reservations to the backward sections but also strengthening of the public education system and employment opportunities together with the implementation of the land reforms. All the concerned citizens, especially youth 'for equality', if they are serious about achieving equality should join their hands to realise this agenda. They have to denounce discrimination based on caste and shun all the feudal value systems. The fight for social justice has to go along with the fight for economic equality and real equality cannot be achieved without social justice.

It is another matter that if they take up this agenda the media that has taken upon itself to "supply anti-reservationists with banners and posters free of cost" will black them out and the "over 50 corporate houses and private hospitals of the likes of Batra, Fortis and Apollo" sponsoring them with "funds, fans, coolers and mineral water" will despise them. Rest assured real India will be standing by you. Come, let us together take the 'broom' to 'sweep' away all the evils from our society and not the 'roads'.

18

Merit of Reservation

KANCHA ILAIAH

Ever since Arjun Singh, the Union Minister for Human Resource Development, announced in the first week of April 2006 that the government is likely to provide 27 per cent reservation to other backward classes (OBCs) in admissions to the central educational institutions, including the Indian Institutes of Technology (IITs), Indian Institutes of Management (IIMs), and medical colleges, the national media started instigating anti-reservation agitations. Upper caste intellectuals who believe in the theory of merit began lambasting Arjun Singh and the reservation policy itself. Upper caste medical students began an agitation against reservation. Why is upper caste youth not willing to tolerate the sharing of government educational facilities with youth coming from historically oppressed communities? They view the proposed reservation as an instrument to limit the share of the future generations of their families and castes. The same upper caste youth have never agitated against private medical, engineering and management colleges selling seats to the rich for money. An anti-caste policy like reservation is being projected as an anti-national policy. The OBC youth who are going to get the reserved seats belong to this nation as much as these upper caste youth. They will not be worse in terms of merit than those who buy their seats. The question is not whether they become socially useful doctors, engineers, managers and so on, but which family and caste benefits. The agitating upper caste students and the mainstream media backing them are not interested in better healthcare services. At no point of time the students of these institutions have agitated about the lack of healthcare facilities for the masses in rural and urban India. They are not concerned about the nation or the quality of education All they seem to be bothered about are the opportunities of their own families and castes. In this article we examine the issue of reservation in the context of the nation.

Backdrop

In 1990 the V.P. Singh government reformulated the ideological discourse on reservations by granting 27 per cent reservation to OBCs in the central services. The notion of social justice became integral to the system, repositioning of the relations between various castes. In a society hierarchically divided along caste lines – castes are "enclosed classes" – the principle of reservation was aimed at engendering organic intellectuals who engage with the state and civil society with altogether different assumptions. The principle of reservation as ideologically constructed by B.R. Ambedkar and Periyar Ramasamy during the nationalist period was meant to create an educated intellectual group that emerges out of the historically oppressed castes. Right from the times of the Kautilyan state and Manu's legal code, Brahminism had denied the oppressed castes access to education and employment. Hence, the process of engendering organic intellectuals from the ranks of the oppressed castes had to be gone through; it was the Mandal agenda that provided the impetus. Since then, civil society has been shaken up. There has been a clear polarisation of society along caste lines, with a "war of position". Each political party and institution is divided along caste lines. Caste has become an ideological anchor around which the discourse began to be conducted. Given that, among other things, caste culture nurtures the mental faculties of individuals, each person has to search for a secular self or an egalitarian self. Ideologically, reservation policy was/is aimed at the expansion of democratic spaces. Pre-Mandal, Indian democracy was essentially an upper caste democracy. Though the SCs/STs were given reservation in the electoral, educational and employment spheres, they were relegated to the margins. SC/ST reservation was seen as a mechanism to overcome untouchability and tribalism. It did not address the caste system and it was not linked to the modern notion of social justice. The Brahminical intellectuals did not come to terms with the discourse of social justice because this posed a real danger of displacing them in many realms of knowledge and institutional authority. They began to attack the notion of social justice as a retrograde and "casteist" step. Anything that displaces the Brahminical elements from their positions of power and privilege gets characterised as retrograde.

The Bharatiya Janata Party (BJP) worked out its "Kamandal" agenda to nullify the "Mandal" agenda. The Congress, under the leadership of P.V. Narasimha Rao and Manmohan Singh, brought privatisation on the agenda to minimise the effect of reservations in the state sector. The BJP demolished the Babri Masjid and organised communal riots to galvanise the OBCs by pitting them against Muslims. They sought to project "casteist" Hinduism as homogeneous and wanted to stop the OBCs from getting Mandalised and organised into an independent political force. Quite interestingly, the Brahmins and Banias in all parties oppose reservations, while the Kshatriyas, who have a small space in the Indian power structure, have taken the initiative in setting the reservation agenda. V.P. Singh then, and Arjun Singh now, have taken that initiative. The Brahminical media has been projecting them as villains. Let us not forget the fact that Gautam Buddha was also condemned in the same manner by his Brahminical contemporaries

Can They Stop It?

Neither Kamandal forces nor the anti-reservationists mindset of the upper castes could stop the process of Mandalisation of the state and civil society. The principle of social justice of an Indian variety, different from what was postulated by John Rawls, came into operation. The response of the upper castes to that was more privatisation. The National Democratic Alliance (NDA) government deployed rabid anti-reservationist, Arun Shourie, as minister of disinvestment. This necessitated a more sustained demand for reservation in the private sector. Since Hindu nationalists were selling Indian companies to foreigners, the Dalit-Bahujans had to ask caste-based reservations in the multinational companies setting up facilities in India. The UN Durban Conference of 2001 and the US House of Representatives Committee hearing of 2005 were used for that purpose. Thus, the issue of caste and untouchability also got globalised.

In the backdrop of the discourse on Mandal, the issue of 33 per cent reservations for women in Parliament and the state assemblies came up. Quite interestingly, there was no opposition to women's reservation from the upper caste intelligentsia and the media on the ground of merit. It was the OBC leadership that demanded women's reservations based on the principle of female social justice called "reservation within reservation". The hypocrisy of the upper caste intelligentsia and media was quite clear when they remained totally supportive of women's reservation but not of SC/ST/OBC reservations.

Myth of Merit

The debate on OBC reservations now certainly gets crowded with the demand for reservations in the private sector. The cobwebs surrounding reservations in the private sector will, to some extent, get cleared with the implementation of OBC reservations in all the central educational institutions. If the present ideology of merit in IIT, IIM and medical education is nailed, the private sector will have to fall in line. The notion of merit must be reset in relation to the levels of living of the masses and improved productivity in both the agrarian and industrial sectors. Development of innovative technologies and evolution of non-discriminatory management systems in all spheres of life do not depend on marks-centred merit. They depend on social connectivity, socially relevant knowledge and good institutional training. The SC/ST/OBC youth are better suited for that kind of a transformational role. The Brahminical theory of merit is like the Adi Shankara's theory of 'maya'. It is dissociated from improvements in the living conditions of the people. It is generated in the dual policy – English and regional language – of education and in costly coaching centres. It is not the kind of merit reflected in the generation and dissemination of innovative knowledge and improvements in productivity. It is merit based upon imported textbooks and mugged up reproduction. In this method of recitation and reproduction, as a Hindu priest does from the Vedas in a temple or on a ritual occasion, a regenerative nation is not going to be constructed. The upper caste theoreticians of merit are again saying that "merit is once again at peril in higher educational institutions" as it was with jobs in 1990. At that time they said that if the reservation snake creeps into R&D organisations and into the military apparatus, the nation would be in danger. If the present attack of the upper castes continues, the lower caste youth will have to look for model of struggle akin to that of the Maoist movement in Nepal. Since the Nepali caste system did not allow social mobility, the lower castes had to resort to violent struggles as an alternative. In India, the system of reservations provides a mechanism of peaceful transformation of the caste centred system and a redefinition of merit.

After the reservations for OBCs in jobs began to be implemented, not a single upper caste intellectual has been able to establish that those OBC candidates who entered through the reservation route undermined those institutions in terms of merit. They have also not been able to prove that the institutions headed by the upper castes had produced high quality output. On the other hand, the reservationists have been arguing that with upper caste intellectuals heading all the major national institutions over the years and endowed with Brahminical merit, these institutions have not been able to deliver with respect to the goals set, whether that of enhanced productivity or distributive justice. Brahminical merit led the nation to foreign debt peonage and dependence. In China the former working class youth (akin to our lower castes) occupied all the key positions after the revolution and successfully developed science and technology through self-reliance. Where does Indian upper caste merit stand in comparison with that of the merit of the socially mobile working class of China?

Diabolic Education Policy

After independence the Brahminical centre declared Hindi as official national language, but ran all its central institutions in English. For deceptive ideological reasons English is also being projected as a colonial language. The children of the SCs/STs/OBCs, who (with a great difficulty) study in government schools, are forced to remain away from the English language. English has become the national language of the upper castes. For the productive mass that lives in the villages, English education is projected negatively. Ambedkar nailed this thinking by writing extensively in English. But, subsequently, the leaders who emerged from the Dalit-Bahujan castes did not realise the importance of the English language in challenging upper caste hegemony. English is the medium of instruction in private and selective central schools, but the OBCs/SCs/STs are excluded for, by and large, they cannot afford that education. Thus, English plus money (that provides coaching at every stage of the child's life) confers merit and the productive mass is excluded. The Dalit-Bahujan and tribal mass have been relegated to the margins. As a result, for a long time, no middle class has emerged from among the Dalit-Bahujan castes, as they were carrying the historical burden of illiteracy of centuries. They are confined to "compartmentalised" artisan professions, with some traditional skills, but even now, they are not being allowed to develop modern skills, nor are they being allowed to acquire modern knowledge and English education. The system must let every child learn three subjects in English and three subjects in regional languages across the country, with a uniformly structured syllabus, from class one. If such a school system is put in place, and if all the tutorial institutions are banned, over a period of 25 years from now reservation can be done away with. Reservation, till then, remains the main avenue to social mobility and access to modern education for the OBCs/SCs/STs, which are preconditions for the modernisation of India.

Merit in IITs and IIMs?

The rural SC/ST/OBC student community is in close interaction with nature. They are not too deficient in mathematics. A number of such students who got the opportunity to educate themselves in reasonably good institutions have proved their merit beyond any doubt. The so-called premier institutions, like the IITs, IIMs and medical schools, whose students are agitating against reservation, have so far not worked to improve technology in rural India, or management in rural areas, or the public healthcare system. Most of the graduates of the IITs and IIMs join US or Western European multinational companies and/or migrate to Western Europe or the US. So far, not many who have been trained in these institutions have worked for the improvement of the nation's technological and management structures.

If the OBCs with less marks at the entry level are allowed to share the seats in these institutions, that in itself is not going to make a substantial difference in terms of creativity and productivity of these institutions. Given the creative interaction of the boys and girls coming from lower castes with nature and the means of production, having entered into such institutions, they might show exceptional talent in discovering new ways of doing things that could enhance the knowledge base of the country. The educational institutions of India must provide a wide interactive base for people who have rich experience of involvement in multiple productive activities since their childhood. Most of the first generation educated Dalit-Bahujan youth have that kind of childhood experience. These minds need to be exposed to systematic thinking and analysis. Modern institutional education provides that kind of scope, but in the name of merit many creative minds were not allowed to enter these institutions for several decades. The reservation system opens up that kind of opportunity for some creative minds among Dalit-Bahujan youth who were deprived of such opportunity for centuries. In fact, the nation would stand to gain a lot from their entry into these institutions.

Further, when reservations coming into force in all the central educational institutions, they will get democratised and more creative interactions among youth from diverse backgrounds would take place. Reservations are a democratic means to avoid social unrest based on caste discrimination. If the people sitting in the central educational institutions and the private companies keep on harping on the merit of marks but not of opportunities to all, the anger of Dalit-Bahujan castes is bound to increase. That in itself is likely to lead to civil strife as it happened in Paris last year.

Reservation and Development

Reservations and nation-building are not antagonistic. The South Indian experience has proved that. Reservations in South India have been more deeply entrenched. The difference between the northern and southern Indian states is quite stark in terms of the participatory levels of the lower castes in institutions and markets. Mumbai, Bangalore, Chennai and Hyderabad could become the more modern centres because of better participation of the SCs/STs/OBCs in all kinds of markets. Delhi and Kolkata, which remain predominantly Brahminical cities, are backward because their participation in the higher-level structures of those cities is minimal. Unless the productive castes come to terms with modernity, they cannot unleash their productive energy. The nation becomes more knowledge-oriented only when shining examples emerge in the villages and shake up the village level caste communities, which have enormous common sense and logical thinking but no exposure to institutional education. The higher dropout rates at the IIT and IIM kind of institutions are not because the SCs/STs/OBCs cannot perform in their respective subjects, but due to the Brahminical cultural environment that these institutions had inculcated. The Indian institutional-cultural environment is worse than the white cultural environment in America or South Africa. In this discriminatory cultural environment the innovative cutting edge of the Dalit-Bahujan youth gets lost and they slip into a withdrawal syndrome. If a biased and prejudiced professor humiliates an SC/ST/OBC student, the student keeps blaming her/his own birth into a particular caste but not her/his inability to hard work. In fact, such humiliation kills her/his motivation to hard work. And, at the societal level, the culture of caste humiliation has destroyed the creative energies of the nation.

If the IITs and IIMs want to produce innovative talent, they must come to terms with reservation. The national identity of these institutions should not be based on what kind of jobs their graduates get in the US or Western Europe. It should be based on the innovative technologies and trans-formational management systems they develop. Reservation does not reduce the scope of national innovativeness. The merit of a scientific or technological community does not lie in mere adoption of the developments in science and technology invented/innovated by others but in indigenous inventions/innovations that are then adopted elsewhere in the world. If the democratic and rational course evolved by Ambedkar is not allowed to achieve that goal, an anarchist trend is bound to set in among the SCs/STs/OBCs. Let the upper castes decide which course is better for the progressive transformation of this nation.

19

Why Reservation for OBCs is a Must?

V.B. RAWAT

Ever since the Union Human Resource Development Minister Arjun Singh declared government's intention to fix a quota for the other backward castes (OBCs) in the premier government educational institutions like the Indian Institutes of Technology (IITs) and Indian Institutes of Management and other institutions of higher learning, the responses have been perplexing. While one know very well the intentions of Arjun Singh and his Congress Party, which was in the forefront of anti-Mandal agitation in 1990, it is important to analyse the nature of protest and fury of the upper castes in India. Why the same upper castes who burnt themselves today keep silent. Whether Arjun Singh and his party is just working on tokenism and refuses to learn lesson that the cry from the Dalits and backwards today is political power which has not yet been over despite the fact that they had chief ministers and ministers. The administration remains strongly in the hands of the upper castes.

A revisit to events in 1990: A hero became villian

On August 7, 1990, when Prime Minister Vishwanath Pratap Singh announced that his National Front government was going to implement the Mandal Commission recommendations in education and jobs, there was not much fury in the beginning. Slowly, a slanderous media campaign was launched particularly to attract circulation. A middle class newspaper like *Indian Express* and its loud mouth editor Arun Shourie became mouthpieces of the upper caste contempt to the Dalits and backwards. Shourie worked not as an ethical journalist but as a hired lawyer who had to defend his case. Upper caste students and their parents went on rampage in North India. Suicides were committed by the innocent students as young as eight years of age who might not have known what Mandal was and what was the meaning of reservation for the downtrodden. Clearly, two big Brahmanical parties of the country the Congress and the Bharatiya Janata Party (BJP) used this opportunity to target the government. Lal Krishna Adavani decided to go on a *Rathyatra* to 'unite' the Hindu society, which was 'divided' by V.P. Singh and his actions. There was a wave of anti-Muslim sentiments in the middle classes. Advani became hero who revived the Hindu society and V.P. Singh became 'dushman number one' of the upper castes in India. Yes, the prime minister of the popular votes of India became the target number one because of reservations. All his merits became non functional once he ordered the implementation of the Mandal recommendations.

Commentators after commentators condoned the Hindutva and their thugs, their misdeeds and anti-national act of spreading hatred and violence but none of them could ever muster the courage to support a prime minister who dared to go ahead against all odds. Yes, one may not agree with V.P. Singh and his style of politics but one needs to see his track record as an efficient minister and an honest Member of Parliament. It was for the first time in history of India that a government fell because it defended a shrine and committed its constitutional duties. Yes, Ayodhya's October 1990 events led to fall of V.P. Singh government. It is not for nothing that he decided to stay away from the parliamentary politics, disown prime ministership and is persistently being seen with the growing mass struggles in India when the so-called mainstream politicians are busy with their castes, religious sentiments. How many of them come and support Narmada or the cause of dying farmers. When the slums were being dislocated none of the politicians dared to come out and challenge the court. But these things do not matter for the journalists who have decided that they have to oppose anything, which brings social justice. V.P. Singh is nowhere in mainstream politics but his Mandalisation process has spread all over. That is the great achievement because the composition of our parliament has changed. Dalits and backward communities are asking for their share in power. The political parties have to listen to them and come to the reality.

Conspicuous silence

Fifteen years later when the same Arjun Singh informs the journalists about the reservation policy, there is not much war by the upper castes though there is resentment by the 'meritorious' industrial houses who run on a monarchical basis. Again, the same talks of merit being affected and non-availability of the students from the backward and Dalit communities. It is amusing how people change their stand. Industrialists like Rahul Bajaj, known for the Hindutva lineage, remarked that reservation in the private sector would damage the credibility of big companies in India. The Bajajs should tell the world why most of the business works in India is done by the Bania community. North, East, South, West, it is the Marwadis and Banias who have captured the major institutions with Brahmins as their Gurus. The opponents of reservation should also inform why the scavenging work is fixed for the Valmiki community in India. Why is this 'Intellectual Property Right' over certain work while ignoring others. Social scientists should also explain why no other community person is seen as doing scavenging work or carrying night soil over head. This meritorious upper caste would then hang their head in shame.

What is happening is most astonishing and show double standard. In 1990, the Dalits were in the forefront of supporting the Mandal Commission recommendations meant for the backward communities. Today, a number of Dalit intellectuals, who would like to parade Dalit capitalists in Delhi, are asking for a creamy lawyer theory to implement the Mandal Commission Report. An example is being given here of the lone dissenter: why should the dissenter argument be taken into account? Mandal gave a report and government accepted it in toto. A person like S.S. Gill, who was member-secretary of the Mandal Commission, today condemns V.P. Singh for implementing it with political motivation. It is amusing when commentators write of political motivation. Why should any work not be done with political motivation? Did the backward communities not voted for the government? It is also important to analyse as why some of the Dalit intellectuals are crying for fixing quota for the most backward communities (MBCs). Arun Shourie, who spearheaded anti-Mandal agitation through his reckless writings and was later rewarded by the Sangh Parivar for persistently abusing the minorities through his newspaper columns, would never had imagined that Mandal would eat his own party. He might never have foreseen the growing assertion among all communities after it. Why was India burning in 1990 and quiet in 2006.

To be sure, in 1990, the people realised that the government of that time was determined to give the Dalits and backwards their due share in power. One need not to remind that ministers like Ram Vilas Paswan and Sharad Yadav had become very powerful proponents of the Mandal Mantra. The government did not stay there only. It was bringing a bill in parliament for labour reform, particularly related to labours participation in management, bill on electoral reform under Dinesh Goswami, autonomy to Prasar Bharati apart from putting Dr. Ambedkar's statue in parliament and honouring him with Bharat Ratna. Each of these acts had loud messages. It is this time that the Buddhist converts got right in job reservations. Mandal in 1990 changed the politics of the country. It gave an unprecedented and lethal weapon for the Dalits, backwards and Adivasis to come together. Every party had to understand the power of Mandal. Over the years, despite talks of globalisation and Hindutva, the Mandalisation process continued. In the process, the upper caste leadership of the Hindutva gangs have to play second fiddle. Right from Uma Bharati to Kalyan Singh and Narendra Modi, caste has forced the Sindhi Lal Krishna Advani to ponder over his own future and he is again on another *yatra,* knowing fully well, that he has lost his caste battle. The upper castes are silent and protesting just in front of the cameras. A few papers that do not sale much are again trying to instigate people to protest but those who get everything at home cannot protest. Secondly, they know, they have their own government and their opposition. A government which just pretend to work for the Dalits and backwards and has no real intention to do so. Most of the people know that in Manmohan Singh's safe hand their interest are safe and would be looked after. Afterall, Arjun Singh's own track record for social justice is ridiculous and his politicisation of HRD ministry is well known. The tricks of anti-Hindutva do not work all the time in the same way as the anti-Muslim card of Advani failed miserably.

Why opposition to reservation for backward communities

One needs to understand the psychology of opposition to Mandal. Reservation for Dalits was never implemented properly before 1990. Every time it was informed that due to lack of non-availability of the candidates, seats remained vacant and quota was filled by the upper castes, particularly those close to the people in power or with big bags. The 1990s changed that the backlog has to be filled with the candidates from the same community. Therefore, 1990 is a watershed in the history of India and implementing the Mandal Commission Report V.P. Singh might have become the most hated politician of the country despite his impeccable credentials, yet, the politics of India has changed. Later, when Narasimha Rao crookedly with the help of the Hindutva brigade tried to undo what the Mandal had done. He went overboard to implement the privatisation process and added fire to the Hindutva. Therefore, both the demolition of Babri Masjid and growing privatisation were part of the Narasimha Rao era which some of our pen pushers termed as glorious. One need not to inform the readers here how Narasimha Rao died. Not a single tear was shed for him.

When the jobs are nowhere and everything is going private, then, why are the upper castes angry at reservation for backward communities? The fact is that seats for Dalits were rarely fulfilled and we had seen huge backlog. There has been no protest. It was easier to curtail the protest of the Dalits because of their numbers and social background. Now, the reservation for backward communities being a reality, the powerful backward communities will hit and break the bone of the upper castes. That is the fear of these. They know that there are enough students from these communities who will join the great institutions of technology and management. Today, these pen pushers pretend that reservation should only for the Dalits. Similarly, Dalit opportunists also dance to the tone of their Brahmanical masters when they condemn reservation for the backward communities. It is a fact that many of the backward communities should not have been there in the list. But that is not a way to justify that there should not be reservation.

Discrimination despite merit

It is completely a lie to say that Dalits and backwards are not doing business today or they lack ability. To say that there is no discrimination in India on the basis of caste is again a great lie which only insensitive caste Hindus can tell the world. Four years back I investigated a case of a very bright Dalit student Jyoti Prakash Vishwas who passed out from R.K. Mission School in Kolkata and was working as an engineer in a central government public sector company. His Bengali bosses used filthy language against him and suspended him on various charges, which were found absolutely untrue by a team of human rights activists including me. Vishwas was not allowed to join a well-paid job in a reputed private company. His wife, who was working with Government of West Bengal, was not given medical compensation as per company's rule. After our fact-finding report came out, the management tried to strike a cordial note. Vishwas, who by then had never knew what exactly was Dalit movement and discrimination, realised what is the identity of a bright Dalit scholar. Two years later when he left Delhi, one day he sent me a mail from Saudi Arabia where he was working as an engineer. He wrote: "Sir, I thank you for standing with me in my struggle against injustice. I know Dalits would not be able to get justice as long as they are part of Hindu system. I have decided to embrace Islam, a faith which give me strength and inner peace." Those votaries of 'merit' should understand clearly well that things are not as easy as they think. A few days back when I was in Chhatisgarh and a Dalit student from National Law University, Raipur came to me and informed me about the harassment he faced in the university. Despite the fact that he was the only candidate in his course of M.Phil/Ph.D/LLM, it took three years for the board of the college to accept his M. Phil and then deny him right for Ph.D. Yes, I talk about Abhishek Priya Anand, a student who completed his M.Sc. from Hyderabad and qualified and ranked 8th in the merit in the National Law College entrance test, today, face a caste prejudiced Vice Chancellor and his bureaucracy.

Will the Indian merit mongers ever think why they want to shut every door for the Dalits and backward communities? If a Dalit converts to other faith, the Hindutva brigade is up in arm against it. There is no reform movement within Hindu dharma where they can get justice. The jobs, which were reserved for them, have been privatised. Educational institutions rarely fulfil their quota. So demeaning are the upper castes that they are ready to get forged certificate of Dalit quota to get admitted in the university. In Delhi, a prominent doctor of a famous medical college got his MBBS degree on passing an entrance test under the SC quota. He produced a false certificate of adoption by a Dalit father. The fact was that his father's servant happened to be a Dalit. This upper caste doctor used his leverages and asked his servant to 'adopt' him to get admit. A similar case of admission has been found in Lucknow by a Brahmin girl.

Creamy layer theory is dangerous at the moment

Unfortunately, some of the Dalit intellectuals have also jumped in to condemn the quota for the Dalits. These commentators are talking in terms of creamy layer theory. Question is let the government first implement the reservation only then creamy lawyer theory could be implemented. If the creamy layer theory could be implemented in the Mandal, then, the same should be true for the Dalits also. And, the same should be true for the upper castes also in the general seats. It is a dangerous preposition. It is a fact that the power elite of a community are the first to get the benefits of education and quota. Did not the Brahmin got it from the upper castes initially? There are so many of them but many of them have little representation in power structure. Same is true about Dalits and backward communities. Of course, the politics of quota is dangerous. Arjun Singh's intention has been like that of his party. I am sure he knows it well that Dalits and backwards are thoroughly politicised and are not going to be just 'vote bank' of any party. They are today running with confidence and asking for a share in power. While the political parties may not have implemented the reservation fully, the MBCs in Uttar Pradesh have learnt a lesson from Bihar. The MBCs have already revolted against the political elites of the state and asking for their fair representation in power. Today, power is the real need of the people. As far as jobs are concern, let the government bring a white paper on reservations and give us ideas as how long will it take it to complete its backlog. When can we see 17.5 per cent IAS officers from Dalits, 27.5 per cent from backward communities and 7.5 per cent from tribals? Once the government fulfil its promise, we can think of new ideas to give representation to MBCs and oppressed Dalits particularly women from these sections of society.

Reforms mean de-Brahmanising India

In a welfare state, the government cannot shy away from implementing reforms. Where are government reforms for land, forest and water? If reform means giving precious national assets to a few cronies of the power elites, then, the government has to be ready to face protest of various forms. Reform means that the government demolishes its Brahmanical structure. Reform truly means de-brahmanisation process of India. It means India's corrupt caste structured village structure is hit from below the belt. For that a strong land reform measures need to be carried out. Our corrupt and casteist industrial magnets are not ready for the same therefore face resistance from the people. Reform means that the upper castes should learn that time for hegemony has gone and it is time they learn to live together and respect diversity of India. Reservations are going to stay as long as government does not reform itself and Hindu system remain caged in the age old myopic vision of division of work based on caste. Let us truly reform our society and work for a truly democratic India where every community participates in power and every person go to school irrespective of caste and creed.

V

State and Equal Opportunity Policies

20

Moments in the History of Reservation

BHAGWAN DAS

The subject of reservations is a vast one. Even in terms of a historical account of reservations in India, it would be impossible to cover most of its aspects in the space of one paper. This article, therefore, provides brief entry points into some of the more significant historical and legal moments concerning the development of a reservation policy in India, all of which require much more attention and analysis. A great deal has been written against reservation policies since the acceptance of the Mandal Commission Report in 1991 in favour of reservations in higher education and government services for the other backward classes (OBCs) of India. Very little has been written by the beneficiaries of reservations, whether in book form or in the form of articles in the national press. Those who are vociferous and loud in their criticism of reservations invariably belong to the dominant groups, who have been enjoying the benefits of, if not a monopoly over, education, wealth, land and public services. On the other hand, the worst victims of the condemnation, persecution and exploitation of contemporary society have been the shudras, dalits (untouchables, unseeables and unapproachables) and women. There is a difference between the bird's point of view and the worm's point of view. There are many scholars and intellectuals in India whose vision get easily stigmatised by phrases and slogans bor-rowed from the west and other lands. Writers belonging to the Hindu upper castes – not Muslims, Christians or Buddhists – have often asserted that it was the British who introduced the policy of 'divide and rule' in India. The phrase 'divide and rule' was in fact originally deployed by the dominating classes of Rome who conquered a large portion of the world and had to devise ways and means to maintain their empire and supremacy. But if we seriously and earnestly study the history of man, the principle of 'divide and rule' was really devised by the Brahmins in India who framed laws and rules in the name of Dhamma and Brahma to divide society vertically and horizontally and exploit large numbers of people – poor, deprived, ignorant and divided – so that a few on top may continue to enjoy the good things of life – power, prestige, priviledges. Reservations were not introduced, as some Hindu writers have asserted, so that the British could 'divide and rule' Indians. The reservation or quota system was introduced in Malta before it was even mentioned in India. Yugoslavia had five nationalities and six linguistic groups. Power had to be shared and a kind of quota system was established to keep the country united. Americans, whether they admit it or not, were influenced by the Indian experiment and 'affirmative action' was introduced in the 1960s with a view to giving a share to the discrimination – African-Americans, Native Americans and other ethnic minorities. Other countries of Europe including Great Britain are now thinking along the lines of some reservation or affirmative action for ethnic and other minorities who are victims of discrimination by the dominating groups.

In the Indian context, reservations were introduced during the last decades of the 19th century at a time when the sub-continent could be broadly divided according to two main forms of governance – British India and the 600 princely states. Some of these princely states were progressive and eager to modernise through the promotion of education and industry; and by maintaining unity among their own people. Mysore in South India and Baroda and Kolhapur in western India took considerable interest in the awakening and advancement of the minorities and deprived sections of society. It should not surprise us then that the very first records of implementing reservation policies are from these princely states.

British India was facing problems right from the 18th century when Lord Cornwallis took over as Governor General in 1786. The East India Company was reeking with corruption. Administrators often find scapegoats and Cornwallis was no exception. He blamed the Indians for maladministration and inefficiency, which resulted in large losses of revenue. Cornwallis introduced certain reforms and closed the doors to employment for the Indians, except in the lower ranks of administration. Scions of the upper castes and affluent families turned to other professions, especially the profession of law. Another event which affected Indians in the services was the introduction of English as the official language by Lord Macaulay. It was decided in the council with Lord Macaulay as law minister that while Madrassas and Sanskrit schools would be allowed to function, official business was to be conducted in English.

"The cause of English was still further advanced by the regulation introduced by the first Lord Hardinge that all public services were to be filled by an open competition examination held by the Council (the successor of the Committee of Public Instruction), preference being given to the knowledge of English. Virtually, English education was made the only passport to higher appointments available to the Indians, and hence its popularity and rapid progress were equally assured" (Mazumdar, *An Advanced History of India*: 818). While the benefits of English education were reaped by members of affluent and newly emerging middle class people, the masses remained ignorant and backward.

Brahmins in the Madras presidency and the Bhadralok in the Bengal presidency took advantage of the new educational policy and the central place of the English language within it and occupied most of the posts available in the administration. Brahmins in Madras comprising barely 3 per cent of the total population occupied more than 80 per cent of the posts. In the princely state of Mysore the Tamil Brahmins monopolised all the jobs, whereas Kannadiga Brahmins had a very small share in public services. The maharaja of Mysore was well advised by his ministers and the resident and some reforms were introduced with a view to giving a larger share to the Kannadiga Brahmins, Vokkalligas and Lingayats besides the untouchable castes and the Muslims. Reservations were thus introduced in 1918 in favour of a number of castes and communities that had little share in the administration. The introduction of

English as the official language antagonised the Muslims, who perhaps unwisely decided not to learn the language of the infidels. It was through the efforts of the famous Muslim leader Syed Ahmed Khan that education was given prominence and schools opened. As the largest religious minority, Muslims had a grievance that they had very little share in the administration of the country. The British had also changed their attitude towards them. Upper caste Hindus, on the other hand, were taking advantage of the educational facilities provided by the British as well as the Christian missionaries and were organising and agitating for political power. They had a large share in the bureaucracy.

Muslims, however, appreciated the importance of political and administrative power. A delegation of Muslim nawabs, landlords and prominent persons led Agha Khan, leader of the Ismaili Sect, waited upon the viceroy and presented a memorandum demanding a share in the administration in proportion to their population. The viceroy gave it sympathetic consideration and provisions were made in the Government of India Acts of 1909 and 1919 granting the Muslims due share and other facilities. The untouchables – or the depressed classes as they were then called – had joined the presidency armies and fought battles under the command of British officers. They had contributed a great deal towards the creation of the British empire. In the army, untouchable soldiers got their first opportunity to learn to read and write and were also exposed to new ideas. Untouchables also worked as camp-followers and domestic servants – as cooks, butlers, bearers, sweepers, gardeners, 'ayahs' and so on – for British families in their cantonments. The Brahmanisation of the Bengal Army led to mutinies and also to a reduction of soldiers of untouchable origin in the Bengal army. They, however, continued to be enlisted in the presidency armies of Bombay and Madras. The British changed their recruitment policies according to their political needs. Christian missionaries contributed a great deal towards awakening the untouchables and promoting literacy, in spite of discouragement by the British officers, many of whom thought that missionary work was a nuisance. Some of them changed their attitude later on.

Ibbetson, the famous Census Commissioner, wrote, "untouchables are politically not important". This was because they were asking for concessions and facilities for their upliftment and had not organised themselves as a political force. It was only with the arrival of Ambedkar that they acquired a leader of stature and education who could also make a political difference.

Provisions of Communal Award

The question of reservations was also discussed in the round table conferences and provisions were made in the Communal Award of 1935 in spite of opposition by Mahatma Gandhi. Seats were reserved in the legislatures in favour of Mohammedans, Sikhs, Marathas, Europeans, Parsis, Anglo-Indians, and Christians. As regards the depressed classes, the following provision was made:

> Members of the 'depressed classes' qualified to vote will vote in a general constituency. In view of the fact that for a considerable period these classes would be unlikely by this means alone, to secure any adequate representation in the legislature, a number of special seats will be filled by election from special constituencies in which only members of the 'depressed classes' electorally qualified will be entitled to vote. Any person voting in such a special constituency will, as stated above, be also entitled to vote in a general constituency.

It is intended that these constituencies should be formed in selected areas where the depressed classes are most numerous, and that, except in Madras, they should not cover the whole area of the province. Mahatma Gandhi saw a danger to Hinduism in these specific provisions of the communal award in favour of the most deprived and disadvantaged sections of society and threatened to go on a fast unto death. Under this pressure an agreement was signed between the Hindu leaders and the leaders of the depressed classes to save the life of Mahatma Gandhi. This agreement is known as the Poona Pact, and its provisions included the following:

1. There shall be seats reserved for the depressed classes out of the general electorate seats in the provincial legislatures as shown below:

Madras	30
Bombay with Sind	15
Punjab	8
Bihar and Orissa	18
Central Provinces	20
Assam	7
Bengal	30
United Provinces	20
Total	148

2. Election to these seats shall be by joint electorates, subject however, to the following procedures:
   All members of the depressed classes, registered in the general electoral roll in a constituency will form an electoral college, which will elect a panel of four candidates belonging to the depressed classes for each such reserved seat, by the method of the single vote; the four persons getting the highest number of votes in such primary election shall be candidates for election by the general electorate.
3. Representation of the depressed classes in the central legislature shall likewise be on the principle of joint electorates and reserved seats by the method of primary elections in the manner prescribed for in clause 2 above, for their representation in the provincial legislature

As regards the share in the administration, the following provisions were made in the Poona Pact:

> There shall be no disabilities attaching to any one on the ground of his being a member of the depressed classes in regard to any election to local bodies, or appointment to the public services. Every endeavour shall be made to secure fair representation of the depressed classes in these respects subject to such educational qualifications as may be laid down for appointment to the public services.

As against the 78 seats allotted to the depressed classes in the state legislature, the Poona Pact gave 148 seats. However, untouchables lost the right to elect their own representatives and this right was transferred to the Hindus. The result was that those who were elected remained faithful to the parties and leaders who adopted them as candidates and funded their elections.

The Poona Pact had far reaching effects and obstructed their progress in other fields also. The government issued orders regarding reservation in services vide resolution F 14/17-B 33 dated July 4, 1934 (*Gazette of India,* part I, July 7, 1934). Reservation in public services was provided for all minorities excepting the depressed classes.

In regard to the depressed classes it is common ground that all reasonable steps should be taken to secure for them a fair degree of representation in the public services. The intention of the caste Hindus in this respect was formally stated in the Poona Agreement of 1932 and His Majesty's Government in accepting that agreement took due note of this point. In the present state of general education in these classes the Government of India considers that no useful purpose will be served by reserving for them a definite percentage of vacancies out of the number available for Hindus as a whole, but they hope to ensure that duly qualified candidates from the depressed classes are not deprived of their opportunities of appointment merely because they cannot succeed in open competition.

Ambedkar was appointed as the member of the Viceroy's Executive Council and he submitted a memorandum 'On the Grievances of the Scheduled Castes' detailing their grievances, and also demanding reservation in public services, scholarships and stipends for study within the country and abroad, a share in contracts, and so on. This was duly recommended by the viceroy and referred to the secretary of state, who accepted the recommendations. The scheduled castes were allowed 8.5 per cent reservation in central services and other facilities for the first time in the history of India in 1942.

As already mentioned, under pressure from upper caste Hindus and also for political reasons, the doors of the armed forces were closed to the untouchables in the early decades of the 20th century. However, the British needed more mercenary soldiers during the Second World War. People were therefore liberally enlisted in the Air Force, Navy and Army besides in units such as Supply Corps, Engineering Units, Civil Pioneer Force and so on. After the transfer of power in 1947, a drafting committee with Ambedkar as chairman was set up to draft the Constitution of India. Some members of the Constituent Assembly were opposed to the provision of reservations in favour of the scheduled castes. Scheduled caste members, mostly belonging to the Congress, were worried about it because Sardar Vallabhbhai Patel, president of the minority committee, was also opposed to reservations. They approached Ambedkar, who in turn advised them to speak to Mahatma Gandhi, and remind him about the promise made in the Poona Pact. Provision was made in the Constitution of India for reservation in the legislature for 10 years ending in 1960. This has recently been extended up to 2010. Provision was also made for reservation in public services. This has no time limit. Surprisingly, prime ministers, political leaders and journalists have been making speeches and writing articles giving the impression that it is reservation in public services which has been extended for ten years. Reservation made under Article 335 read together with Article 46 has no time limit prescribed under the Constitution. Reservation was also made in favour of Anglo-Indians for a shorter period in view of the difficulties and disabilities peculiar to them.

Constitutional Provisions

Article 46 contains the provisions regarding the interests of the weaker sections of society. Accordingly, the state shall promote with special care the education and economic interests of the weaker sections of the people, and, in particular of the scheduled castes and the scheduled tribes, and shall protect them from social injustice and all forms of exploitation.

Who is a member of the scheduled castes and scheduled tribes has been defined under Article 366 of the Constitution.

Under Article 366(24) 'scheduled castes' means such castes, races or tribes or parts of or groups in such castes, races or tribes as are deemed under article 341 to be scheduled castes for the purposes of this Constitution. Similarly, 'scheduled tribes' means such tribes or tribal communities or parts or groups within such tribal communities as are deemed under Article 342 to be the scheduled tribes for the purposes of the Constitution. Initially, only members of the scheduled castes professing Hinduism and four castes among the Sikhs (Kabirpanthis, Ramdassias, Sikligars and Mazhbis) were included in the list in accordance with the provision made in the scheduled castes order appended to the Constitution. In 1956 it was extended to include all scheduled castes professing Sikhism. Ambedkar revived Buddhism and started mass conversion to Buddhism in October 1956. The Government of India issued orders declaring them ineligible to any of the concessions admissible to scheduled castes. In 1990 scheduled castes professing Buddhism were also included among the scheduled castes. There is no such restriction with regard to the people belonging to the scheduled tribes who return themselves as animists, Hindus, Christians or Buddhists. Article 14 guarantees equality: "The state shall not deny to any person equality before the law or the equal protection of the laws within the territory of India." Article 15 concerns discrimination against any citizen on grounds of religion, race, caste, sex, place of birth or any of them. Article 16(1) guarantees equality of opportunity in matters of public employment etc. Reservations in public services and educational institutions were created with a view to giving a share to the members of society who had been denied opportunities in the past. This naturally antagonised those sections of society who had been enjoying the monopoly of power. Immediately after the adoption of the Constitution, the provision of reservation under Article 16 was challenged through a writ petition filed in Madras High Court (*State of Madras vs Champakam Dorairajan*, April 1951). The case later came before the Supreme Court of India. It was held that the communal government order of the Madras government fixing the proportion of students of each community that could be admitted to state educational institutions was ultra vires under Article 29(2) (which states that no citizen shall be denied admission into any educational institution maintained by or receiving aid from the state on grounds only of religion, race, caste, or language) and was not saved by the provisions of Article 16. There was considerable protest in the southern states as the result of which the Constitution was amended for the first time, and clause 15(4) added, according to which nothing in this article or in clause (2) of Article 29 shall prevent the state from making any special provision for the advancement of any socially and educationally backward classes of citizens or for the scheduled castes and scheduled tribes.

Those who are opposed to reservations in public services have challenged all orders issued by the government under Article 15(1) or Article 16. Article 226 (on the enforcement of fundamental rights by a High Court) or Article 32 (concerning moving fundamental rights before the Supreme Court) are invoked and writ petitions are filed before the High Court. Sometimes the government comes before the Supreme Court, and sometimes it is the petitioners, if they feel aggrieved, who do so. Judicial process has routinely and effectively been used to obstruct the progress or to delay the implementation of reservation orders.

Post-independence India has witnessed many landmark cases which have affected the administration as well as interests of the scheduled castes, scheduled tribes and other backward classes. In the famous case of Balaji vs Mysore state in 1962, reservation orders were challenged on the grounds that the lists of backward classes were prepared only on the basis of caste and that this was unconstitutional. The Supreme Court struck down the Mysore backward classes list. Similar claims were again taken up in the Chitralekha case (*Chitralekha vs State of Mysore*, 1964). In this case, the Supreme Court interpreted the Balaji case somewhat differently. It was pointed out that two principles were prominent from the observations in Balaji's case, namely (1) "the caste of a group of citizens may be a relevant circumstance in ascertaining their social backwardness", and (2) though it is a relevant factor to determine the social backwardness of a class of citizens, "it cannot be the sole or dominant test". In another landmark case, namely, *Jayasree vs State of Kerala* (1976), the Supreme Court accepted the logic of the Kerala High Court that economic backwardness plays a part in social and educational backwardness. In the Thomas case (*State of Kerala vs N.H. Thomas*, 1976) the Supreme Court upheld caste-based reservation. The apex court also observed that the aim of the Constitution is to eliminate caste from the affairs of the state. Yet certain backward castes have to be recognised and classified for compensatory measures so that caste can be abolished ultimately.

The implementation of the recommendations of the Mandal Commission was challenged and opposed not only by angry students belonging to the Hindu upper castes, but also by the Supreme Court Bar Association. A writ petition was filed in the name of Indira Sawhney, one of the practising advocates in the Supreme Court.

Even though the rights of scheduled castes had nothing to do with the subject of the OBCs in the Mandal Commission Report, certain items affecting them were included as issues. Justice Ahmedi raised an objection and did not comment on the issues during the proceedings. The promotion of scheduled castes was discussed and the Supreme Court held that there should be no reservations in promotion. In spite of all the opposition to Mandal, reservations in favour of the other backward classes to the extent of 27 per cent was upheld and the agitationists were disappointed.

Besides these, there are landmark cases like the Rangachari case (*Rangachari vs General Manager*, 1962), Devadasan case (*Devadasan vs Union of India*, 1964, which was ruled out in the Indira Sawhney case), Hira Lal case, and the recently decided PGIMS Chandigarh case (reservation in medical colleges) and Ajit Singh Janjua case (seniority in promotion case) which have adversely affected the interests of the scheduled castes and scheduled tribes. Reservations were originally provided for the scheduled castes and scheduled tribes. It was extended to the other backward classes at the national level in 1993. Several states have passed their own laws and granted reservations to backward sections of society. It was held by the Supreme Court of India that reservations can be made under an executive order. However, in view of the recent judgments of the Supreme Court affecting the scheduled castes which have stirred the minds of the scheduled castes and scheduled tribes, the government is under pressure to enact a law so that the judiciary may not decide against the deprived and disadvantaged sections of society. Besides the scheduled castes, scheduled tribes and other backward classes, Christians of dalit origin and backward sections of Muslim society are also staking their claim for a share in governance. After independence and the creation of Pakistan, Muslims have not been able to enter public services. There is a genuine need to make provisions in order to make the bureaucracy more representative. Women who comprise about 49-50 per cent of population also deserve consideration for reservation not only in the legislatures but also in the bureaucracy.

As in the olden days some people raised the various cries, like 'religion is in danger', 'dhamma is in danger' or 'Islam is in danger', nowadays a new slogan is being raised: "abolish reservations because merit and efficiency are in danger". This is often heard in the Supreme Court also. Those who have been opposing reservations in public services and educational institutions do so because their personal interests are in jeopardy. Those who made the provisions in the Constitution had the interest of the nation in view. If more and more people take part in decision-making – which also means in the execution and implementation of these decisions taken in a democratic manner – the country will benefit. Those who want to maintain the status quo and consider their personal interests above the national interest, oppose reservations. Dominating groups who have been enjoying a monopoly of power are also notorious for corrupt practices. Be it said to our shame that our country's name appears among the most corrupt countries of the world. One wishes this pernicious development had also attracted the attention of the patriots and champions of merit.

21

Equality in Higher Education

The Impact of Affirmative Action Policies

S. SRINIVAS RAO

The educational disparities among different social groups in India have been both cause and consequence of difference in their levels of socio-economic development. Since achieving independence in 1947, India has sought to address this education challenge, motivated by concern for the well-being of the socially and economically deprived groups and for the health of the new nation. It was recognised that order for the nation to develop its human resources, it would need to ensure that all segments of the population received even handed attention and support. The social cohesion of the society depended on even distribution of resources among individuals and groups.

The builders of independent India also believed that education bore a special responsibility for transforming India's rich diversity into a constructive social force. They believed that higher education in particular constituted a mechanism for conferring socio-economic mobility on the socially and economically disadvantaged sections. Socio-economic mobility would in turn produce social integration and cohesion. As India became increasingly a "knowledge society" the need to broaden access to higher education became more urgent. Unfortunately, progress has occurred at a slower pace than one might have expected from the affirmative action policies of the government.

Post-independent India's doctrine of equality and social justice was embedded in a constitutional provision that established the reservation policies. The Constitution of India rightly notes that unless the inequalities are addressed through such policies and provisions, the declaration of equality and social justice for all citizens in the preamble of the Constitution, it would be meaningless and futile. Thus, the Constitution of India identifies certain groups that are deprived of access to education and other social and economic opportunities. They are referred to as Scheduled Castes (SCs), Scheduled Tribes (STs), and Other Backward Classes (OBCs). The reservation policy was designed to ensure that a certain level of access to these opportunities would be reserved for these groups. The policy was the linchpin of an emerging democracy's substantial commitment to social justice and equality.

This paper examines the impact of affirmative action policies in higher education during the fifty years after independence. It is divided into six sections. The first section deals with the nature and types of social inequality in India, while the second traces the evolution of affirmative action policy. The third section presents an overview of the status of Indian higher education and the position of historically deprived groups within it. It also specifies the representation of these groups in higher professional education, such as engineering and medicine, which are the most sought-after fields of study and the also most valued by contemporary Indian society.

The next section of the paper focuses on issues and problems related to the admission, retention and performance of students from the scheduled groups. It also describes the patterns of unequal treatment and discrimination that sometimes affect their entry, persistence and performance. The fifth section describes recent debates in the country over the implementation of affirmative action policies. The issues include demands for the inclusion of additional groups under the umbrella of the reservation policy, disagreements over the distribution of reserved spaces among groups, and the trade off between equality and excellence. The final section examines the position of scheduled groups and the affirmative action policy itself in India's emerging 'knowledge society' and offers some concluding observations.

Social Inequities in Indian Society

Caste is the most pervasive dimension of social stratification in India. A caste is a hereditary, endogamous, usually localised group of Hindus, with a traditional association with an occupation and a specified position in the local hierarchy of castes. Relation between the castes is governed, among other things, by such concepts as purity and pollution, division of labour, and segregation. Those at the top of the hierarchy of castes – the Brahmins – are believed to be the most clean and pure, while those at the bottom – the former "untouchables" – are impure and unclean. The untouchables were actually considered to be outside the "varna" system that divides all of relationship with the rest of the social hierarchy and forced them to live a life of social exclusion and isolation.

The practice of untouchability is reported even today in certain parts of the country and from time to time it evokes a national outcry of condemnation. Sometimes it results in violent conflict between the upper castes and the ex-untouchables. While it should be unthinkable in the present age of egalitarianism, civil democracy, and postmodernism that such a social perversion to persist in India. It condemns a section of Indian society to live from generation in deprivation and humiliation. The groups that experienced the worst deprivation in the past are now referred to as Scheduled Castes (SCs) and are covered under the affirmative action policy. They include the former untouchables, whom Mahatma Gandhi called "Harijan" or "children of the god". Their position has a major impact on the social structure of Hindu society. While they differ from region to region, from city to village, and among various occupations, their extreme poverty reflects general conditions in India, where an economy of scarcity has given rise to acute inequalities. In the past, education was completely denied to these segments of the population.

Another social group that remained beyond the reach of education comprised of the so-called Scheduled Tribes (STs). Most of the STs live in settled communities away from towns and villages, often in mountainous and forest regions. They are isolated, culturally and economically, but the isolation is imposed primarily by geography rather than by socially enforced tradition.

In addition to the SCs and STs, there are caste groupings that are somewhat higher in the hierarchy, but still bellow the present shudras. They include artisans, such as blacksmiths and barbers, cow herders and washermen. They are also educationally deprived, and are referred to as Other Backward Classes (OBCs). They too are covered by the affirmative action policy. In certain parts of contemporary India these groups fare better than the upper castes in term of ownership of land and political and economic power. It is interesting to note that these groups, like their upper caste counterparts, use oppression to enforce their dominance.

Evolution of Affirmative Action Policy in India[1]

The concern for the welfare of disadvantaged groups in India is not a post-independence phenomenon. It has a long history of advocacy and implementation even before 1947. The rigid Hindu caste structure and hierarchy were contested even in ancient times. The emergence and spread of such religions such as Buddhism, Jainism and Sikhism, and of the Bhakti movement gave impetus to the opposition. In the late nineteenth and early twentieth centuries, the cause was taken up by nationalist leaders and enlightened social reformers like Ishwar Chandra Vidyasagar, Raja Ram Mohan Roy, Gandhiji, Jyotiba Phule, and communities even before the colonial rulers took legislative action to ameliorate the living conditions of these deprived groups.

In the Caste Disabilities Act of 1850, the British rulers in India first introduced the principle of equality of all citizens before the law. In 1885, the provincial government of Madras made a provision for education of children from disadvantaged groups. Somewhat later, the Madras government reserved positions for non-Bramhins in government services. Another significant development came in 1918 when the Maharaja of Mysore appointed a committee for the upliftment of non-Bramhins. The committee recommended that within a period of not more than seven years, at least half of the higher and two-thirds of the lower appointments in each grade of government service, and so far as possible in each office, were to be held by members of non-Bramhin communities (Karnataka 1990).

The Montague-Chelmsford Reforms of 1919 envisaged representation of deprived groups in several local government and public bodies. Further, the legislative assemblies for the depressed castes, reservation for SCs were made for the first time in 1943, when a government service for them. The reservation quota was raised to 12.5 per cent in June 1946 to correspond with the proportion of members of Scheduled Castes in the population (Chanana 1993:

122). Special assistance to the backward classes was offered in education as well through a programme of scholarships introduced in 1945 for Scheduled Castes and extended three years later to Scheduled Tribes (GoI 1984: 55).

In Indian Constitution, the commitment made to social justice and equality emerged out of the conviction that education is a basic instrument of social mobility. Article 46 of the Constitution requires the state to "promote with special care the educational and economic interests of the weaker sections of the people, and in particular of the Scheduled Castes and Scheduled Tribes and [to] protect them from social injustice and all forms of social exploitation". Various commissions and policies on education in independent India explicitly stated the commitment mandated by the Constitution. For example, in 1949, the Radhakrishnan Commission on University Education stated that "education is the great instrument of social emancipation by which a democracy establishes, maintains and protects the spirit of equality among its members" (GoI 1950: 49). The Education Commission of 1964-66 provided the vision of Indian education as a mechanism for achieving civil society. The Commission observed that one of the important social objectives of education was to equalise opportunity, enabling the backward of underprivileged classes and individuals to use education as a leveller for the improvement of their condition. Every society that values social justice and is concerned to improve the lot of the common man and cultivate all available talent, must ensure progressive equality of opportunity to all sections of the population. This is the only guarantee for building up of an egalitarian and human society in which the exploitation of the weak will be minimised (GoI 1966).

Education is also viewed as an instrument for promoting social equality for all groups through the pursuit of social justice and integration (India 1986). This objective was also shared by two commissions appointed by the government, namely, Kalelkar and Mandal Commissions. The Mandal Commission, however, succeeded in defining the category of Other Backward Classes (OBCs) and established criteria for assigning castes to the category. It also recommended reserving 27 per cent of government jobs for groups in the category. The recommendation was shelved for a decade until the government under V.P. Singh decided to implement it. The decision evoked violent demonstrations by students belonging to upper castes. This percentage of reservation was in addition to the reservation provided for the Scheduled Castes (15%) and Scheduled Tribes (7.5%) The recommendation was not implemented until 1990 after much public debate and expressions of resentment.

After independence, in response to the special obligation placed on the Government of India by Article 15 (4) of the Constitution to make special provision in education for the disadvantages groups, the Ministry of Education sent a letter in 1954 to the Chief Secretaries of all state governments suggesting that 20 per cent of seats in educational institutions be reserved for the Scheduled Castes and Scheduled Tribes, and that minimum qualification grades for admission be reduced by 5 per cent. This was slightly modified in April 1964, when the reservations for Scheduled Castes were sets at 15 per cent and for Scheduled Tribes at 5 per cent. At the same time, the Ministry of Health and Family Welfare called upon the vice-chancellor of universities with medical faculties to reserve 15 per cent of seat for Scheduled Castes and 5 per cent for Scheduled Tribes and to reduce the minimum qualifying grades for admission to medical and dental programmes by 5 per cent. The University Grants Commission (UGC) also issued guidelines to the universities and colleges under their control to ensure that students from these groups received special consideration in all undergraduate and graduate programmes. The percentages of reservations for Scheduled Tribes were revised upward from 5 per cent to 7.5 per cent in 1982. At present, 15 per cent and 7.5 per cent of seats are reserved for students from Scheduled Castes and Scheduled Tribes respectively in all educational institutions.

Besides establishing reservation, the Government of India took additional steps to improve education of Scheduled Castes and Tribes. New institutions were established in areas where these groups live, student housing facilities were built, scholarships were made available, and academic support programmes were developed, all of which contributed a great deal to raising educational levels. The academic support programmes have focused on improving the students' general academic skills and linguistic proficiency, and raising their level of comprehension, especially in subjects where quantitative techniques and laboratory work are involved. Yet, another important step taken by the UGC in recent years was the appointment of a monitoring committee to oversee the implementation of reservation policies in universities under its control. For state universities, the UGC has set up regional committee to monitor the implementation of affirmative action policy. In a recent directive to the universities that are not implementing the policy in student admissions and faculty appointments that they may risk losing their funding.

The reservation policy does not envisage reservation for OBCs in national institutions. Individual states, on the other hand, have established varying reservations quotas for these groups. For example, Tamil Nadu, which has the highest percentage of reservations in the country, reserves 50 per cent of seats in state institutions for backward classes and a group designated as Most Backward Classes (MBCs). It reserves an additional 18 per cent for Scheduled Castes and one per cent for Scheduled Tribes. By contrast, Andhra Pradesh reserves 25 per cent of seats for the OBCs. Karnataka also reserves seats for this category in its educational institutions.

Higher Education in India

The expansion of higher education in India has been rapid since the achievement of independence. In 1947, there were twenty universities and 636 colleges in the country (NCERT 1961: 48). In academic year 1950-51, enrolments at the undergraduate level totalled 1,40,000, and at the graduate level 20,000. By 1998, the number of universities had grown to 237.

Over the past 25 years student enrolment has grown at the rate of 4.2 per cent per year (UGC 1994: 98). It more than doubled between 1974 and 1994 rising from 2.3 million to an estimated 5 million. But, the annual growth has not been uniform, and some observers find the pattern of growth as discouraging.

Eighty-eight per cent of students in the higher education system are enrolled at the undergraduate level. The percentage of students enrolled in graduate level courses is 9.4, while a very small proportion (1.1%) is doing research. Only 1.3 per cent are enrolled in diploma or certificate courses. In terms of areas of study, four out of ten students are in science courses. Another 20 per cent are in commerce courses. Thus, eight of every ten students are enrolled in science, arts, and commerce. The enrolment in engineering and technology education is very low, but has been increasing, especially since 1990. The study of agriculture as a discipline has not been prominent in India, despite the fact that India has a predominantly agricultural economy.

Scheduled Castes and Scheduled Tribes in Higher Education[2]

There is no doubt that the enrolment of students from scheduled groups has risen considerably since the establishment of the reservation system. But many observers find this progress inadequate in light of the large proportion of the scheduled population that has no access to higher education, or, for that matter, to minimum levels of literacy. This section reviews the programmes over the years with regard to the implementation of affirmative action policy in the country.

Table 1

Enrolment of Scheduled Groups in Higher Education

Year	*Non-Scheduled Castes*	*Scheduled Castes*	*Scheduled Tribes*	*Total*
1978-79	2,337,221(91.35)	180,058 (7.3)	41,081(1.6)	2,558,360(100)
1988-89	3,488,087(90.90)	279,720(7.29)	69,169(1.8)	3,836,976(100)
1995-96	5,532,998(89.24)	496,872(8.01)	170,239(2.74)	6,200,109(100)
1996-97	5,898,407(89,49)	512,291(7.77)	180,142(2.73)	6,590,840(100)

Figures in parentheses are percentages.

Sources: 1. Twenty-Eighth Report of the Commissioner for SC/ST, 1986-87, Government of India, New Delhi, 1987.

2. Select Education Statistics: 1988-89, Ministry of Human Resources Development, Government of India, New Delhi, 1989. Annual Report, 1996-97 and 1997-98, Ministry of Human Resources Development, Government of India, New Delhi, 1997 & 1998.

The data in Table 1 show that the enrolment of Scheduled Castes in higher education is very low. Though the actual enrolment increased from 1,80,058 in 1978-79 to 5,12,291 in 1996-97, the percentage of total enrolment did not show much improvement. On the other hand, the enrolment of Scheduled Tribes showed stronger growth, though from a significantly smaller base. Their share of total enrolment grew from 1.6 per cent in 1978-79 to 2.7 per cent in 1996-97.

While the period from 1978-79 to 1988-89 showed only a marginal increase in the percentage of Scheduled Castes and Scheduled Tribes, growth was considerably stronger during the period between 1988-89 and 1995-96. But, what these figures reveal most dramatically is that the enrolment of the SC/ST students in higher education is still far below the stipulated quotas of reservations, i.e., 15 per cent for Scheduled Caste and 7.5 per cent for Scheduled Tribes. Inter-state differences are also quite significant. In 1979-80, Uttar Pradesh had the highest percentage – 11.6 – of Scheduled Caste students enrolled at the undergraduate level, followed by Tamil Nadu (9%), West Bengal (8.4%), and Punjab (8.29%). The state of Meghalaya in the North East, where Scheduled Tribes are predominant, had the highest percentage – 66.9 – in this category, followed by Bihar with 6.86 per cent and Assam with 6.86 per cent (UGC 1990).

Unfortunately, a detailed report on the higher education of Scheduled Castes and Scheduled Tribes was last compiled by the UGC in 1990. Neither the UGC, nor the Ministry of Human Resource Development, nor the Scheduled Castes and Scheduled Tribes Commission has produced a subsequent report. The UGC attributes this situation to the failure of colleges and universities to submit timely data in usable form. In any event, the author had to compile data from different sources to get an idea about the situation of Scheduled Castes and Scheduled Tribes in higher education.

As stated earlier, nearly nine out of ten students from Scheduled Castes and Scheduled Tribes are enrolled at the undergraduate level in general programmes in the arts, sciences, and commerce. Their participation has been far lower in the more prestigious programmes – law, medicine, engineering, technology, and education – that lead to higher paying professional careers. In fact, the percentage of Scheduled Caste students enrolled in medicine actually declined between 1978 and 1997.

The enrolment of the SC students at the graduate level presents a similar picture. About 95 per cent of the SC students were enrolled in science and commerce programmes in 1978-79. The proportion of the SC students in professional programmes at the graduate level is still very low. For example, only 0.8 per cent, 0.5 per cent, and 1.6 per cent of the SC students have enrolled in graduate courses in education and engineering respectively. High rates of attrition among these students contribute to the problem.

As indicated above, the enrolment pattern among the undergraduate students from Scheduled Tribes is the same as that of Scheduled Castes, with about 90 per cent enrolled in arts, commerce and science programmes. In 1996-97, the proportion of Scheduled

Tribe Students at the undergraduate level in medicine, engineering, technology, and education was very low.

The pattern is clear. In response to the constitutional mandate for affirmative action, students from Scheduled Castes and Scheduled Tribes are admitted in substantially larger number into the general programmes in the arts, science and commerce, which prepare them least well for competition in the job market. Their enrolment in professional courses, for which the job market is attractive, is extremely low. The proportion of the SC/ST students in such emerging fields as information technology and biotechnology is at best negligible.

Scheduled Caste/Scheduled Tribe Students in Elite Technical Institutions

Indian Institutes of Technology (IITs) are the elite institutions that provide high quality technological and engineering education. IITs were first established in 1952, and for the first two decades admission into these institutions was based exclusively on performance in the national-level Joint Entrance Examination (JEE). It was only in 1973 that a policy of reservations was implemented. At present, 15 per cent of seats in IITs are reserved for Scheduled Castes and 7.5 per cent for Scheduled Tribes. Candidates from these groups are admitted if their score in the JEE is at least 60 per cent of the minimum score required for general admission. Student from the scheduled groups who score lower can enter a preparatory programme. If they complete it successfully, they are automatically admitted to the IIT.

But, despite all these efforts, the enrolment of SC/ST students in IITs is low (Table 2). At IIT, Delhi, for example, only 132 of the 355 seats reserved for Scheduled Caste undergraduate were filled in the academic year 1994-95. The shortfall was 62.82 per cent. It was even greater – 88.64 per cent – for Scheduled Tribe undergraduates. The situation was even worse at the graduate level. IIT, Kanpur showed the same pattern for undergraduates, but at the graduate level 79.6 per cent of seats reserved for Scheduled Castes were filled, while, surprisingly, not a single tribal student was enrolled at the graduate level.

Table 2

SC/ST Students in Elite Technical/Engineering Institutions (1994-95)

	UG	*PG*	*UG*	*PG*	*UG*	*PG*	*UG*	*PG*	*UG*	*PG*
Total seats	2457	483	375	53	527	450	348	261	408	422
Numbers of seats reserved for										
SC	355	72	53	19	28	67	57	40	61	17
ST	176	35	26	10	3	33	29	20	31	9
Number of candidates selected										
SC	132	21	19	14	28	54	28	48	32	0
ST	20	3	3	0	3	7	3	13	4	0
Shortfall percentage SC	62.82	71	64.2	21.4	0	19.5	51	Excess 20%	48.6	100
ST	88.64	92	88.5	100	0	78.8	90	35	871	100

UG: Undergraduate; PG: Postgraduate.

Source: Report on the Reservation for Employment of SCs/STs in IITs including Reservation for SCs/STs in Admission therein. Standing Committee for Welfare of SC/ST. Fifth Report. (1998-99). Lok Sabha Secretariat, New Delhi, pp. 21, 23, 25, 27, 29.

At IIT, Kharagpur all the seats reserved for scheduled groups were filled at the undergraduate level. However, at the graduate level, the shortfall was 19.5 per cent for Scheduled Castes and 78.8 per cent for Scheduled Tribes. Some of the differences between institutions are particularly striking. IIT Chennai, for example, had more Scheduled Caste students in graduate course than the number of seats reserved for them, while at IIT, Mumbai there were no SC or ST students at the graduate level.

Scheduled Caste and Scheduled Tribe Women in Higher Education

The participation of women in general programmes of higher education is far from satisfactory. Analysis of data from 1971 to 1994 reveals that the enrolment of men in general higher education increased from 1.2 million in 1971 to 2.7 million in 1994 (IAMR 1995: 68-69). Though the number of women in general higher education has shown some sign of progress, it is far behind the number of men. For instance, a survey published in 1997 showed there were 52 women for every 100 men enrolled in higher education in India (UGC 1997: 160). But, since 1971, the gap has been narrowing. In

1971, the number of men in general higher education was almost three times the number of women. It was 2.5 times as great in 1981. In professional programmes the situation is much worse. In 1981 the number of men in professional education programmes was six times that of women, and it had not improved by 1991 (IAMR 1995: 68-69).

Table 3

Proportion of Women in the Total Enrolment

Year	*Men*	*Women*	*Total*
Non Scheduled Castes			
1995-96	3,546,366 (64.09)	1,986,632 (35.90)	5,532,998 (100)
1996-97	3,771,100 (63.93)	2,127,307 (36.06)	5, 898,407 (100)
Scheduled Castes			
1995-96	363,783 (73.21)	133,089 (26.78)	496,872 (100)
1996-97	371,783 (72.57)	140,508 (27.42)	512,291 (100)
Scheduled Tribes			
1995-96	119,911 (70.43)	50,328 (29.56)	170,239 (100)
1996-97	127,378 (70.7)	52.764 (29.2)	180,142 (100)

Figures in parentheses indicate percentages.

Source: Annual Reports: 1997-98, Ministry of Human Resource, Government of India, New Delhi, 1997 & 1998.

The enrolment of women from Scheduled Castes and Scheduled Tribes is still worse (Table 3). Women from these categories constituted only 27.42 per cent and 29.2 per cent of the total enrolment from their respective groups in 1996-97. This compares with 36.06 per cent of non-scheduled students who are women. This shows that women in the scheduled categories are even more seriously disadvantaged with respect to access to higher education than are non-scheduled women.

One way to assess the seriousness of these inequalities in Indian higher education is to consider the case of a woman from a Scheduled Caste or a Scheduled Tribe from a village in a backward region. Her chances of finding a place in higher education are extremely remote (Chanana 1993). What holds true of women is equally true for other disadvantaged population? The lower the position of a person in the social hierarchy, the greater the chance that the he or she will be denied access to higher education.

Issues and Problems

Access/Retention/Performance. A very pertinent question arises at this juncture: Who has benefited most from the expansion of education? J.P. Naik, an eminent educationist, answered it this way.

> At the *elementary stages,* the weaker *sections of* the *community* get *very* little *benefit;* it *appears* that the quality *of* education *provided* at the *secondary stage is far* less than at the *elementary stage...* At the university *stage, the top* 5 per cent *of* the *social strata* take *more* than 70 per cent *of the seats* (Naik 1965: 108).

The Education Commission (1964-66), in its study of the socio-economic background of students, substantiated this observation. The situation in technical education is much more appalling. The marginal representation of students from Scheduled Castes and Scheduled Tribes is, even today, an indicator of unequal educational opportunity. In other words, the reach of the higher education system is not commensurate with the national goal of equality.

The problems of poor access and low retention begin in the lower schools (Chanana 1993: 144). The single most important factor is the absence of schools in many areas where Scheduled Castes and Scheduled Tribes reside. In recent years the government has sought to address this issue by creating more schools in areas to which scheduled groups have access.

It is also noteworthy that higher education in India has an urban bias. Those who spent most of their lives in urban areas have an overwhelming majority in higher education. Students in the general higher education programmes from Scheduled Castes and Scheduled Tribes, on the other hand, are largely from rural backgrounds and tend to be first-generation participants in higher education. Their parents tend to be in low-status occupations and have little or no education. Their educational opportunities are thus crippled by the lack of economic resources in the family and the competing pressure to help the family eke out a living.

Caste, class and gender all play a role in limiting the educational opportunities of the scheduled groups. While gender bias may affect girls from all socio-economic strata, factors related to caste and class are also influential. In the case of boys, they are expected to engage directly in economic activities that benefit the family, which in some cases provides an incentive to purse higher education, but in other cases may compel them to forego education in favour of an immediate economic gain.

Where schools are available to the members of scheduled groups, their quality is an important factor in determining educational outcomes. The quality of schooling that most Scheduled Caste and Scheduled Tribe students receive is inferior to the schooling available to the more privileged children who find their way into the prestigious courses and institutions (Chitnis 1988: 161).In recent years, efforts have been made to raise achievement levels among Scheduled Caste and Scheduled Tribe students by setting up residential schools. The students who are admitted to these schools receive extra coaching designed to overcome their social and educational deficiencies. Remedial coaching is also provided in subjects such as language, mathematics and science. Special coaching is also available to prepare students for the entrance examinations required by many higher education institutions.

The Scheduled Caste and Scheduled Tribe students in the professional colleges and institutions usually hailed from families with middle or higher occupational status. This gives rise to the argument that the professional educational institutions are socially exclusive and that they are accessible only to groups occupying higher positions in the socio-economic hierarchy, regardless of caste affiliation. This situation is described in the author's doctoral thesis on "Equality and Excellence in the Institutions of Engineering and Technology in India" (Rao 1997). In the words of a Scheduled Caste student,

> Since my childhood, I see my village worse than slum. Even if the reservations are continued for next fifty years, it doesn't matter. They are at least providing opportunities far some of them to get into good institutions. Most of the depressed group people in my area are not even aware of the facilities (ibid.).

Yet another Scheduled Caste student focuses on the lack of proper literary home environment as a cause of poor access and retention of Scheduled Castes and Scheduled Tribes in higher education. He notes:

> For example, I found a dictionary printed in 1940s in one of my forward caste, Brahmin friend's room and it belongs to his great grandfather. That means in 1940s itself, my friend's ancestors are well educated. But, whereas my father is the only person who studied. He was able to study because of reservations which helped him getting free hostel, mess, books and then a job (ibid.).

The factors related to caste, class and gender that affect access and retention of students from scheduled groups also affect their performance levels. The differences between the performance levels of Scheduled Caste and Scheduled Tribe students and students from non-scheduled groups become apparent at their entry into the higher education institutions either in an entrance examination or in the grades they received in prior courses of study. The experience at the Indian Institutes of Technology (IITs) is a very good illustration. In order to be admitted to an IIT, a student from a Scheduled Caste or Scheduled Tribe must achieve a score that is at least 60 per cent of the lowest score achieved by a non-scheduled student who is admitted. The large performance differential has brought into the institutions a significant number of academically deficient students who have considerable difficulty in coping with the system in spite of remedial measures (Indiresan and Nigam 1993: 357-58). Further, of those admitted, almost 25 per cent are asked to leave the institutions due to their poor academic performance. The Twenty-Sixth Report of the Commissioner for Scheduled Castes and Scheduled Tribes (1978: 39) describes the problem in the following words:

> It is reported from various studies that the performance of these (Scheduled Caste and Scheduled Tribe) students after admission was not very satisfactory. Even after the special coaching, several students left the course and a number of them could not withstand the strain of a five year course.

Attempts to narrow down the performance gap have included special preparatory courses, coaching programmes, faculty improvement, summer sessions, and mentoring programmes involving older students. But, the problems often persist and prevent students from being promoted to the next class. Some students drop out of courses, and some leave the institution.

Kirpal and Gupta (1999) have recently studied the issue of academic performance of students from scheduled groups and its linkages with socio-economic background, educational background, and deficiencies in English. They noted that the Scheduled Caste and Scheduled Tribe students feel alienated from mainstream students because of differences of caste and class and they do feel financially inferior. At the same time, they feel that they are not able to meet the academic standards expected by the institutions. They feel helpless and their motivation is undermined, which further alienates them from the mainstream and widens both the social and academic gaps. But Kirpal and Gupta concluded that it was the social divide that affected the students most deeply (Kirpal and Gupta 1999: 32).

As we have seen, higher education is still not accessible to a large proportion of the socially disadvantaged population of India. We have also noted that enrolment patterns vary widely, from state to state, from institution to institution, among programmes and disciplines. It is clear that the policy of reservations is implemented more fully in some instances than in others. This is clearance in the dichotomy between general programmes in the arts, sciences and commerce, and professional programmes in such fields as medicine and engineering. It is often explained in terms of the low number of students from disadvantaged groups who apply for professional courses. The explanation is used by institutions to absolve themselves of responsibility for the discrepancies. But, if the goal of upward mobility for the disadvantaged population is to be credible, and if the national commitment to the ideals of social justice and equality is to be realised, the current situation is unacceptable.

The problems of access, retention and performance represent the challenge of socialising the underserved population into the social and academic pattern of the education system. The challenge is to assimilate the Scheduled Castes and the Scheduled Tribes into a higher education system that is poorly matched to their learning needs and inhospitable to them culturally and socially. The problems are especially acute in the most prestigious institutions and the most demanding academic programmes (Chitnis 1988: 163). These students are not adequately equipped to cope up with the academic pressure and competitive climate of the institutions. Furthermore, they are students who would not, but for the policy of reservations, have found their way in.

The Practice of Discrimination

Discrimination is defined here as unequal treatment that is detrimental to the socially disadvantaged groups in higher education. Discrimination towards the Scheduled Castes and Scheduled Tribes has a negative impact on their psycho-social integration and development. While discrimination is not rampant in all educational institutions, prejudice related to caste and tribal affiliation certainly exists. Discrimination by non-scheduled students against the scheduled group – is often born out of resentment over what appears to be preferential treatment of scheduled groups. They are viewed as beneficiaries of the reservation system who got seats despite their poorer academic performance! They get free books, their fees are waived, they receive financial assistance, and they have an advantage in getting good jobs. Older students are often a source of discrimination against younger ones, but, in others cases, classmates discriminate, sometimes in unspoken ways (Kirpal and Gupta 1999; Rao 1997).

Teachers are another source of discrimination. The manner in which they discriminate is best explained in the personal experiences of a few Scheduled Caste and Scheduled Tribe students. A student in the College of Engineering, Chennai, observed:

> The teacher knows how to take revenge against Scheduled Caste and Scheduled Tribe students particularly, in awarding marks. Once I was affected by this and then onwards, I lost interest in studies. This happened in the fourth semester. In the, department, about 60-70 per cent teachers show this kind of discrimination. Even if one works hard, this happens. This happens only with the reserved category students (Rao 1997).

Another student in the IIT, Chennai narrates his experience:

> I met a professor to tell my problem that I am unable to understand what he is teaching in the class. The first question he asked me was, "Are you a reserved caste student?" Will he say the same thing if a general category student goes to him with a doubt (ibid.).

These feelings of discrimination often result from a reference to caste, tribe, or scheduled status which assumes that the student is academically inferior. The Scheduled Caste and Scheduled Tribe Commission of the Government of India tries to address these issues when they are brought to its attention. During 1993-94, there were 108 complaints to the Commission concerning educational institutions (GoI 1996: 25). There were allegations of intentional discrimination, failure to follow required procedures, and violation of safeguards by authorities at various levels. There were 26 cases alleging violation of reservation requirements for the admission of students from scheduled groups to engineering, medical and other professional courses. However, the investigation of such complaints by the Commission has proved to be ineffective, for two reasons. First, the follow-up of complaints by the Commission is so slow that it discourages complainants from pursuing their grievances.

Second, many of the complainants appear to be politically motivated or vindictive. In any event, discrimination is a problem whether it is real, perceived, feigned, or a combination of these. It can disrupt the smooth functioning of an educational institution, and it often further alienates students from their academic pursuits and encourages them to drop out.

Recent Debates

Demands for Expansion of the Reservation System

The reservation system is seen as a means to emancipate from abject coordination of living, and all segments of the affected population want to acquire for themselves as large a share as possible of the new wealth and opportunities. As a result, it has become necessary not only to continue the policy of affirmative action, but also to increase its scope. The recent demands for a 30 per cent reservation for women and for proportional representation for the backward classes and minorities are a case in point. Furthermore, those among the beneficiaries who already enjoy the greatest advantages, seek to obtain an even larger share of the benefits.

Five decades of implementation of affirmative action policy in India have thus brought into focus the need to take a fresh look at the system and at the way its benefits are distributed. The current system of distributing the benefits of reservations uniformly does not reflect the fact that some individuals and groups have benefited from reservations to such an extent that their socio-economic circumstances rival those of the upper castes. For example, the Mahars of Maharashtra, Malas of Andhra Pradesh, the Pariahs of Tamil Nadu, the Chamars of Uttar Pradesh and the Meenas of Rajasthan are now better off than most of the castes and tribes in the scheduled category. This has occurred because the reservations are assigned to the scheduled category as a whole rather than assigned proportionally to a group within the category.

The specific case of Andhra Pradesh is interesting because it has recently brought the issue of proportional representation within Scheduled Castes into the national debate. Two major castes, the Malas and the Madigas, together constitute 80 per cent of the total Scheduled Caste population in the state. While the Madigas are concentrated in the backward Telangana region, the Malas are the major Scheduled Caste in the districts of coastal Andhra. In the third region, Rayalaseema, the Midas and the Madigas comprise more or less in similar proportions. Traditionally, the Malas have pursued agricultural labour and claim purity on the basis of the nature of their work. Madigas, on the other hand, remove the skin from dead animals, which is later processed into leather. By the very nature of their occupation, the Madigas rank lower than the Malas in the caste hierarchy.

Malas were exposed to education earlier than the Madigas for two reasons. First, educational reform activity reached them earlier. Second, since Malas were engaged in a seasonal occupation dependent on the monsoon and successful harvests their income was not steady and it was difficult for them to depend exclusively on agricultural labour. As a result, they had to look for alternatives to eke out their living, and modern education provides an answer. Madigas, on the other hand, had steady income and were not forced to look for alternative sources.

The relative levels of development of the Malas and Madigas is reflected in their respective shares of reserved appointments in public services and reserved admissions to educational institutions. The Malas have benefited more, and the resultant antagonism between the two groups has virtually split the entire category of Scheduled Castes into two warring factions. One favours the current system, which benefits them disproportionately, whereas the other favours a system that would assign reservations to the individual groups within the category rather than to the category as a whole.

What this feud ignores is the fact that in relation to the upper castes, both Malas and Madigas remain disadvantaged. Of those who have obtained positions in the civil services, most are in low-paying jobs. Another important dimension that these groups have not considered is that the market for the government jobs subject to the constitutional provisions for reservations is shrinking. As more and more of them are privatised, the benefits to the scheduled category will diminish. Thus, the debate over the distribution of reservations may in the long run exacerbate the current problem of social exclusion in the country.

The Debate on Equality versus Excellence

The contemporary debate over affirmative action has also brought into focus the perceived trade-off between equality and excellence. While the one argument pleads for the equalisation of educational opportunity in higher education, the other argues that the development of a society depends more on the quality of goods and services produced than on equality of educational opportunity. It is generally believed that the pursuit of equality causes excellence to suffer, and vice versa. It is also argued that the pursuit of equal access would siphon resources away from the achievement of excellence. How do we foster excellence and yet maintain equality? What are the trades-offs when we emphasise one goal over the other? What is the relationship between the two goals in institutions of higher education that assign a higher priority on excellence?

It is interesting to note some of the perceptions of students in IITs and colleges of engineering where the debate on equality versus excellence is intense. My study on equality and excellence in the institutions of engineering and technology (Rao 1997) revealed some of the contradictions in the debate and its explosive nature. Those who argued in favour of affirmative action noted that the reservation system compensates for the environmental deficiencies that prevent students from the Scheduled Castes and Scheduled Tribes from getting an education. They also argued that reservations are necessary to uplift the weaker sections of society from utter poverty and oppression. The contention of these students is best represented in the words of a few students. For instance, a Scheduled Caste student from an IIT states:

> The policy of reservations is good. In my family, I am the first person to get into IITs. Most of the Scheduled Caste and Scheduled Tribe students are the first members of their family to get exposed to IITs. Other students' parents or brothers or sisters are already exposed to good education.

On the other hand, the respondents who were against the policy of reservation, argued that caste should not be the basis of reservations in admissions. They favour using the economic status of the family of a student as the basis for reservations. According to them, the reservations have so far catered only to the students from scheduled families that are economically well-off. They also contended that reservations deny admission to the academically deserving. An IIT student from a non reserved caste argued:

> The present policy of reservations is ridiculous because an IAS officer's son who is academically weak has a preference over a lorry driver's son who is bright and academically sounds, just because the former is from the reserved caste and the latter from the non-reserved caste.

Another such student argued eloquently:

> I am against reservations in top institutions of India. Elsewhere, reservations should be made on the basis of economic background as well as on the merit of student and the percentage of reservations should not exceed 25 per cent in any case. Reservations should be based on economic criteria because it will help the country realise the ideal of economic equality and narrow down the disparities between different sections.

Other opponents of reservations argued that they lower academic standards and the reputation of the institution. According to them, the emphasis in admission to IITs should be solely on an individual merit and competence, irrespective of caste or class background. An IIT student from a non-reserved caste put forward the following argument:

> Firstly, isn't it frustrating that a guy after putting much hard work cannot get into an institution, while his classmates whose academic records were not as good as his, can get through, without putting much hard work, just because he had the necessary certificates (Scheduled Caste, Scheduled Tribe, etc.)with him? Secondly, think of the situation in medicine and engineering. Isn't it sad that we are producing inefficient doctors and engineers because of the folly of policy makers, who may be risking the life of a human being or a nation? Thirdly, reservations in admission had to be followed by reservations in government jobs. Doesn't the inclusion of inefficient people jeopardize the efficiency of the government departments and offices?

In summary, the arguments in favour of affirmative action centre around the socio-economic and educational backwardness of Scheduled Castes and Scheduled Tribes that has resulted from age-old social oppression and segregation. Since the economic backwardness of each individual is difficult to measure in a country like India, caste is taken as a surrogate criterion that can easily be identified and positioned in relation to other castes. The opponents to affirmative action argue that the current system favours those at the top of the scheduled category and thus reinforces stratification. They also argue that reservations lower standards and give the less meritorious and therefore presumably less intelligent an advantage that is not only unfair, but also inefficient.

Conclusions: Future of Affirmative Action in India

The debate over excellence and equality leads us to another pertinent question: What is the future of affirmative action policy in a country that aspires to be both a "knowledge society" and a civil society? An exclusive focus on merit or excellence is questionable as a criterion for the distribution of a scarce commodity, such as high quality education, in a democratic country like India. On the other hand, an exclusive concern about quality and social justice is questionable if it denies individuals or groups opportunities to acquire knowledge and achieve success in 21st century India. This dilemma is obviously of great concern to the social and educational policy makers guiding India's transition to a knowledge-driven society.

An important development in the Indian economy in recent years is that the service sector consisting of trade, commerce, transport, construction, communications, banking, insurance, public administration, defence and the professions now contributes more than half of the real Gross Domestic Product (GDP) in the country (Kurien 1999). Its share in the GDP exceeded the combined contribution of the other two sectors, viz., agriculture and manufacturing. This is remarkable in an economy that usually claims agriculture as the backbone of an emerging industrial power. This new development in the economy reflects the contribution of skill-intensive services that add high value. The bulk of the service sector – trade, communications, banking, and insurance – represents a spurt in technological progress in these fields. This has obviously induced a shift in employment patterns from agriculture and industry to the service sector.

A related development in higher education in India is the growing demand for courses related to electronics software, computers, and information technology. Today, even a typist needs computer skills, and India is known all over the world for producing a sizeable proportion of the world's software professionals. These developments are leading India toward becoming a knowledge society. A knowledge society requires an open system of continuous learning characterised by flexibility and availability without regard to time or place. Every aspect of life, at both the individual and social levels, offers opportunities for both learning and doing. Therefore, learning does not stop with the award of a degree, and the highest educational achievement is in fact to "learn to team". The implication of this for higher education is that the colleges and universities change from "teaching systems" into "learning systems".

But, in this context, where do we place the educational advancement of the Scheduled Castes and Scheduled Tribes in India? The participation of Scheduled Castes and Scheduled Tribes in the sectors of higher education contributing to the emergence of a knowledge society, namely, electronics, information technology, software development, and the like, is likely to remain very low. This is because these courses are offered either in the elite public institutions of technology and management or in self-financing private institutions, both out of reach for these students. Most of the courses in these institutions and employment in these fields are not effectively covered under the system of reservations, either because the system is circumvented or because the opportunities lie in the private sector. As more and more government jobs are privatised through government reforms, the large number of students from scheduled groups that graduate with general degrees in the arts, sciences and commerce will be increasingly marginalised and redundant in the job market. The situation will be further aggravated if the students graduate without a basic understanding of information technology. Today, the question is not whether one group is unjustly exploiting another, but whether historically depressed groups will become invisible in a knowledge society that has denied them the information and skills for meaningful participation. The priority of the affirmative action policy must therefore be to give the Scheduled Castes and Scheduled Tribes effective access to the knowledge society.

Yet another crucial question is what will happen to the social stigma that is attached to these scheduled groups as they gain wealth and power. It has been my experience that increasing levels of education have not really changed the attitudes of hatred and discrimination in the minds of the so-called upper castes. A Scheduled Caste officer is not simply referred to as an officer by his position, or by his name, but by his ascriptive status, no matter how brilliant he is at his job. Even, at the village level, the education of students from the scheduled groups is seen not as a positive development for the marginal group, but as a negation of the traditional authority of the upper castes. This conflict has manifested itself in political agitation, legal battles, public protests, and sometimes violent clashes. There have been massacres of disadvantaged groups by upper castes and instances of retaliation by the disadvantaged groups against the upper castes. These conflicts reflect a growing negative caste consciousness that pits groups against each other. These hatreds and vindictive attitudes vitiate trust among the groups and make it more difficult to cultivate a positive understanding of diversity that leads to mutual benefits. We must ask, will the emerging knowledge society contribute to a more just and civil society, or will it further widen the gap between oppressors and the oppressed? That is a question to be debated and answered by the policy makers of 21st century India.

One of the major factors that a new policy must address is the distribution of socio-economic distress and deprivation within the Scheduled Castes and Scheduled Tribes. The deprivation may differ from region to region, sub-caste to sub-caste, tribe to tribe, as well as between genders. Because of this diversity of conditions and attitudes, it may not be feasible to have a uniform policy across the country. There is, therefore, a need to evolve indicators that could facilitate fair distribution of benefits and avoid their concentration in a single social stratum. There is an urgent need to identify the neglected sub-groups within the category of Scheduled Castes and Scheduled Tribes and provide them with educational supports that will create an educational pathway for them into the knowledge society. This will require new schools and programmes, beginning at the primary level and extending through higher education. The policy should pay special attention to the psycho-social needs of first-generation learners, scheduled groups, and women.

India needs a new policy on affirmative action to respond to basic changes occurring in the economy and society. The new policy must continue to address poverty, wages, land rights, protection of traditional occupations, and the like. But, it must also address the increasing inequality that threatens to damage the members of the very castes and tribes the original policy was designed to help. A new policy can pave the way for India to emerge as a vibrant egalitarian civil democracy in which each citizen has a valued role to play in the nation's development in the 21st century.

Notes

1. There is a difference in the way the term 'affirmative action' is used in the United States and India. In the United States affirmative action refers to the preference given to deprived groups, all other things being equal. In India, affirmative action refers to the special privileges or concessions that are reserved for designated groups. The policy is known as the "reservation" policy or the policy of "positive discrimination".
2. The Constitution of India establishes the categories of Scheduled Castes and Scheduled Tribes. It also contains provisions for "other socially and educationally backward groups" in its 1978 report on affirmative action. The Mandal Commission used the category Other Backward Classes extensively and included the artisan castes in it. The term "class" was used to underscore the fact that in Indian affirmative action law, inequalities and preferences are ascribed only to groups, not to individuals

Reference

Chanana, K. 1993. Accessing higher education - the dilemma of schooling: Women, minorities, scheduled castes, and scheduled tribes in contemporary India. In S. Chitnis and P. Altbach, eds. *Higher Education Reform in India: Experience and Perspectives.* New Delhi: Sage Publications.

Chitnis, S. 1988. Educating the weaker sections of society. In A. Singh and P. Altbach, eds. *Higher Education in India: The Social Context.* New Delhi: Konark Publishers.

Galanter, M. 1984. *Competing Inequalities.* Delhi: Oxford University Press.

Government of India. 1950. Report of the University Education Commission: December 1948-August 1949. New Delhi: Ministry of Education.

—. 1966. Report of the Education Commission'(1964-66). New Delhi: Ministry of Education.

—. 1984. Report of the Commissioner for SC/ST; Twenty-sixth Report (April 1983 - March 1984). New Delhi: Ministry of Education.

—. 1986. National Policy on Education. New Delhi: Ministry of Human Resources Development.

—. 1987. Report of the Commissioner for SC/ST, Twenty-eighth report (1986-87). New Delhi: Ministry of Education.

—. 1989. Selected Educational Statistics, 1988-89. New Delhi: Ministry of Human Resources Development.

—. 1996. Report of the National Commission for Scheduled Castes and Scheduled Tribes, Second Report: 1 April 1993 to 31 March 1994. New Delhi: Ministry of Education.

—. 1997a Selected Educational Statistics, 1996-97. New Delhi: Ministry of Human, Resources Development.

—. 1997b. Annual Reports: 1996-97. New Delhi: Ministry of Human Resources Development.

Indiresan, P.V. and N.C. Nigam. 1993. The Indian Institutes of Technology: Excellence in Peril. In S. Chitnis and P. Altbach, eds. 1993. *Higher Education Reform in India: Experience and Perspectives.* New Delhi: Sage Publications.

Institute of Applied Manpower Research (lAMR). 1995. *Manpower Profile India: Year book.* New Delhi: IAMR.

Kamat, A.R. 1985. *Education and Social Change.* Bombay: Somaiya.

Karnataka, Government of. 1990. *Report of the Karnataka Third Backward Classes' Commission,* Volume I. Bangalore.

Kirpal, V. and M. Gupta. 1999. *Equality Through Reservations.* Jaipur: Rawat Publications.

Kurien, C.T. 29 September 1999. The surging services sector. *The Hindu.*

Naik, J.P. 1965. *Educational Planning in India.* Delhi: Allied Publishers.

National Council of Educational Research and Training (NCERT): 1961. *Review of Education In India* 1947-1961. First Yearbook of Education. New Delhi.

Rao, S.S. 1997; Equality and excellence in the Institutions of engineering and technology in India. Ph.D. Dissertation. New Delhi: Jawaharlal Nehru University.

University Grants Commission (UGC). 1990. Report on the facilities to SCs and STs in Universities and Colleges. New Delhi.

—. 1990. Annual Report: 1989-1990. New Delhi.

—. 1994. Annual Report: 1993-1994. New Delhi.

—. 1997. Annual Report: 1996-1997. New Delhi.

22

Reservation and Casteism

C.P. BHAMBHRI

It is a truism that public life in India is conditioned and controlled by caste identities. It can be stated unambiguously that 'casteisation' of politics has become a reality because the political class has nurtured and manipulated caste versus caste identities to win an election on the basis of assured caste-based social constituencies. While the emergence of casteism as an ideology has been attributed to the technologies of electoral politics followed by the political class, it has not been an issue of public discourse that the policy of reservations might have also contributed to the solidification of casteism in India. Hence, it deserves to be stated that the linkage between reservation policies and the growth of casteist consciousness should be examined in a dialectical manner. While affirmative action or preferential policies have been implemented to deal with the inherited caste-based injustices and discrimination, its negative consequences have not been properly analysed because reservation which has created vested interests in caste identities has been kept out of the public discourse.

'Politically Correct' Discourse

Public discourse on the issue of reservations for dalits in public institutions has become politically correct because any critique or concrete suggestion for an alternative approach to the issue of affirmative action evokes a very hostile response from the champions of reservations for dalits. It deserves to be clearly stated that the doctrine of affirmative action, popularly known as the policy of reservations in India, had elicited multiple intellectual and political opinions in the US beginning from the 1860s to the middle of the 1960s when the then President John F. Kennedy had to order 'federal forces' to put some sense into the racist southern states. Americans not only hotly debated and discussed the multiple dimensions of affirmative action for about a century, they arrived at a kind of intellectual, political and judicial consensus only at the beginning of the 1960s when the US economy had arrived at a 'golden phase of capitalism' as described by historian Eric Hobbawm. Not only this. Every step forward towards affirmative action brought US presidents from across the political spectrum face to face with the Supreme Court because conservative judges had to be dealt with by the President 'nominating' judges who were in tune with the changing public opinion in the country. Unlike US judges, the Indian judiciary has played a constructive and moderating role to arrive at a proper balance between the social need for reservations and the adventurism of vote-seeking politicians.

The demand for extending reservations to the private sector has once again created a mood of political confrontation between a section of the political class and the captains of industry represented by FICCI and CII. Ram Vilas Paswan of the Lok Jan Shakti Party, Meira Kumar of the Congress along with many dalit MPs have launched a political campaign for a policy of reservation in the Indian private sector which so far has been outside the purview of such a quota system in recruitment. A few arguments advanced by the supporters of such a new policy on reservations deserve to be stated to understand the real intentions of the dalit political leaders. First, dalit leaders have maintained that the economic policy of 'liberalisation, globalisation and privatisation' (LPG) has led to the 'shrinkage' of the state and public sector jobs are therefore becoming limited. Second, not only are employment opportunities in government services decreasing, India has been witnessing growing unemployment. Third, while job opportunities are expanding in high technology sectors, the manufacturing sector is not able to absorb the new entrants to the job market and the decrease in capital investment in agriculture in the 1990s has hit employment generation in rural India. In such a pessimistic scenario, the private industrial sector should take on new social responsibilities of hiring dalits on a preferential basis by fixing a quota as in the case of public sector undertakings. On December 10, 2004, on a private member resolution on reservations for SCs/STs in the private sector, the Minister of Social Justice and Empowerment, Meira Kumar told the Rajya Sabha, "There is no need for the government to impose reservations". A letter was also sent to 218 industry and trade organisations by the Secretary in the Ministry of Social Justice to elicit their response to the idea of affirmative action by the private sector.

Voluntariness is a mask worn by politicians who have to cater to their specific social constituency and its elite for winning an election. The cat was outside the bag when Ram Vilas Paswan, a great champion of reservations, announced on November 27, 2004 that the winning formula for his Lok Jan Shakti Party to counter Lalu Prasad's Rashtriya Janata Dal in Bihar was to lead a 'Muslim-dalit' coalition to confront the 'Muslim-Yadav' combination of Lalu Prasad. The argument of social justice for dalits advanced by the Paswan and Meira Kumar fell to the pieces when Paswan declared on November 27, 2004 that "this time the state will see how successfully the Muslims and dalits can bring about a change by putting LJP at the top". Along with dalits, Paswan played the Muslim card by proclaiming, "If the LJP comes to power, this government will provide 10 per cent reservation to Muslims in jobs. Besides it will also set up a Central Muslim University in the state to provide adequate academic platform to the Muslims." India is witnessing a raw, vulgar and naked election politics by the use of vote banks by the proponents of reservations for dalits. Not to be left behind, the other backward caste (OBC) MPs have also demanded a quota of reservations in the private sector.

Profitable Political Platform

It deserves to be clearly stated that neither can the claimants for reservations take refuge behind the spurious argument of 'social justice for the dalit' nor can the opponents maintain that 'meritocracy' is the sole criterion of employment in the private sector. Public discourse on reservations for the socially disadvantaged has to be rescued from both the proponents of social justice and champions of 'meritocracy' because both of them are hiding more than they are revealing to the public. Politicians are only worried about their vote banks and it is only the elite among the dalits who are the real concern of the dalit political leadership. It is only the makers of the Constitution who were genuinely interested in providing reservations for the SCs and STs as a 'transitory' phenomenon because during the freedom struggle the issue of acute social discrimination against the dalits had assumed great importance for the nationalist leadership. Further, the British colonial rulers, in their policy of divide and rule, were determined to fragment India by showing special preferences for dalits, Muslims and the princely states. The post-independence political class has found reservations to be a profitable political platform as witnessed clearly in August 1990 when V.P. Singh announced the acceptance of Mandal Commission Report on reservations to divert the attention of his opponents in his ragtag government of 1989-90.

V.P. Singh sang the song of empowerment of the backward castes by accepting the Mandal Commission recommendations on reservations and he was not worried about the caste war in North India. The politics of social division and fragmentation has been the staple diet of sectarian casteist and communalist leaders who play the card of reservations and 'Hindutva' to win an election. The public discourse on extending reservations to the private sector has to be rescued from the social justice versus meritocracy campaign and it deserves to be clearly stated that caste as an identity marker by the political class has completely casteised Indian society and polity and the goal of establishing a casteless society has been derailed by the Indian state by making caste a point of entry to claim public resources. If the Indian state was really interested in the 'empowerment' of the historically discriminated strata of caste society, it should have pursued secular public policies of guaranteed employment to all the poor and the state should have supported compulsory education for children of the deprived. A survey conducted by the National Council of Applied Economic Research (NCAER) in the mid-1990s and National Sample Survey Organisation (NSSO 1999) makes pathetic reading while informing us about the state of education of the dalits. If the uplift of dalits was the real concern of the Indian political leadership, secular development programmes like food for work and free food for school-going children should have been honestly implemented and its positive results would have been seen in 2005. Human resource development policies concerning socially deprived dalits have been a showpiece of the Indian governing classes and every concerned MP, MLA and bureaucrat knows that developmental programmes for the dalits have been a mere eyewash and budgetary allocations have been projected as evidence of so-called concerns. Further, rising unemployment in India should be the concern of public policy-makers who are searching for short cuts to ensure a few jobs in the private sector by a policy of reservation for the dalits. If employment is showing signs of slowing growth, the distribution of a limited number of jobs on the basis of reservations is political tokenism and politicians know that their real concern is not welfare of the dalits but winning elite support in dalit constituencies.

The central question is: Have we strengthened casteism during the 60 years in post-independence India and have we really achieved the goal of eradicating caste discrimination? The answer to this question is an emphatic no because caste politics and caste-based social policies as followed during the past-independence years cannot lead to the erosion of the pernicious caste system. A very important lesson from the US experience is that affirmative action has not at all helped in eradicating racism or changing the attitudes of the white US citizens towards the 'poor' Afro-American. The black elite is the only beneficiary of US policies and he has seceded from his poor and underprivileged fraternity. Paul Sweezy was once asked: "Why is it that the most important capitalist country does not have a socialist or labour party in the 20th century?" Sweezy responded that racism in America has obstructed the unity among the working classes which gets divided between 'blacks' and 'whites'. This is precisely what has happened in India, otherwise the Supreme Court would not have to say that the 'creamy layer' among the reserved category should opt out of the caste-based privilege of reservations. It deserves to be stated that neither the Ambedkarites nor the neo-Buddhist dalit leadership is committed to the eradication of casteism as perceived by Ambedkar or Buddha because caste has received governmental stamp of approval. Incidentally, Ambedkarites have been unfair to him because he wanted fundamental rights under the system of 'state socialism'. Because without an appropriate economic structure, political rights including reservations will remain hollow for everyone including the dalits. The upshot of the above is that concern for dalits should be articulated by following secular public policies and not by token policies of reservations. The state should guarantee education, health facilities and employment to every deprived citizen and this would take care of the genuine interests of the dalits. The poor should be the real target of secular public policies and this is the only way to build a new modern casteless secular India.

Token Support

The plea is that the poor of India should be the concern of public policymakers, irrespective of their caste, religion, gender or language labels. Unfortunately, India does not have a powerful constituency to support secular anti-poverty public policies as it has once again been witness to a lukewarm and token political support by the political class to the National Rural Employment Guarantee Bill, 2004. It is extremely surprising that the Bill seeks to provide 100 days of employment in a year to one member of every poor household in only the poorest 150 of India's 593 districts. Even, the communist parties which are natural supporters of anti-poverty secular programmes are not taking a public stand against caste-based preferential public policies of reservations. Lenin had maintained that trade unions were schools for the growth of class consciousness of the proletariat. In India, on January 31, 2005, caste-based trade unions came out in support of reservations in the private sector for the dalits. A joint action committee of the federation of Scheduled Caste, Scheduled Tribe, Other Backward Caste and most backward caste employees unions of state and Central governments met at Salem in Tamil Nadu on January 31, 2005 to demand reservations in the private sector as a 'fundamental right'. Every socially progressive strata of society should be disturbed that caste-based reservations have led to the emergence of fragmented caste-based trade unions. Is it not empirically correct to maintain that caste-based reservations have directly hit the socially progressive parties and the trade unions of the working classes? The growth of caste consciousness has hurt the development of progressive social consciousness among the oppressed and exploited millions of the labouring classes because caste ideology has made workers casteists and not fighters for secular anti-poverty programmes.

VI

Debating Merit

23

Exclusive Inequalities

Merit, Caste and Discrimination in Higher Education

SATISH DESHPANDE

The most acute and extensive examination of compensatory discrimination policies in independent India describes them as being framed by "competing equalities".[1] This essay, divided into three sections, argues that the notion of "exclusive inequalities" provides a comparable heuristic framework for analysing similar policies in the specific context of higher education in 21st century India. Section I begins to spell out this argument with a description of what precisely is at stake in the recent conflicts over other backward class (OBC) reservations in elite higher and professional education. Section II outlines the reasons why the specificities of higher education require us to think in terms of inequalities and exclusion (rather than equalities and competition), and what implications this has for affirmative action policies. Section III takes up the key ideas of merit and caste and their centrality to the ideological contestations and the practical manoeuvring going on in publicly funded higher and professional education today.

I
The Problem

What is at Stake in Mandal II?

It is hardly surprising that the recent decision to introduce 27 per cent reservation for the OBCs in elite institutions of higher and professional education met with such determined and vociferous resistance. Nor is it surprising that the anti-reservation views that dominated the media described the move as motivated by "vote bank politics" designed to benefit a particular caste bloc, which is also an electorally powerful constituency. Although, in this particular instance, the Congress Party on the whole appears to be more of a bemused spectator than a wily conspirator, the charge may well be true in the larger sense. However, to begin the story here is to begin in the middle; but this suits the anti-reservationists very well, for they would much rather forget the beginning.

In the Beginning

The Table 1 shows where the "Mandal II" story really began. It shows the number of graduates and postgraduates (including diplomas and other technical qualifications) in urban India who were identified in a sample survey done by the National Sample Survey Organisation (NSSO), done in 1999-2000. This was one of the "big sample" five-yearly surveys covering the entire country, but the data shown here are for urban India only, since that is where higher education is concentrated. The survey covered about 2.24 lakh people which, when adjusted for the relative weight of the particular segment of population covered, amounts to about 1.51 lakh persons. The first column lists castes and communities, while the last column gives their percentage share in the total urban population as estimated by the survey. The middle columns give the caste/communitywise number (in normal lettering) and the percentage share (in bold letters) of graduates and postgraduates in the agricultural sciences; engineering and technology; medicine and related fields; and all other fields, including the natural sciences, social sciences and humanities.

You need to read only one row – that for the "Hindu upper castes" to get the basic story line. Looking at the percentage share figures first and reading right to left from the last column, this row tells us that according to the NSSO, the Hindu upper castes formed almost 37 per cent of the total population of urban India. But, they accounted for almost 66 per cent of all non-technical subject graduates, more than 65 per cent of medical graduates, almost 67 per cent of engineering and technology graduates, and about 62 per cent of graduates in agricultural sciences. In sum, the Hindu upper castes are a little more than one-third of the total urban population, but around two-thirds of professional and higher education degree

Table 1

Sample Number and Proportion of Persons with Graduate/Postgraduate Degrees

Castes and communities	*Number and percentage share of graduates in various discipline in the sample*								*Caste/Community share of total urban population (percentage)*
	Agriculture		*Engineering*		*Medicine*		*Other Subject*		
Hindu STs	26	**2.4**	18	**1.3**	10	**1.8**	229	**1.3**	2.6
Hindu SCs	41	**3.8**	30	**2.2**	10	**1.8**	629	**3.6**	12.9
All Muslim	101	**9.4**	68	5.0	54	10.0	1,006	5.7	17.0
Hindu OBCs	108	**10.0**	202	**14.9**	56	10.4	2,402	13.7	24.2
Hindu Upper castes	669	**62.1**	908	**66.8**	350	**65.3**	11,529	**65.9**	36.9
All Christian	90	**8.4**	70	5.2	35	**5.2**	707	4.0	2.8
All Sikh	18	**1.7**	30	2.2	11	**2.2**	419	2.4	1.6
All Other	25	**2.4**	33	2.4	10	**2.4**	581	3.3	2.0
Total	1,078	100.0	1,359	100.0	535	100.0	17,501	100.0	100.0

Notes: 1. Figures in bold letters show caste/community share of graduates in urban India.
2. Includes persons with postgraduate degrees.
3. Cells show rounded and multiplier weighted sample numbers and proportions.
4. Columns may not add up due to rounding.
5. Total unweighted and multiplier weighted sample sizes are 2.24 and 1.51 lakh persons respectively.

Source: Computed from NSSO 1999-2000 data.

holders: their share in the highly educated is about twice their share in the general population We already know from this information that since the Hindu upper castes are heavily overrepresented among the highly educated, some other castes and communities have got to be underrepresented. This is indeed true for all the rows above the Hindu upper castes row – the Hindu Scheduled Tribes (STs) and Scheduled Castes (SCs), Muslims and Hindu OBCs are underrepresented among the highly educated relative to their share of the total urban population. Hindu SCs are the most severely affected – almost 13 per cent of the urban population, they are less than 4 per cent in all fields, and only around 2 per cent in engineering and medicine. It is clear that Muslims and Hindu OBCs too are severely underrepresented in higher education in urban India. On the other side, the rows below the Hindu upper castes are all overrepresented, whether slightly like the "other religions" (Parsis, Jains, Buddhists), or quite significantly like the Sikhs and specially the Christians. However, though overrepresented in proportional terms all these communities are very small in absolute terms and together account for fewer than 6.5 per cent of the urban population. By contrast, the underrepresented groups – the Hindu lower castes and tribes (STs, SCs, OBCs) plus Muslims – account for well over half (about 57%) of the urban population. Indeed, the caste divide in urban higher education is even worse than what it looks like here because the table ignores the well-known caste divisions within the non-Hindu communities.[2]

But, the story is not just about the caste divide – the punch line is the overwhelming dominance of the Hindu upper castes in higher education. This is brought out very starkly by the figures for the sample numbers. Although the point is already made by the percentage share figures, the sheer weight of the Hindu upper castes is palpable when you compare its absolute numbers with those of the next biggest category – the Hindu OBCs. In the total sample (about 1.51 lakh persons in urban India), there were 1,359 persons with engineering degrees, of which as many as 908 belonged to Hindu upper castes; the next highest figure is 202 for Hindu OBCs – less than one-fourth the former figure. Similarly, Hindu OBCs include 56 doctors out of the sample total of 535, but the Hindu upper castes have as many as 350 doctors, or more than six times the OBC figure! Among the non-technical graduates 11,529 out of 17,501 are Hindu upper castes, which is more than four and a half times the figure for the OBCs at 2,402. The nature and extent of this dominance is reflected in the fact that the Hindu upper castes alone have roughly double the total number of graduates among all other castes and communities put together. And yet this measure may be an understatement is because the table includes all types of educational institutions and all types of degrees from the humble BA upwards. If we were to do a survey of postgraduate and professional education in elite institutions, it is a safe bet that the extent of Hindu upper castes dominance would be much more.

This is where the story of Mandal II really begins – in the undeniable fact that, more than half a century after the formal adoption of a Constitution that explicitly forbids recognition of caste (except, ironically, to provide compensatory discrimination to the lower castes), the dominance of the Hindu upper castes in Indian higher education is still substantial, while the lower castes and Muslims are significantly underrepresented. The story begins here, but, as they say, this is only the beginning.

From Inequality to Injustice

The table (or other evidence of this sort) surely proves that Hindu upper castes and the underrepresented groups are definitely different and unequal in terms of their access to higher education. Since differences of this magnitude appear to have survived for so long after the "abolition" of caste, the table also proves that these must be the product of durable, self-reproducing mechanisms that are systematic (i.e., not accidental or random) and systemic (i.e., relating to system properties rather than to the attributes of individuals).

In other words, looking at this phenomenon from another angle, it is clear that there is something in the gate-keeping mechanism which regulates entry into higher education that makes it discriminate in favour of the "upper" and against the "lower" castes.

However, the existence of inequality and discrimination may be necessary, but it is not sufficient to prove the existence of injustice. For there are many kinds of inequalities and of discrimination that are considered just and desirable. Most people believe, for example, that those who work more should be paid more, and vice versa, i.e., they believe in unequal pay for unequal work. (This is actually a corollary of the popular slogan, "Equal pay for equal work".) Similarly, Indian cricket fans would hope and pray that the national selection committee systematically discriminates in favour of more talented players and against less talented players. In fact, the word "discrimination" bears both good and bad meanings – prejudiced or malicious bias, as well as discernment or the ability to distinguish better from worse, etc. (The contrast with "indiscriminate" also brings this out.)

So, there may be inequality and discrimination behind the dominance of the Hindu upper castes in higher education, but how do we know that it is not legitimate or "good" discrimination? If the gate-keeping mechanism is favouring the upper castes, is it because it is doing its job well or because it is malfunctioning? This is essentially the nature of the split between the two opposing sides in Mandal II. While the fact of upper caste dominance is undeniable and implicitly or explicitly conceded by sides, one claims that this dominance is perfectly justified and the other claims that it is unjust. Seen in reverse, the reservation for OBCs in elite institutions of higher education is seen by the upper castes as a travesty of justice – indeed, as the perpetration of injustice. The lower castes, on the other hand, see it as the long arm of justice finally catching up with the unfairly privileged upper castes.

We are now at the point where the anti-reservationists wanted to begin the story of Mandal II. In order to proceed further with the story we need to understand the specificities of higher education as a sector and their consequences for affirmative action.

II
Specificities of Higher Education

It may be useful to divide the specificities of higher education as a sector into those that apply in any context, and those that are peculiar to a poor and populous country like ours. These are discussed in turn below.

General Features of Higher Education

First of all, unlike primary education, healthcare or similar "basic needs", higher education is not a matter of right, leave alone a fundamental right. No person of any caste or community has a right to become a doctor, engineer or other kind of highly educated person. Everyone has the right to aspire to such status and to fair and equal consideration in the admission process, according to specified norms of fairness and equality. But no one has an a priori right to actual admission.[3]

Second, by its very nature, higher education is a selective field – its elitism is an integral aspect of its nature, not necessarily or only the perversion of this nature. From the point of view of both efficiency and ethics, higher education is not an "universalisable" resource. Although the relative numbers and proportions that determine ideal or desirable levels will be different in each case and although we need much larger numbers than what we currently have, it is nevertheless intuitively clear that only a very small (sometimes minuscule) proportion of the population will ever be neurosurgeons, space scientists, architects, or even generic non-technical PhDs. However large (relative to present levels) the ideal number or proportion is, it will still be small relative to the population. We do not need more; we cannot afford more; and there do not seem to be any obvious moral-ethical reasons why we should want to change this state of affairs.[4]

If the pattern of economic rewards and social prestige associated with higher education-based professions (relative to the rest of society) does not change drastically, it seems reasonable to suppose that the number of aspirants who wish to enter such fields will not decline and is likely to rise. In combination with what has been said above, this leads logically to the conclusion that higher education will necessarily remain a selective or elite sector. In other words, there will always be a funnel effect here – more will want to get in than can be accommodated, so at least some and probably very many will have to be turned away. The important point is that this is true and will remain more or less true even if India miraculously turns into a rich and overdeveloped nation tomorrow.

It would seem therefore that because higher education is inherently an exclusive field, modes of exclusion are built into its fundamental structure as a matter of principle. Discrimination in the sense of principled exclusion is thus a defining feature of higher education. This in turn means that concrete modalities for selection and rejection are a critical component of its institutional design. How these modalities work, how they are perceived by differently placed parties, and how they respond to the pressure of conflict and contestation are thus important questions of both principle and practice.

Given the centrality and contentiousness of the modalities of discriminating (rather than indiscriminate) selection to higher education, it is not surprising that their design follows the same general pattern. In most societies and contexts, institutional mechanisms regulating entry into higher education are based practice on some form of scholastic *examination*, and in principle on some notion of *merit*. The idea of merit is particularly important as it bears the heavy ideological burden of legitimising a system explicitly based on exclusion by discrimination. However, despite the extensive domain of beliefs, values and norms that merit invokes, in concrete practice it depends on the mundane mechanism of the examination or some variant thereof. In modern societies, degree of dependence on the examination increases in direct proportion to the pressure of demand for scarce higher educational opportunities. The more sought after and competitive a field, the greater the likelihood that entry will be regulated by examination. The role of merit and examinations will be discussed in detail in Section III.

A third general feature of higher education in all societies is its role as the institutional context responsible for creating and nurturing an intellectual vanguard entrusted with the task of thinking on behalf of society and preparing the present to meet the future. This abstract and rather grand description provides a telegraphic summary of what is expected of "criticism", "research" and related activities. Not all of higher education is devoted to such pursuits, nor need all such pursuits necessarily be located within higher education. But, there is undeniably an institutional affinity between higher education and the research function, regardless of whether and how well higher education manages to support it. The main implication that is commonly drawn from this is that higher education, or at least some segment of it, can legitimately claim exemption from the "normal" rules and responsibilities imposed on other sectors of public life. I will return to this point later in the argument.

Higher Education in a Big and Poor Country[5]

First, in countries like India, higher education is almost entirely state funded and is still among the most important avenues of mobility for all classes including the affluent class. This is particularly true of elite professional education in India, despite the growing importance of private actors both domestic and foreign. In India, the affluent (largely upper caste) elite have seceded from school education long ago and are beginning to send their children abroad for general undergraduate education. The middle classes (with a more mixed caste composition, but still tilted towards the upper end of the status hierarchy) are now abandoning state schools, but they still need state-run colleges and universities. But institutions like the IITs, IIMs and AIIMS are still in demand by everyone from the affluent elite downwards because they offer credentials encashable in the "first world" at "third world" prices. That is why, unlike primary or secondary or even general tertiary education, institutions of specialised and professional education are being subjected to enormous political and social pressure.[6]

This is happening because the long-standing monopoly of the upper caste and upper class elite over these resources is now being challenged by politically resurgent lower castes and classes. Previously, this monopoly worked through something akin to the "silent compulsion of economic relations" that Marx spoke of. The modalities of merit went with the grain of society so to speak; they "naturally" favoured the privileged and in effect handed over elite education to them by default. This status quo, consisting of a *de facto* monopoly masked by the *de jure* presence of open competition, is now being questioned "by any means possible".

The second feature is very closely related to the first but is important enough to be considered a distinct point. This is the fact that in a poor country with limited avenues for capital accumulation, state-funded higher education provides the safest, most legitimate and least regulated method of privatising public resources. The end product produced by the IITs, AIIMS and similar institutions is a "credentialed" individual who is a free agent but by virtue of the state's investment in him/her now owns a kind of capital that is perfectly portable and (in this instance) internationally encashable. Being a free agent, the credentialed individual can put this capital to (almost) any kind of use (almost) anywhere – the particular state and society that made the investment may or may not gain. Compare this to land or industrial capital, and the differences become clear. Although it is obvious that the importance of credential capital has increased greatly in the era of globalisation, we must not forget the special historical role of this process. Massive expansion of state-funded higher education in the Nehruvian era saw the upper caste middle classes convert their landed capital into credential capital. The state at that time fuelled both the demand and supply sides of the higher education equation – it provided educational opportunities and training, as well as employment. The castes and classes, who were in the right place at the right time in the early decades of independence, got to occupy an empty and expanding state sector. This kind of historic opportunity is a once only phenomenon, and no other generation will get it. While this may be treated as "historical luck", it should be kept in mind when trying to interpret the strife and acrimony that marks the present.

A third important feature of higher education in poor and populous countries is that it tends to be associated with various kinds of discrimination in practice. These may be collectively called "resource discrimination", i.e., discrimination born out of inadequate endowments of the resources required to access and succeeds in higher education. It is well known, for example, that higher education is biased against the poor, and against the lower castes or other groups who suffer from social disadvantages in society. This is true in developed countries as well, but is more starkly relevant in countries like India. By its very nature, higher education presupposes access to a minimum level of economic, cultural and political resources. Only those who already possess such resources can realistically expect to benefit from it. That is why, the "creamy layer" argument needs to be made with care. Providing access to higher education is not a method for tackling poverty; by the same token, poverty cannot be made a qualifying condition for granting special access to it. Indiscriminate use of the creamy layer argument thus risks disqualifying precisely those segments of socially disadvantaged castes and communities who have a good chance of succeeding. Conversely, with minor exaggeration, one could claim that heavy handed use of creamy layer arguments would end up admitting students whose cumulative disadvantages make it highly probable that they will fail, thus discrediting the affirmative action programme itself.

This combination of merit discrimination, or discrimination in principle (discussed above), and discrimination in practice, or resource discrimination, produces a situation where one kind can in fact masquerade as another, or where claims to this effect can be made regardless of the facts of the matter. The permanent potential for misrecognition of one kind of discrimination for the other kind makes the issue very contentious and also very hard to resolve because merit discrimination is considered legitimate and desirable while resource discrimination is considered illegitimate and undesirable. While higher educational institutions and administrators are very eager to claim and to demonstrate that they practise merit discrimination, they are as anxious to deny that they are complicitous in the practice of resource discrimination. Similarly, victims of merit discrimination may claim to be victims of resource discrimination, or beneficiaries of resource discrimination may claim to be meritorious. Finally, a fourth feature of the higher education sector in poor countries with large populations is that it must take on the additional burden of supporting aspirations for mobility. This is somewhat different from the point made above. Because in our context the number of desirable formal sector jobs is always much less than the number of job seekers, applicants must constantly seek to improved their credentials. One way of doing this is to acquire more degrees and this leads to "credential inflation". A significant proportion of those in higher education are there simply to improve their career prospects in non-research related fields. Thus, in a poor country, higher education must also accommodate these legitimate aspirations which are forced to take the route of higher education because of prevailing market and social conditions.[7]

One consequence of this feature is that it counterbalances the special claims made on behalf of higher education because of its responsibility to pioneer cutting edge research for the future. To the extent that higher education functions as an avenue of mobility, it must be subject to the social justice or other obligations imposed on public institutions. Exemption from these obligations means that this route to mobility is embedded in a system that is inaccessible for many.

III
Meanings and Roles of Merit

We are now in a position to return to the question of merit and its critical role as the principal source of legitimation in a field inevitably marked by discrimination and exclusion of various kinds. What does merit mean in the context of Indian higher education?

Examinations and Merit

Denotations

We are now in a position to return to the question of merit and its critical role as the principal source of legitimation in a field inevitably marked by discrimination and exclusion of various kinds. What does merit mean in the context of Indian higher education?

At the denotative (concrete, literal) level merit usually refers to a certification of competence, aptitude or knowledge acquired through an examination of some kind. In most instances, what is actually involved is the relative rank obtained in the examination. What really matters is not really how "well" one does in the examination, but how much "better" (or worse) one does compared to others taking the same examination. The matter does not end here. In the context of entrance examination for professional educational institutions, for example, the critical factor is getting a high enough rank to qualify for admission. Suppose an institution called XIT has 3,000 places avail-able to be filled through an entrance examination. Then, "merit" for XIT – and therefore for the candidates aspiring to enter it – means all ranks from 1 to 3,000. From the point of view of XIT, ranks lower than 3,000 are all equal or the same in the sense that they all belong to the category of "did not qualify", which is indistinguishable from the category "without merit".[8]

The dreaded "cut-off point" is the guillotine that severs the candidate pool into the mutually exclusive categories of "meritorious" and "without merit". But how is this cut-off point determined? By the number of places available. In short, the number of meritorious candidates is pre-determined; the examination is only a means to identify who they will be. How is this identification to be made? By ranking the candidates. The first social function of the examination is to produce or elicit evidence of inequality from the candidates. The examination is thus an implacable device for generating inequality along a continuous scale, the measurement units of which can be infinitesimal – three decimal places are now commonly reported. But, a curious reversal takes place once this inequality is successfully generated and the ranking done – then, the obsessively continuous scale suddenly transforms into a dichotomy with the guillotine of the cut-off point creating two internally homogeneous but mutually exclusive groups. The second social function of the examination is to provide an ideologically defensible method of saying "No" to large numbers.

Connotations

At the connotative (symbolic, figurative, ideological) level, merit functions as a kind of entitlement, a moral claim on society. It is simultaneously a claim in the sense of an assertion about myself (my capabilities, competence, and at the broadest level, moral worth); and a claim in the sense of an expectation or demand addressed to the rest of the world. Merit at this broad symbolic level functions as the *raison d'etre* of the examination. Or, to put it the other way around, the third social function of the examination is to identify merit. But, where the first two functions were latent (i.e., unrecognised by or opaque to the actors involved), this third function is a manifest function (i.e., explicitly recognised or stated).

We can now resume the discussion about how higher education inherently involves exclusion, and how the merit examination. Combination bears the burden of legitimising such necessary exclusion. From the point of view of allocation of scarce higher education resources, merit discrimination is justified as the method of identifying persons who (a) are best prepared and qualified to enter specialised higher education; and (b) will produce the best return on this social investment. These are actually two distinct claims, but are frequently conflated – it is possible, but not necessary, that the best prepared person in the sense of scholastic aptitude will also be the person who will make the best doctor, engineer or whatever.

In principle, examinations identify merit, and merit provides sufficient justification for discriminating in favour of its bearers and awarding them admission in preference to others who do not have merit. In practice, examinations coercively generate inequality expressed in a rank ordering, and they help to persuade both the "selected" and the "rejected" that the division is fair. However, as long as they succeed in practice, examinations are presumed to have succeeded in principle. In other words, the only thing an examination *must* produce is a rank ordering that is not disputed by candidates; this is a necessary and also a sufficient condition for the system to succeed. Everything else is an optional matter of assertion and counter assertion.

(Imagine what would happen if, with only 50 seats available, the AIIMS entrance examination produced a result where the top 100 candidates had the same mark…)

To put the argument sharply, the merit discrimination system functions on the basis of formal differentiation of a candidate pool through an examination; it is institutionally required to ensure such a differentiation. It is not *required* to ensure or defend a substantive differentiation of candidates. What must be produced is a differentiated ranking; it is not necessary to explain what meaning the differentiations carry. More accurately, as long as they are present, it is permissible to simply assume that the differentiations mean whatever they are supposed to mean. This is the underlying system that, under the pressure of large numbers of aspirants, produces the arcane world of third decimal point differences and cut-offs that are accepted as justifying large claims about the presence or absence of merit.

In effect, one could say that the preceding argument establishes that the examination rank method is of dubious reliability. This still leaves open the question of validity – do entrance tests really measure what they are supposed to measure, i.e., aptitude, likelihood of succeeding, etc? Here we are on familiar ground, for it is well known how difficult it is to devise tests with good predictive power in this sense. We may know a good doctor or engineer when we see him at work, but we do not really know how to predict this before the fact.

To argue that a system is arbitrary is not to say that it is useless or more important, that obvious alternatives exist. The purpose of this argument was to show that the moral weight that is placed on merit is in practice borne by examinations, and that examinations cannot but be arbitrary under the conditions imposed on them. Appreciation of this arbitrariness should temper one's opposition to reservations or similar proposals that appear to interfere with this system. When opponents of reservations (who have themselves survived such a system) use emotive language like "murder of merit", they are trying to leverage the moral potency of merit to foreclose tempered responses. They are suppressing or disowning their own intimate knowledge of the heartbreaking arbitrariness of merit discrimination. They are endorsing the guillotine mentality and refusing to acknowledge that the ranking game starts with the play of infinitesimal gradations.

How much "compromise" with merit a reservation scheme will entail ought to be recognised for what it is – an empirical question. How much further down the rankings will we have to go? What is the substantive meaning of this distance in marks or ranks, i.e., how much of a difference does it make in terms of the quality of candidates? It is only after we have asked and answered such questions that we will be in a position to respond in a reasoned manner to proposals like the recent one for OBC reservations.

Merit and Resource Discrimination

The preceding argument has kept within the limits of the "merit only" position; it is time now to move beyond this self-imposed limitation.

If we return now to the argument in Section I and the figures in the table, the skewed distribution of access to higher education was explained as being due solely to merit by the anti-reservationists. How-ever, the flaws in this argument are too obvious to need much rebuttal. As Marc Galanter has pointed out, three broad kinds of resources are necessary to produce the results in competitive examination that qualify as indicators of merit: (a) economic resources (for prior education, training, materials, freedom from work, etc); (b) social and cultural resources (networks of contacts, confidence, guidance and advice, information, etc); and (c) intrinsic ability and hard work. It is some combination of these that allows people to "acquire merit". When it is said that merit alone is responsible for the dominance of the upper castes, what is meant is that economic and cultural resources are not important, but it is differences in sheer intrinsic ability alone that make for the inter-caste differences. This is a position that is indefensible, for it cannot be argued today that large groups numbering in the millions are more or less intrinsically able than other such groups. We have to look to inequalities in the other factors to explain the difference.

Once we recognise the causal contribution of other inequalities towards the unequal distribution of merit and hence of higher educational opportunities, this opens the door to considering interventions for their redressal. (Because these reasons for inequality cannot be called "just discrimination"; it is to foreclose this that the "merit as the only criterion" argument is made.) Once we begin to talk in terms of gradations – as we must – it becomes possible to move towards a more realistic and transparent policy framework where we can discuss the different social objectives that higher education can accommodate without excessive costs or damages being imposed on it. The present framework of debate – marked by Manichean dichotomies between merit and incompetence (as though there were nothing in between, or that each was such a singular monolithic category) – will not take us forward.

By way of conclusion, it would seem that while more conceptual work definitely needs to be done on these questions, what we need even more perhaps is more and thicker empirical descriptions. Most of all, we need good descriptions of the everyday practices that help produce and reproduce social capital and link caste to privilege or disprivilege in durable ways.

Notes

1. The title and this essay itself are a tribute to Marc Galanter's classic work, *Competing Equalities: Law and the Backward Classes in India* (Oxford, New Delhi, 1984). It is to his credit – and to the collective embarrassment of my "caste" of social scientists and specially my "sub-caste" of sociologists and social anthropologists – that more than two decades after its publication, his superb survey still remains by far the best analysis of "compensatory discrimination" in independent India. Its own example and the events of the "Mandal decade" should have been advantage enough for us to at least match the analytical precision and careful scholarship of *Competing Equalities*. Whatever the reasons why this has not yet happened, I hope that "Mandal II" will provide collective inspiration to overcome them. This is a very preliminary version of work in progress and should be read as such. For more immediate incitement, encouragement and critical engagement I am grateful to Mihir Shah, Yogendra Yadav and Mary E. John.
2. These differences are sharpest among Christians and Sikhs, and least among Muslims. The other religions in this table include Buddhist dalits.

   (Since SCs are limited to Hindus), and they too would be sharply differentiated from the Jains, other Buddhists, and Parsis.
3. The strict implications of this are often glossed over, as was evident in the less than even-handed application of this logic to the two sides in Mandal II.

4. Unless we reach a stage of social development where the wishes of individuals or groups to be involved in higher education for its own sake are considered sufficient to justify investment to expand this field.
5. The features noted here are not necessarily absent in a rich small country, but their effects in a poor big country are of much greater consequence.
6. This argument is made by Mary John; see 'Schooled in Inequality' in *The Hindu*, May 30, 2006.
7. This also happens in rich countries, but to a much lesser extent. No one needs a postgraduate degree merely to reach the average standard of living.
8. This is because, after the ranking is done and results declared, the XIT cannot meaningfully differentiate between different "amounts" of merit that are less than whatever was needed for being the 3,000th candidate. In other words, it has nothing (or the same thing) to say to all ranks higher than 3,000 – "Goodbye, better luck if you try next time". There is thus no demonstrable difference between saying "Not enough merit" and "No merit".

24

Merit is My Mother Tongue

KANCHA ILAIAH

With Union Human Resource Development Minister Arjun Singh declaring that there is a consideration to provide 27 per cent reservation to the OBCs in all the central government educational institutions, including IIMs and IITs, a new attack started on the question of OBC reservations. The print and electronic media have gone to town about the issue of merit in the premier institutions of the nation. Hence, the debate.

Surely, these institutions have remained the property of the Brahminic castes ever since they were established. Though the SC/ST reservation has been in vogue in these institutions, the upper castes who manned these institutions have been using all kinds of methods to see that the SC/ST seats do not get filled. Whatever seats are filled with the SC/ST candidates they use the stick method without involving the carrot to force them to drop out. They are now showing the statistics of drop out rates of SC/ST candidates and the 100 per cent pass out rate of the upper caste candidates as reason enough to not extend reservations to OBCs.

Their entire argument is based on the premise that passing out and dropping out are not political and ideological questions. They want to tell us that all those who pass out are nationalists and all those who drop out are anti-nationals.

Almost all the national English dailies editorially opposed the Arjun Singh proposal. All kinds of progressive intellectuals opposed the proposal as a retrograde step. Every so-called progressive man/woman coming from an upper class background in Delhi and other cosmopolitan cities is worried about the future of merit in central institutions that have brought academic and intellectual name and fame to the nation; and, of course, dollars and pounds to their families by the meritorious graduates of these prime institutions. We need to raise some simple questions in this regard.

Why it that while English as a language is not yet recognised as an Indian national language, all these central institutions teach, evaluate students and do research only in English? Is it not a fact that starting with central schools to IITs and IIMs, they orient the student community to ape America and Europe through the means of the English language? Why is it that the same English medium-educated and English-speaking, and in most cases foreign-educated intellectuals, who are now "beating their chests" about the death of merit in these premier institutions, have never asked the governing forces to teach rural children studying in government schools in English?

When SC, ST and OBC students have been asking for English education in the government schools, the same media and intellectuals bring up the issue of colonialism versus nationalism. They say, no, English is a colonial language and we must preserve the national languages through government schools! They imply that nationalism should be preserved by the SCs, STs and OBCs, as they are the ones who study in government schools in the villages and urban slums. But, the urban upper castes train their children in the colonial language without entering into a debate about the language issue. They are like the revolutionary pigs in George Orwell's *Animal Farm,* which revolt against the two-leg animals and then they themselves slowly learn to walk on two legs.

Everyone knows that Hindi is now a national language but no single IIM or IIT conducts teaching and evaluation in Hindi or in any other Indian language. Interestingly, education is divided between central and state government subjects and all the central educational institutions are reserved for English language based education by design, which, in other words, is reserved for the upper castes.

Thus, English is their first and foremost stepping stone into the merit house of success and power and that is denied to vast SC, ST and OBC students who can study only in the state government schools in regional languages. The second basement of this merit is 'money' and exposure to western cultures. Most public schools run by upper caste Hindus and upper caste Christians are based on money power and childhood training in Euro-American cultures. One can clearly see the consequences of this structural difference.

The OBC leaders whom the upper caste intelligentsia portray as rich and powerful, who could easily rob the quota benefits are Mulayam Singh Yadav, Laloo Prasad Yadav, Sharad Yadav, Uma Bharti, Kalyan Singh, Nitish Kumar and so on. None of these leaders can speak fluent English and carry no westernised cultural idiom. On the other hand, witness how anglicised leaders like Arun Jaitley, Jairam Ramesh, Mani Shankar Aiyar, Sitaram Yechuri, Prakash Karat, etc., use English and the western idiom. Cutting across party ideologies, this is a class of leadership that combines English education, imperial culture and money as a back up to their childhood upbringing and later privileges. They all come from upper castes. Thereby, caste, English and money nurtures a particular mode of merit. The OBCs, leave alone SCs/STs, lack that background.

The present education system cannot change the relations between the upper castes and the lower castes because these communities send their children into two different school systems. Added to this is the OBC/SC/ST leadership's lack of vision about English education. They too have not realised the need for seeking English as a national language and making it the medium of instruction in all state government schools, especially wherever they rule. Indeed, they remained primitivist and thus destroy the future of children going to government schools.

The intellectuals who are opposing OBC reservation in the central educational institutions never define what constitutes merit. About 80-90 per cent of IIT and IIM graduates settle down in America and Europe and that has been the life ambition of that class/caste of people. From childhood onwards, they are mostly Indian-Americans or Indian-Europeans. When we ask why they leave the country after getting hugely subsidised education with the taxpayer's money – OBCs too contribute a lot of money to the state exchequer – the elite argument is that they are not being provided suitable jobs by the state. If they are so meritorious and brilliant, why are they looking for a job in the state sector?

As per the neo-liberal logic, these meritorious guys should have become self-employed and thereby created millions of jobs for the not so meritorious SCs/STs/OBCs. Ideally, their innovations would have eradicated mass poverty and would have created a bubbling nation of equal opportunities. Instead, these premier institutions produce a skilled technical and a management labour force that basically serves the American and European economy. With the dollar and Euro currency that these meritorious forces earn, their families benefit, not the nation. The media is losing its marbles about the placement opportunities that these fellows get in America and Europe. This cannot be defined as merit. If technical skills are not given with English as a speaking and writing language, no country in the world will recognise their skills and they will not get these jobs.

Hence, for the rural youth who get their education in regional languages, an opportunity needs to be given to learn in English in a friendly environment. That is what the SCs/STs and OBCs need urgently. They do not have an equal opportunity to study in English medium schools and their paying capacity is always much too low. They cannot go to good schools, or to costly tutorial institutions. Once English is recognised as a language of the nation and a neighbourhood school system is established where a rich Brahmin child and a poor dalit child can study in the same school, nobody will ask for reservation.

In the contemporary context, reservation is being asked on caste-based criteria because caste also decides the social, economic and educational status of people. The upper caste intellectuals, instead of getting worried about merit where it does not exist, must talk about uniform English (and English alone) medium schools all over the country. Then, let us see which castes will control the Indian institutions. Till then, let there be caste-based reservations in all institutions as that creates a level playing field in employment and education. If that is not allowed, every city may become a Paris of 2005.

25

The Question of Merit

SANDEEP PANDEY

The question of merit and excellence being discussed in the debate raging on reservation needs to be examined critically. What is this merit in reality and of what use is this to the society? Since we are talking about reservation in higher education institutions, some of the best of which are funded by the government with public money, we assume that students graduating from these institutions have some social responsibility.

The brightest minds from our schools enter the higher education institutions because most of the admissions to these institutions are based on competition or the so-called merit. Since only 9 per cent of our population makes it to the college level education, an overwhelming majority of India is not in the category of meritorious. The numbers who make it to the elite professional careers like administration, engineering, medicine and management is even smaller. Some people belonging to this segment of the society are quite worried about the dilution of quality if reservations are implemented for OBCs in higher education institutions.

This small segment of the society, who are among the brightest students of their class, prepares itself for jobs in the service sector. The irony is that for delivering their service to the society we have to pay them exorbitant salaries compared to what a common citizen of the country can earn, provide them with all facilities, perks, etc., and often common citizens of the country have to render their services to be their servants, drivers, housekeepers, gardeners, etc. This service sector elite is completely incapable of serving the society without an extensive paraphernalia at public expense. And, the fact of the matter is that in spite of their quality service the situation of the common citizen, who they purport to serve, has not improved since the independence of this country. The gap between the rich and the poor has increased, farmers are committing suicides, people are dying of starvation and TB, gender ratio is deteriorating, small children are being forced into prostitution, natural resources are running out or getting polluted and there is increase in crime and terrorist violence. Still, in every next Pay Commission, this service sector expects a hike in their salaries and benefits, whereas, there is no guarantee for a minimum income level for those outside this prestigious service sector.

The engineer is least interested in ensuring that his knowledge is of any use to the society. Some of the brightest of them graduating from the IITs, flee the country at the first opportunity and prefer to serve a more prosperous US society. The ones who remain behind are interested in advancing their careers on commissions that they can get from mega projects. People who decide to object to what is going on, like in the case of Satyendra Dubey, have to pay with their life or job.

The doctors, who are supposed to be next only to God, are more interested in making the money rather than improving the health of the society, especially the poor. The poor patient is cheated by the private pathological/clinical testing laboratories and drug companies, which route back a portion of their profit to the doctors, who have no qualms in being a part of the system. Is this an ethical earning?

The managers graduating from IIMs are clearly out there to make money for themselves. They are taught to maximise profit. It does not matter whether they have to sell cigarettes or Coca Cola, which is depriving the farmers of the country of ground water, or other products which are harmful to human health, environment and society. Managers are also infamous for indulging in manipulations and malpractices. And, when one of them, S. Manjunath, decided to question the adulteration at a petrol pump in Lakhimpur Khiri, he was eliminated.

The administrative officers are the worst. Guardians of the system meant to ensure that the spirit of the Constitution is implemented, they have perpetuated an oppressive system inherited from the British in which the common masses still find themselves as subjects rather than empowered citizens of a democracy and have promoted corruption so much that the system has been virtually sabotaged. No legitimate work of a common citizen can get done in the normal course through the system. Strings have to be pulled or bribes have to be paid to move things. What is worse is that even illegitimate things can be accomplished by adopting these methods.

The learned judges of the courts are delivering anti-people judgments more frequently than before, whether it the denial of right to rehabilitation of those being displaced by Sardar Sarovar dam, crushing of daily wage workers fighting for their employment rights, slum dwellers being bulldozed in modernisation drive or cycle rickshaws being banned in Chandani Chowk in Delhi.

The intellectuals, professors, etc., also prefer to play a lame role. The scientists are busy thinking of the most anti-people projects, like the nuclear weapons, nuclear power or interlinking of rivers. They have poisoned our fields with artificial fertilisers and pesticides and are helping the private corporations to make money from GM seeds at the expense of common farmers.

Now, most of these self-serving brightest minds happen to be upper caste people. They have abdicated their responsibility of making a social intervention to lay the foundation of a just human society. In fact, the more educated one is the more socially irresponsible, insensitive to fellow human beings and corrupt. What is one then to make of the merit of these bright minds? They seem to be doing more harm to the society than good. Was it not their responsibility, since they are the ones who make policies and implement programmes, to ensure that their dalit and backward caste fellow citizens get equal opportunity? It is time for them to reflect and make amends for the historic injustice done to these communities by supporting their empowerment through the process of reservation.

If our Constitution can be credited for one thing it is establishing the value of equity in a caste-ridden fragmented hierarchical society. Aided by the Constitution and a policy of caste-based reservations the Indian political scenario has dramatically altered since independence. We now see organic leadership among dalits and backwards and an assertion demanding equality. Whereas the reservations in jobs might have helped only a limited number of dalits and backwards but it has brought about a tremendous transformation in their self-confidence to participate in the democracy on equal terms.

This churning of the society must continue, if we are to rid ourselves of the ignominy of the caste system, in the form of more reservations until dalit and backwards find representation in elite institutions and services of this country in proportion to their population and the domination of upper caste within the ruling elite ends. Only then can we claim to be a fair society.

26

The Sociology of Merit

AMMAN MADAN

The concept of merit is in very common use these days. It is central to the way we think of excellence in education and also to much of the debate on the issue of reservations. Most people, however, treat the concept of merit in a too simple manner: a students who tops a given examination is said to have merit and the others do not. Sociologists of education, however, think quite differently about it. Things are not as simple as they seem.

To begin with, it is now quite well accepted by social scientists that all humans are born equal. If you leave aside a very few extreme cases, most people are born with an equal capacity to achieve very high levels of excellence. If people are given lots of encouragement, set high goals to aspire to, and given enough resources, most people can do very well indeed.

The basic problem then is that of why all are born equal, but become unequal in later life. If all are born equal (more or less), then, why is it that only some students get admission into an IIT every year? In every class there are some students who always do better than others. What is one to make of this? The popular answer is that only a few have merit, but like many popular answers, it hides more than it reveals.

Racists would say that differences in abilities are due to the differences between races. There are indeed some minor biological differences among different communities and also between men and women. However, biological advantages need supportive environments to get "turned on" and also in how well developed those advantages become. The environment seems to play a much larger role than biology. Further, biological advantages are usually only in the realm of one out of the many kinds of attributes needed to become say, a great cricketer. To become Sachin Tendulkar, for instance, apart from being born with a superb muscular coordination, one also needs dedication, regularity, strategic understanding of the game, a mastery of tactical options, the ability to ignore empty criticisms and sheer raw courage. All these other qualities are learnt by human beings as they grow up in society and go through a variety of experiences. Biology is best seen as the platform on which society and culture act. It is not decisive in itself.

A more accurate answer is that all are born with an approximately equal capacity to learn, but differences in social environments lead to that being converted into different kinds of abilities. Examinations are set up to identify some (not all) of those abilities. Merit, then, is not what it seems – it is not a quality possessed by an individual alone. It is also the product of what kind of community one comes from and of the history of that community. The differences which have been created by history are of great importance. Of course, the individual will is quite important – the will to push oneself, to work hard, to work in a planned and selective manner. But that will, too, is being expressed through a historically created medium. Regularity in sitting at one place and applying oneself to books, for instance, is a quality more easily found in communities that have a culture of studying sacred books. It is not so easily found in communities that do not read anything and may celebrate their religion only through song and dance, or may have been historically banned from access to reading. Of course, given the right environment, regularity in studying books is quickly learnt. But it should not be forgotten that all individuals live their lives through a web of cultural and social influences. Some threads in that web hold us back and some threads can pull us forward.

A major contribution of the sociology of education has been in revealing in detail how our social environment influences merit. The most basic way is through economic and political inequality. About a third of our population still lives a precarious, hand to mouth existence. They have little access to economic resources and are routinely ignored by political formations. Living in desperate circumstances, they have to struggle to come to school and then to keep coming regularly. They fight against terrible odds to convert their talent and capacity into merit. How severe the odds are can be seen by the fact that the proportion of young people who are in the relevant age group and can actually make it up to the class XII examination is in the order of 15 per cent. So, when one looks at entrance examination to various vocational courses, it is important to realise that roughly 85 per cent of India is not even getting the chance to apply, what to talk of living up to its fullest potential. It may not be wrong to argue that the biggest enemy of merit in India is inequality.

The obstacles created by poverty and inequality to the fuller expression of one's abilities and talents have been well studied. For one thing, even government schools are not really free. A recent study by a team of scholars, led by Santosh Mehrotra of the UNDP, revealed how high were the out-of-pocket costs of schooling for the poorest income slab of rural India. Varying across different states, they were equivalent to at least several days' wages for the poorest of the poor. And this was only at the primary school level. To this must be added the opportunity costs of sending away to school hands that could have taken care of younger siblings when the adults went out to scratch a living and so on. As several studies have pointed out, when a family looks around at the probable future a child will have after finishing class V, then it often has to take difficult decisions. The first to lose out are girls and the children of those castes which have historically been discriminated against.

The ability to acquire merit is further denied by the problem of getting physical access to schools. The simple fact of how far one has to walk to get to a school acts as a severe filter against several crores of children. Again, after primary school one has to go to middle school. We have in our country roughly one-third as many middle schools as we have primary schools. Our country's bravest soldiers, our village primary school teachers, have a thumb rule – if the middle school is not in the same village as the primary school, then, the number of their beloved pupils who will continue with their studies will simply get halved. And, no prizes for guessing who drops out first – girl children and castes with lesser resources. This process is repeated again when these children have to move to high school and to senior secondary school.

We can better understand the implications of such processes deciding who is able to acquire "merit" and who is not, by taking up the example of say, Amartya Sen. He was born to scholarly parents and had the great fortune of being brought up at one of our finest educational institutions – Shanti Niketan. Of course, he is a remarkable person, with extraordinary clarity of thought and determination of purpose. But it was simply a matter of chance that he was born where he was. Remember that today only about one out of eight Indians is even able to finish class XII. Do you think Professor Sen would have been able to repeat his successes if he were to be born again in today's India. I think Professor Sen would himself say that the odds are greatly against it.

There is much more to the denial of talent and the shaping of merit in our country. The social environment operates on merit in complex and subtle ways. One of the least understood and yet very important factors is that of culture: the culture of a community and the culture of the school. We shall discuss that in the next instalment of this article.

Merit and Culture

It would be correct to say that the biggest factor in deciding who gets "merit" and who does not lies in the nature of the social structure. Individuals located in certain parts of the social structure must swim against severe odds. The most obvious way by which the social structure affects merit in India is through the lack of access to schools and the inability of the poor to send their children regularly to class. Then, there is a further pruning done by the poor functioning of the schools which many millions attend. I have previously referred to the fact that only somewhere around 15 per cent of our youth manage to make it up to class XII. But, apart from the above, there also occurs a less visible, but equally insidious process of filtration within those who do come to school. This occurs through the domain of culture, for instance, the different values attached by teachers and schools to the ways of different communities and classes.

The concept of culture has for long been central to sociology and anthropology. It commonly refers to the various beliefs, values, practices and other symbolic behaviours that human beings learn as they grow up. Earlier, it was thought that different communities have different cultures. Now, it is clear that cultures are not like watertight compartments. Differences between communities are more in terms of degrees of emphasis in their cultural traits rather than in basic, fundamental divides. However, the importance of culture cannot be overstated. All the joys and sorrows, jokes and jibes of our lives are formulated and practised through cultural, symbolic processes. They are all the more effective for often being just below the level of our consciousness. Teachers, after a few years, hardly notice how a student greets them as they pass but let someone say just one word with a slightly different tone and the entire meaning of the student-teacher relationship immediately changes.

With the coming of independence in India, equality became an officially accepted principle of our national culture and our education system. Schools in India were seen as a great example of the open society which we were striving to become. The formal rules of this institution are such that ability and achievement are stressed rather than the social group within which one is born. However, sociologists have revealed how, in schools and classrooms, cultures became a very effective ground for invisibly influencing selection and discrimination. They still are quite effective in deciding who will eventually be declared meritorious and who will not. Many of the processes seen in this are such that even the teachers are barely conscious of them.

In our apparently open and achievement-based schools, the most common cultural process of discrimination rests on the basic cultural premise of the caste system: that people are basically different from each other and some are higher and others are lower. This is acted out in how most primary school teachers, for instance, when dealing with an active and raucous group of children, quickly divide them into two mental groups – the good children and the bad children. Supportive and encouraging attention is given to the good, while it is thought that the bad only deserve to be controlled sharply and periodically told that they are of little worth and need to improve themselves. Thus is expressed the principle of hierarchy, which is typical of caste systems. The consequence of this is that differences which appear in early years get amplified and continue to leave their scar for the rest of one's school life. Our behaviour here is sharply different from the way school classrooms get organised in less unequal societies. A society where egalitarianism is taken more seriously, for instance UK, emphasises that all students have the capacity to do very well and teachers are encouraged to pay special attention to those who are not doing well, just the reverse of the Indian practice.

The basis of defining good and bad students itself reveals further cultural prejudices. Students who accept power quickly and sit submissively quickly get positive vibes from teachers. Learning the alphabet and textbook-oriented knowledges is valued much more than, say, being good at articulation or at games or making things with one's hands. Students who participate enthusiastically in the latter kinds of activities are soon labelled as noisy and boisterous. The support which young children get from their homes predisposes which kinds of activities they would be more comfortable with. Family background and caste thus have a clear presence in the apparently open and merit-based school.

Students who are dressed neatly and practise etiquettes closer to the cultural ways of the teachers are known to get greater approval and support. Proficiency in reading is closely associated with opportunity to read at home and those who lag behind at school get only discouragement and stigmas. This is accentuated further in the divide between the official language of the school and the different languages spoken at home. The sharpest influence of this is seen in tribal households. Similarly, those with little opportunity to practise arithmetic skills at home do not do as well in school, too. Culture and family, the basic building blocks of caste, play an important role in the selection processes seen in school.

The ability to sustain boredom for long periods of time is an essential resource for doing well in schools. It is necessary to be able to sit quietly through droning lectures, hour after hour and to still focus on what the teacher is saying. Children from assertive, active and confident backgrounds will be more reluctant to do so. This often means that children from farming, animal rearing and artisan communities get declared as poor learners and non-studious. In situations of bad and painful teaching, a culture of fearing and revering teachers becomes an asset to survive schools.

Families with a history of prioritising book-based learning tend to do much better in schools than families with different histories. Researchers across the world have pointed out that children should not be forced to write before the age of 5-6. Before this age their hand muscles are not developed enough to be hold writing instruments properly and may cause ache and pain. In our country, we expect children as young as 3 to write the alphabet. Schools which do not give such homework to 3-4 year olds are considered inferior and incompetent. Certain kinds of families and castes tend to be more willing to push and bully their children into doing their homework and the rest of the children are told that they are bad.

Culture, then, not only decides who gets merit, but also decides what is merit. The practices which lead to selection may not be useful or correct in themselves, but still may become the basis of differentiation into the meritorious and the non-meritorious.

It is now well known that many students who become engineers have little love for engineering. The selection system, the way merit is defined, is tilted in favour of certain knowledges and not others. Those students who do well in bookish maths, physics and chemistry easily get selected for such courses. However, students from families which predispose them to working with their hands, to designing and making physical objects, to playing with shapes and forms, cannot be said to have no knowledge assets. Yet, their knowledges and cultures get no weightage in the way engineering colleges define merit. The definition of merit, then, also gets influenced by a variety of extraneous factors.

It is often assumed that merit is a personal quality. That a student has merit and enjoys it because of purely personal efforts and abilities. Of course, hard work and individual efforts are very important. But to see this as a purely personal quality and with no link to one's social background is not a correct picture. Merit has a very strong social dimension to it. It is humbling to realise how much one's family and the kind of position one's community has held within our society contributes to one's apparent merit.

But there is another humbling dimension to merit, too. Which has to do with the ways by which its defining features get chosen. Certain cultures take up greater importance than others in deciding what is merit, without necessarily being any better. This is an expression of the unequal structure of society itself. The greatest aid for an unjust society comes when those at the bottom believe that they deserve to be at the bottom. And when those at the top believe they deserve to be at the top. The sociology of culture and merit exposes the mistaken character of this belief.

Merit and the Middle Class

Many social scientists believe that behind the idea of merit often there lies a hidden terrain of injustice. A denial of merit to most Indians is done, not through their laziness or stupidity, but just through a lack of access to schooling, and an inequality of resources. Merit itself may be defined in unfair and incorrect ways through a distorted curriculum or a curriculum which biases selections in favour of certain cultures over others. In a society with so many different strata and so many kinds of inequalities, some will have an unfair advantage over the rest in gaining the label of merit. Assuming, of course, that the label does correspond to what is inside the bottle, and is not just another case like the botany topper who had no idea how to raise a plant.

Yes, many would agree that in our society merit is not to be taken at face value. But why then is it so deeply moving a concept? Merit is what inspires millions of students and their parents to come out into the streets in its defence. What is the fault, they say, of the hardworking person who toils day and night to finally gain entrance to a prestigious institute, only to be pipped at the post by a reserved quota candidate. This scenario disturbs them greatly and challenges their most deeply held values. The opponents of reservation feel violated and injured. Some of them go so far as to declare the denial of merit through reservations as an assault on our nationhood itself.

The idea that merit should decide the distribution of rewards and positions in society is a relatively recent one. India had seen for many centuries just the reverse – the Mughals, for instance, restricted positions at the top to Turks, Afghans and Iranians and, sometimes, extended this reservation to Rajputs as well. The caste system developed the world's most detailed system of reservations, strictly stipulating who could and could not aspire to higher ranks. It is a rather new idea that we can and should compete in an open examination, which does not ask who one is born as, but only examines what one has become.

The open, meritocratic system was brought to India by the British, by the same British whom we never cease to blame for all the problems in our education and culture. Whatever else they may have messed up here, the open examination system was definitely a great improvement in terms of a legal guarantee that no one would be discriminated against. Among the British, too, this was not an ancient tradition. Like in India, the notion of merit had always existed in a narrow and restricted form. There had been accepted the idea of equality within a circumscribed community – all adult males of a certain age were equals within a 'jati' in India – and selection of a leader took place relatively freely within that. But not across all communities in a country. When it first came, it was a revolutionary idea in England to select men for public service on the basis of open examinations.

The previous system in England, just like India, was one of patronage and nepotism. Rich and influential members of the ruling aristocracy would appoint their relatives and followers to important positions in the state. While ability was important, the family of one's birth was a sharp demarcation and lines of descent formed a boundary around the privileges of the powerful. In the 18th and 19th centuries, the rise took place of commercial and manufacturing classes and they, too, demanded a share of the pie. The rising middle classes led the demand to open up the closed circle of power. Science was an important aid in this campaign. It provided convincing arguments and evidences that the differences between people were created by society and not by a special god-like being. Science was a very compelling weapon for demolishing the special rights claimed by the aristocracy. If all were born equal, then, none could claim special status merely by birth to privilege. Thus emerged the claim to merit.

The professional, trading, manufacturing groups demanded that positions in the state be opened up to those with qualities achieved through hard work, study and special ability. The middle and upper-middle classes were going in increasing numbers to study in universities and the definition of merit began to be done in the symbols of the university. Desirable qualities were typically defined in terms of the curriculum and examinations acquired there. The basis of legitimacy for power began to change. Merit was now increasingly seen as the source of legitimacy, much more than birth into royal families. As a society this marked an important step in the transition from a closed, inheritance based society into an open, achievement based one.

England saw in the 18th and 19th century a marked increase in the freedom of many men. Science and merit were important contributors to that process. However, merit had another side to it, which quickly emerged.

The first large-scale open examination which recruited people on the basis of merit was set up for the Indian Civil Service. The directors of the East India Company resisted this fiercely, but the British Parliament finally prevailed over them in 1853. Within Britain itself, the British elite managed to stave off competitive examination for their internal civil service for many more years. Yet, the dilemma in merit may be seen from those early times – the administrators of India were chosen on the basis of their knowledge of Greek and Latin! The ICS examination was held in England for many years, sharply curtailing the number of Indians who could sit for it. It took a long struggle for it to be held in India as well. The British middle classes were willing to push for equality and merit so long as it served their interests. But they were quite reluctant to support the same demand from their own poor or from the residents of their colonies.

When the British brought their educational system to India, examinations were an integral part of it. Communities with previous histories of literacy and of service to the rulers of the older states were amongst the first to adapt to the new system. The radical step of open examinations was typical of the British contribution to dissolving dividing walls in this country. Not that they had an unblemished record in this regard, since they were also active in devising other kinds of religion and community based quotas for recruitment to their army, etc. Yet, it was the British educational system and their system of government employment which gave a strong impetus to renewing a vision of human equality in India. Processes like these were responsible for eventually leading Indians to question the special status of the British themselves. Thus emerged the Indian freedom struggle and the Constitution of a free India that guaranteed the equality and freedom of all.

The history of merit as a concept helps us to understand its appeal and its role in the culture of the middle class. It was central to the rise of middle class and gave it its legitimacy. Merit was embedded in a vision of people rising up on the basis of hard work and acquiring educational certificates which gave the stamp of correctness and justice on their newly acquired power and wealth. However, like many popular beliefs, merit also hides dark secrets: it hides the inequality built into the system. This is easy to see in a now distant example: the few who became members of the ICS thought themselves to be deserving and meritorious. The many who were left out because they could not sail to England for the examination thought otherwise.

The legitimacy of merit is based on several half truths. It is based on the denial of opportunity, on a system which insists that only some can be meritorious and not many, on a system which certain knowledges get privileged over others only because of the distribution of power in society. That the Indian middle class finds this lack of legitimacy difficult to digest is hardly surprising. It goes against the grain of the culture which sustains and motivates them. Questioning merit means to question individualism, to question the justice of the job market, to question the justice of consumerism. These are all central to the middle class culture today. Yet, equality and freedom, too, continue to be attractive principles. Perhaps, they may still inspire greater honesty and courage in us.

Merit may be a great improvement over nepotism, but it is now in the need for serious re-examination. The challenge before us is how to create a society where merit really speaks for equality of opportunity and does not serve as a label that legitimises systemic inequality and injustice.

Merit as an Ideology

The common sense understanding of merit is that it is real, objective and easily measurable. The common sense thinks it as obvious that those who top an examination have merit and they deserve all the rewards they can get. However, a famous scholar once pointed out that if external appearances were the same as inner realities, then, there would be no need for science. The social sciences help us to peel apart the myths that are embedded in many common sense perceptions. They can help us to see that merit is part of an ideology.

Many social scientists use the concept of ideology to refer to how culture takes up a dimension of power. Culture is made up of an interconnected mesh of symbols and practices and may often prioritise certain interests over others. Certain meanings are brought to the front and others pushed back, all the while maintaining an impression of normalcy and naturalness. Thus, fairness gets to be seen as the mark of beauty, over all other shades of skin in India. The ways of the rich and powerful begin to be equated with style and eventually with goodness. Ideologies are believed to be present in not just political parties. Cultures have invisible strings that pull, in an often unconscious manner, to strengthen certain hands and weaken others. The commonest way to do this is by the process of legitimisation. The strength of British rule was their having persuaded us that their ways were superior and correct. Thus, the ideologies of colonialism held us under their spell as no amount of guns and swords could. This explains why one of the main strategies of our freedom struggle had to be the encouraging of self-respect and faith in our own ways.

Merit, too, acts ideologically in today's India. It defines the desirable qualities for entry to prestigious and powerful positions. It celebrates the few who are selected and they are declared the rightful and just occupiers of those special positions. In this manner, the notion of merit magnifies the qualities of the selected, thereby brushing under the carpet the systemic deficiencies that prevent other more or less equally good candidates from also being selected. This may be best illustrated through an angry protest by some MBBS students who were agitating against reservations in a postgraduate departments. They pointed that that there were just five seats, of which just two would be left after various quotas had been filled. This was a denial of merit, they argued. The hold of ideologies is remarkable: they were willing to agitate against reservation, but not against the fact that there were so few seats in the first place! The first was to them clearly illegitimate. The second was probably seen as only "natural".

The real issue behind a shortage of jobs, a shortage of college seats and the lack of dignity for most job-seekers is the structure of inequality in society. We have a political system that gives power to a few and not to most. We have an economic system that gives wealth to a few and not to most. Instead of asking why there are so few jobs or why there are so few seats in colleges, we quibble over the criterion of selection.

Entry to the state, the corporate sector and the professions is about the selection of a few and the exclusion of many. In all cases selection is said to be done on the basis of certain qualities. And, in all cases, the justification of exclusion is at least as important as the supposed utility of those qualities. If there are a thousand qualified applicants for just one post, then, how is one to decide? The notion of merit provides a gloss of legitimacy. It claims that the selection is correct because of some standard of measurement. The successful candidate is said to out-distance the rest by a real and substantial difference. Assuming that the selection was done on the right and relevant criteria, there is the problem of the absurdity of one per cent differences and how much results vary with each repetition of a test. But, there is another basic problem in this: many of the rest were rejected not because they were unsuitable for the job. They were rejected because the jobs were not enough for all of them.

The acceptance of inequality and its justification is one of the prime functions of ideologies of domination. Merit is part of a much broader culture that sees inequalities as normal and legitimate. This has become part of our motivation system. A well-wishing friend sitting with me in my car once tried to persuade me to get rich quickly. Why, I asked him? Why not, he countered, don't you want to drive a Mercedes? I was puzzled at that then: he would still be sitting with me and we would still be crawling through city traffic. What would we gain by a Mercedes? I understand that better now. Our motivation systems are less about what we will get by doing something, and more about how much superior we will become to others. As our society becomes more and more unequal, with a certain kind of economic growth, inequality itself becomes our driving force.

Our advertisements are saturated by the desire to be different. In this consumerist milieu, our middle and upper-middle classes do not seek long-lasting satisfaction. To become content means the end of consumerism. That would be disastrous to the growth of our economy. No, what we seek is to be, well, different. And not different as an equal, but different as a superior. To eat better than others, to drive better cars than others, to wear better clothes than others. Superiority is defined by quick labels and there is little desire or inclination to examine the content. The label of merit shares the qualities of the various other symbols of a consumer society: the label is what validates and legitimises and the brand is what gives value. The content is secondary.

Even when the content of merit is important, its implications are deliberately pushed out of mind. Getting ahead in life needs us to get certain kinds of jobs. And for those jobs we need to be submissive, manipulative and opportunistic. That is what merit is often all about. When 1,00,000 people sit in a competitive examination for 100 seats, then people with the above qualities will have an edge. The greater the competition, the more difficult will become the selection of students with healthy, all-round interests, or even a practical interest in say, making things with their hands, or taking care of the ill or unhappy. The tougher the competition, the more likely will it be that the meritorious will be the completely focused, the single-minded and the studious. That also means they must be moral cowards who are submissive to the mindless demands of the system, have little interest in real world matters and little practical orientation. This is why, we need to fight systemic inequality: it leads to the distortion of even our most cherished values.

Of course, all these suit selecting institutions fine. Such students are not trouble-makers, can be easily controlled and can be counted on not to rock the boat. They also make excellent employees for the corporate sector. However, they do not make particularly good human beings and we see that all the time in our hospitals and in the actions of our private sector.

The ideological weight of merit acts to strengthen the power of those who are endowed with its halo. The professions, for instance, are actually characterised by a powerful exclusionary tendency. Doctors insist that they and only they have the capability and the moral right to heal. They seek to exclude others from the realm of healing. This is central to all professionalisation – the demarcation of boundaries and the desire to monopolise control within them. Criticisms of the medical profession get drowned under the pressure of merit. Doubts over intrusive medicine and the violence of hospitals get crushed. Pointing to the dehumanisation, greed, selfishness and exploitation rampant in medicine is futile. The best are selected for this profession on the basis of merit. How can they be wrong? If the IIMs and IITs are selecting the most meritorious students in our country, then, how they be responsible for anything less than a perfect pollution-free environment and a just, equitable society?

Merit, as an ideology, can hardly be understood without examining the larger contours of contemporary society and the kind of selections it wants to make. Gandhi understood this very well. When he debunked British education, he said that he could understand why people were still reluctant to quit British-designed schools and universities. They gave entry to the charmed circles of power. The nature of those circles of power continues to be central to understanding the hold and meaning of merit. The roots of merit lie in the egalitarian ideal of a meritocracy, where merit is what counts and inherited privileges cease to matter. However, in an unequal society, with continued distortions in the sharing of resources and opportunities, merit becomes a fig leaf. It becomes an ideology to cover up the deficiencies of a system which is pretending to distribute rewards in a just manner. The hope of justice which merit had once held out continues to go unrequited.

27

Democracy, Disagreement and Merit

PRATAP BHANU MEHTA

The current dispute over extending reservations for OBCs in central educational institutions has raised a question that is being little discussed. The question is this: Assume that many people agree on the objective of creating a socially inclusive education system, where students are not deprived of the relevant opportunities because of their financial and social backgrounds. But assume further that even serious minded people disagree over the best instruments to use for this purpose. How should this agreement be accommodated in a democratic polity? How does one move beyond the banal statement that reasonable views must be respected, and give these views some institutional space. It seems that, at this juncture at any rate, this question requires some consideration. Unfortunately, in the reservation debate, the distasteful attribution is made that people hold the views that they do because of their caste identity. But, let us assume that there might be reasonable disagreements over the subject even when people make good faith arguments.

Although the empirical data on this subject is deeply inadequate, I suspect that in the end even empirical data is not going to do too much to resolve these disagreements. This is partly because we seem to have gone from the presumption that in a democracy everyone is entitled to their opinions to the assumptions that everyone is entitled to their own facts as well. We need to reflect on why reference to empirical argument has become more of a rhetorical tool than a serious exercise in reflection. But it is also likely that data may underdetermine policy options. We can always turn any argument on its head. If we find that existing quotas are not being fulfilled, we can see this as a failure of quotas, or evidence that there is no will to enforce them. Perhaps like the divisions over religion, divisions over this matter will be irresolvable and deep. I do believe that nothing is more dangerous for sound doubt that at the moment, there is serious disagreement.

We also disagree over the consequences of reservation as practised. Does it produce more social integration by giving access, or does it re-entrench caste by making it an axis of social distribution? Does reservation extend a genuinely helping hand, or is it merely a politics of condescension? Is it a way of saying to backward castes, "We don't think giving you resources and removing the obstacles that stand in the way of realising your policy than the assumption that anything goes under the name of social justice and that there are no such things as relevant facts and cogent arguments." But, in the final analysis, we cannot deny the possibility of fair minded disagreement

Gamut of Issues

After all, our disagreements on affirmative action run the gamut of issues. While we can all agree that we share the same goal, building a more socially inclusive education system, we disagree over the most effective instruments for doing so. There are also disagreements over the objective of affirmative action policy. Some think that the creation of equal opportunity should be limited to anti-discrimination measures. On this view, we need to ensure that, other things being equal, no candidate is discriminated against for being who they are. This is probably a baseline aspiration on which all can agree. But beyond this aspiration things get more complex. Some think of reservation as, rather implausibly, an instrument to fight poverty. Some think of it as creating equality of opportunity. Others still think that it is simply an instrument for creating a middle class of dalits and OBCs even though reservations do not achieve a generalised equality of opportunity. Some think that we must go beyond equality of opportunity to something closer to equality of outcomes. It is intrinsically desirable that jobs and educational institutions roughly mirror social cleavages in society. It is not simply enough that certain disadvantages be compensated for, or certain obstacles to opportunity be removed, but that the only test of success is that institutions are literally mirror of society. We also disagree over exactly how much weightage to grant different forms of deprivation. We can debate whether these are the aspirations we should have, and we can debate whether reservations are a plausible way of achieving these goals. But there is no talent will be enough. You will also require these additional "crutches" as one scholar has called them. Does being identified through a caste tag harm the interests of those students from backward classes who are able to make it in the general merit list? The list of relevant questions could go on. We also disagree over the relevant target groups that should be included. Are the claims of SCs/STs the same as those of OBCs? How much sub-group differentiation should there be? How are intra-caste differences as opposed to inter-caste differences to be accommodated? What are the other groups that need to be brought into the discussion of deprivation? Or further still, what do we mean by merit? How do we weigh the relative importance of granting autonomy to institutions to experiment, with the objectives of social justice? There is one way of diagnosing these disagreements. This is simply to assume that our positions in this debate are structured by our caste or class interests. While there is no doubt that many individuals and groups strategically seek to advance their interests, the idea that all our disagreements can be traced to who we are is insidious for a democracy. It makes reasoned discussion and argument, reciprocity and mutual acknowledgment almost impossible. If we are so sure from the start that our identity structures our arguments why even bother having discussions at all. Are all of us going to be diminished and miniaturised, because we have no possibility for speaking for any identity or interest other than our own? If all our concepts are mere ruses of power, is there going to be any possibility of public reason? The way that arguments over reservation have proceeded over the last few weeks makes this question unavoidable. It is not that there are no better or worse arguments; public reason would not survive if we did not believe that. But, in these complicated matters, there are so many underlying causal assumptions and judgment calls about how the world works, so many diverse ways in which our experience impinges upon us, that it would be fatuous to expect agreement. At this juncture, even before we discuss what effective access policies should look like, we need to clear some space and ask: How will we handle disagreement in this domain? For fundamentally, the reservations debate has become a debate about the character of democracy, in more ways than we recognise. It would be too easy and tempting to give a moral psychology for why disagreements on this subject are so deep and passionate, but I think it is time that we reflected on one aspect of the way in which this debate is structured. Part of what gives the reservation debate such an edge is the fact that it has become an all or nothing affair. It proceeds on the assumption that there is one correct model of affirmative action policies, and this model should apply more or less to all institutions across the board. Whether this model is numerical quotas, or numerical quotas minus creamy layer or whatever, the assumption is that almost all institutions, other than minority institutions should adopt this model. It is a "winner takes all" approach to public policy. So, the stakes in the debate are extremely high. Perhaps more than arguments for or against reservation, we need to work out mechanisms for lowering the stakes in this debate. By lowering stakes I do not mean minimising the importance of the question about how to build socially inclusive educational systems; by lowering I mean simply that different sides have space to try out different experiments, and not feel institutionally shut out.

Diversity

It is something of a mystery that the one thing we seem not to acknowledge is that a concern for diversity is a concern for a diversity of institutional forms. Diversity need not be limited to a diversity of opinion where we say to each other, without quite meaning it, that we respect each other's views. Surely, there is more room to have those views, within some baseline limits, express themselves in diverse institutional forms. What those baseline limits are can be a subject of debate. They should not be set so low that serious moral values like non-discrimination are compromised. But they should not be set so high either that the range of permissible options shrinks to zero. Why should all institutions adopt exactly the same model of admissions? Why should they all perform exactly the same social role? Could we not think of different institutions as performing different roles and catering to different needs and demands? For instance, there could be institutions where the state feels numerical quotas are important, there could be institutions where other kinds of deprivation indexes are used, there could be institutions that have open admissions and take it upon themselves to admit anyone who cares to show up, and there could be institutions that have very stringent criteria of entry. The lack of diversity in institutional forms in higher education extends beyond access policies as well; arguably ours is amongst the most homogenised large education systems in the world. For a country that prides itself on its diversity, there is a surprising fear of institutional diversity on any measure of the term diversity. We have reduced the idea of diversity to the idea of recognising different identities, but not recognising that they can be accorded recognition in different ways. How might bringing this form of diversity into the debate help? For one thing, it would be a more honest acknowledgement of the standing of all the parties in the debate as citizens. It will be a truer reflection of views in society. It appears to me that this would be a more honest way of not only dealing with our genuine disagreements, but will foster more creativity and encourage pedagogic honesty. Second, it will lower the intensity of the debate, at least somewhat. It would be possible for all kinds of institutions to exist simultaneously. If some feel strongly that numerically mandated quotas are the only way to express commitment to social justice, they can express this commitment in the institutional forms they choose; if others find this notion anathema, they could have their own institutional forms that express their preferred mode of social justice. Some might have reservations for 33 per cent, some for 50; some might target dalits, some OBCs. The diversity of institutional forms was a default position of institutions in India, which has been progressively eroded. What the current quota proposal, of extending reservations to OBCs in all central institutions, does – and the reason it elicits such opposition – is that it threatens to erode the pockets of institutional diversity.

The third advantage of bringing the diversity of institutional forms into the debate is this. One of the weaknesses of current affirmative action programmes is that institutions simply do not respond to the presence of socially marginalised groups in the way they should. Even in India's top universities (or rather one should say especially in top universities) there is a conspiracy of silence around the problems of students who arrive through affirmative action. Some of them will do well, but in many cases the system will pass these students through. There is a glaring contradiction in the self-image of these institutions. On the one hand, they think they are being bastions of social inclusiveness just because they have given access to socially marginalised groups, but whether they effectively help these students take full advantage of the opportunity that access gives is another matter.

Relating with Students

There are several reasons for this. Most of the pedagogic techniques in Indian universities are not aimed at the specificities of different students. We talk at students rather than talk to them and so are unable to discover or respond to the appropriate level a student requires. There is frankly no way of flexibly responding to the needs of students in ways that are appropriate for them. What goes by the name of remedial programmes and support systems are frankly a joke that often infantilise students who go to them. So, we violate the first canon of good teaching that you have to start at the point the students are at. The problem is that the greater the disparity of starting points in the classroom, the more likely is that students are to be left out of real teaching. In our debates, while we have recognised the importance of diversity of identities, we underestimate the challenges huge disparities in starting points produce in the classroom. Our answer to this challenge is simply to ignore it; to shuttle people through.

A diversity of institutions can help address this huge but unacknowledged problem in our education system. Rather than clubbing all institutions under one rubric, institutions will become more self-conscious of the kinds they are, the kinds of students that come to them, and the pedagogy appropriate to those student bodies. For instance, in California, the higher end of the state system, the Berekelys, etc., teach in one way; while the Long Beach model, which is required to admit every student with minimal qualifications, teaches another way. But both address their students rather than shunt them through.

Is there a danger that this plea for diversity will promote unintentional ghettoisation of students? Not really, at least if some background conditions obtain. Nothing in this plea for diversity should be read as suggesting that the state will not have to provide adequate resources at all levels of education so that no child is deprived of the education he or she deserves because of financial or social disadvantages. If even a modicum, and not a full measure of those background conditions obtain, you would expect students from different groups being able to make it to different institutions. If these institutions are, within their own premises, well run, they will attract all kinds of students – privileged and not so privileged. Second, we would have a more refined concept of equal opportunity. Equal opportunity does not necessarily imply that every student should have access to the same kind of institution; it implies that every student should have access to the institution most appropriate to them. The important thing is that the institution contributes to a substantial enlargement of opportunities and abilities. It does not let the student simply pass through, knowing that there is no accountability at all. Third, nothing in this proposal is prejudging which institutions will be good and successful. It may turn out that institutions with reservations are better if not as good as institutions without; and there is more demand for them, rather than less. Nor is this proposal suggesting that some of these institutions should be endowed on the criteria of the kinds of policies they adopt. Indeed, there is something unjust about the current allocations, where a handful of IITs get more than 15 per cent of central allocation on higher education, while institutions that cater to much larger numbers are starved of resources. It need not necessarily follow that institutions of particular types be funded more than others.

Finally, this diversity will help us get around the confused thinking we have on merit. Let us assume that merit is randomly distributed across castes and classes – a baseline assumption that no democracy can reject. Given the right institutional conditions this merit can be discovered and nurtured. But, both sides in the affirmative action debate have a valid point. Proponents of reservation argue, rightly, that relaxing standards in admission is not necessarily incompatible with merit. Opponents of reservation argue, plausibly, that relaxing standards at admissions leads to inferior outcomes on the output side. Both observations may be true if one condition obtains, namely, the institution does not contribute to development but is simply a screening device. So, if institutions do not help less qualified students improve their abilities, then, they will go out as they came in. What is the evidence of this phenomenon? Frankly, this is an area that does need more empirical investigation. But some studies suggest that institutions do not in fact contribute to improvement; relaxed standards in, relaxed standards out.

'Output' Merit

If this is happening, then, we need to interrogate the pedagogy in our institutions more. But, the fundamental point is this: what is the appropriate point at which merit should be measured, assuming it should be. The peculiarity of the Indian debate is that we lay inordinate stress on measuring merit on the input side; whereas the genuinely relevant measure should be on the output side. For society what matters less is what marks someone got it with; what matters more is the competence they graduate with. Unfortunately, in professional schools for instance, output testing is less stringent. The result is that even well-to-do students, from recognised institutions, get off scot-free. But, if our output licensing requirements were credible, it would matter less what criteria students got in with. The important thing is that institutions be held accountable for the outputs. Unfortunately, if the chain of reservation extends from education to jobs, and reserved students can easily get access to reserved jobs, the chain of accountability on the output side breaks down. This is not to suggest that these students are necessarily inferior in quality; it is simply that there are no credible signalling mechanisms that can validate them. I suspect the advantage of more stringent output testing rather than an obsession with criteria for admission would be a far fairer picking out of potential. The practical difficulty in a scheme that has the buzzword diversity is that it still leaves us with difficult questions about allocative decisions. How many institutions of what kinds should there be? Are there principled criteria by which we can determine which institutions should have what kinds of policies? This question is particularly acute since most institutions are likely to be state institutions, and the state needs some criteria to allocate funding. But, the fact that this question is not easy to answer is no reason to suppose that a one-size-fits-all solution is an honest answer to our problems. Allowing for a diversity of institutional forms, is a better and more honest way of encouraging innovation, creativity and pedagogic appropriateness. I have my views on what kinds of policies will produce better access than numerically mandated quotas. But, the pressing call of our democracy at the moment is to remember that honouring diversity may well be the best way to mitigate conflict. Freedom does not always produce perfect social justice.

VII

Better-off, Worse-off and Creamy Layer

28

Examining the Creamy Layer Principle

S. SUBRAMANIAN

In a recent verdict, a Constitution bench of the Supreme Court has upheld the validity of the 77th, 81st, 82nd and 85th constitutional amendments on reservation for Scheduled Castes (SCs) and Scheduled Tribes (STs) in the matter of promotion in government employment. This verdict has generated afresh a debate on the merits of the so-called "creamy layer" criterion in determining eligibility to the benefits of affirmative action. Abstracting from the specificities of the judgment, a matter of general concern it provokes relates to the principle that in any scheme of group-based reservation, the creamy layer ought to be excluded from preferential treatment.

Indeed, this principle, which, for convenience, will here be called the "creamy layer principle" has been held out by many forward caste persons as an argument against providing reservation in education to the creamy layer segments of the "backward castes". Once the validity of the creamy layer principle is acknowledged in any one dimension of application, or as an axiomatically appealing principle of equality at an abstract level, it would be inconsistent to deny its validity in other spheres of application. It therefore becomes a matter of some importance to submit the appeal of this principle to critical scrutiny.

One means to this end is to work through a particularly simple illustrative example, and to examine the analytical implications it has for considerations of group equality. This is a method which Amartya Sen has called the "case-theoretic method": it involves constructing counter-factual, though conceivable, situations, and testing our moral intuition against the outcomes dictated by this or that principle when applied to this or that situation. The idea is not to build a complex and nuanced moral or political theory on the basis of a simple example, but rather, at a preliminary level, to provide an anchor for certain ideas which, at the present moment, are not exactly distinguished for their clarity or freedom from ambiguity.

With this in mind, let us imagine that society can be partitioned, along caste lines, into a backward caste (which has been historically discriminated against and oppressed) and a forward caste; and, along economic lines, into the poor and the rich. We are interested in assessing what sort of mechanism of compensatory discrimination might assist the cause of justice in the allocation of scarce educational opportunities among competing contenders for them. That is, whom, and to what extent, is a system of preferential treatment toward those who are disadvantaged by caste and/or income-deficiency likely to assist?

One Judgment, One Assumption

To answer this question requires one to make some plausible judgments and assumptions. I shall make one judgment and one assumption. I shall judge that caste backwardness is a more crippling disability than is income insufficiency, and, in particular, that the "capability gap" between a rich backward caste person and a rich forward caste person is greater than that between a poor forward caste person and an economically better-placed person of his own caste. Further, I shall assume that poor cohorts of the backward caste group would, because of their social and educational disadvantage, typically not fare academically well enough to be greatly aided by the availability of compensating concessions in their behalf. Under these circumstances, the implementation of a "creamy layer" corrective is likely to exacerbate prevailing caste disparities in the access to education. The example furnished below is intended to illustrate this conclusion. It is important to stress that the example is just that an example, whose role is to clarify a certain line of reasoning, and not serve as a precise and literal replication of reality.

Suppose, then, that four candidates appear for a competitive examination for admission to a professional college and that only two seats are available. Imagine that one of the candidates is a "poor backward caste" person (whom we shall refer to as PBC), one is a "rich backward caste" person (whom we shall refer to as RBC), one is a "poor forward caste" person (whom we shall refer to as PFC), and the fourth is a "rich forward caste" person (whom we shall refer to as RFC). Let it be the case that a candidate has to secure a mark of 80 per cent in order to qualify for admission. This, however, is only a necessary condition. Among those that qualify, only the two top-ranked candidates will be selected. In what follows, we consider a certain hypothetical distribution of marks among the four candidates, and alternative schemes of compensatory discrimination, together with the outcomes they lead to, in terms of the candidates selected.

Suppose, the distribution of marks is as follows: 70 for PBC, 81 for RBC, 83 for PFC and 85 for RFC. This distribution simulates the commonly observed phenomenon that, other things equal, academic performance improves with each of economic and caste status. Suppose, further, that no mechanism of compensatory discrimination is in place (Case I). Then, clearly, the selected candidates will be PFC and RFC. Next, suppose that we have a scheme of extra marks allotted to a person suffering from the disadvantage of caste backwardness (Case II); specifically, assume that a backward caste person is given 6 extra marks. Then, the "effective" marks of PBC and RBC respectively will be 76 (= 70 + 6) and 87 (= 81 + 6), while the "effective" marks of PFC and RFC will remain at 83 and 85 respectively. The chosen candidates, in this situation, will be RBC and RFC.

Consider a third case (Case III), in which caste-based preferential treatment is given to a backward caste person (6 extra marks), *but only if s/he happens to be poor*: this scheme upholds the creamy layer principle. Then, the effective marks of PBC, RBC, PFC and RFC will be, respectively, 76 (= 70 + 6), 81 (no extra marks for RBC because he belongs to the creamy layer by virtue of being rich and is excluded from preferential treatment), 83, and 85. In this situation, the selected candidates will be PFC and RFC. Finally, consider a scheme (Case IV) in which an extra 6 marks are allotted for caste backwardness and an extra 3 marks for poverty: both caste and economic status are seen as grounds for preferential treatment. In this situation, the effective marks of PBC, RBC, PFC and RFC will be, respectively, 79 (6 extra marks for caste backwardness and 3 extra marks for the condition of poverty), 87 (6 extra marks for caste backwardness), 86 (3 extra marks for poverty) and 85 (no extra marks at all), and the selected candidates will be RBC and PFC. These details are conveniently summarised in the Table 1. (Notice that the table reflects the judgment and the assumption we started out with.)

Table 1

Selected Candidates under Alternative Schemes of Compensatory Discrimination

Scheme of Compen-satory	*Effective Marks of Poor Backward Caste (PBC) Candidate*	*Effective Marks of Rich Backward Caste (RBC) Candidate*	*Effective Marks of Poor Backward Caste (PFC) Candidate*	*Effective Marks of Rich Backward Caste (RFC) Candidate*	*Qualifying Mark*	*Selected Candidate*
I	70	81	83	85	80	PFC RFC
II	76	87	83	85	80	RBC RFC
III	76	81	83	85	80	PFC RFC
IV	76	87	86	85	80	RBC PFC

Let us consider each of the schemes of compensatory discrimination in turn. Scheme I, which does not allow for any group-related preferential treatment whatever, is the sort of scheme that would be favoured by an undiluted belief in the virtues of meritocracy: notice that it is the two members of the forward caste who are selected under this scheme. No doubt, there are large numbers of individuals – of predictable caste and class affiliations – who would approve of Scheme I. We shall, however, take the view that Scheme I does not belong in any reasonable discourse on social justice: it is a bit late in the day to deny, for instance, the historical and contemporary reality of the disadvantages imposed by the caste system.

An acknowledgement of this reality is compatible with a scheme of compensatory discrimination such as Scheme II, which endorses preferential treatment in the event of caste disadvantage. For the example we have considered, the candidates who are selected under this scheme are RBC and RFC. Given a certain perspective, this outcome is unfair to PFC: the poor, forward caste person is seen as having been forced to lose out unjustly to the rich, backward caste person. This perception plays an important role in upholding the creamy layer principle, which underlies Scheme III. Notice that the distribution of effective marks under Scheme III is different from what it is under Scheme I: in particular, PBC's effective marks are higher (at 76) in Scheme III than in Scheme I (at 70), and this fact can serve as a basis for upholding the "justice" of the scheme. For all practical purposes, however, neither of the backward caste candidates is helped by Scheme III: PBC's "raw" marks are too low to be aided by the preferential treatment to which he is eligible, and RBC, by virtue of being rich enough to belong to the creamy layer, is not eligible for caste-based preferential treatment at all. The outcome of Scheme III is that it is the two forward caste candidates that are selected. This outcome is identical to the one corresponding to Scheme I: consequentially, it makes no difference whether it is Scheme III that is implemented or a scheme that does not allow for any caste-related preferential treatment.

Combining Caste and Economic Status

In judging the merit of any principle of social justice, there is a strong case for being guided (even if not exclusively) by consequentialist considerations. By this reckoning, the creamy layer principle underlying Scheme III puts up a pretty poor showing. If the grievance with the Scheme II outcome is that the poor, forward caste candidate has not been adequately compensated for his disadvantaged economic status, then that grievance is badly served by invoking the creamy layer principle: the solution does not reside in asserting that the social and educational disadvantage of a backward caste group is obliterated at some (sufficiently high) level of income. Assuming there is merit in the grievance just described, a more rational approach to the problem would consist in basing preferential treatment on grounds of both caste and economic status. This, precisely, is the view that underlies Scheme IV. Under this scheme, the outcome is that the selected candidates are RBC and

PFC. Notice that, of the two rich candidates RBC and RFC, Scheme IV favours the candidate disadvantaged by caste; and of the two forward caste candidates PFC and RFC, Scheme IV favours the candidate disadvantaged by poverty. This, one would imagine, is as it should be: the outcome respects the "other things equal" clause in the arbitration of competing claims. The grievance with the Scheme II outcome, reviewed earlier, is rectified under Scheme IV: the poor, forward caste person is now selected. We are also now enabled to see that the sense of PFC having been forced to lose out to RBC under Scheme II is a misguided one: it is more meaningful to see PFC as having lost out to RFC, an aberration that is corrected under Scheme IV, which avoids also the aberration, under Scheme III, of having RBC lose out to RFC.

The outcome under Scheme III has the further effect of widening the gulf between the backward and the forward castes. In course of time, the need for preferential treatment to the backward castes would reassert itself with vehemence. When this need is sought to be addressed, a so-called creamy layer of the backward caste may be expected to manifest itself again. If this calls forth a proscription of preferential treatment to the rich among the backward caste, then one would have to fall back once more on a Scheme III mechanism of compensatory discrimination. One can look forward to a perpetual oscillation between Schemes II and III. The need for caste-based preferential treatment will then be never-ending. And this would be a consequence of disregarding a dictum (here paraphrased) of Baba Sahib Ambedkar's: that one has to have preferential treatment in order to annihilate preferential treatment.

It is at least a little ironical that the creamy layer principle is often invoked alongside an impatient demand for a time-bound cessation of caste-based preferential treatment, when precisely this principle may be expected to grant preferential treatment an indefinite lease of life. And quite apart from this, one would imagine that an elementary level of social maturity, combined with a sense of proportion, would dictate vastly more urgent deadlines for a cessation of caste atrocities than for a cessation of the phenomenon of reservation.

There is a real and a professed rationale for the creamy layer principle, the former of which has been reviewed above (and found seriously wanting). A professed rationale often held out is based on a concern for a fairer distribution *within* the backward caste group. This rationale, when it is not insincere, is certainly paternalistic and condescending. First, the issue of group-related preferential treatment is, by its very nature, an issue of social justice addressed to the question of *inter*-group equality, not *intra*-group equality. As such, the concern should essentially be with group averages of relevant indicators of well-being, not with questions of how the total is distributed within any group. For, no matter how distributed, if the average for a currently disadvantaged group rises sufficiently over time, then that should be a signal for moving the group out of the ambit of preferential treatment. (Indeed, for the average to rise over time, any presently observed "layer" would have to thicken with time.)

Notice that the discourse is about including groups within, or excluding groups from, the scope of preferential treatment, and not about including or excluding individuals within particular groups. On the other hand, if it is fair to import considerations of within-group inequality into the discourse, then, there is a strong case for being even-handed in the matter – indeed, the more so because it is well known that the intra-group distribution of resources is more unequal among the forward than the backward castes. The forward caste concern for inequality within the backward caste group is a fit candidate for the advice: "Physician, heal thyself". (A less classically restrained injunction would be the American colloquialism: "Mind yer bizness".)

A large part of the appeal of the creamy layer principle resides in the principle's nomenclature. The image of overweight, indolent, dishonest, and undeserving elements among the backward castes which the creamy layer appellation conjures up, is one which inhibits the need for a more detailed scrutiny of the principle as an acceptable tenet of social justice. Such a slightly more careful examination suggests that the principle is a misguided one from both logical and sociological perspectives.

29

Creamy Layer Principle: A Comment

K. SUNDARAM

In an elegant note (*EPW*, November 11, 2006), S. Subramanian offers a strong case for not excluding the so-called "creamy layer" from the benefits of affirmative action for the socially disadvantaged groups in India. In arguing his case, Subramanian sets up a mechanism of compensatory discrimination in a format akin to a handicap race with a common finishing line with only those crossing that line being selected – in his example, for admissions to higher education courses. In particular, in his scheme, there are no pre-assigned quotas for any socially disadvantaged groups. Now, the issue of exclusion of the 'creamy layer' has come up precisely in the context of a quota regime with strong restrictions on the transferability of seats/jobs from the quota pool to the general category. In the context of admissions to the graduate and postgraduate courses, typically, this regime is operated with lower eligibility requirements for the reserved category students. To illustrate, for admission to the master's programme in economics in Delhi University, while the minimum eligibility requirements for the general category is 50 per cent in an honours programme, for the reserved category student, it is a pass in the BA programme. In this respect, the reservation system in operation is similar to the scheme of compensatory positive discrimination outlined in Subramanian's note. However, and this is the crucial difference, in a quota regime, the quota seats will first be filled from all eligible reserved category students, with the further provision that, all those among them making the "cut" on the basis of the cut-offs for the general category students are not to be counted towards the filling-up of the quota. It is only when the number of eligible applicants falls below the number of reserved seats that they get transferred to the general category. In fact, in the matter of jobs, the reserved jobs are not transferable at all.

In the sort of quota regime outlined above, two issues seem to be important in deciding on the creamy layer principle. First, whether, in a non-quota regime, the creamy layer gets a fair representation in, say, the admissions to the undergraduate and postgraduate courses. Second, whether the exclusion of the creamy layer so depletes the pool of the eligible candidates that there are not enough of them to fill the quota. Both of these are essentially empirical questions. In seeking an answer, it is important to define the creamy layer more narrowly than a simple poor-rich categorisation where the latter category covers over 50 per cent of the population – over 70 per cent in the case of the OBCs. Extending the analysis reported in my recent paper (*EPW*, December 16-22, 2006), I have looked at the picture for those located in the expenditure class interval that defines the top 5 per cent of the total population as per the NSS 55th Round Survey, 1999-2000.

To form a judgment of outcomes in the absence of a quota regime, I will focus on the OBCs.

Focusing on the urban youth in the 17-25 age group (the relevant age group for analysing representation in higher education) in the expenditure class defining the top 5 per cent of the all-India urban population, the OBCs, with a 19.4 per cent share of the total population (all social groups taken together), have a 20.3 per cent share in the population with a higher secondary certificate in that expenditure class and, a 20.6 per cent share of those attending undergraduate courses with higher secondary as their highest level of completed education and located in that class interval.

Clearly, in such a situation, the creamy layer among the OBCs would, as they indeed did in 1999-2000, have their fair share of undergraduate seats even when they are kept out of the ambit of a quota system.

Among the OBCs, those located in the expenditure class defining the top 5 per cent of the total all-India urban population (with a 3.1 per cent share in the total OBC population in the 17-25 age group) accounted for 7.9 per cent of the OBCs in this age group with a higher secondary certificate and for 12.2 per cent of OBCs with a higher secondary certificate and attending undergraduate courses, also in the same age group. Excluding this creamy layer of the OBCs from the ambit of quotas will, therefore, still leave over 92 per cent of the OBCs with a higher secondary certificate available to fill the "quota" seats without "risking" transferring seats to the "general category" and, without denying those in the creamy layer their fair share of seats in higher education.

Table 1

Intra-Social-Group Inequality in Access to Higher Education of Population in the 17-25 Age Group in Urban India: 1999-2000 Value of Gini Coefficient

Access to higher education	*Social Groups*			
	ST	*SC*	*OBC*	*Others*
Completed higher secondary	0.3577	0.3951	0.2816	0.2397
Attending "graduate and above" courses	0.5466	0.4756	0.3966	0.3247
Completed "graduate and above"	0.6501	0.4610	0.4527	0.3534

In such a scenàrio, with the creamy layer getting their fair share of seats in the absence of a quota and their exclusion still leaving enough number of eligible candidates from the disadvantaged groups to fill the quota seats, it is less than obvious that the exclusion of the creamy layer from the ambit of a quota regime will exacerbate prevailing caste disparities in the access to higher education.

Finally, a brief comment on Subramanian's assertion: "It is well known that intra-group distribution of resources is more unequal among the forward than the backward castes" (p. 4645). This again is an empirical issue. In the area of higher education (whether in terms of completed levels of education or in terms of access to higher education in terms of proportions attending undergraduate courses), the evidence does not support this assertion. As can be seen in the above table in respect of urban youth in the 17-25 age group, relative to the distribution of population of each social group across expenditure groups defining quintiles of the total urban population, the distribution of population with a higher secondary certificate or of those currently attending undergraduate courses or of those with a "graduate and above" level of completed education, is in fact more unequal among the backward castes than among the forward castes. So that, even as one accepts the need to address inequalities in access to higher education among the forward castes by substantially expanding the availability to them of means-based scholarships, there is a strong case for excluding the creamy layer of the backward castes in a quota regime. Such an exclusion will significantly raise the access to higher education of the overwhelming majority of eligible backward caste population, even as their creamy layer gets its fair share of opportunities for higher education while being kept out of the quota regime.

30

Demystifying the Anti-Creamy Layer

K. RAVI SRINIVAS

The editorial ('Myopic Oversight', *EPW*, November 4, 2006) and the article by S. Subramanian ("Examining the 'Creamy Layer' Principle", November 11, 2006) show that the creamy layer principle is an irritant to most supporters of reservation for OBCs. In this response I would examine only the article by S. Subramanian for reasons of space.

Contrary to the widely held view, the question of "creamy layer" is not decided on economic criterion alone. Even a cursory look at the criteria would show that the idea was to ensure that socially and educationally advanced persons do not corner reservations in the name of social justice for OBCs. The rationale for excluding the creamy layer has been debated at length since the early 1990s although the idea is much older.

In the Indra Sawhney case, of the nine judges in the bench, eight were in favour of excluding the creamy layer. A reading of the judgment would show why but for one judge all were in favour of such exclusion. The Central government has implemented the creamy layer norm. Many state governments have implemented it. Thus, by now it is a well-settled principle and practice. Lest it should sound that the creamy layer principle was advocated only by the courts, one could point out that in 1990 itself, CPI(M) took the position that creamy layer should be excluded. Hence, there is no need for a "case-theoretic method" using counterfactual situations to examine the consequences of applying the creamy layer principle. Anyway, for the sake of argument, one can accept the method. The problem with the example given by the author (Subramanian) is that it amounts to an exercise in tautology. The gap of 15 per cent between poor backward and rich forward candidates flies in the face of facts. If at all anything, the gap between cut-offs for OBCs and open quota cut-offs have been diminishing over the years. In Tamil Nadu the backward caste (BC) and most backward caste (MBC) candidates corner a lion's share of the seats available under the open quota, i.e., seats that are available to all irrespective of caste.

If there are four such candidates (PBC – poor backward caste, RBC – rich backward caste, PFC – poor forward caste and RFC – rich forward caste), then, the situation in reality is very different. Those who score more than the cut-off marks for BCs can compete for the seats available to all while those who score less than or equal to the cut-off marks for BCs are selected, based on their marks in descending order for seats under the quota for BCs. The situation is the same whether the quota is divided between BCs and MBCs. For example, in Tamil Nadu, the 50 per cent quota is divided as 30 per cent for BCs and 20 per cent for MBCs.

In reality, what happens is that the RBC candidate will have an edge over RFC candidate as (s)he can compete for seats in the BC quota if the mark is equal or less than that of the cut-off marks for that quota or can compete with RFC in open competition if the mark is more than the cut-off for BC quota. In other words, BC candidates are much better placed than FC candidates. If one gets less marks one can compete with other BC candidates in the reserved quota, and if one scores very good marks one can compete in the open competition also. The PFC and RFC have no such choices. Most state governments provide many facilities to BC students including hostel facilities, scholarships that are not normally available to poor FC students. BC students are doubly blessed by the quota system as well as the other facilities that the state provides, ranging from hostel facilities to free coaching for competitive exams. About the condition of PFC the less said the better. The author would like us to believe that the reality is otherwise.

'Capability Gap'

The author's assumption about the capability gap is just an assumption. One can assume that the poor irrespective of caste fare worse because of their educational and social disadvantages, a consequence of their economic backwardness. For example, the picture dramatically changes if one assumes that the PFC gets 81 per cent and RBC gets 83 per cent. Since the RBC is entitled to compensatory discrimination he would score 87 per cent, more than the RFC. Both the RFC and PFC have to compete with others for seats, which may be 50 per cent, or less. The purpose of excluding the creamy layer is to ensure that the benefits of reservation are available to the most deserving among BCs. Those BC candidates who are thus excluded can still compete for what is open for all. In this the PFC has to compete with RBC as well as RFC. But since excluding anyone at this stage on any criteria like caste or poverty would be absurd, the creamy layer principle cannot be applied. One solution would be put the most disadvantaged among the PFC, RFC and RBC first and categories them accordingly. But this would go against the constitutional principles of equality and non-discrimination.

If all the groups classified as backward classes are equal to each other and get reservation benefits equally, there would have been no need to divide the reservation quota further. Many states have quotas earmarked for BCs, MBCs, etc. This shows that the author's argument about equality within groups is flawed. Then, B.R. Ambedkar was not for a reservation system in which a majority of the seats would be under reservation. He did advocate preferential treatment but the reservation system today with quotas of 50 per cent and above resembles reverse discrimination rather than preferential treatment. For reasons of space I would not examine Subramanian's other views. My reasons for this rejoinder were driven by some theoretical flaws in his argument which do not appear substantiated by solid empirical evidence.

31

A Reply to Sundaram and Ravi Srinivas

S. SUBRAMANIAN

I am grateful to K. Sundaram and to K. Ravi Srinivas for having taken the trouble of commenting on my article. In what follows, I shall try to respond to their criticisms as best as I can. Given constraints on space, I shall mainly address Sundaram's discussion, which strikes me as being more straightforwardly directed at my article, while making references, where relevant, to Ravi Srinivas' comments. I believe Sundaram's comment can be seen in the light of three major points he makes. First, he suggests that my argument is located in the format of a "handicap race" rather than in one of a "pre-assigned quota"; the latter is what is relevant to the context of discussion. Second, he suggests that skimming off the creamy layer among the backward caste group need not necessarily compromise the extent of backward caste representation in aggregate educational attainment. Third, he suggests that, contrary to my assertion, within-group inequality, at least in the matter of certain aspects of educational achievement, is more pronounced for the backward than for the forward castes. I address each of these points in turn.

'Handicap Race' vs 'Pre-assigned Quota'

As I had tried to indicate in my article, my objective was to examine some possible implications of the creamy layer prescription for between-group equality, at a certain abstract level of the underlying principle involved. I had also warned that my approach was not intended to encompass nuance nor complexity, nor a literal representation of reality. The idea was simply to convey (and to convey simply) the essential logic of a certain line of reasoning. Having said this, I believe it should be possible, at the expense of a little incremental complexity, to reformulate my "handicap race" argument into a corresponding "pre-assigned quota" argument. Imagine, as before, that there are two castes (backward and forward: BC and FC respectively) and two economic classes (poor and rich: P and R respectively). Suppose four seats are available for admission to a professional college, and that there are 10 candidates competing for the seats. Of these, let us suppose that three candidates are PBC, three RBC, two PFC and two RFC. The distribution of marks is: 70 for each of the three PBC candidates, 76 for each of the three RBC candidates, 83 for each of the two PFC candidates, and 85 for each of the two RFC candidates. In the absence of any quota provision for those that may be perceived to constitute disadvantaged groups, and assuming a qualifying mark of 82 (Case I), the selected candidates will be the two RFCs and the two PFCs. Suppose now that a 50 per cent quota is reserved for the backward caste, with a qualifying mark of 75 for the reserved category and one of 82 for the open category (Case II). Then, the selected candidates will be the two RFCs and any two of the three RBCs. Next, suppose we have a scheme of 50 per cent reservation, with a qualifying mark of 75, for backward caste persons, but provided only that they are also poor, and a qualifying mark of 82 for the open category (Case III). Then, the caste quota will be of no avail to the three PBC candidates because of their low marks, while the three RBC individuals, because of their creamy layer status, will have to compete in the open category, where they will lose out to the two RFC and the two PFC candidates. Finally, consider a scheme (Scheme IV) in which 50 per cent of the seats are reserved for caste backwardness, with a qualifying mark of 75, and 25 per cent are reserved for economic backwardness (irrespective of caste affiliation), with a qualifying mark of 80, while the qualifying mark in the open category is 82: in this case, and given the specific, assumed distribution of marks across the castes and the classes, two of the three RBC candidates will be selected under the caste quota, one of the two PFC candidates will be selected under the "poverty quota", and one of the two RFC candidates will be selected in the open category. In Cases I and III, the backward caste candidates find no representation in the set of selected persons (the creamy layer criterion is consequentially equivalent to the no-compensatory discrimination outcome); and Schemes II and IV ensure that 50 per cent of the selected candidates belong to the backward caste, with Scheme IV ensuring that the open category seats are not confined to the rich among the forward caste. These "pre-assigned quota" outcomes are very similar to their original "handicap race" counterparts dealt with in my article.

I might as well state here, explicitly, that I have carefully selected the numbers required to yield the above results. The example I have dealt with was intended to illustrate the proposition that implementation of the creamy layer principle could exacerbate caste disparities in access to education. If, in line with Ravi Srinivas' complaint, this is an exercise in tautology, I am afraid there is no help for it. An example explicitly intended to illustrate a certain proposition must presumably end up illustrating it. I would imagine this is in the nature of things. Arising from which, if there is little to be said for making a virtue of necessity, then, there is equally little to be said for making a vice of necessity. On the other hand, if the BC-FC gap in academic performance is quite narrow, one wonders what to make of the common FC lamentation that "quality" and "merit" are being crucified at the altar of reservation.

Creamy Layer Criterion and Backward Caste Representation

The second point, which Sundaram makes, is grounded in useful empirical work. (Ravi Srinivas complains that I myself have not offered any findings from empirical study. Apart from the fact that I did not make any claims to the contrary, all I can say is that I am very happy for him, or anyone else, to engage in the requisite empirical research.) The import of Sundaram's databased analysis can be reformulated in the following simple terms. Let Q stand for the number of seats allotted to the backward caste under a quota reservation system, and let E be the number of eligible candidates from the backward caste. One of the "essentially empirical questions" which Sundaram suggests should be addressed in assessing whether the implementation of a creamy layer criterion could adversely affect backward caste representation in admissions, is that of the relative magnitudes of Q and E. If E is greater than Q, then – Sundaram seems to infer – the basis for the apprehension just mentioned is removed. Let us suppose that E is indeed greater than Q, and let D be the (positive) difference between E and Q. Further, let CL be the size of the identified "creamy layer". The positivity of D is just one of the empirical questions that needs to be checked. Another important question is the size of CL. If CL is greater than D, then the basis for the apprehension outlined earlier is not removed. Why should one object to implementation of a creamy layer criterion if $CL \leq D$? This begs a prior question: why have a creamy layer criterion at all? Once the legitimacy of the principle is acknowledged, it is a matter of the camel's head in the tent. The debate will quickly shift to where the size of CL should be pitched. One should be possessed of an uncommonly large stock of naivete to believe that the aggressive, broomstick wielding votaries of the creamy layer principle will have any use for that principle if CL is identified in such a way that $CL \leq D$. Empirical information is available not only in columns of data in census or NSSO publications, but out there on the streets as well! But, apart from instrumental reasons, there are also intrinsic ones for treading warily in the presence of the creamy layer principle.

I would like to reiterate the point made in my article – that affirmative action relates to questions of inter-group, not intra-group, equality. Restricting the creamy layer principle to cases in which $CL \leq D$ can only be motivated by a pure concern for within-group equality among members of the backward caste. It is one thing to express this concern in exhortatory terms, but another to seek legislative endorsement for it; also, there is a strong case for permitting these concerns to emerge more "organically" from within the backward caste community itself.

Second, if concerns of within-group equality must be imported into the discourse, why restrict these concerns only to the backward caste? Sundaram does seem to endorse a more even-handed approach to the issue of intra-group equality when he says: "...even as one accepts the need to address inequalities in access to higher education among the forward castes by substantially expanding the availability to them of means-based scholarships, there is a strong case for excluding the creamy layer of the backward castes in a quota regime." Why is the redress of forward caste inequality located in "substantially expanding the availability of means-based scholarships", while the redress of backward caste inequality is located in skimming off the creamy layer? Notice that the eligibility criterion, in terms of qualifying marks, would become more stringent for the backward caste creamy layer members if they were graduated out of the quota ambit into the open category. A more consistent approach would be to either (a) simply substantially expand the availability of means-based scholarships to the more disadvantaged members of the backward caste or (b) implement a creamy layer criterion (subject to $CL \leq D$) for the backward caste and implement a similar equality-preferring scheme of differentially higher qualifying marks for the forward caste creamy layer. One has to wonder if all the complexity of backward and forward caste creamy layer identification, together with the problem of coming up with a satisfactory scheme of differentiated eligibility criteria, would indeed be worth the trouble.

There is no question of refusing to acknowledge that some defendants of the creamy layer principle are motivated by a pure concern for within-group backward caste equality (though, as argued above, it is not clear that implementation of a creamy layer criterion is the appropriate solution to their problem). Having said this, I would reiterate a point made in my earlier article: that, often enough, there is a difference between the real and professed reasons for favouring the creamy layer principle. It is not even always evident that votaries of the principle are, in fact, themselves self-consciously aware of the difference. In this connection, I shall confine myself to observing briefly that Ravi Srinivas holds both of the following views: "The purpose of excluding the creamy layer is to ensure that the benefits of reservation are available to the most deserving among BCs" and "even a cursory look at the [creamy layer] criteria would show that the idea was to ensure that socially and educationally advanced persons do not corner reservations in the name of social justice for OBCs....BC candidates are much better placed than FC candidates". The concern for equality within the backward caste group is apparently not so narrow as to exclude a note of grievance on behalf of the forward caste group. Incidentally, the remark that "[i]f all groups classified as backward classes are equal to each other and get reservation benefits equally there would have been no need to divide the reservation quota further" is misplaced: it seems to take no account of the point I had made in my earlier article, that "...no matter how distributed, if the average for a currently disadvantaged group rises sufficiently over time, then that should be a signal for moving the group out of the ambit of preferential treatment".

Within-Group Inequality

Finally, I address Sundaram's third point on the empirical validity of greater within group inequality in the distribution of resources for the forward than for the backward caste. I am afraid there is a straightforward misunderstanding here. I did not say that there is greater inequality in the distribution of educational attainment in the forward caste group than in the backward caste group – I could not have, for a reason which I will discuss in the next paragraph. What I did say is: "...if it is fair to import considerations of within group inequality into the discourse, then there is a strong case for being even-handed in the matter – indeed, the more so because it is well known that the intra-group distribution of resources is more unequal among the forward than the backward castes." For instance, data in the 1991-92 NSS survey on Assets and Liabilities of Rural and Urban Households suggest that at the all-India level, in each of the rural and urban areas, both the Gini and the Theil indices of inequality in the distribution of household assets were lower for the scheduled caste and tribe group than for the non-scheduled caste and tribe group. Yet, there is little evidence of prescriptions for within-group redistribution of assets among the forward caste group – which marks a strong contrast from the strangely solicitous concern for inequality in the distribution of educational attainment within the backward caste group. In any event, and for the point I was stressing, it suffices that there be a finite level of inequality in the distribution of resources among the forward caste; it is not necessary that this level be higher than what it is for the backward caste.

Insofar as the within-group distribution of educational attainment is concerned, one should expect, at the outset, that the Gini coefficient of inequality will be higher for the backward than for the forward caste, and a reverse-claim would be a priori indefensible. The reason for this is discussed in what follows. When, for example, we speak of those with or without a higher secondary certificate, we are speaking of a binary variable, which takes the value 0 for those who are deprived, and the value 1 for those who are not deprived. For a population of size n, if the mean of the distribution under review is m, and if n is sufficiently large, the Gini coefficient.

G can be approximated by the expression $1-(2/n^2 m)\sum_{i=1}^{n}(n+1-i)x_i$, where x_i is the ith poorest person's resource level. If x_i is interpreted as the ith poorest person's headcount ratio of access to a given state of educational achievement, then xi is either zero or one, and it is very easy to verify that G is simply H, where H is the proportion of the population without access to the educational achievement in question. One must expect H – and therefore G – to be lower for the forward than for the backward caste group. For the distribution of a binary (0-1)-valued variable, it just so happens that G (an index of disparity) coincides with H (an index of deprivation): the group with lower inequality is simply the less deprived group. In such a situation, within-group inequality is just a manifestation of group poverty.

The above considerations are relevant for Sundaram's finding that "in respect of urban youth in the 17-25 age group, relative to the distribution of population of each social group across expenditure groups defining quintiles of the total urban population, the distribution of population with a higher secondary certificate or of those currently attending undergraduate courses or of those with a 'graduate and above' level of completed education, is in fact more unequal among the backward castes than among the forward castes". I take it that the Gini coefficients reported in his table relate to the caste-wise distribution of educational attainment across expenditure groups; and if this is so, the result he obtains is not surprising in a situation, as is generally the case, where educational attainment is an increasing function of income.

For example, let $(x_1, \ldots, x_{10})$ be a tenvector of income levels arranged in ascending order, viz, $x_1 < x_2 < \ldots < x_{10}$. If the headcount ratio H of, say, failure to enter college, is 70 per cent (call this Case A), it is likely that the entrants to college will be the three richest persons, namely individuals 8, 9, and 10. If the headcount ratio declines to 50 per cent (call this Case B), the likely entrants would be the five richest persons, namely individuals 6, 7, 8, 9 and 10. As deprivation declines, concentration also tends to get diluted with a percolation of educational attainment down the income ladder. Since deprivation in the forward caste is lower than in the backward caste, one must expect there to be less income-related concentration of educational achievement in the former than in the latter.

Interestingly, this suggests that there could be two ways of diluting concentration. Going back to Case A, let us imagine that it describes the backward caste distribution in a situation where there is a 30 per cent quota and all of it has been "cornered" by the richest individuals (8, 9 and 10). One could now aim at one of two stratagems. First, one could retain H at 0.7 and arrange – by, say, skimming off the creamy layer (persons 9 and 10) – for persons 6, 7 and 8 to enter college. Alternatively, one could seek to reduce the educational deprivation rate from 0.7 to 0.5, and dilute concentration by transiting from Case A to Case B. The latter stratagem, surely, is preferable. One obvious means to this end would be to increase the size of the quota (from 30 per cent to 50 per cent) – a possible prescription that flows out of Sundaram's finding. Somehow, I get the feeling that Sundaram may not endorse the prescription!

Concluding Observations

In the end, it is vitally important that positions should be advanced, or defended, or rebutted, through recourse to logic and reasoning. But, surely, a fine-grained sense of arithmetic is only aided by a sense of perspective as well. The latter should assist in recognising that, in the matter of caste in India, there are rather more urgent issues of justice to contend with than resisting a perceived "unfairness" in some particular arrangement of preferential treatment. In a very general way, such a recognition, informed as it would be by a little less flintiness and a little more generosity of spirit, can create the conditions for a vastly more productive discussion of issues relating to compensatory discrimination than appears now to be the case. I cannot hope to improve upon the sentiment expressed by my well-remembered friend S. Guhan, when he said: "There can be constructive debate on these practical matters but what is of prior importance is to agree that philosophically and politically social discrimination in India has to be corrected through concrete measures for social justice. The process is bound to be painful, but we should accept the pain as the necessary concomitant of the maturation of our society and nation."

Contributors

A. Ramaiah, Associate Fellow, Tata Institute of Social Science, Mumbai.

A.R. Vasavi, Professor, National Institute of Advanced Study, Bangalore.

Ambrose Pinto, Principal, St. Joseph's College, Bangalore.

Amman Madan, Department of Humanities and Social Sciences, Indian Institute of Technology, Kanpur.

André Béteille, Chairman, Indian Council of Social Science Research, New Delhi.

Aashish Mehta works with the Asian Development Bank.

Ashwini Deshpande, Associate Professor of Economics, Delhi School of Economics, Delhi.

Bhagwan Das, lawyer and prominent Dalit activist.

C.P. Bhambhri, Former Professor, Centre for Political Sciences, Jawaharlal Nehru University, New Delhi.

Dipak Basu, Professor in International Economics, Nagasaki University, Japan.

Jayati Ghosh, Professor, Centre for Economic Studies and Planning, Jawaharlal Nehru University, New Delhi.

K. Ravi Srinivas, Professor, Department of Economics and Social Science, Indian Institute of Management, Bangalore.

K. Sundaram, Professor, Delhi School of Economics, Delhi University, Delhi.

Kancha Ilaiah, Professor, Department of Political Sciences, Osmania University, Hyderabad.

Keith Jones, columnist associated with the World Socialist Web.

Kranti Kumara, columnist and writes for the World Socialist Web.

Narender Kumar, Faculty Member, Political Science, Motilal Nehru College, University of Delhi, Delhi.

Neera Chandhoke, Professor of Political Science, University of Delhi, Delhi.

Partha S. Ghosh, Professor of South Asian Studies, Centre for South, Central, Southeast Asian and Southwest Pacific Studies, School of International Studies, Jawaharlal Nehru University, New Delhi.

Pratap Bhanu Mehta, President and Chief Executive Officer, Centre for Policy Research, New Delhi.

R. Arun Kumar, columnist and works with the Communist Party of India(M).

Rana Hasan works with the Asian Development Bank.

Rohini Somanathan, Professor, Delhi School of Economics, University of Delhi.

S. Srinivas Rao, Asstt. Professor, Zakir Hussain Centre for Educational Studies, Jawaharlal Nehru University, New Delhi.

S. Subramanian, Madras Institute of Development Studies, Chennai.

Sandeep Pandey, Ex IITian & Ramon Magasasay Awardee.

Satish Deshpande, Professor of Sociology, Delhi School of Economics, Delhi University.

Sukhadeo Thorat, Chairman, University Grant Commission, New Delhi.

T. Pradeep, Professor, Department of Chemistry and Sophisticated Analytical Instrument Facility, Indian Institute of Technology, Chennai.

V.B. Rawat, columnist and leading activist.

Yogendra Yadav, Professor, Centre of Study of Developing Societies, Delhi.

Index